The Book.
A History of
the Bible

D1338694

illummo
mea et sal
mea qm
mebo Dñ
ptector m
te mee aq
trepidab

Dum ap
piant sup
me noce
tes ut eda

The Book.
A History of
the Bible

CHRISTOPHER DE HAMEL

Phaidon Press Limited
Regent's Wharf
All Saints Street
London N1 9PA

Phaidon Press Inc
180 Varick Street
New York
NY 10014

www.phaidon.com

First published 2001
© 2001 Phaidon Press Limited

ISBN 0 7148 3774 1

Design by Ken Wilson
Printed in China

Frontispiece: detail of Pl. 76; title page: Pl. 90; this page: artists
mixing pigments and painting an initial in the Dover Bible, *c*.1150
(Cambridge, Corpus Christi College, MS. 4)

The following abbreviations have been used:

BL   London, British Library
BNF   Paris, Bibliothèque nationale de France
Munich Munich, Bayerische Staatsbibliothek
ÖNB   Vienna, Österreichische Nationalbibliothek

Contents

Introduction

THE HISTORY OF THE BIBLE is perhaps the biggest subject in the world. This statement can be understood both theologically and practically, for probably more has been written about the Bible, over a longer period, than about any other subject. More manuscripts of the Bible, or parts of the Bible, survive from the Middle Ages than any other tangible artefacts. The Bible was the first substantial book to be printed in Europe, completed in Mainz by Johann Gutenberg probably in 1455-6, and it has remained in print ever since. It is generally and credibly asserted that more copies of the Bible have been published since then than any other text, and that even now it continues to be the best-selling text across the globe. It is more widely disseminated than any other written text, and there is probably hardly a person in the world now without achievable access to a copy, usually even in their own language. That cannot be said of any other written text. Many of the stories recounted in the Bible are part of our common cultural heritage and, in various forms, the Bible provides a documentary basis for Judaism, Christianity and, to a lesser extent, the prehistory of Islam.

The present *History of the Bible* is not a theological book. It acknowledges, for it must, that many people who have used the Bible throughout its long history have regarded its text as having been divinely inspired, and that this very unusual status has been one reason why the Bible has been so widely promoted and read. It would be a mistake to underestimate this. At the same time, others have considered use of the Bible to be dangerous and even subversive. The history of the Bible also includes accounts of burning and deliberate destruction. The present book offers no position on whether or not the Bible was actually dictated or endorsed by God, or even whether its circulation is morally good or irrelevantly futile. That is not the job of a historian. While I was writing the text, people

RA
T
ER
AM
BRO
SIVS

would from time to time ask me what I was working on. If I had been able to reply that it was a book about the manuscripts of Dante, for example, or the publication of Shakespeare, the response would doubtless have been interested but neutral. The moment I said that it was a book about the Bible, there was always a sudden tension. Was I a religious fundamentalist? Would I ridicule the Bible? What was my own position? Why should I be interested in the Bible at all if I was neither defending nor attacking it? Almost no other subject could provoke such fervent partisanship, and the fact that the Bible still has this emotionally charged place in popular imagination, even in our apparently secular age, tells us a great deal about the Bible as part of our long cultural legacy.

   This is a history of the Bible as a book. It is the story of a literary artefact. This is not an account of the writing of the Bible, or of the events in the ancient Near East and in Palestine which are described in the text of the Bible itself. The title, which has evolved several times during the writing of the text, is *The Book, A History of the Bible*, but it could as well be *The Bible, A History of the Book*, and it opens at a time when the Bible was already regarded as a recognizable entity. The Bible exists simultaneously in many languages (in this it differs from many holy texts of other religions) but its actual text has hardly changed at all in thousands of years, except for the occasional disputed phrase here or there, or a delicate realignment of emphasis. This will reassure those who believe and use the Bible now. The same biblical text, however, has appeared in many guises. It has been conveyed by papyrus scrolls, parchment manuscripts and printed books on paper. It has comprised dozens of little books and single gigantic volumes. It is as if the same object has been moulded and reshaped in each age of history. The Bible has sometimes been a public symbol and sometimes a book of extremely private devotion. It has been remote and sacred; it has been aggressively popularized. The Bible has been used by emperors, nuns, professors, ploughboys and imperialists, for hugely different purposes, all in the absolute belief that their use was the right one. It has been copied in stately languages which were no longer spoken or even understood by those who used and promoted the Bible; and it has been translated into the daily speech of nearly every street corner in the world. It has appeared attached to long explanatory commentaries, or with none at all. It has been enormously expensive and extraordinarily cheap, or free, all for good reasons. Its component books have been rearranged at various periods into entirely different sequences, to suit the needs of the time. The Bible has been austere and unadorned; it has been illustrated with some of the very finest works of Western art. The Bible – exactly the same Bible – has survived through almost all the recorded history of Europe, tossed and rolled over and over, as it were, resurfacing in an endless variety of shapes and structures and for different purposes, but formed from an identical original text. This constant reshaping of the same text makes the Bible so fascinating as a book.

   The word 'Bible' is from the Greek, simply meaning 'books' or 'scrolls' (it

1 previous page
Saint Jerome's prologue to the Latin Bible is an introduction to the whole text. This is the opening of the prologue in the giant Bible of Bury St Edmunds Abbey, illuminated in England by the artist Master Hugo, c.1135 (CAMBRIDGE, CORPUS CHRISTI COLLEGE, MS. 2)

originates at a time when the terms were interchangeable). It is not necessary to have read the whole Bible to follow its history as a book, but we need to know that the Bible is not a single narrative but a series of often unconnected or loosely associated groups of short books. Those who are familiar with the text will know that even an exact definition of these individual components is not always easy. Lists of the books of the Bible appear on pp. 22–4 and 120 below. There are elements there which are universally accepted as being part of the Bible, such as the first five books of the Old Testament, Genesis to Deuteronomy, for example, or the Psalms. These are included in the official canon of the Bible both for Jews and Christians. The books of the New Testament, however, are uniquely Christian. There are also texts which some Bibles include and others reject as spurious or doubtful. These are often known as the 'Apocrypha'. The archaeology of the twentieth century may have added little to the text of the conventional Bible but it has furnished many unknown texts which look and read disconcertingly like the familiar Bible but which were never gathered up into the sacred anthology which is defined by the title of Bible. The important point is to remember that the Bible is a collection of texts, and that the inclusion or rejection of books and the arrangement of the components into particular sequences all form part of the Bible's history.

It is quite obvious that no narrative of the Bible's transmission can hope to mention every known manuscript or printed edition, or even every translation, for there are very many thousands of these. Such a text would be unreadable. We can only hope to focus on certain principal topics which represent the Bible at particular moments of its great journey through time. These provide a narrative sequence which is approximately chronological. We begin in the fourth century. By then the Bible already existed in more or less its present form, with the accepted texts of the Old and New Testaments. From that moment onwards, the Bible has an unbroken tradition which can be witnessed at every stage by surviving manuscripts or printed editions. We can look back at the Bible in ancient Greek and Hebrew and can see how the old texts were edited into Latin by Saint Jerome and how this version conveyed the Bible, hesitantly at first, through what we call the Dark Ages into the time of Charlemagne. In the eleventh century the size of Bible manuscripts grew larger and more massive than ever before or since, until they were so vast they could hardly be lifted. In the thirteenth century, Bibles went very small. This is probably the turning point of the whole story, for then the Bible was for the first time assembled into a size, order and format which is still in use. We look at the medieval understanding of the Bible, through commentaries and biblical pictures. The Bible, at least in Western Europe, was mostly still in Latin, by then used by fewer and fewer people. This gave it authority but obscurity. That too is an interesting theme. We begin to find revolutionary initiatives to translate the Bible into currently spoken languages. In England, especially, this was deeply mistrusted by the established Church, and Wycliffite translations, as they were called, were rapidly declared illegal and heretical. They and their owners were burned.

In the mid-fifteenth century, Gutenberg invented printing with movable type. His principal publication was the Bible. We will look very closely at that innovative book. Until that moment, all Bibles had been copied out by hand by scribes who inevitably made occasional mistakes and errors of transcription. In theory, at least, every printed book in an edition was identical. Gutenberg initiated a stampede of printed texts which was captured and harnessed by the first Protestants. Martin Luther validated the Reformation by re-translating the Bible into current German from published editions of the original Greek and Hebrew texts, thus giving it authority even older than that of the Latin Bible, and he promulgated it with printing. Both the Luther Bible in German and the English Authorized Version of 1611 marked major stages in the establishment of modern literary language. The English translation, however, became entangled with problems of copyright. Americans defied such restrictions after the Declaration of Independence from Britain in 1776, and the Bible multiplied prodigiously in the United States. In the meantime, European forms of Christianity were being promoted across the world by evangelical missionaries, using translations of the Bible for their purpose. The Bible became part of the triumph and burden of colonialism. In the nineteenth century, however, the historical authenticity of Bible stories was first seriously called into question. Darwin and others began to undermine the Bible's version of Genesis, and many people sought reassurance in biblical archaeology. They found texts and fragments of original manuscripts in Egypt and around the Dead Sea which took the Bible far beyond Saint Jerome, back into New Testament times. The apparently limitless public appetite for many relatively small finds is uniquely modern. No medieval theologian would have been interested in the Dead Sea Scrolls. The unbroken line of the Bible's descent may have begun around 400 AD, but the thrall of its real beginning belongs in the history of the twentieth century.

The Bible is by far the most international of literary texts. Chapter 1 traverses the western world from Bethlehem to Jarrow and south and westwards as far as Naples and Spain. Chapter 2 is set in the eastern Mediterranean. Chapter 3 takes place mostly in Italy and central Europe. Chapter 5 is centred firmly in Paris, then the largest city in Europe. Chapters 4 and 6 take us around Europe, especially to France. Chapter 7 is set in England. Most of Chapters 8 and 9 concern events initiated in Germany. A good part of Chapter 10 is set in North America. Chapter 11 includes the Far East, the South Pacific and Africa. The final chapter looks mainly at Egypt and the Near East.

At times the later chapters of the tale may seem to be especially focused on Bibles made in Protestant England and North America. European and Catholic readers should not feel neglected. A narrative history must be selective. The Eastern Orthodox and Catholic Churches always used the Bible devoutly and conscientiously but the form and wording of the Bible changed relatively little in their care. Some would regard this as a positive achievement. Protestants, however, constantly promoted new manifestations of the Bible text and therefore they figure more prominently in an unfolding history. We record what happened, without judgements of denominational virtue.

The story here begins with scribes and it ends with information technology.

The Bible, however, is a text which crosses extraordinary frontiers, back and forth across the centuries. Let us give one example – a Catholic one. In September 1998, the Benedictine monastery of Saint John at Collegeville, Minnesota, formally commissioned a Bible. It is a manuscript. The book is conceived in seven large volumes, 635 by 405 mm (25 by 16 inches), double column, 54 lines, copied by the British scribe, Donald Jackson. The manuscript is on parchment. From its inception, it was expected to take six years to complete. The text is in the English language, in the New Revised Standard Version, originally a Protestant translation. The book has dazzling illuminated pictures in contemporary style. St John's is a university as well as a monastery, and is probably best known internationally for its Hill Monastic Manuscript Library, an enterprise set up to record medieval books by photography and now by digital scanning. There is something very reassuring about the fact that a religious community, with all the resources of technology at its disposal for studying medieval books, resolved to commission its most modern Bible in the ancient form of a manuscript.

I myself began looking at antiquarian books in about 1964 in Dunedin, New Zealand, when I was 13. My guide was old Mr A.H. Reed, afterwards Sir Alfred Reed (1876–1975), who had specifically collected Bibles from a Christian standpoint and who had presented his collection to the Dunedin Public Library. I was entranced by these venerable books. Mr Reed encouraged me to open the glass cases and to look more closely at the books and to turn their pages. The collection includes no monuments of world-class importance but it spans much of the period covered by the present book. There is a fragment of papyrus, the first I had ever seen. There are specimen leaves of a ninth-century Evangeliary and great Romanesque lectern Bibles. There are four thirteenth-century Vulgates, and a handsome Wycliffite Gospel Book (Pl. 134). There is a single leaf from a Gutenberg Bible and there are wide-ranging printed Bibles of the Reformation, and of the early missions, including those to New Zealand in the early 1840s. The collection was assembled to illustrate the history of the Word of God, but to me it opened up the whole world of manuscripts, scribes and illuminators, printing and bookbinding and collecting, and the history of language, literature, craftsmanship and art, and, in short, of Western civilization. I dedicate this book to the memory of those exhilarating sessions after school with A.H. Reed.

2

The most recent monumental Bible, still in progress as this book goes to press, is a vast illuminated manuscript, commissioned from the contemporary scribe and illuminator, Donald Jackson. The illustration shows an illuminated page in the form of a Jewish Menorah depicting the genealogy of Christ at the beginning of St Matthew's Gospel. In the foreground is a burnisher for polishing the gold leaf

1 | Latin Bibles from Jerome to Charlemagne

IN THE BEGINNING, in the late fourth century, Saint Jerome translated the books of the Bible from Hebrew and Greek into Latin. He arranged the various texts into order, and he translated them into what was then the every-day language of people living in Western Europe. Jerome's edition was used almost unchanged for more than a thousand years, until Latin was long obsolete as a spoken language, and it carried the Bible from the ancient world into the Renaissance of the sixteenth century. Of course, Jerome was not the author of the Bible. Every word of the Bible, as it survives now, already existed in his time, in Hebrew, Greek and even in rough Latin translations. The actual beginnings of the Bible text were very much older. The Hebrew Old Testament had been assembled in many stages, parts of it up to a thousand years earlier, in the deserts and ancient cities of the Near East. The Jewish scriptures had then been supple-mented with the four Gospels and other New Testament books written in Greek by various authors within a century of the lifetime of Christ. These texts, the Old and New Testaments of the Christian Bible, were already in wide circulation by the time of Jerome.

So much of the very early history of the Bible is made complicated by credulous legends and assertions made from a religious perspective, rather than from a historical one. Since the fourth century, without question, the Bible has existed as a single entity in a continued and unbroken tradition. It is represented in every period since then by surviving manuscripts. It is sensible, therefore, to begin with a real person. Jerome actually existed. We therefore start this immense epic with a text, which still survives, and with a securely identifiable historical figure.

Eusebius Hieronymus, Saint Jerome, was born near Aquileia in approximately 342. Aquileia, in Dalmatia in the extreme north-east of Italy, was then a major

Roman city and the centre of an early Christian diocese, reputedly founded by Saint Mark. This was the period when the ancient Roman Empire was starting to break up, fractured along its northern and eastern frontiers by barbarian raids. For almost 300 years since the lifetime of Jesus, Christianity had been spreading as a religion around the Mediterranean and along trade routes through the provinces of Rome. It had sometimes been harshly persecuted, driving groups of early Christians into catacombs and other places of hiding. As the Roman Empire began to disintegrate, its emperors lost the self-confidence and authority to suppress Christianity. They began instead to see its merits as a faith which would unite the Roman world as it struggled to adapt and survive. Christianity was finally adopted under Constantine the Great, emperor 312–37, shortly before the birth of Saint Jerome. By the mid-fourth century, Christianity was the national religion of the late Roman Empire.

Jerome's own native language would probably have been Greek, but both Greek and Latin were then languages of everyday speech. As a boy of about 12, Jerome was sent to Rome where he studied Latin under the famous grammarian Donatus. The textbook which Donatus wrote became the most popular guide to the Latin language throughout the Middle Ages. When many centuries later Gutenberg perfected the art of printing, the schoolboy grammar of Donatus and the great Bible translation of Jerome became two possible candidates for the first book ever printed in Europe. It is intriguing that Jerome and Donatus knew each other. Jerome himself wrote clear and fluent Latin, but it may say something about the success of his literary style that his Latin teacher provided the first knowledge of Latin to almost every Bible reader in Europe for over a thousand years.

Having mastered Latin, Jerome set out on travels and study in other parts of the Roman Empire. He visited Palestine and the Near East where he perfected his Greek and began to study Hebrew. Many medieval and Renaissance paintings show him as a hermit in the Syrian desert, with a lion at his feet, surrounded by books. The tale of the lion is an agreeable medieval fiction; so too is the tradition that Jerome was a cardinal. Pictures of Jerome often show a medieval cardinal's red hat laid on the ground or hung from a peg. What is certainly true is that Jerome soon held some kind of office in the papal household in Rome, apparently as secretary to Pope Damasus, bishop of Rome 366–84. The popes were already established as the administrative leaders of Christendom. Damasus himself worked tirelessly to promote the city of Rome as the Christian capital of Europe, constructing buildings and churches there and honouring the early Roman martyrs. Jerome was working for Damasus by 382, and while he was in Rome he seems to have first begun revising the text of the Bible.

Many medieval Latin Gospel manuscripts preserve copies of a preface which Jerome addressed to the 'most blessed pope Damasus', referring to the fact that Damasus had evidently commissioned him to prepare a revision of the text of the four Latin Gospels. There were already various renderings of the Gospels into

3 previous page

Saint Jerome is shown here in his study, removing a thorn from the paw of a lion, in a detail from a painting by Niccolò Colantino, c.1450 (NAPLES, SAN GIORGIO SCHIAVONI)

Latin then available in Rome. These had been copied so many times that countless minor variants had crept into the text. Jerome's preface informs Pope Damasus that there were then almost as many versions of the Gospels as there were manuscripts. He exaggerated, as editors do, for the differences between manuscripts were doubtless often very slight. The preface does, however, introduce a recurring theme in the history of the Bible. Almost anyone copying out by hand a text as lengthy or as complicated as the Bible will occasionally misread a word or two or will accidentally corrupt the text by attempting to correct the apparent mistranscriptions of an earlier scribe. The next copyist is likely to repeat these errors and then to introduce others. This process is unending, and the topic of ever-multiplying variants will recur time after time in the course of the following chapters, at least until the invention of printing.

The papal household of Damasus would at this time have had two principal versions of the Gospels. One would have been in Greek, the language in which the texts were first written. The first Christians in Rome had probably spoken Greek, for it was a cosmopolitan city (and Saint Paul, of course, had written his Epistle to the Romans in Greek, confident that they would understand it). Out towards the edges of the western Empire, however – along the coast of Africa and up into Spain and Gaul – there had evolved various different Latin versions of books of the Bible for use by converts who did not know Greek. The most common was what is generally called the 'Old Latin' version. It was provincial and inconsistently translated. To judge from quotations from writers such as Saint Cyprian (d.258), bishop of Carthage in North Africa, all parts of the Bible were available in the Old Latin versions by the third century. Pope Damasus himself was of Spanish descent and doubtless knew the Old Latin Gospel texts from childhood. When the Roman Empire became Christian and the popes were reasserting the primacy of Rome, it was natural that there should be a need for a Bible in the metropolitan language of government. The Old Latin was brought in to fill the gap. This is the text, however, which Jerome found to be especially corrupt and in need of redrafting into accurate and idiomatic Roman Latin.

There survive a number of fragments and defective manuscripts of the Old Latin Gospels which are actually as early as the time of Jerome. They give us an idea of the sort of manuscript he might have used. One defective manuscript of part of the Old Latin Gospels is the so-called *Vercelli Codex*, still in the cathedral library of that city. It was preserved there as a relic of Saint Eusebius of Vercelli, who is reputed to have copied it himself. The script suggests that the book is probably old enough to have belonged to Eusebius, who died in 371, and so it is contemporary with Jerome and Pope Damasus. Another manuscript of the same text is extant only as separate and charred pieces in the Biblioteca Nazionale in Turin (cod. G.VII.15). It was once in the monastery library at Bobbio and it too dates from the late fourth century. It may have been brought to Italy from North Africa.

Books like this, then, if we can imagine them intact, are the sort of Old Latin manuscripts which Jerome confronted in Rome in the 380s. They are quite small volumes, almost square, written on thin parchment in rather untidy script with almost no punctuation or even spaces between the words. The script is known as 'uncial', formed of small capital letters. The lack of word division looks strange to modern eyes, and the sentences have to be read aloud to extract their meaning. The textual variants of fragments like these seem to justify Jerome's comment that there were as many versions as manuscripts. We can take a small example, chosen at random from easily available published plates of these two manuscripts. The Vercelli manuscript at Matthew 10:21 reads that 'brother shall deliver brother *in mortem*' ('to death', Pl. 4), whereas the Turin manuscript at the same point reads 'ad mortem': the meaning is the same, but the actual words are slightly different. Jerome chose *in mortem* as his preference. Furthermore, the scribe of the Turin book evidently misread an uncial 'f' as 'e', and what he actually wrote was that 'brother (*frater*) shall deliver *eratrem ad mortem*', nonsense, of course, as any reader could tell, unless, say, Eratres was a person being delivered to death. The name is improbable, but the Gospels are full of names unfamiliar to fourth-century Italians and there were no larger letters to mark the opening of proper nouns. Without word division, a reader might even think *erat* was a verb, separate from *rem*, strange and meaningless grammatically but composed of recognizable Latin words. One can see how easily, even in a simple and unimportant verse, a tiny variant could creep into circulation and become immortalized by precedent.

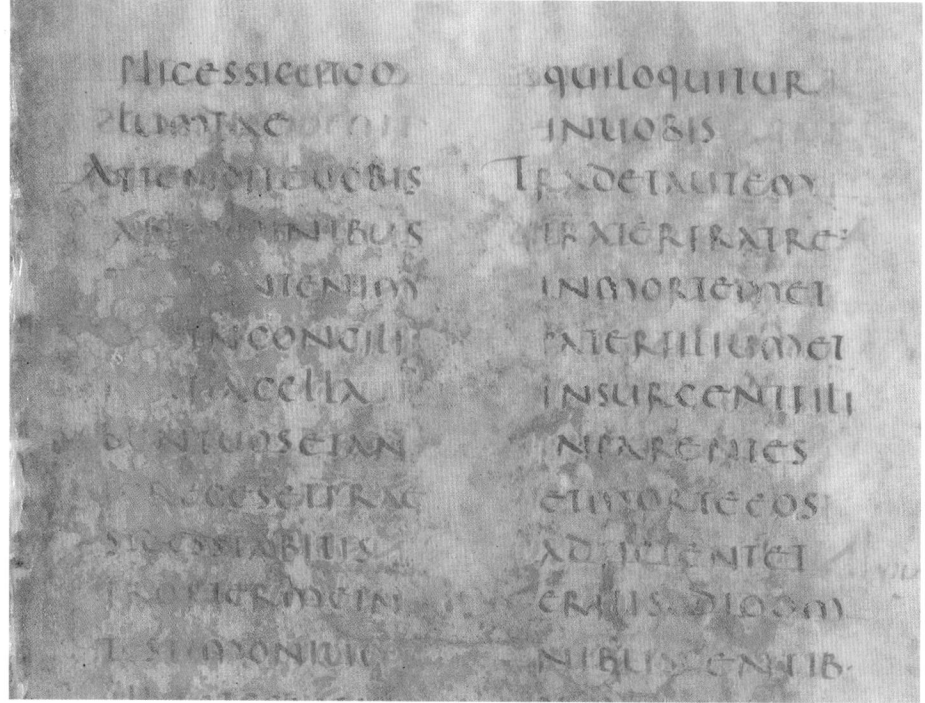

4

The Vercelli Codex, *a frag-mentary manuscript of the Old Latin text of the Gospels writ-ten in Italy in the second half of the fourth century. The detail here shows the text of Matthew 10:21 in the fourth and fifth lines at the upper right* (VERCELLI, BIBLIOTECA CAPITOLARE, S.N.)

5 opposite

Canon Tables in a Latin Gospel Book of the mid-eighth century, copied by the scribe Lupo in southern Italy (LONDON, BL, ADD. MS. 5463)

Saint Jerome also, of course, could have checked the meaning of Matthew 10:21 against the same sentence in Greek. There can have been no shortage of Greek Gospel Books in Rome in the fourth century. We know that Jerome used some of the latest Greek texts because he copied and translated one of their innovative features. This was the group of Eusebian canon tables, invented not long before by Eusebius of Caesarea (*c.*260–*c.*340). Jerome's preface, addressed to Pope Damasus, explains their purpose. Each of the four Gospels recounts a similar narrative in a slightly different form. The tables comprise a series of coloured diagrams drawn rather like an arcade of arches in an early church (Pl. 5). Between the pillars were numbered chapter references to parallel passages in the Gospels. The reader could run a finger across the columns to match up references to the same story in the other Gospels. The canon tables furnished a convenient aid for readers which became attached to the Gospels for many hundreds of years.

If Jerome was working for Pope Damasus from only 382 until the pope's death in 384, there can have been little leisure for extensive biblical research. He apparently completed a Latin text of the Gospels during this period and he worked extensively on the Psalter. The Latin edition which he prepared of the Psalms is almost certainly the one which survives under the name of the 'Roman Psalter', traditionally because it was adopted for use by the early medieval papal court in Rome. It is possible, but not certain, that Jerome may at this time have begun revising other parts of the New Testament, from Acts to Revelation.

After Damasus died, Jerome set off again on academic wanderings to North Africa, Antioch and Palestine. He finally settled in Bethlehem, no less, in 386. Here he took on responsibility for a monastery and spent more than 30 years working on a comprehensive translation of the Bible. Jerome recalls in his letters that he had collected manuscripts throughout his life. He must have surrounded himself with books in Bethlehem. He certainly had multiple copies of the Bible in Greek. The New Testament had been written in the Greek language. The Old Testament, the Bible of the Jews, was originally in Hebrew but was translated for Greek-speaking Jewish communities in the third and second centuries before Christ (we will return to this version in the next chapter). Jerome also had other Greek translations from the Hebrew made by Aquila, Symmachus and other writers of the second century. We know almost nothing about them except their names. Jerome had copies of their translations in an enormous six-column manuscript of the Bible known as the *Hexapla*, prepared by the famous Greek scholar and theologian, Origen (*c.*185–*c.*254). The first column was in Hebrew. The second was in the Hebrew language but transliterated into the Greek alphabet. The third to sixth columns comprised four different Greek translations of the same text. It sounds a remarkable book, and many biblical scholars have wished they could recover this lost text. Jerome states that he found Origen's original manuscript of this giant work in Caesarea, on the Mediterranean coast of Palestine, and the implication is that he carried it back to Bethlehem.

In the course of the later 380s, Jerome, surrounded by his collection of manuscripts, began again revising the entire Bible, concentrating now especially on the Old Testament. He also wrote extensive commentaries on individual books of the Bible. These will be described in Chapter 4. The value of the commentaries in reconstructing the history of Jerome's scholarship lies in the fact that he often cites the Bible in his text. By collecting these citations in order, one can approximately reconstruct the state of the Bible version he was using at the time. Jerome had evidently prepared for his own use a second version of the text of the Psalms, collating it against the Greek and the *Hexapla* text, and it is this version checked against the Greek which survives under the epithet of the 'Gallican' Psalter (for it became widely used in Gaul). He revised the book of Job on similar principles, and probably worked on Chronicles and the Books of Solomon.

Around 390, Jerome began to realize that he had been wasting his effort if he really aspired to a definitive Latin version of the Old Testament. He decided it was pointless to take this from any form of Greek. It would be more authentic, he decided, if he could eliminate the middle versions altogether and to translate directly from the original Hebrew. For about fifteen years, therefore, from about 390 onwards, Jerome devoted himself to this massive task. The project included a third translation of the Psalms, in Jerome's 'Hebrew' version (Pl. 7). At this point we simply have to trust Jerome's account of his sources, for no biblical manuscripts in Hebrew now survive from between the time of the Dead Sea Scrolls (unknown in Jerome's time, of course) and the ninth or tenth century. Therefore we cannot check independently what kind of Hebrew texts were available to Jerome. There is every reason, however, to accept that Jerome, by now fluent in Hebrew, translated carefully and painstakingly from his Hebrew sources. If we can judge from later Hebrew manuscripts of the same text, Jerome was as conscientious as his Hebrew Bibles must have been accurate.

Jerome's increasing trust in the Hebrew scriptures brings us to another important and complicated point in discussing the history of Bibles. This is the problem of defining what texts should or should not be part of the Bible. Today most people tend to think of the Bible as an entity and seldom question the presence of its various components. We are likely to accept or dismiss the whole corpus of texts. Early readers of the Bible had no such certainties. Scholars wrestled desperately with decisions about which individual parts should be regarded as genuinely sacred, in some way inspired or endorsed by God, and which were merely devotional. The question will recur again in Chapter 12 below, when we consider the mass of strange texts which are disconcertingly similar to parts of

6 opposite

Jerome writing the prologue to the Latin Bible, miniature from the fifteenth-century Bible of Borso d'Este
(MODENA, BIBLIOTECA ESTENSE E UNIVERSITARIA, COD. EST. LAT. 422)

7

Jerome prepared three different Latin translations of the Psalms. This early thirteenth-century manuscript of the Latin Vulgate preserves two of them as parallel texts, the so-called 'Gallican' and 'Hebrew' versions
(PRIVATE COLLECTION)

the Bible and which evidently circulated freely in the early Christian Church.

Jerome found that the Hebrew scriptures did not include the books of Tobit, Judith, Wisdom, Ecclesiasticus, I-II Maccabees and Baruch, all of which were in the common Greek translation. He had already prepared Latin texts of Tobit and Judith from the Greek. However, Jerome now eliminated these books from his definitive edition of the Old Testament and he downgraded them as apocryphal. The word 'apocrypha' means the 'hidden' books, texts to be put aside from the official Bible. He similarly questioned the authenticity of some parts of other books, including Esther 10:4 to 16:24 and chapters 13 and 14 of Daniel. Jerome used the Hebrew text as his standard, and rejected any parts of the Bible not found there. He partially rearranged the sequence of the books of the Old Testament, to bring it in line, more or less, with the order of the Hebrew Bible.

The component parts of the New Testament were less controversial by the time of Jerome. The so-called 'Muratorian Canon' (an early Christian text named after the biblical scholar who first published it) shows that most of what we now recognize as the New Testament had already been accepted by Christians in the late second century. The Epistles of James and I-II Peter had not yet joined the list of official texts. By the time of Jerome, however, they were safely in place. Jerome worried privately, as New Testament scholars still worry, over the genuineness of the Epistle to the Hebrews, but overall he accepted and endorsed the New Testament in its received structure.

Jerome's work in translating the New Testament focused principally on the Gospels. He had first prepared these for Pope Damasus in the early 380s, and he continued to revise this translation while living in Bethlehem. It is not quite clear how far he worked through the rest of the New Testament. The Latin text as it survives from Jerome's period might, in fact, be the work of one or more anonymous editors in Rome. Even faced with a surviving text and the name and biography of Jerome, we cannot be absolutely certain that Jerome worked entirely alone.

Jerome died in 420, aged nearly 80. His writings were already being copied and circulated around Europe in his lifetime. Jerome or his literary friends (he had many) tidied up his biblical revisions into the order he had proposed and they presented what seemed to be the most definitive and authentic texts of the Bible then known, translated into excellent and fluent Latin. The endorsement and editorial judgements of Jerome conferred authority. At a very early date – probably not in Jerome's lifetime – prologues were grafted on to the text. The prologues do not pretend to be part of the Bible. These are short introductions to each biblical book, or coherent group of books. In most Latin Bibles these are explicitly attributed to Jerome by name (Pl. 6). This is accurate, but they were mostly excerpted from other books by Jerome rather than designed originally for inclusion with the Bible. Some were extracted from the letters written by Jerome to his disciple Brother Ambrosius (Epistles 52–3 in printed editions). Others came from Jerome's book on famous writers, *De Viris Illustribus*. Like the Eusebian canons, these Bible prologues provided aids to the reader. They are simply intended to assist the reader in understanding the context and authorship of each book. The prologues explain briefly the subject of the books, often discuss Jerome's reasons for accepting or rejecting books from the authentic Bible, and explain the variant orders of the texts in the different ancient languages. His prologue to the books of Kings, for example, is where we find his statement on rejecting the apocrypha not found in the Hebrew.

Here, then, follows the great irony of Jerome's Latin Bible. The supreme value of Jerome's scholarship as editor lay in his skill in assessing textual authenticity and in eliminating books and passages which he deemed inauthentic. Jerome produced a Bible which was a model of scholarly caution and care. His judgements still carry weight. However, throughout all periods, members of the Bible-reading public have always been reluctant to sacrifice any familiar passages of scripture in bouts of textual spring-cleaning, however justified. Any sacred text is more likely to accumulate additions than to lose parts which might be authentic. To incorporate passages of unproven authenticity always seems less fearsome that to risk eliminating what might be divine text.

Jerome's Bible, pruned against the Hebrew original, proved too purified for public acceptance. At some early stage, as it came to be copied and recopied and as it entered the life of the Latin-speaking Church, all the rejected books and passages found their way back in again. The position becomes even worse. Jerome's saintly bones would revolve in their reliquaries if they could have seen what happened next. Not only were the apocryphal texts reinstated into their old places, but the form in which they re-entered the Bible was none other than that of the archaic Old Latin, for Jerome had allowed them no other. Texts like Wisdom, Ecclesiasticus, I-II Maccabees and others slipped back into Jerome's edition, in exactly the wording of a translation so corrupt that it had inspired Pope Damasus to appoint Jerome in the first place. Good portions of the Old Latin survive for no other reason than that Jerome utterly excluded them.

The final Latin Bible, known as the 'Vulgate', is actually rather more of a hybrid than its reputation suggests. The name simply means the 'popular' version. Although not every part was necessarily the work of Jerome alone, the Vulgate was certainly all credited to him in most manuscripts. The monumental Vulgate edition of the Latin Bible came into use in most of Western Christendom through-out the Middle Ages, it was published by Gutenberg, and is still in print. It is now available on the Internet.

To summarize before proceeding, manuscripts of the Latin Vulgate in the Middle Ages would comprise a complicated series of multiple texts, mostly based on the work of Jerome. The list here gives characteristic components. The order varies slightly from one manuscript to another, especially in the placing of the texts which Jerome himself did not translate or those which he rejected as apocryphal.

Prologue to the whole Bible, by Jerome, beginning 'Frater Ambrosius …'	
Prologue to the Pentateuch, by Jerome, beginning 'Desiderii mei …'	
GENESIS EXODUS LEVITICUS NUMBERS DEUTERONOMY	translated by Jerome from the Hebrew.
Prologue to Joshua, by Jerome, beginning 'Tandem finito …'	
JOSHUA JUDGES RUTH	translated by Jerome from the Hebrew.
Prologue to Kings, by Jerome, beginning 'Viginti et duas …'	
I SAMUEL (I KINGS in Latin) II SAMUEL (II KINGS in Latin) I KINGS (III KINGS in Latin) II KINGS (IV KINGS in Latin)	translated by Jerome from the Hebrew.
Prologue to Isaiah, by Jerome, beginning 'Nemo cum prophetas…'	
ISAIAH,	translated by Jerome from the Hebrew.
Prologue to Jeremiah, by Jerome, beginning 'Ieremias propheta…'	
JEREMIAH LAMENTATIONS	both translated by Jerome from the Hebrew.
BARUCH	rejected by Jerome; supplied unchanged from the Old Latin.
Prologue to Ezekiel, by Jerome, beginning 'Ezechiel propheta…'	
EZEKIEL	translated by Jerome from the Hebrew.
Prologue to Daniel, by Jerome, beginning 'Danielem prophetam….'.	
DANIEL	translated by Jerome from the Hebrew.
Prologue to Hosea, by Jerome, beginning 'Non idem ordo …'	
THE 12 MINOR PROPHETS	all translated by Jerome from the Hebrew, *with prologues by Jerome, to Joel (beginning 'Joel filius …'), Amos (beginning 'Amos propheta …'), Obadiah (beginning 'Abdias qui interpretatur …'), Jonah (beginning 'Ionas columba …'), Micah (beginning 'Micheas de Morasti …', Nahum (beginning 'Nahum consolator …'), Habakkuk (beginning 'Habacuc luctator …'), Zephaniah (beginning 'Sophonias speculator …'), Haggai (beginning 'Aggaeus festivus …'), Zechariah (beginning 'Zacharias memor …) and Malachi (beginning 'Malachias aperte …').*

Two prologues to Job, by Jerome, beginning 'Cogor per singulos…'
and (usually) 'Si autem…'

| JOB | translated by Jerome from the Hebrew. |

Prologue to the Psalms, by Jerome, beginning 'Psalterium Rome…'

| PSALMS | the 'Gallican' Psalter, the second of Jerome's three versions, translated from the Greek, not the Hebrew; his third and final 'Hebrew' Psalter version, intended as part of the edition, occasionally occurs in a parallel column beside the Gallican Psalter but not as the Psalm text on its own. |

Prologue to the books of Solomon, by Jerome, beginning 'Tres libros Salomonis…'

Prologue to Proverbs, by Jerome, beginning 'Iungat epistola…'

| PROVERBS | translated by Jerome from the Hebrew. |

Prologue to Ecclesiastes, by Jerome, beginning 'Memini me…'

| ECCLESIASTES
SONG OF SONGS | both translated by Jerome from the Hebrew. |
| WISDOM
ECCLESIASTICUS | rejected by Jerome; supplied unchanged from the Old Latin. |

Prologue to I Chronicles, by Jerome, beginning 'Si septuaginta…'

| I CHRONICLES
II CHRONICLES | both translated by Jerome from the Hebrew. |

Prologue to Ezra, by Jerome, beginning 'Utrum difficilius…'

| EZRA (I ESDRAS in Latin)
NEHEMIAH (II ESDRAS in Latin) | both translated by Jerome from the Hebrew. |
| III ESDRAS
IV ESDRAS | rejected by Jerome; supplied unchanged from the Old Latin. |

Prologue to Esther, by Jerome, beginning 'Librum Esther…'

| ESTHER | translated by Jerome from the Hebrew. |

Prologue to Tobit, by Jerome, beginning 'Chromatio et Heliodoro…'

| TOBIT | translated by Jerome from the Greek but afterwards rejected by him. |

Prologue to Judith, by Jerome, beginning 'Apud Hebreos…'

| JUDITH | translated by Jerome from the Greek but afterwards rejected by him. |

| I Maccabees
II Maccabees | rejected by Jerome; supplied unchanged
from the Old Latin. |

Preface to the Gospels, by Jerome, addressed to Pope Damasus, beginning 'Beatissimo papae Damaso ...'

Prologue to the Gospels, by Jerome, beginning 'Plures fuisse ...'

Canon Tables to the Gospels, translated by Jerome from Eusebius of Caesarea.

| Matthew
Mark
Luke
John | all translated by Jerome
from the Greek. |

Prologue to Acts, by Jerome, beginning 'Actus apostolorum nudam ...'

| Acts | translated from the Greek, perhaps by Jerome,
probably by an unknown but contemporary translator. |

Short prologues to all the following books were commonly ascribed to Jerome in manuscripts but none is authentically from any text of Jerome.

James
I Peter
II Peter
I John
II John
III John
Jude

Revelation (Apocalypse in Latin)

Romans
I Corinthians
II Corinthians
Galatians
Ephesians
Philippians
I Thessalonians
II Thessalonians
Colossians
I Timothy
II Timothy
Titus
[Laodiceans]
Philemon
Hebrews

Since Jerome's monumental Latin version was without doubt the most authentic biblical text assembled up to that time, and since Jerome's reputation as a scholar and Doctor of the Church was without reproach, one might reasonably expect that Jerome's text would have been instantly adopted in the Latin west. It was not. At no period in the history of Bibles has there ever been an easy balance between the recovery of an accurate text and the alteration of sacred words which have been familiar since every Bible reader's childhood. No other text in Europe is capable of provoking in practice such mistrust of textual correction, and yet no other text is universally agreed in theory to be in such need of meticulous textual authenticity. There is almost no compromise between the two. This is a theme unique to Bibles. In his preface to Damasus, Jerome himself describes how his revision of the Gospels, prepared in Rome, was the subject of hostility from many who thought it sacrilegious that he should tamper with the words of the scriptures.

Jerome wrote in the current Latin of his time, the language of the western Roman Empire as it was used in the late fourth and early fifth century. It is a curious fact that at many stages in the Bible's history, contemporary translations into current languages have often been regarded with unease. The words of the Old Latin translation, by contrast, must by Jerome's time have sounded archaic, and therefore seemed to many people to be more fitting for a biblical text. It is interesting that the Vulgate never really gained acceptance until its language too began to seem archaic. In the period when its supporters defended it most fanatically, the late Middle Ages, it was obsolete.

For centuries after Jerome's death in 420, then, the Vulgate text actually struggled for survival. Very early manuscripts are extremely rare. The oldest is a copy the Vulgate Gospels written in Italy in the early fifth century, probably within Jerome's lifetime. It survives now as a group of about 110 leaves and pieces mostly preserved in the library of St-Gall in Switzerland (cod. 1395, and others, Pl. 8). Its original marginal notes give variant readings in Latin and Greek, and it is generally assumed to have been a book made for personal rather than public or liturgical use. It was probably owned by a biblical scholar. It is even possible that its

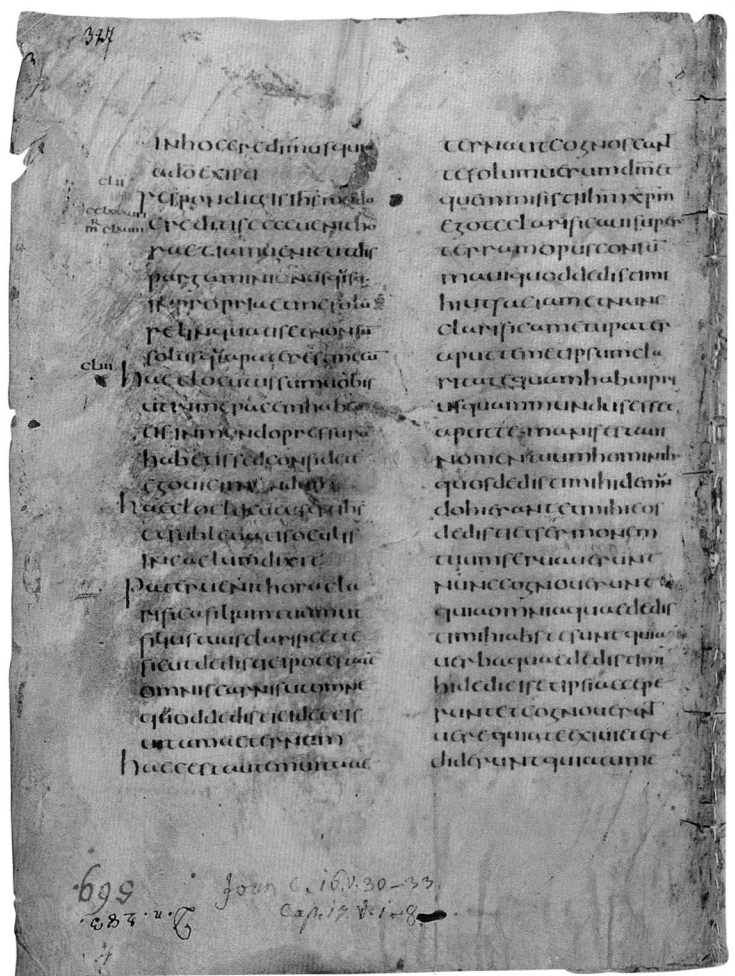

8

One fragment of the Gospels in Jerome's translation, written in the first half of the fifth century, possibly from the lifetime of Jerome and perhaps even annotated by him
(ST-GALL, STIFTSBIBLIOTHEK, COD. 1395)

9

A small Gospel Book in Jerome's translation, probably made for personal use. The manuscript was made in Italy but had reached France by the ninth century
(LONDON, BL, HARLEY MS. 1775)

annotations might actually be in Jerome's own hand. Another very early Gospel Book in Jerome's translation which survives intact is London, BL, Harley MS. 1775, made in the sixth century (Pl. 9). This is a small thick book, about 160 mm (6¼ inches) high, written on widely spaced lines in small script in pale brown ink. It is a book suitable for holding in the hand, and was probably made for private use.

By contrast, a number of the very great Gospel Books made for public ceremonies, some written centuries later, still used the manifestly faulty and archaic Old Latin text. Among these are several of the famous early Irish Gospel Books, including the oldest, the First Ussher Gospels (Dublin, Trinity College, MS. A.4.15, probably early seventh-century), and the Book of Dimma (*ibid.*, MS. A.4.23, late eighth-century) and the Garland of Howth (*ibid.*, MS. A.4.6, eighth- to ninth-century). The text of all these follows the Old Latin version of the Gospels. Christianity had reached Ireland by the back door, as it were, perhaps brought by missionaries up the Atlantic coast in the fourth century. Evidently the books they brought with them belonged to a tradition older than that of Jerome.

Other luxurious early manuscript Gospel Books were made in the centre of the Christian world, and yet they still used the same Old Latin text. Some of these were written in gold or silver script on purple vellum, including the *Codex Palatinus* (Trento, Museo Provinciale d'Arte, n. 1589, fifth-century), the *Codex Vindobonensis* (Naples, Biblioteca Nazionale, cod. Vindob. lat. 3, late fifth-century), the Verona Gospels (Verona, Biblioteca Capitolare, cod. VI, late fifth-century), the *Codex Brixianus* (Brescia, Biblioteca Civica Queriniana, early sixth-century, Pl. 10), the fragmentary *Codex Sarzanensis* (pieces of an early sixth-century Gospel Book, now in the parish library of Sarezzano), and even the famous Anglo-Saxon *Codex Aureus* in Stockholm (Kungliga Biblioteket, MS. A.135, late eighth-century). These are all manuscripts written on coloured parchment in gold and silver for public display; and all are copies of the Old Latin text. Jerome himself in his prologue to the book of Job disapproved of writing manuscripts in gold or silver on purple parchment, protesting that accuracy of text was more important than the frivolity of the trappings. Books which have acquired a dignity and status from their noble appearance are unlikely to be subjected to the impertinence of textual scrutiny. Some portions of the Old Latin were certainly preserved for their use in luxury and ceremonial manuscripts.

It might be argued that grandly illuminated manuscripts made for public display are more likely to survive than everyday copies of the same texts, and so (it might be thought) the Old Latin might be disproportionately represented among extant manuscripts. Yet this does not seem to be the case. We can sometimes find evidence of lost manuscripts by identifying palimpsests. At certain periods in the early Middle Ages some scribes used to erase texts from the pages of obsolete manuscripts so that the parchment leaves could be recycled for use again. Portions of at least ten fifth-century manuscripts of parts of the Old Latin scriptures have been partially recovered as under-texts in palimpsests, and there are others from later centuries. Such discoveries are evidence of deep entrenchment of the Old Latin version of the Bible across Western Christendom. If we know where the upper text was written, we can plot how far into the monasteries of medieval Europe the Old Latin text must have reached. This does not necessarily mean the Old Latin was used there (perhaps even the opposite), but it shows the books themselves moving across the West. They were presumably discarded as the Old Latin was gradually ousted by the Vulgate. Thus we know that at Bobbio in north Italy around the year 700 the monks were discarding fifth-century Old Latin manuscripts of Genesis, Kings, Proverbs and twenty leaves from Acts and the Epistles of James and I Peter. At St-Gall in Switzerland at the same time they erased a fifth-century Jeremiah. At Freising in Germany

10

Many luxury manuscripts retained the Old Latin text long after the time of Jerome. This is the Codex Brixianus *made in Italy in the first half of the sixth century. It is written in silver and gold ink on purple parchment*
(BRESCIA, BIBLIOTECA CIVICA QUERINIANA)

the monks rewrote other texts on top of 28 leaves from a late sixth-century Old Latin text of Saint Paul's Epistles, written in Spain or possibly North Africa. In Salzburg in the eighth century they erased and reused a fifth-century Gospel of Saint Matthew. A large Old Latin manuscript of Acts, the Catholic Epistles and the Apocalypse was erased perhaps at Fleury Abbey in western France. At Luxeuil in northern France around 700 they reused 48 leaves from a very fine fifth-century Prophets, together with other fifth-century manuscripts of the Pentateuch, Proverbs, and Pliny's *Natural History*.

11

Fragments from a fifth-century Italian manuscript of the Prophets in the Old Latin translation, once in the library of Reichenau Abbey on Lake Constance
(OSLO AND LONDON, THE
SCHØYEN COLLECTION, MS.
46)

12 opposite
Books of the Bible were always an essential part of church services, both for public reading and symbolic display. This French ivory book cover dates from about the tenth century. It shows a priest in church holding a book before his congregation
(CAMBRIDGE, FITZWILLIAM
MUSEUM)

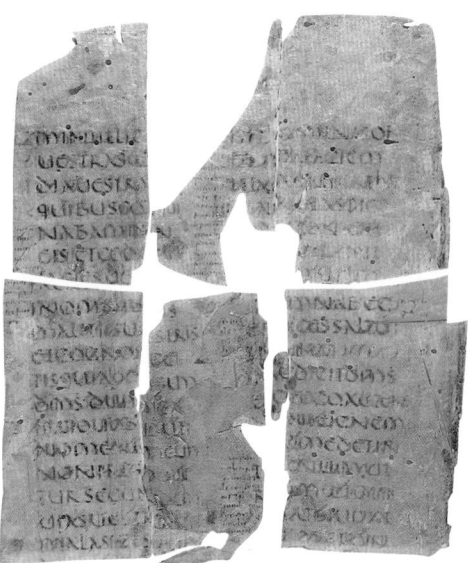

Similarly, waste leaves of obsolete manuscripts were sometimes reused as flyleaves, endpapers or strengthening pieces in later bookbindings. From these we can point to portions of the Old Latin scriptures being discarded mostly in the late Middle Ages in Bobbio again, St-Gall (a fifth-century Old Latin Gospel Book which must have come up from Rome in the eighth century), Sagen (in Silesia, where they had a manuscript of the Old Latin Maccabees probably from Verona), Salzburg, Benedictbeuren, Quedlinburg, Lorsch, Corbie, and so on. Taking these together, we have a traces of a good clutch of lost Old Latin manuscripts of the Bible, many of them – to judge from their script (which is almost universally uncial) – written in Italy. Part of 46 leaves from bookbindings survive from a fifth-century Italian manuscript of the Prophets in Old Latin, clearly once in the library at Reichenau on Lake Constance (Pl. 11). The early ninth-century library catalogue of Reichenau describes what is probably the same book of Prophets intact, adding 'which Hiltiger brought from Italy'. This gives a glimpse of one Old Latin manuscript on its travels.

One by one, however, Old Latin manuscripts were discarded and texts of the Vulgate version replaced them. It took several centuries, until, in practice, the Vulgate of Jerome's time had acquired a patina of age and of archaic language. By then, the Roman Empire was destroyed and Latin was no longer the universal tongue. Approximately 370 biblical manuscripts or fragments in Latin survive from before about the year 800. In the fifth century, within a hundred years of Jerome's translation, only about a third of those that survive are from parts of the Vulgate. By the middle of the sixth century, manuscripts of the Vulgate start to outnumber those of the Old Latin by about two to one. In the seventh century, the ratio has risen to about six to one. By the eighth century, there are about a dozen manuscripts with part of the Vulgate Bible to every one written in Old

Latin. Even still, the Old Latin had not quite died out. The enormous and strange *Codex Gigas* in Stockholm (Kungliga Biblioteket, MS. A.148), written in Bohemia towards the end of the twelfth century – there is an old tradition that it was copied by the Devil – still uses the Old Latin for Acts and the Apocalypse.

The Vulgate version of the Bible text must have received a huge and self-perpetuating endorsement when it began to be used for readings during the services in church, collectively known as the liturgy. As this tells us something about the history of early Bibles, and how they were used, it is worth looking back briefly into the Bible as a liturgical text. The public reading and discussion of the scriptures goes right back to the beginning of organized Christianity. The custom is alluded to in the first Epistle of Timothy 4:13, and was certainly common practice by the second century. Some early fragments of the Old Latin text, like the fifth-century book of the Prophets which Hiltiger brought to Reichenau, cited above, appear from their contemporary marginal notes to have been prepared for recitation in the liturgy. The Gospels had an especially important liturgical function. The reading of chapters from the Gospels has always been an integral part of the Christian Eucharist (the Mass or Communion service, commemorating the Last Supper), and the Gospel reading appeared in the culminating position of honour in the service, after the Epistles or any other readings from the Bible. A deacon would usually carry the Gospel Book in procession to some kind of raised platform or (at a later period) a reading desk, and he would read or chant a prescribed text for the day, with the congregation standing (Pl. 12). In the course of the fifth and sixth centuries, the cycle of appropriate Gospels readings gradually became standardized, at least within the cultural reach of the Church in Rome. The Rule of Saint Benedict (*c*.540) made provision for scriptural readings during meals and during the daily round of services ('offices') in monasteries. By the seventh century at the latest there had evolved the practice of reading through the whole Bible in church during the cycle of a year, in addition to the Gospels at Mass. They began with Genesis in the Sundays before Lent, and divided the text where possible so that the readings coincided with the themes of appropriate seasons, such as Jeremiah and Lamentations during Lent, and Isaiah's prophecy of the Messiah during Advent. The version used in this liturgy was the Vulgate.

The implications of this for the history of Bible manuscripts are enormous. Manuscripts of the four Gospels account for almost half of all biblical manuscripts surviving from before the ninth century, which may not necessarily mean that the Gospel narratives were studied privately more than any other part of the Bible, but simply that the Gospels were essential for the Mass. It may also be an accident of survival, of course, or the especial reluctance of librarians at all periods to discard books as holy as the Gospels. Many biblical manuscripts show added markings or scratched indentations which correspond with the beginnings and

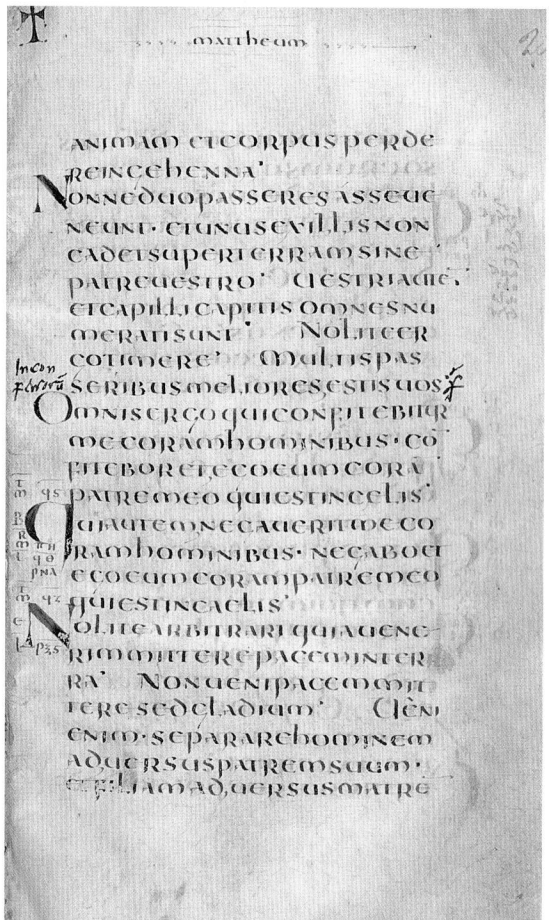

13

Headings added in the margins
of manuscripts can show which
passages were read in church.
This north Italian Gospel Book
of the second half of the sixth
century is marked up at
Matthew 10:32 for reading
during the feast of a confessor
(MILAN, BIBLIOTECA
AMBROSIANA, COD. C.39.INF.)

ends of liturgical readings. They give a valuable clue as to how the books were commonly used. A sixth-century Vulgate Gospel Book now in Milan was certainly in liturgical use by the seventh century, and it has marginal notes pointing probably to use in the diocese of Aquileia (Biblioteca Ambrosiana, cod. C.39.inf., Pl. 13). It is fitting, though coincidental, that this was the district where Jerome was born. Another in Milan, a seventh-century Gospel Book from Bobbio, was apparently still being used liturgically right up until the late fourteenth century, to judge from the marking-up of the Holy Week readings in a hand of that date (Biblioteca Ambrosiana, cod. I.61.sup.).

The triumph of the Vulgate text over the Old Latin probably had a great deal to do with the dissemination of the Roman liturgy from Italy. This is an important point. The Vulgate became the translation of the Italian missions. The sixth-century Gospel Book brought to England from Rome for the conversion of England under Saint Augustine of Canterbury (d.604/5), for example, uses the text of the Latin Vulgate (Cambridge, Corpus Christi College, MS. 286, Pl. 14). One of its two remaining full-page illustrations shows the Passion of Christ arranged around an image of Christ instituting the Eucharist at the Last Supper. Another almost contemporary Gospel Book brought with the Italian evangelists to England is in the Bodleian Library, Oxford (MS. Auct. D.II.14). It too follows the Vulgate text and is full of liturgical markings, both original to the book and added as late as the eighth or ninth century, including musical neumes, suggesting that it was used for chanting during services. A third is the sixth-century Vulgate Gospel Book which must have come from Italy to Northumbria by the late seventh century, and from there with the Anglo-Saxon missionaries to Würzburg, where it still survives (Würzburg, Universitätsbibliothek, Cod. M.p.th.f.68, Pl. 15). Liturgical readings were indicated in red ink both by its original scribe in Italy and by Anglo-Saxon

14 left

The sixth-century Gospel Book brought to England from Italy in the mission of St Augustine of Canterbury, long preserved on the high altar of the abbey founded by Augustine (CAMBRIDGE, CORPUS CHRISTI COLLEGE, MS. 286)

15 right

Another Italian sixth-century Gospel Book brought first to England and then by Anglo-Saxon missionaries across to northern Europe for the conversion of Germany (WÜRZBURG, UNIVERSITÄTS-BIBLIOTHEK, COD. M.P.TH.F. 68)

scribes during its time in Northumbria. Once familiar from liturgical chanting, then, the Vulgate translation moved across Europe.

The Gospels were generally written in a single volume with all four texts. They are the most common early manuscripts of any kind. Manuscripts of other parts of the Bible mostly also circulated in separate books, or clusters of books, such as the Octateuch (the first eight books, from Genesis to Ruth), or the books of Solomon, or the Prophets, or the Epistles. Acts was often accompanied by the Apocalypse. Psalters usually appeared as separate volumes and became relatively more common in the seventh and eighth century, which may say something about private devotion (or this may too simply be a chance of survival, for they are often pretty books). Biblical manuscripts gradually became larger in their dimensions between the fifth and the eighth century, a trend found in all books at this time but which may also reflect the increasing use of the Bible text in public reading.

Manuscript texts always have a tendency to become ever more inaccurate, as one copy is taken from another. Various local textual families of Vulgate biblical books can be loosely identified, often in trends that cross and re-cross each other as one text is copied from one source and then perhaps checked against another.

Manuscripts are very portable and were moved easily across Europe. It is never completely simple to assert that textual variations prove a manuscript to come from one centre or another, but sometimes a cumulation of variant readings can be used to suggest that a text belongs to a family which is common in Spain or Ireland or southern France, for example.

At certain stages in the history of the Latin Vulgate, medieval scholars attempted to restore the purity and uniformity of its text. There was an old tradition that one Peregrinus revised the Vulgate in fifth-century Spain. Other than noting a distinct strain of Spanish Vulgate Bibles hundreds of years later, we do not know what he did. Victor, bishop of Capua (just north of Naples) from 541 to 554, devised an intriguing edition of the Gospels in which all four narratives were conflated into one. It was formed of lengthy extracts from each of the four evangelists according to the Vulgate text, arranged so that one biblical quotation follows another and creates a single narrative, with appropriate citations in the margins. His own manuscript, apparently dated 546–7, belonged later to Saint Boniface (680–754), who annotated it, and it happens to survive among the relics of that saint (Fulda, Landesbibliothek, cod. Bonifatianus 1). It is the oldest dated Latin biblical manuscript known.

We have more knowledge, although probably not the actual manuscripts, of Cassiodorus (*c*.485–*c*.580) as an editor and promoter of the Vulgate text. Flavius Magnus Aurelius Cassiodorus was a late Roman senator who in his mid-50s retired from the civil service and founded a very civilized monastery on his family estate near Naples. It was called the *Vivarium* ('fish pond'), named after the water gardens in the grounds. He furnished the monastery with three complete sets of the books of the Latin Bible. Cassiodorus had probably not altered the text as such, but he certainly selected the translations with care and had standardized the grammar and spelling, and he devised quite distinct formats for each of the three sets. He describes these in some detail in his *Institutiones*, a textbook which he wrote on Christian education. The first set comprised the Bible arranged into a set of nine matching volumes. Presumably these followed the standard Vulgate text. The second he calls his *Codex Grandior*, the 'larger codex'. It was written in big script and contained the whole Bible, with the Old Testament in Jerome's intermediate version (taken from the Greek rather than the Hebrew). It is described as being made up of 95 gatherings of 8 leaves, a total of 760 vast leaves (1,520 pages), and it included a plan of the Temple of Jerusalem and a diagram showing the different ways of arranging the books of the Bible. The third book was a one-volume Bible, presumably the Vulgate again, in small script, fitted into 53 gatherings of 6 leaves, a total of 318 leaves. All these details are recorded in the *Institutiones*.

Like many ideological institutions which depend on the personalities of one man, the Vivarium did not long survive the death of its founder. Funds ran out, and within 30 or 40 years it had been disbanded. The manuscripts made for

Cassiodorus seem to have been acquired by an Englishman visiting Rome in the seventh century, Benedict Biscop (d.690), who then brought them back to Northumbria in the very north of England. The *Codex Grandior* was evidently especially admired there. According to a contemporary biography of Ceolfrith (d.716), abbot of Wearmouth and Jarrow, three vast manuscripts were made on the same model, one each for Ceolfrith's two monasteries and one intended for the pope in Rome. Their text was copied according to the final Vulgate text of Jerome, and

it is striking that this was still described as the 'new translation', 300 years after Jerome had prepared it. Ceolfrith himself set off in June 716 to carry the pope's copy to Italy, but he died on the journey. The manuscript survives. It is known as the *Codex Amiatinus* (Florence, Biblioteca Medicea-Laurenziana, cod. Amiatino 1). Now, at last, we have one surviving manuscript with a format and a design based on the edition of Cassiodorus. It even includes copies of the diagrams which Cassiodorus so carefully describes.

The *Codex Amiatinus* is one of the purest and best copies of Jerome's Vulgate. From the sixteenth century onwards it has been accepted and used as the most reliable manuscript for editors of Jerome's translation. There are two important points to be made about it. The first observation is that it is a complete Bible, or 'pandect'. This is a word which will occur a number of times in the first few chapters of our story. The word is from the Greek, *pan* (all) and *dekhesthai* (to receive), and a pandect is an all-inclusive Bible, or a complete text of every book combined into a single comprehensive volume. Complete Bibles, as we would recognize them, with all the books of the Old and New Testaments contained in a single volume, were almost unimaginable at this time. The books of the Bible would usually have circulated in multiple volumes. Sometimes these were evidently made to form matching sets, as was likely at Bobbio in the seventh century (flyleaves in Milan, Biblioteca Ambrosiana, cod. D.30.inf., and cod. D.84. inf.). The famous frontispiece to the *Codex Amiatinus* itself shows the scribe Ezra seated in front of a book cupboard with nine matching volumes on the shelves, doubtless echoing the idea of Cassiodorus's own nine-volume Latin Bible (Pl. 17). The *Codex Amiatinus*,

17

The frontispiece of the Codex
Amiatinus *shows Ezra seated
by a book cupboard, with a
9-volume Bible on the shelves
beside him*
(FLORENCE, BIBLIOTECA
MEDICEA-LAURENZIANA, COD.
AMIATINO 1)

18 opposite

*The Echternach Gospel Book
was made in England in the
eighth century, but claims to
have been corrected by comparison with a manuscript which
had belonged to Jerome
himself. The symbol of Saint
Matthew is a man (Imago
Hominis) shown holding a
book*
(PARIS, BNF, MS. LAT. 9389)

however, is one vast volume, 1,030 leaves (2,060 pages), 505 by 340mm (20 by 13¼ inches), encompassing all the books of the Bible, with a diagram showing the Holy Ghost clasping it its beak a sort of net linking the whole of the eloquence of God in a single unit. It is the oldest surviving manuscript of the Latin Bible as a single volume. It dates from three centuries later than its original translation by Jerome, and it marks a turning-point not only in book production but in the abstract concept of the Bible as a unity.

The second notable point about the *Codex Amiatinus* is that was made in England. The idea of a one-volume pandect of the Bible was evidently imported from Cassiodorus in southern Italy, but English scribes seized the concept as no one else had done, and they multiplied the text. The *Codex Amiatinus* text, in turn, provided the direct model for the Lindisfarne Gospels (London, BL, Cotton MS. Nero D.IV) and for other biblical books subsequently disseminated by the Anglo-Saxon missionaries across northern Europe in the eighth century. The Echternach Gospel Book (Paris, BNF, ms. lat. 9389, Pl. 18), perhaps made in Lindisfarne, north of Jarrow, has a curious subscription claiming that it was corrected against a codex which had belonged to Jerome himself and which was in the year 558 in the library of the priest Eugipus. This priest has been tentatively identified as a man recorded as abbot of a monastery near Naples. We cannot trust the statement itself, but it is evidence of Northumbrian scribes attempting to get back to a pure and ancient text, perhaps through a source in southern Italy. Another extremely important surviving southern Italian manuscript is bilingual copy of Acts in Greek and the Old Latin, dating from the sixth or seventh century. It shares so many unique readings with the text of Acts as quoted by Bede (*c.*673–735), that we must assume that this actual manuscript too was brought to Northumbria where Bede must have used it. It is now Oxford, Bodleian Library, MS. Laud Gr. 35. Probably, even if the mechanics are lost to us, there was a careful programme of studying the sources of the Bible text in north-east England. Northumbria seems to have played a remarkable part in the dissemination of Jerome's translation. It is tempting to see the Venerable Bede, Doctor of the Church, like Saint Jerome, as having a role too in completing the publication of the Vulgate.

Bede died in 735, the year that Alcuin was probably born, in York, 75 miles south of Jarrow. In 766 Alcuin became master of the cathedral school in York.

In 781 he met Charlemagne, who summoned him to Aachen as the administrator of a whole royal programme of religious reform. The entry of Alcuin in this story takes us into the last part of this chapter. Charlemagne (*c*.742–814) was the founder (or re-founder, as he preferred to see it) of the Holy Roman Empire. By the eighth century, the ancient Roman Empire had entirely disintegrated, and all Europe had been overrun by what the classical Romans would have called barbarians; we now call this period the Dark Ages. Christianity, however, survived. It had managed to maintain and develop its structure of papacy, bishoprics, churches and monasteries, and gradually converted the invaders. In doing so, it preserved the language and some of the prestige and authority of Rome. Charlemagne now hoped to re-create the spirit of this once great empire. Although Latin had passed out of daily use, Charlemagne promoted its retention with Alcuin's help, and the Vulgate suited his purpose for it represented imperial antiquity and consistency. He was concerned to unite his kingdom through active promotion of cultural uniformity, which was then enforced. His proclamation of 789 identifies the need for correct and standardized Latin manuscripts of the liturgy and of the Bible.

There is evidence of three distinct campaigns of biblical reform in Charlemagne's kingdom in the late eighth century. The first is associated with Maudramnus, abbot of Corbie, who commissioned a series of books of the Bible on a grand scale, edited 'for the convenience of readers' (as the colophon at the end of Maccabees asserts). Five volumes and part of a sixth from the set survive, mostly in Amiens (Bibliothèque Municipale, mss. 6–7, 9, 11–12, and Paris, BNF, ms. lat. 13174, Pl. 19). The project began on a grand scale, and the books adopt a new script – a small, round and legible hand now known as Carolingian minuscule. The volumes, however, began decreasing in size and expense as the text progressed through the Old Testament, and presumably the Bible was more or less abandoned when Maudramnus died in 781, before beginning the Gospels.

The second attempt at biblical reform is associated with Theodulf of Orléans (c.750–821), a Spanish theologian who was abbot of Fleury. It is represented in its original phase by two complete Bible manuscripts, luxury pandects, from around the year 800 (Paris, BNF, ms. lat. 9380, and Le Puy, Trésor de la cathédrale, s.n.). The huge manuscripts are very similar to each other, in two columns of 62 lines of minuscule, with illuminated prefaces in gold writing on purple vellum, and with variant or doubtful readings of the text carefully marked in the margins. However, this second project evidently also failed to catch the imagination or the necessary finance of patrons.

Charlemagne's vision of a uniform and accurate one-volume Bible text was finally brought into realization in its third attempt, masterminded and promoted by Alcuin of

York. In 796 Alcuin was appointed as abbot of St Martin's Abbey in Tours. He refers to books being sent over from York in 797, and it is clear that Northumbrian biblical manuscripts were a principal source for Alcuin's edition. There is a reference in the year 800 to Alcuin being involved in the 'emendation' of the Old and New Testaments. Probably Alcuin's task was not so much in changing the words of text (wisely, if he was to succeed) as in editing the spelling, punctuation and grammar into a standard form throughout the Bible. Alcuin uses the term 'pandect' and he clearly conceived of the Bible as a single publication, a unit, whether in one volume or split into several matching volumes created as a continuous set of books in a fixed order. Carolingian library catalogues start to use the word '*bibliotheca*' for a Bible, the same word as for a 'library', a complete collection of books. From the very first years of the 800s, the new big revised 'Alcuin' Bibles were being sent out across the Carolingian Empire from the monastic scriptoria of Tours.

No fewer than 46 whole manuscript Bibles and 13 Gospel Books attributable to Tours have actually survived from the first half of the ninth century, and there are references to many others (Pl. 20). This probably represents the production of something like two entire Bibles every year, for fifty years. The manuscripts are generally extremely consistent in format, comprising the whole Bible in about 420–50 leaves, written in two columns of 50 to 52 lines. Between two and 24 scribes worked on each manuscript. Alcuin himself died in 804 and Charlemagne in 814, but the production of Bibles continued relentlessly at Tours under abbots Fridugisus (804–34), Adalhard (834–43) and Vivian (844). They are often very richly illuminated and illustrated books. The expense involved must have been enormous; availability of funds was one reason for their success. Some were evidently paid for by the monks, who presented copies to rich patrons in expectation of favours in return. Others were commissioned by princes of Church and state, in order to be presented to other monasteries in the hope of spiritual reward. The initial purpose of the ninth-century Bibles may well have been political and strategic, but the result was that the Latin Vulgate text, in Carolingian minuscule script, was promoted, adopted and then recopied throughout the empire of Charlemagne and his successors, Louis the Pious (814–40) and Lothair (840–55). All the great monasteries of northern Europe seem to have owned pandect Bibles by the mid-ninth century, and there were already copies at Laon, Aachen, Paris, St-Denis, Metz, St-Gall (where we saw palimpsests of the Old Latin Bible struggling for survival centuries earlier), Monza, Trier, Hildesheim, Bamberg and elsewhere.

In conclusion, it had seemed for some centuries as though Jerome's translation of the Bible would hardly make headway against the conservative Old Latin editions of the Scriptures. It had been written in the daily language of the time but only gained in popularity as Latin became archaic. The Vulgate was gradually adopted into public use in the liturgy of Western Europe. This really secured its position of eminence. From time to time, attempts were made to revise the biblical texts and to bring them into consistency with each other. By the period of Charlemagne, the books of the Bible had evolved into a consistent whole, and the translation is principally that of Jerome. By now, after four hundred years, the very name of Saint Jerome and the antiquity of his text conferred unimpeachable authority. Let us end this first chapter then with a miniature from the First Bible of Charles the Bold, sometimes called the Vivian Bible, made in Tours about 846 (Paris, BNF, ms. lat. 1). One of its full-page prefatory illustrations (Pl. 21) shows Saint Jerome, with a golden halo, sailing to the east, working on his Bible, explaining it to his disciples who begin to copy it, and finally Jerome himself again, like Moses on Mount Sinai, distributing manuscripts of the text to the left and to the right to monks who hurry off with their one-volume Bibles into their churches. We have come a long way from what actually happened in Bethlehem in the late fourth century, and we have brought the Latin Bible into a shape in which it will be recognizable for the rest of the Middle Ages.

21 opposite

A full-page illustration in the First Bible of Charles the Bold, Tours, c.846, shows the work of Saint Jerome in translating and distributing the Latin Bible

(PARIS, BNF, MS. LAT. 1)

2 | The Bible in Hebrew and Greek

A TRANSLATOR does not eliminate an original text by turning it into another language. In preparing the Latin Vulgate, Saint Jerome had used manuscripts of older versions of the Bible in Hebrew and Greek. These were languages still spoken then by people who lived in and around the Near East, where Jerome was working, and their texts of the Bible existed before and after translations were made into Latin. The Vulgate text was assembled in Palestine, but it was used in Western Europe. Hebrew and Greek speakers still kept their Bibles with the wording and arrangement of the text unaltered, and these Bibles too left manuscript descendants which still exist. This chapter considers the early history and continued survival of the Scriptures in their original languages.

Let us lay out the ground extremely simply first, for the evolution of the Bible in Hebrew and Greek is complicated. Then, we can return to greater detail. It begins in ancient history. Most of what is now called the Old Testament had originally been written in the Hebrew language, centuries before Christ. Jews today still use the Hebrew text, apparently unaltered. Jewish readers of the Bible would not use the term 'Old' Testament, because for Jews there is no other part. It is simply the Bible. The ancient Jews, however, did have access to this Hebrew Bible in a Greek translation. This was the version known as the 'Septuagint', which was originally used by Greek-speaking Jews, still before Christianity. When the New Testament was compiled, it was written in Greek from the beginning. There was no New Testament in Hebrew. Many of the first converts to Christianity had been brought up as Jews, familiar with the Bible. Early Christians rapidly adopted the old Greek Septuagint, as if it had been intended for them all along, and they twinned it with their new Scriptures to form a complementary pair of sacred collections in a single language, now called the Old Testament and

ΥΝΙ ... Ρ...ΟΧΟΙΟΥ...ΓΥΝΑΙΚ... ... ...ΘΗΝΑΠΟ...ΟΝ...ΠΑΝ ICΟΑΛ...
ΗΛΠ...ΤΗ ... CΟΤΗ... Η ... ΤΙ ΜΕΚ... ... ... ΙΑΝΟΚ...Η
CΟΝ ΤΑΙ ΥΜΩΝ ... ΟΦΕ ΛΑΜ... ΛΚΙC...ΘCΕ... Κ... Cε...ΙΝ ...
ΚΟΝ ... Cε ΛΑΟΜ... ΓΑ...ΠΟΝΗ... ...ΤΑΙ ΠΑ CΟ ... ...
ΤΟΥ ... ΛΟΜΕΙΟΒΡ...ΩCIN Η ... ΙΟΤ... CΕΟ ΠΟ ... ... ΦΕ ΛΑΜΟΙCΙΑ
ΚΜΟΡΘΟΝ CC... ΤΗΝ ΤΟΥΙ CΑ ... Λ ΟΗΙΚ...Κ... ... ... C ... ΟΜΑ ΓΥΝΗ...
ΤΟΥ ΚΑΡΠΟΥΑΥΤΟΝ CΘ ΦΑΓΕ... ΚΑΙ ... ΑΥΓΕ... ... ΤΙ ΤΩ Α Μ... Ρ...
ΑΥΤΗ C ΜΕCΑ... ΤΗC ΤΟΝ CΟ ... ... Η ... ΥΛ... ΤΑΡΑ ΧΟΗ...ΟΑΛ...
ΟΙ ΟΟΘ ΚΑ ΜΟ ΓΤ... ΛΛ Ο ΙCΕΡ... Η ... C Κ ΝΑΟΘΙΟΥ Μ...Ο ΤΗC ΓΑ ...CΑ...
ΕΡ ΜΑΝΟΥ ΤΑ ΛΙ CΥΓΛΛΔΟΗ... ΚΑΙCΟΝ... ΑΜΕ...Τ ΟΥΠΕΡΙΖ Τ ...ΤΑ
ΚΛΗ ΜΑ ΤΟΟΗΡΙΝ ΚΟ ΧΟΥ ΜΕΝΗ C... ... Τ ΕΝ ΟΥC Ο ΑΙ ΟΙCΚ Cε ΚΤΙ Κ CΟΛ ... CΕ NIC ⲥ̄
Ο ΓΟ ΝΑ Α ΛΛ Ι CΟ...Ο Π ΕΝ ΑΥΤ ... ... C Ο CΤ... CΑ... ΚΑ Μ Ο ΤΤ Η CΟ ΦΑ Ι NHCT Υ
Γ Η ΚΟΥ CΑ Λ Ε ΦΟ ... C...Η ... ΗΤΗΝ ... ΓΥΝΙΚ CC ... ... Κ Ε ΚΤΥΒΗΗ... Cε ΙΘΕΝ ΥΤ
ΑΝ Η ΠΙ ΓΛ ΝΟ C ΠΓ ΓΜ ΝΟ Ο Β ... CΕ ΧΑ ΤΙ Ο ... Α... ΧΥ ΛΟΥ ... ... ΤΑ ΛΛ ΑΛΙ Ν CΟΙ
Cε ΙΠ Ο ΤΥ ΤΟ Υ ΓΥ ΝΑ Ι ΚΑ ... Μ ΛΑ ΡΙ ΗΝ ΑΠ ΛΓΑ Λ ... CΕΟΗΗ C ... C Η ... Π Ο ... ΛΛΙ Η ΓΥ Ν
Η ΝΕ Δ ΩΚΑ C ΜΟΙ Cε Ε ΜΟΥ ΑΥ ΤΗ ΜΟΙ Ε ΔΩ ΚΕΝ ΑΠΟ ΤΟΥ ΓΥΛΟΥ Ι ΦΑ ...
ΚΛ Ε Ι ΠΕ ΝΟ ΘΟC ... Η ... ΙΥ ΜΗ ... ... Υ ... ΤΤ C ΟΥ ΤΟC ΕΠΟΙΗCΕ ΙΕ... Ε NΟ Ο Φ...ΛΤ... ...

the New Testament. Christian Bibles therefore used both parts, the old Jewish and the more recent Christian scriptures, all in Greek.

Following the Jewish revolt of 66 AD, the Romans sacked Jerusalem in 70 AD, destroyed the Temple, and expelled the Jews from their homeland (Pl. 23). This was the beginning of the extraordinary exile of the Jewish people, the longest and most restless journey in history, which lasted until the final establishment of the modern state of Israel in 1947. The Jews took their Bible on their travels. The Bible in Hebrew, regarded as unalterable and absolute, became a unifying symbol of Jewish identity in exile. There is evidence of an important council of Jewish rabbis held in Jamnia, south of Jaffa, around 100 AD, which apparently settled for all time the components and exact wording of the Hebrew Bible. One of its leading members was the great biblical interpreter, Rabbi Akiba (c.55–132). There is much speculation but no certain knowledge of what was resolved at Jamnia. The Greek Septuagint was put aside and the sacred text was henceforth defined as being in Hebrew. That decision must have had an incalculable effect in preserving the Hebrew language and thus the cultural unity of all future generations of Jews, in every part of the world. It may be that parts of the Hebrew Bible known today were actually translated at the time of Jamnia back into Hebrew, based on the Septuagint, or were at least revised and standardized against the Greek text. The council seems to have made a final ruling on what books were or were not to be included in the Hebrew Bible. Some ambiguous texts, such as the Song of Songs, were accepted as biblical. Others, which had been in the Septuagint translation, were eliminated. These included the books of Wisdom, Ecclesiasticus, Judith, Tobit and Baruch. The rejected books survived only in the Greek, which had by then been adopted by early Christians, and thus their texts are preserved outside the Jewish tradition. The council at Jamnia

ruled that any future decisions about the wording and use of the purified Hebrew Bible would be subject to the *Masorah*, or unquestionable rabbinical tradition. The endorsed Hebrew Bible was thereafter known as the 'Masoretic' text.

It has always been difficult to follow the subsequent history of the Bible in Hebrew because, until recently, no manuscripts of the Hebrew Bible were known earlier in date than the ninth or tenth century, eight or nine hundred years later than the Council of Jamnia. Modern archaeological discoveries of much earlier Hebrew fragments will have to be deferred until Chapter 12 below. For most of the history of Bible scholarship, therefore, the early history of the Hebrew text has always been reconstructed by speculating backwards from very late manuscripts. Hebrew Bibles are extremely conservative, right across different strands of Judaism. Hebrew Bibles are much more consistent in structure and text than any manuscripts of the Christian Bible. The Masoretic customs first established at Jamnia for the safe transmission of the Hebrew text seem to have been followed scrupulously.

Surviving Hebrew Bibles are relatively common from the late twelfth century onwards. They often bear evidence of heart-rending histories, as their owners moved from one persecution to another around Europe and the Middle East. The manuscripts are written in the ancient Hebrew alphabet, running from right to left. There are no equivalents of capital letters in Hebrew script, and the neat columns of writing give the appearance of extreme austerity, without the colourful initials which often enliven Latin Bibles. There are usually no illustrations in Hebrew Bibles. Although artistic invention has always been permitted in Jewish lore (indeed an artist Bezalel ben Hur was appointed by God in Exodus 31:1-5), the second of the Ten Commandments seemed to proscribe the depiction of living creatures. This prohibition was applied especially to Bibles. Some manuscripts have decorated borders or ornamented title-pages, usually without human figures. In many medieval Hebrew Bibles the margins are filled with lines of writing in tiny script. These record the *Masorah*, statements of the inherited rabbinical rules on the correct methods of reading and accenting the text. Sometimes these lines of minute text are bent upwards and downwards and are shaped into forming wonderful patterns swirling and criss-crossing around the edges of the pages. The lines the *Masorah* are sometimes ingeniously formed into outlines of pictures of flowers, animals (Pl. 25), and even people. Because the lines are composed entirely of writing, such ornament escaped the prohibition of illustrating the Bible.

The texts of Hebrew manuscript Bibles are traditionally arranged into clusters of books, to which different levels of sacred importance are accorded. The most holy texts are the first five books of the Bible, Genesis to Deuteronomy, known as the Books of Moses, or, more usually, the Torah. The Samaritan sect broke away from mainstream Judaism in the ancient world. The Samaritans were already a distinct and mistrusted ethnic group in the time of the Gospels. The only part of the Bible which the Samaritans accepted as authentic was the Torah, and so presumably they had split off from the Jews when only the Torah existed. The break occurred sometime between the fifth and the first century BC. It pro-

vides a clue to the fact that the Bible must have acquired its texts cumulatively and that there was once a time when it comprised the Torah alone. Simply by order of precedence, if nothing else, the Torah is rightly assigned to the most important status.

The Prophets are accorded the second level of sacred importance in the Hebrew Bible. For convenience, the prophetical books are subdivided into two further groupings, of equal rank. These are called the 'Former Prophets', which are Joshua, Judges, Samuel and Kings (mostly historical narratives) and the 'Latter Prophets' (Pl. 26), which are Isaiah, Jeremiah and Ezekiel, and all twelve minor prophets, Hosea, Joel, Amos, Obadiah, Jonah, Micah, Nahum, Habakkuk, Zephaniah, Haggai, Zechariah and Malachi. All other books of the Hebrew Bible are assigned to a third ranking. In Hebrew Bibles these are called the 'Hagiographa', or holy writings. This third and lowest level of sacred status includes the Psalms, the books of Solomon, Daniel, and various other historical texts such as Ruth, Chronicles and Esther.

The division of the Hebrew Bible into three categories presumably dates back to antiquity, for Jesus seems to allude to it in Saint Luke's Gospel, before the Ascension (Luke 24:44). He says there that the events of his life had all been predicted by the Law of Moses, the Prophets, and the Psalms. (The Psalms form the opening book of the Hagiographa.) Medieval Hebrew biblical manuscripts often comprise only one of these three classifications of books. If all three parts are present, they are usually separated from each other by clear visual breaks or by groups of what are called 'carpet pages'. These are full-page ornaments of softly coloured patterns of decorative interlace, resembling oriental tapestries, which mark the openings of each section of a manuscript (Pl. 27). They are especially common in medieval Hebrew Bibles from Spain and Portugal. Turning a group of carpet pages is like lifting layers of precious textile before revealing the sacred text.

From the perspective of the modern Christian Bible, the choice of texts within the second and third sections of a Hebrew Bible is unexpected. The definition of 'Prophets' seems very broadly interpreted, if they can include historical narratives such as Samuel and Kings, and yet assign the very similar books of Chronicles to the Hagiographa. The book of Daniel, which is quite explicitly prophetical in its text, is not included among the Prophets at all. This is usually taken as evidence that the Hebrew Bible originally expanded in fixed stages. Since Daniel probably dates from around 165 BC (even Jerome accepted this

26 opposite

The opening of Isaiah, the first text of the 'Latter Prophets' in a Hebrew Bible illuminated in Florence in the late fifteenth century
(PARIS, BNF, MS. HÉB. 15)

27

The clusters of texts in Hebrew Bibles were often graphically separated by full-page decorations known as 'carpet pages'. This example is from a Bible completed in Lisbon, Portugal, in 1483
(LONDON, BL, OR. MS. 2628)

approximate date), the Prophets must already have been by that time a self-contained entity in the Hebrew Bible, with no scope for supplements. Daniel seems to have been a late entrant. The Hagiographa was still flexible in the second century BC, and probably its composition was not finally settled until the council of Jamnia.

The best indication of the contents of the Hebrew Bible before the Jewish exile is to be found in the Septuagint, translated for the many Jews who spoke the Greek language. The legend of the Septuagint's origin is recounted in the so-called 'Letter of Aristeas', a Jew who claimed to have been a court official under King Ptolemy Philadelphus, king of Egypt 285-247 BC. Aristeas tells that the king commissioned from the Jews a translation of the Hebrew Pentateuch into Greek for inclusion in the library of Alexandria. It was carried out with the support of Eleazor, high priest in Jerusalem. The tale reports that 72 Jewish elders, six from each of the Twelve Tribes, were sent to sit on separate sand-banks in the harbour at Alexandria, and each was asked to prepare a complete translation of the Hebrew Torah. After precisely 72 days every single translator found he had prepared an identical translation. The name 'Septuagint' means '70' in Latin, and the version is commonly abbreviated in writing as the 'LXX' (acknowledgement of the final two of the 72 supposed translators seems to have dropped off the name). Although originally it comprised only the five books of the Torah, Genesis to Deuteronomy, the name 'Septuagint' is generally applied to the whole Old Testament in late classical Greek.

So far as can be judged, the translation into Greek must have evolved over several generations, perhaps beginning around the third century BC. A full and composite Septuagint text was certainly available by the first century before Christ. The date of Ptolemy Philadelphus is at least chronologically plausible for the beginning of the undertaking. By the time it was completed, the Septuagint contained all of what we know as the Old Testament. There is still some uncertainty about the book of Daniel, the last-minute prophet who was nearly left behind. The version as it appears in the Septuagint may have been inserted from a later translation from the Hebrew, after the revision of Jamnia.

The first Christians knew and used the Septuagint in Greek. It was the only body of Scripture known to Saint Paul, for the Gospels did not yet exist as a written text when he was first preaching Christianity. His listeners spoke Greek. The Epistle to the Hebrews was doubtless written in Greek, not Hebrew. When Saint Paul invoked the Bible, he did so by reference to the Septuagint. The Gospel writers used it too. When the author of Saint Matthew's Gospel cites the prophecy of Isaiah in Matthew 1:23, he uses the phrasing of the Septuagint which differs very slightly from that of the text in Hebrew.

Many of the names of the books of the Bible, familiar to us now as if they were proper nouns, are actually Greek words surviving from the Septuagint. Examples include *genesis* ('creation' in Greek) and *exodos* ('going out', the exit from Egypt). The title of Deuteronomy is from the Septuagint translation of Deuteronomy 17:18, in which a good king is enjoined to write out a second copy of the Law and to honour and keep it. The two words *deutero nomon* literally mean a 'second law', for that fifth book of the Bible was seen as a reaffirmation of the Law of Moses. The book of Psalms too has a title from the Septuagint, *psalmos* in Greek meaning 'plucking with fingers', for these were hymns sung to the harp. Even the designation 'Bible' is a Greek word. The Jews had no generic title for the Scriptures. There is a reference to earlier prophecies in Daniel 9:2, where Daniel says he looked 'in the books', *ha-sefarim* in Hebrew. That is as near to a title as the Old Testament gives itself. It is translated *en tois bibliois* in the Septuagint, from the plural noun *ta biblia*. In Greek this literally meant 'the scrolls'. The Septuagint gives us the word 'Bible' by describing it as a collection of scrolls.

The scroll or roll book was the usual format of a text in the classical world. To judge from the Dead Sea Scrolls and other fragments from sites in Palestine, many ancient Jewish texts were written on animal skin, either leather or parchment. This was being used as a writing material in the Near East by the third century BC. The ancient form of a roll book has a remarkable living fossil in the Jewish practice of writing Torah Scrolls today (Pl. 28). A modern Sefer Torah, or Torah Scroll, is still made by hand from parchment, which even now is scrupulously prepared from the inner layer of the skin of a kosher animal. The writing in a Sefer Torah still reflects the script of the ancient world, without the Masoretic apparatus grafted elsewhere into the Hebrew Bible after Jamnia. Torah Scrolls are attached to wooden rollers at each end, so that the text can be unfurled horizontally between two hands. Many rituals are attached to Torah Scrolls today and some, including the format and material, are likely to echo practices of extreme antiquity.

Bibles in the ancient world were usually written as scrolls. This format still survives in the traditional Hebrew Torah Scroll for the sacred books of the Law. The illustration shows a Jewish scribe in New York

There are a number of explicit references to scrolls in the New Testament. In Luke 4:17 and 4:20, for example, Jesus unrolls and rolls up again a scroll of Isaiah. There is a wonderful image in Revelations 6:14 in which the sky is described as disappearing, 'like a scroll rolling up'. It is extremely likely that most or all of the New Testament was originally made on scrolls. The early Christians, looking outwards onto the Greco-Roman world, probably mostly wrote on papyrus rather than on animal skin. Papyrus was the normal writing material around the shores of the Mediterranean, common in Egypt, Greece and Italy. The use of papyrus is important in the original development of the New Testament, for its limitations imposed restrictions on the length of books.

Papyrus was formed from broad ribbons of pith which were cut from the stalk of the papyrus reed. These were laid side by side and compressed together with further parallel rows laid at right angles on top. Sheets of papyrus were evidently manufactured commercially in units of about 3 metres long (10 feet). An ancient scribe assembling a book in roll form could either cut the sheet shorter (for a brief text) or could paste several sheets end to end to make a very long consecutive roll for a lengthy text. In practice, a scroll of more than about three sheets (say 10 metres, 30 feet) would have been extremely unwieldy to use. Some short books, like the Epistles of John, could have been written on single sheets. Longer books, like Saint Matthew's Gospel, for example, or the Acts of the Apostles, would probably have required the absolute maximum manageable length of about 10 metres each. It would have been impossible to write all four Gospels (for example) as a single scroll, and it would be inconceivable to consider the whole Old or New Testaments as single entities. From the beginning of Christianity, therefore, the Greek Scriptures must have been formed of separate texts or clusters of texts, and never as a single consecutive unit. This is important in the subsequent history of the Greek Bible.

There is a major contribution to modern civilization which was probably made by the Bible. This is the adoption of the codex as a book format, a shape that is

29

Early Christians adopted the codex format for their Bibles, creating books with pages. This detail from a Greek Gospel Book of 1133 shows Saint John holding a codex
(LOS ANGELES, J. PAUL GETTY MUSEUM, MS. LUDWIG II.4)

30 opposite

Constantinople was refounded in 330 AD. It became the greatest city of the Greek world, filled with churches and monasteries. This illustration is from an Italian fifteenth-century guidebook to the Greek archipelago
(PRIVATE COLLECTION)

with us still (Pl. 29). The codex ('codices' in the plural) is what we would now recognize as a book – a rectangular artefact with separate pages hinged along their inner edges so that they can be turned one after the other to follow a text from beginning to end. This may originally have been a Roman invention, perhaps deriving from bundles of tablets tied together for note-taking, but it was almost exclusively adopted and promoted for copying portions of the New Testament. The format was probably already being used for Greek biblical texts by the early second century. The association between the codex and Christianity is increasingly supported by archaeological evidence. Christian texts dating from about the third century onwards are consistently found in fragments of what were evidently once codices; whereas non-Christian and late classical texts at the same date are almost invariably found in what must still have been scrolls. Many ingenious explanations have been put forward. One theory associates the codex with the publication of Saint Mark's Gospel, the most Roman of the Gospel texts. Another links it with the assembling of Saint Paul's Epistles into a single comprehensive collection. There is persuasive but indirect evidence that the Epistles were edited around 100 AD into a mathematically neat sequence of ten texts addressed to the seven churches of early Christendom, arranged into seven books in order of decreasing length, from Romans to Colossians. Such an extensive compilation would have been far too bulky for a single scroll. The sequence of texts and their universal application across the whole Church would not have been possible if the publication had been in the form of seven separate scrolls, in no fixed order. Therefore, it is argued, the first omnibus edition of the Epistles of Saint Paul must have been conceived as a codex.

Certainly the codex was quickly welcomed by scribes of the early Greek Bible. During the period of the Roman persecution Christians were relatively poor and perhaps the codex was simply cheaper, because it uses both sides of the papyrus. It may also have been a convenience when the books were being used. Biblical books were not primarily single sequential narratives to be read from end to end. They needed to be consulted as works of reference, comparing passages, such as prophecy and fulfilment, and they had to be recited during church services in short but widely separated passages, required in rapid succession. It would undoubtedly have been simpler to compare pages and to mark passages with bookmarks if the Bible had been constructed in the form of a codex.

The first codices were probably all made of papyrus. Constant turning of pages must have rendered papyrus very brittle in the folds. Papyrus is also quite thick

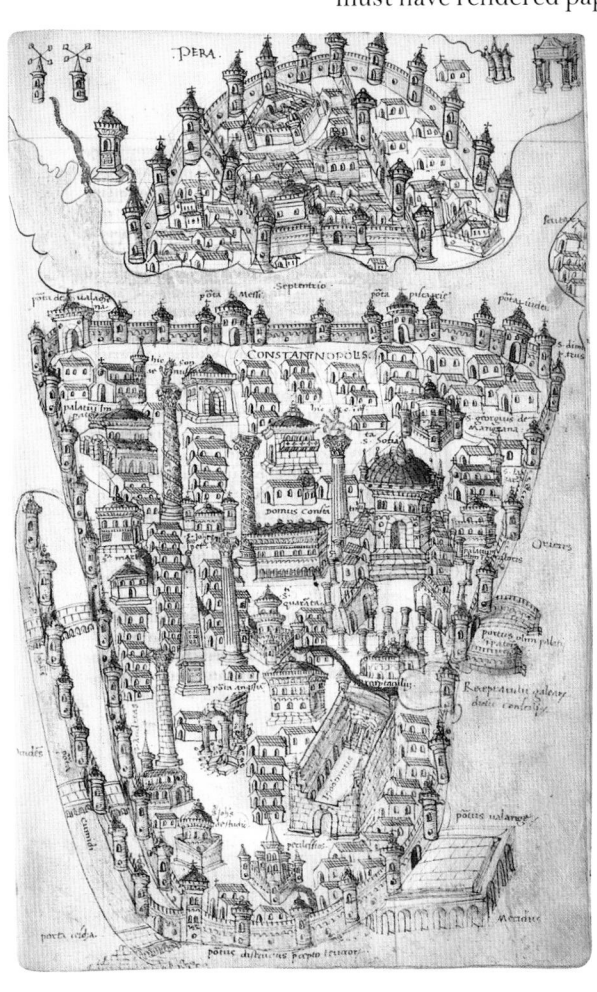

and dense, compared with some of the earliest examples of parchment, and a codex made of papyrus is unexpectedly heavy to hold in one's hand. A papyrus book of very large dimensions would have been extremely weighty. Very gradually, perhaps following the adoption of the Septuagint, fine parchment began to replace papyrus as a common medium for Christian books. Parchment (or vellum, for the terms are interchangeable) was made from animal skin soaked, scraped and dried under tension. By the third or fourth century, many Greek biblical codices were being copied on parchment.

Christianity became the official religion of the Roman Empire under Constantine the Great (d.337), changing in policy from toleration (312) to active promulgation (324). The Council of Nicea took place in 325. The Nicene Creed, which is still used, recites the principal tenets of Christianity. These may be confirmed by reference to the Bible but the Creed says nothing about the status or authority of the Bible itself. In 330 a new joint capital of the Roman Empire was founded by Constantine in Byzantium (Pl. 30), courteously renamed Constantinople in his honour (it is now called Istanbul). The creation of an eastern Empire marks the very beginning of what eventually became, and still remains, a split between the Roman and the Orthodox Churches. The

Pope still resides in Rome and the head of the Eastern Orthodox Church is still the Patriarch of Constantinople, perpetuating the twin cities of the Roman Empire from the time of Constantine.

Although Latin was initially still the language of Roman government and law, the old Byzantium was a long-established Greek-speaking town and had been Christian since the second century. It was natural that Christian observance there should continue in Greek. In 332, two years after its re-foundation, Constantine wrote to Eusebius of Caesaria, who was then in Constantinople, soliciting his help in ordering fifty manuscripts of the Divine Scriptures for the instruction of the Church and for use in the churches he was building in the new city. The manuscripts were to be written, the emperor's letter says, 'on well-prepared parchment by copyists most skilful in the art of accurate and beautiful writing, which must be very legible and easily portable in order that they may be used'.

This is the earliest surviving official statement on the making of Bibles and their function. It is implicit that the texts would be in Greek. The books are to be accurate, which already suggests a standard against which to measure the text. They must be beautiful (they were to be on show, presumably) and easily legible (which suggests public reading). They are to be easily portable, perhaps for use in processions or other liturgical ceremonies. They are on parchment, and they must have been codices. They are being commissioned by a ruler for presentation to churches: this is the first reference to a practice of Bible patronage that has continued in various forms throughout all centuries ever since. What we do not know from the letter is what text the manuscripts were to comprise: 'Divine Scriptures' may simply mean the four Gospels, or some other combination of texts.

Now we shall turn to three of the most famous manuscripts in the world. All three present huge problems at this stage of the story, and they (probably) interrupt our narrative, but they are among the most important surviving manuscripts of any kind. Like the Three Magi at Epiphany, three supreme manuscripts out of the east appear suddenly in a blaze of royal splendour. The three books are the *Codex Sinaiticus* (London, BL, Add. MS. 43725 and fragments elsewhere), the *Codex Vaticanus* (Vatican, cod. Vat. gr. 1209), and the *Codex Alexandrinus* (London, BL, Royal MS. 1.D.V-VIII). All three are (or were) complete Bibles, in Greek, encompassing both the Old and the New Testaments. They open with the Septuagint; they close with the New Testament; the two parts, Old and New, are triumphantly united into single consecutive texts. Here are the earliest Christian Bibles. The *Codex Sinaiticus* and the *Codex Vaticanus* are confidently ascribed to the fourth century, and the *Codex Alexandrinus* to the early fifth century. *Sinaiticus* and *Vaticanus* are especially tantalizing if considered in conjunction with the fourth-century letter from Constantine ordering fifty beautiful parchment Bibles. Could they actually be two of the fifty Bibles of the Emperor Constantine? The question has been asked a thousand times, wrenched back and forth between wildly wishful thinking and unreasoning rejection. The date is consistent or

31, 32, 33 opposite

The three great codices of the Greek Bible of the fourth and early fifth century, respectively the Codex Sinaiticus (LONDON, BL, ADD. MS. 43725), *the* Codex Vaticanus (VATICAN, BIBLIOTECA VATICANA APOSTOLICA, COD. VAT. GR. 1209) *and the* Codex Alexandrinus (LONDON, BL, ROYAL MSS. I.D.V-VIII). *The evolution from the layout of scrolls is illustrated by the number of columns of script, diminishing from four to three to two*

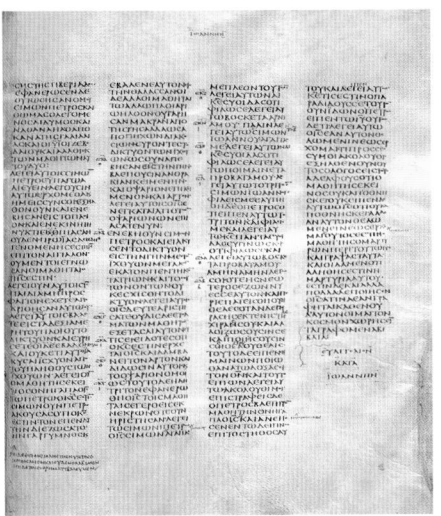

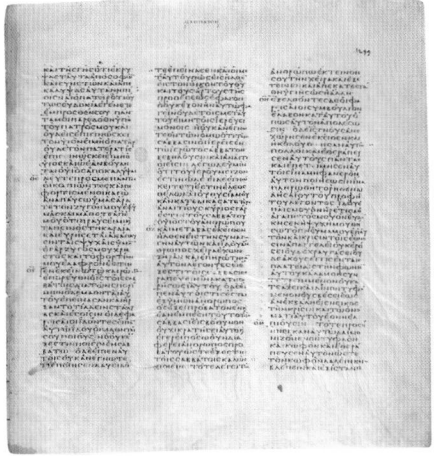

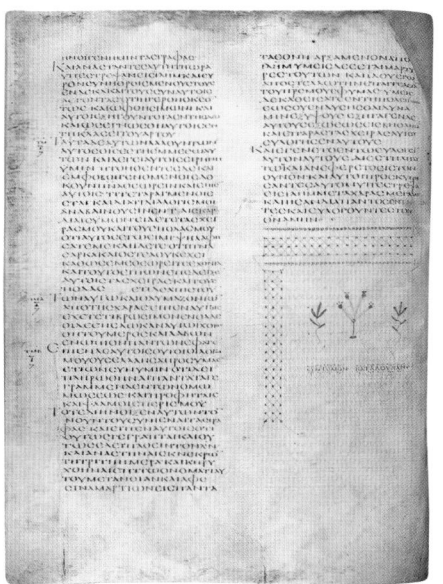

nearly so; the quality is there; but on balance the discrepancies are generally thought to outweigh the likelihood.

The *Codex Sinaiticus* (Pl. 31) is named after the monastery of St Catherine on Mount Sinai in the wilderness between Palestine and Egypt, where the manuscript was discovered in the nineteenth century (see below, p. 298). It is on vast almost square pages of parchment, about 381 by 330 mm (15 by 13 inches). Some 390 leaves survive out of an original estimated total of at least 730 leaves. It is now bound principally in two volumes, not including further fragments in Leipzig, St Petersburg and at Mount Sinai still. It is written in Greek, with four columns on every page. Each opening therefore has a row of eight columns, like pillars of text, resembling the appearance of a scroll held open. The manuscript comprises the Old and New Testaments as well as two apocryphal texts to which we will return in Chapter 12. It was probably copied in Alexandria, though those who favour the fifty Bibles identification have argued for origins in Caesarea on the coast of Palestine, where Eusebius was bishop, or in Constantinople itself.

The *Codex Vaticanus* (Pl. 32) takes its name, obviously, from the Vatican Library in Rome, where it has been since at least 1481. It is currently disbound and the extreme fineness of its parchment is very apparent in its present state. Its loose leaves feel almost weightless. Although it is imperfect at each end and elsewhere (it opens in Genesis 46 and breaks off in Hebrews 9), it too comprises the Old and New Testaments together in Greek. It is on 759 leaves, nearly square, rather smaller than Sinaiticus (265 by 255 mm, about 10½ by 10 inches), with three columns to a page. It too is generally ascribed to Egypt (and if so, to Alexandria), or to Constantinople.

The *Codex Alexandrinus* (Pl. 33) was presented in 1624 to the English royal library by Cyril Lucar, patriarch of Constantinople, who had himself obtained it in Alexandria (hence its name). It had been in Alexandria probably since at least 1308. It is bound now in four volumes. It comprises a total of 772 leaves, 317 by 254 mm (12½ by 10 inches). It is written in Greek in two columns. It is the most complete of the three great Greek Bibles, with all the Old and New Testament as now known, with the Epistles of Clement following the Apocalypse. It is usually supposed that it was written in Egypt, though there is some case for suggesting an origin in Ephesus in Asia Minor.

Between them these three great books are of incalculable value for the history of the Bible text, especially *Sinaiticus*, which was evidently intended to be a model of accuracy. Extreme effort was made by the original scribes of the *Codex Sinaiticus* to check and correct the transcription word by word. It contains traces of some 14,500 corrections (often very minor). One of the correctors added a note claiming that the text from I Samuel to Esther had been compared with an actual manuscript which the martyrs Antoninus (d.310) and Pamphilus (d.309) had themselves checked against the famous *Hexapla* manuscript of Origen, the long-lost third-century manuscript which Saint Jerome had found in the library of Caesarea and later removed to Bethlehem (see above, pp. 17–18). We can almost glimpse that we are getting back tangibly close to the real source material of early Christianity. Variant readings in *Vaticanus* and *Sinaiticus* carry huge weight with textual critics, for these manuscripts are by far the oldest and best and most important copies of the Greek Bible extant.

Having said that, there is a problem. The great handicap in considering *Sinaiticus*, *Vaticanus* and *Alexandrinus* in the history of the Bible, as we now know it, is that all three comprise vast composite texts of all the Old and New Testaments in order. This unity, to us in Western Europe at least, is easily identifiable as 'the Bible'. It is too easy to imagine that they represent the jumping-off point of a tradition which has existed ever since. We might think from a cursory glance at *Sinaiticus* or *Vaticanus* that by the fourth century the building of the Bible text was finished and that from now on all Bibles would or should be in that form.

The three great manuscripts are, in a sense, magnificent freaks. There might once have been a fourth, of which there is part of a shadowy fifth-century New Testament as undertext in a twelfth-century palimpsest in the Bibliothèque Nationale in Paris (ms. gr. 9, the so-called *Codex Ephraemi*). But that is the full extent of once-complete early Greek Bibles or even vast volumes of whole Old or New Testaments. Something like 7,000 Greek biblical manuscripts have been recorded, from all parts of the Old or New Testaments, and there are no others remotely like *Sinaiticus*, *Vaticanus* or *Alexandrinus*. They do not represent the start of a tradition; on the contrary, the three (or four) manuscripts stand alone. As we saw above, the separate books of the Greek Bible were first written as individual scrolls. In the early Church they were copied out as distinct little portable volumes. Several biblical texts might be written in one codex, but the idea of putting every possible biblical text together was almost inconceivable for normal purposes. This is the real difficulty in hoping to identify *Sinaiticus* or *Vaticanus* with the fifty books commissioned by the Emperor Constantine, for the easily portable manuscripts of the Divine Scriptures, which the emperor ordered with some urgency for daily use in his churches, are more likely to have been simply Gospel Books. There was no sustained tradition in Greek manuscripts, before or after the fourth century, of whole one-volume pandect Bibles.

From this point onwards, we take leave of early Christianity and the broad picture of the Roman Empire and we begin to follow the Greek Bible as it evolved after the time of Saint Jerome. The focus narrows to the Greek Orthodox religion of the eastern Mediterranean, where the Scriptures always continued to be used in the traditional Greek, while the Western Church was gradually beginning to adopt the Latin Vulgate. Over the next thousand years and more, from the late fourth century onwards, Greek biblical manuscripts were still made and used in large numbers in the Orthodox Church. Texts were often grouped in clutches of books but they were not whole Bibles in the modern sense. The four Gospels formed the most important unit. Other common and distinct volumes might commonly comprise the Psalms (sometimes with other biblical poetry) or the letters of Saint Paul. Some were formed of Pentateuch (the old Septuagint Torah, now tamed to Christian use), the Octateuch (the first eight books of the Old Testament together, from Genesis to Ruth), or the sixteen books of the Prophets.

Two very early and famous Greek manuscripts, with illustrations (some of the earliest known), simply comprise the book of Genesis alone. One is in London (BL, Cotton MS. Otho B.VI), known as the Cotton Genesis, probably dating from the late fifth century. It once had something over 300 miniatures, in the dramatic sketchy and rather blobby style which resembles that of classical Roman frescoes familiar to us from the finds at Pompeii. The Cotton Genesis was probably made in Egypt, but was in England by the early seventeenth century. The great tragedy is that the manuscript was almost entirely destroyed in a terrible fire in the Cotton Library in London in 1731 and it was burnt into tiny blackened and misshapen fragments. Even these give a hint of what an expensive early Greek book of the Bible must have looked like. Similar but even finer paintings occur in the Vienna Genesis (Vienna, ÖNB, cod. theol. gr. 31, Pl. 22), probably of the sixth century. It may have been made in the Near East and it was apparently brought to Venice during the Crusades. The Vienna Genesis too is now hardly more than a fragment, 24 leaves with illustrations on both sides, but it can be calculated from the text that the whole book would have filled about 96 leaves. The important point is that both the Cotton and Vienna manuscripts were single biblical books, bound as separate volumes, and were not part of some vast complete Bible or even whole Pentateuchs.

The four Gospels were often grouped together as volumes. Gospel Books make up about half of the surviving medieval Greek manuscripts of New Testament texts. There are remains of a number of truly luxurious Gospel Books from the sixth century, richly illuminated. Some are written in gold or silver ink on parchment stained purple. These include large portions of a dismembered Gospel Book in the library of the monastery on Mount Patmos in the eastern Greek islands, of which other detached leaves are now in the British Library (Cotton MS. Titus C.XV) and elsewhere. Another comprises 190 leaves from the Gospels of Matthew and Mark once at Berat in Albania, now in the national archives in Tiranë. Both this and the Patmos manuscript are written in silver. Although the metallic silver has tarnished to the extent that the text now looks fuzzy black on dark purple leaves, it is easy to imagine these books when they were newly written, shimmering like silver moonlight on a wine-dark sea. Two extant portions of closely related Greek sixth-century purple Gospel Books are actually illustrated as well. One is the fragmentary Sinope Gospel of Matthew in Paris, written in gold and illustrated in its lower margins (BN, ms. suppl. gr. 1286, Pl. 34). Another is the magnificent Rossano Gospels, in Rossano cathedral in Calabria in southern Italy (Pl. 35). It is written in silver and includes page after page of virtually full-page illustrations depicting the principal liturgical readings used during Lent, and an entirely full-page miniature of Saint Mark seated in a wickerwork chair, writing his Gospel on a long scroll at the apparent dictation of an angel or female saint (fol. 121r).

The use of gold or silver script on purple parchment was a deliberate symbol

of luxury. We have already encountered it in our discussion of Latin Gospel Books. The Cotton and Vienna Genesis manuscripts use it too. Purple itself was the royal colour from antiquity. Christ himself during his Passion was robed in royal purple. The patriarch of Constantinople, Germanos I (715–30), describes the opening of the Greek liturgy in which the deacon enters the church first carrying before him a manuscript of the Gospels, representing the coming into the world of the Son of God. Therefore the Gospel Book actually symbolized Christ, the king of kings.

Jerome in the late fourth century had criticized the wanton practice of writing biblical books in gold and silver on purple parchment, which (he said) distracted from the message. We will look at this in Latin – it comes from his preface to the book of Job – because Jerome's use of one word in particular is very interesting. He disapproved, in his actual words as they survive, of '*libros vel in membranis purpureis auro argentoque descriptos vel uncialibus, ut vulgo aiunt, litteris*'. In a literal translation, this would mean that he objected to 'books, either laid out on purple skins in gold and silver, or with what are commonly called uncial letters'. Look very closely at that word *uncialibus*. This is the first time that the word 'uncials' appears in any Latin text. Almost all Greek or Latin biblical manuscripts at that date, however, were written in what we now call uncials – neat unornamented majuscules, like capital letters today, formed of gently curved strokes – and Jerome cannot reasonably have objected to normal script. Remember that 'i' was not dotted in the fourth century; and that 't' and 'c' are frequently interchangeable. Re-read the word *uncialibus* as *untialibus*, then separate off the first and fourth curved downstrokes as letters on their own, and join the second and third. It is actually worth trying this experiment with a pencil and paper. Suddenly exactly the same word reads *initialibus*. Was that what Jerome actually wrote, that he disapproved of large initial letters?

34, 35

There are two major sixth-century Greek Gospel Books written in gold or silver ink on purple parchment, illustrated with pictures. The first is the Sinope Gospels (opposite), a fragment of Saint Matthew only (PARIS, BNF, MS. SUPPL. GR. 1286), *and the other is the Rossano Gospels (right), with Saints Matthew and Mark* (ROSSANO, MUSEO DIOCESANO D'ARTE SACRA)

It makes better sense. Some very early copyist of Jerome's preface to Job may simply have hastily misread the word, copied it as nonsense by mistake, and then every subsequent scribe of the passage thought this was an actual word and so repeated it. Thus perhaps the word 'uncial' came into being.

The usual modern method of classifying Greek biblical manuscripts is by whether they are written in uncials or in minuscules. This divides the manuscripts into two distinct groups. Uncial script was used from the early Christian period until about the tenth century (Pls. 31–35). Minuscule means, in effect, lower-case script (Pls. 38–40). It overlapped with uncial and began to appear in Greek biblical manuscripts by the ninth century, and it has been used ever since. Biblical scholars often use this very convenient distinction, for uncial usually means early, and minuscule means late. Approximately 300 Greek manuscripts and fragments of New Testament books are recorded in uncials, of which about 200 are little more than fragments. By contrast, more than 2,800 manuscripts of New Testament texts are recorded in Greek minuscule, mostly complete books, and even this total is not exhaustive.

Greek uncial script originated as a small round hand written with a narrow pen or reed (like that used in the *Codex Sinaiticus*). There gradually evolved an uncial which became thicker and bigger by the fifth and sixth centuries with paragraph breaks and enhanced opening initials. By the seventh century this uncial began to lean to the right, and it loses its roundness. By the eighth and ninth century, most Greek uncial scripts resemble modern Slavonic hands (the type of script used in Bulgaria or Russia), pointed and angular with huge contrast between thick and thin strokes. In fact, the Slavonic alphabet is actually based on this last style of Greek uncial writing, adapted by Saint Cyril (d.869) and Saint Methodius (d.885), who brought Christianity to Moravia.

The end of the uncial period in Greek Bibles corresponds too with the Iconoclastic Controversy which dramatically affected Greek religious culture. We have already encountered the Jewish interpretation of the Commandment at Exodus 20:4 as prohibiting the use of pictorial images in art. For over a hundred years, the Byzantine emperors enforced a similar policy. This was first promulgated in 726 by Leo III (emperor 717-41), ordering the destruction of religious art in Constantinople. The decree remained in force until the year after the death of the emperor Theophilus in 842. Many illustrated Greek biblical manuscripts must have been destroyed by the imperial *eikonoklastes* during this period. The books that were produced during that period are without illustration. To modern eyes, many eighth- to ninth-century Greek biblical manuscripts in those 'Slavonic' uncials are ugly and austere.

One of those who vigorously campaigned for a return to the use of art was Saint Theodore of Studios (759-826), re-founder in 799 of the old monastery of Studios in west Constantinople. Under the abbacy of Theodore, Studios became a centre of monastic reform and of book production. From the beginning of the ninth century onwards there seems to have been a positive campaign to introduce minuscule script into Greek biblical manuscripts, and to replace uncial books with the new script. Theodore of Studios established rules for the accurate writing of manuscripts in his reformed monastery. A scribe whose attention wandered during the task of copying could be punished by a diet of bread and water; a scribe who did not keep his parchment clean could be subjected to 130 penances; a scribe who broke his pen in a fit of temper could be subjected to 30 penances; and so on. Minuscule script lent itself to this new revival of accurate book production. It was small and neat and it

36
After a century of iconoclasm, when Bibles were made without pictures, Byzantine manuscripts were often richly illustrated in the ninth and tenth centuries. This is a detail from the book of Job copied in 905 AD (VENICE, BIBLIOTECA MARCIANA, COD. GR. 538)

37 opposite
The Gospels often open with pictures of each of the four Evangelists writing their texts. They either appear separately, at the start of each book, or together, as here, at the opening of a Gospel Lectionary made in Constantinople in 1070 (PARIS, BNF, MS. SUPPL. GR. 1096)

could be written much faster than uncial, for the scribe could join up letters without raising his pen from the page, and a larger amount of text could be fitted onto a page without loss of clarity or elegance. In the 300 years after the Greek Church emerged from the disruptions of Iconoclasm, the production of Greek biblical manuscripts flourished as never before, or since.

An important development, and one which has no real parallel in the West, is the increasing separation of manuscripts of the Gospels into two forms. The first is the straightforward Gospel Book with the four texts, Matthew, Mark, Luke and John, in biblical order. The second is the Gospel Lectionary. Twenty-two Gospel Lectionaries have been recorded from the eighth century, 123 from the ninth, 147 from the tenth, 231 from the eleventh, and 499 from the twelfth. From the medieval period of Greek biblical manuscripts in minuscule script, Gospel Lectionaries are at least as common as Gospel Books, and thousands survive. Let us therefore take each in turn, for they tell us about the most common manuscripts of the Scriptures in Greek.

Once the period of Iconoclasm was over, Gospel Books were often elaborately illuminated. Usually each of a manuscript's four texts opens with a portrait of its author, generally in the act of writing or receiving divine inspiration. They can furnish us with very interesting images of scribes or illuminators, with all the tools of their trade. The backgrounds are very often of gold. The earliest surviving example of an evangelist portrait is in the sixth-century Rossano Gospels, described above. The idea of an author being illustrated as a frontispiece to a text he wrote probably echoes some ancient Greek prototype, like portraits of the Four Philosophers (Plato, Aristotle, Zeno and Epicurus) or the Four Playwrights (Euripides, Sophocles, Aristophanes and Menander). Sets of four Evangelist portraits certainly became standard when illustrations were re-introduced back into Greek biblical manuscripts from the ninth century onwards (Pl. 37). The pictures are on the verso of pages, facing across the manuscript to the opening of the Gospel on the opposite page. This usually has an elaborate headpiece across the top above the text, like a great illuminated canopy or hanging banner (Pl. 40), and generally a large opening initial which leads into a top line of capital letters. The text is normally written in a single column, in a minuscule script. Chapter divisions are marked with decorated initials.

At the beginning of the volume, most Greek Gospel Books have the canon tables invented by Eusebius of Caesarea, which we encountered in the chapter on early Latin Bibles and which tabulate parallel chapters of the four Gospels. The canon tables too are often elaborately illuminated in architectural designs. Some Greek Gospel Books are also illustrated with cycles of full-page miniatures, usually at the beginning or in clusters at the beginning of each Gospel. High-quality Greek manuscripts are often (and generally on slight evidence) attributed to Constantinople, while those with poorer illumination are ascribed to outlying monasteries and the provinces. Two extremely richly decorated Gospel Books, dating from the late eleventh and early twelfth century, are Paris, BNF, ms. gr. 74, with 372 miniatures, and Florence, Biblioteca Medicea-Laurenziana, cod. Plut. 6.23, with 301 miniatures. Both these manuscripts may have been made at the monastery of Studios itself.

Greek Gospel Lectionaries, however, are quite different. They use the same Gospel text, but break it up and rearrange it according to the portions and order in which the Gospels were chanted during services throughout the whole Church year. Some feasts in the year are fixed to specific days of the Calendar; while others, known as 'movable feasts', are based on Easter, which varies in date from one year to the next, according to the cycles of the moon. Manuscript Lectionaries are therefore usually in two volumes. The first is the *Synaxarion*, with readings for the movable feasts from Easter to Easter (Pl. 38). The second is the *Menologion*, with readings for fixed saints' days and festivals, beginning on 1 September. The *Synaxarion* generally opens with readings from Saint John's Gospel (chanted from Easter to Pentecost on Saturdays, Sundays and on feast days), followed by those from Saint Matthew (chanted from Pentecost to the first week of September), Saint Luke (chanted from the Sunday after 14 September to the beginning of Lent) and finally Saint Mark (chanted during the Saturdays and Sundays of Lent). There are no weekday Gospel readings in Lent; instead there would be readings from the Old Testament, found in a different manuscript. Gospel Lectionaries might also include the Holy Week readings, and Sunday morning readings, all from all four Gospels, varying from one manuscript to another. Each reading is usually introduced by a formula which leads into the text, such as '*To kairo ekeino ...*' ('at that time ...', introducing a narrative passage), or '*Eipen o kurios ...*' ('the Lord said ...', introducing an extract from the teaching of Christ). Lectionaries were often written in two columns. They do not have canon tables. They rarely contain illustrations (and not before the tenth century).

38 opposite

A Gospel Lectionary gives the readings for use in Church services. This is the opening of an eleventh-century Synaxarion, *or Lectionary for the movable feasts from Easter onwards. The illustration shows the Resurrection*
(NEW YORK, PIERPONT MORGAN LIBRARY, M. 639)

EVANGELISTARIVM SEV
EVANG + ANNVM

+ ☩ΆΓΆΚΥ̅Ι̅Η̅Κ̅ ☩Π̅Ά̅C ☩

EKΫ́KATA ΪΩ̅:

μαρχη̅ · η̅μ · ο · λογ̅ +
Kαι ο λόγος · η̅μ · πρ
τὸν θν̅ · Kαι θϲ η̅μ

ὁ λόγος ☩ ὁυτος η̅μ
ο̅ μ αρχη̅ πρὸς τὸν
Αθ̅ + π αύτου · διαυ
τοῦ ἐγένετο ☩ Kαι χ̅
ρὶς αὐτοῦ · ἐγένετο

Some, however, have text ingeniously laid out with a partial column of short lines, then lines right across the page, then another partial column of short lines: the effect is as if the whole page of writing was in the form of a cross. Even the most committed iconoclast would find this ornament acceptable for it consists of nothing but Gospel text. It parallels the *Masorah* of Hebrew Bibles, described above, where the lines of writing themselves are melded into the shape of pictures.

After the Gospels – whether as texts in order or as Gospel Lectionaries – the next most common Greek biblical manuscripts are Psalters. Greek monks recited the Psalms and canticles (or biblical hymns) as part of their daily office, and so these texts too were primarily liturgical. About 80 surviving Greek manuscript Psalters are illustrated, often in the margins, like a kind of pictorial

gloss. A famous example is the Theodore Psalter, with a total of 435 miniatures (London, BL, Add. MS. 19352, Pl. 39). It was completed in February 1066 by the presbyter Theodoros from Caesarea at the request of the *sugkellos* Michael, abbot of the monastery of Studios.

It is true to say that most Greek biblical manuscripts are monastic or for use by priests or monks in church. Quite commonly they are signed by their scribes. Usually such inscriptions comprise simply the scribe's name, perhaps a date, and often some self-deprecating remark on the scribe's unworthiness. We thus pick up isolated names such as the monk Ephraim in the year 948, the presbyter Eustatheios in 967, the monk Ioannes in 992, the monk Nikolaos in 999, the monk Theophanes, a priest of the monastery of Iberon in 1008, the monk Loukas in 1013, the lector and *kaligraphos* Theopemptos in 1045, and so on. A few colophons give glimpses of circumstances under which the manuscripts were made. A Psalter was commissioned in approximately 951 by Georgios, a novice, to give to Euthumios, a priest (Oxford, Bodleian Library, MS. Auct. D.4.1). A Lectionary was completed in January 1027, during the reign of Constantine VIII, by the priest Nikolaos on commission from the priest Ioannes (Jerusalem, Greek Patriarchate, cod. Sabas

82). Another Lectionary was written on 24 June 1068 in the reign of Romanos and Eudocia in the Laura of Hexekontagenes by the monk Leontinos on joint commission from the monks Michaël and Basileios (Oxford, Christ Church, MS. Gr. 15). Another again was completed on 30 January 1070 by Petros, *grammatikos* of the School of Chalkoprateia in Constantinople for the priest Konstantinos (Paris, BNF, ms. suppl. gr. 1096, Pl. 37). A Gospel Book was written by Theodoros in 1129 and decorated by his son Basileios for the monk Leon (Mount Athos, Esphigmenu, cod. 25). A Lectionary was finished in April 1152 by the monk and priest Georgios on commission from the *hieromonachos* Gerasimos, who then donated it to the church of the Mother of God in Tiberias (Jerusalem, Greek Patriarchate, cod. Anastaseos 9). A Gospel Book was completed in July 1156 by Manouël Hagiostephanites for Ioannes, archbishop of Cyprus (Oslo and London, The Schøyen Collection, MS. 231). A Lectionary was completed in February 1167 by the *notarios* Basileios Skenouris for the salvation of his soul and that of the abbot of the monastery of Hagia Kellia in Bethlehem (Sinai, Monastery of St Catherine, cod. 220). Each one of these colophons – and there are many others similar – gives little revealing clues to typical patronage of Greek biblical manuscripts, mostly priests and monks.

The words of the text in Greek biblical books remained almost identical throughout this entire period. Even now a modern printed Greek Bible, still used in the Orthodox Church, incorporates the very text of the Septuagint prepared (as Aristeas had assured us) for the ancient library of Alexandria, and it continues with the New Testament in its original language. That is a remarkable claim, for any written book. The textual transmission of Greek Bibles is not as inflexible as that of the Hebrew Scriptures. Greek scribes attempted accuracy but accepted that little mistakes were common human failings. The signatures of scribes often modestly proclaim their own inadequacies. Certain related families of textual traditions can be detected. Some scribes evidently copied from much older exemplars, and so even a quite late Greek biblical manuscript of the thirteenth or fourteenth century might suddenly supply a reading from a thousand years earlier. One or two passages of the Greek text always remained in doubt. There is much dispute in the Greek Church, for example, as to whether the story of the woman taken in adultery (John 8:3-11) is really an authentic part of the Gospel or whether it is a subsequent insertion into the original narrative. It does not appear in *Codex Vaticanus* or *Codex Sinaiticus*. In some medieval Greek manuscripts it appears, in some it is omitted altogether, and in some it is moved to other places in the text, including (in what is referred to as 'family 13' of the Gospels) to a new position after Luke 21:38. In many Greek Gospel Books it is simply marked in red ink as a doubtful passage.

For a thousand years or more from the fourth century onwards, almost all Greek manuscripts were written on parchment. Often Greek parchment seems thick and coarsely made, and tends to be very shiny on the flesh side. It may have been made from the ancestors of the knobbly goats which still flock the Greek islands and mainland of the eastern Mediterranean. The thickness of Greek parchment may be one reason why it would have been difficult to write a whole Bible in a single volume. The three great exceptions (*Sinaiticus*, *Vaticanus* and *Alexandrinus*) are, by contrast, on extraordinarily thin parchment. The nineteenth-century scholar who discovered the *Codex Sinaiticus*, Constantine Tischendorf, suggested that the parchment for that book must have been made from antelope skin. The general thickness of most Greek parchment, however, meant that it was easy to scrape away a layer of the surface to remove a mistake. Greek pictures of evangelists writing (which one can assume were based on scribes of the artists' own time) always show knives among the essential equipment for writing. The surface of Greek manuscripts is often abraded with corrections. Stout parchment also lent itself to use as palimpsests. The complete erasure and rewriting of old parchment, relatively rare in Western Europe after the Dark Ages, seems always to have been a temptation to Greek scribes. The decrees of the Trullan Synod, which met in Constantinople in 692, condemned the impious practice of erasing biblical texts

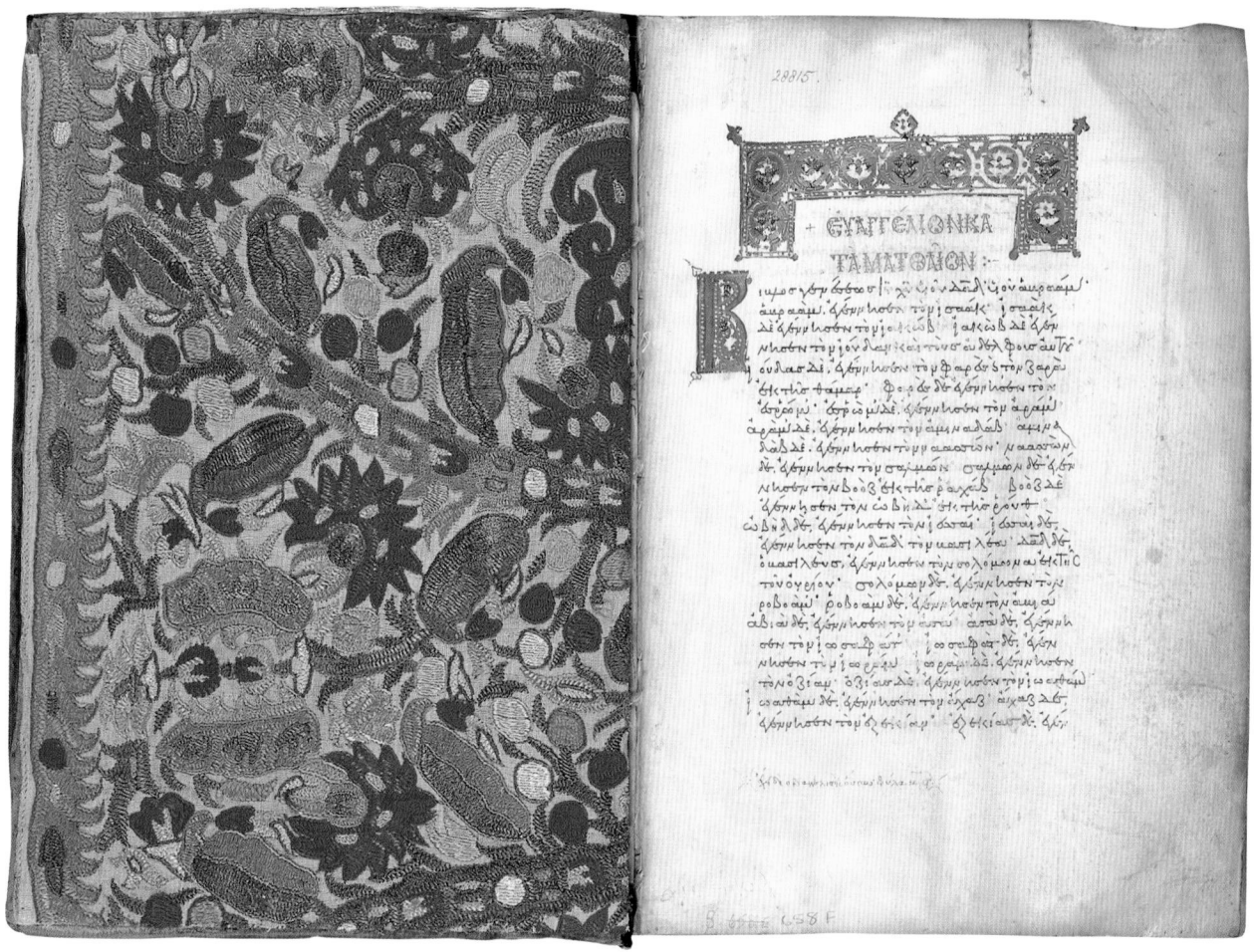

for other purposes. In fact, about a fifth of all extant uncial manuscripts of New Testament texts have survived only because they were later reused as palimpsests.

The general coarseness of many Greek manuscripts (at least from a Western perspective) is often exacerbated by the apparently poor-quality pigments used for illuminating books. Illustrations in Greek biblical manuscripts are often very flaked and oxidized. This may be partly because of the conditions in which the books have been kept, in alternating extremes of hot Greek summers and damp monasteries. Probably also Greek biblical manuscripts are damaged and worn for the very best of reasons, and that is that they were really used by their owners.

If there is one theme which runs right through the history of Greek Bibles (apart from the survival of the ancient and never-changing Greek text) it is that the books were made to be used. They were seldom luxury manuscripts simply for the delight of private owners. They were primarily institutional and mostly liturgical. They were made as separate books or groups of books of the Bible, as they always had been since the time of the first Greek-speaking Christians, principally because that is how the books were used. The Emperor Constantine in 332 had commissioned his fifty manuscripts to be 'easily portable in order …' (and let us emphasize this) '… that they may be used'. We can end then with another commission over 700 years later, that of a wealthy eleventh-century landowner, Eustathius Boilas, who built and endowed a monastery to the Mother of God in northern Asia Minor. His will survives in Paris (BNF, ms. Coislin 263). The remarkable document, dated 1059, lists about 90 books with which he endowed his foundation. It opens with the bequest of 'my highly prized, or rather my priceless treasure, the sacred and holy Gospel, written in gold letters throughout, containing golden pictures of the four evangelists, with enamel decorations, a purple binding and silver-gilt plaits [these are the clasps which hold it shut]; it has a buckle, painted letters, and also a scene from the feast of the Nativity …' He also gave (separate) volumes to the church, including Genesis, Psalms, Proverbs and Acts. Apart from the Gospels, there were three volumes with multiple texts – the Pentateuch, I-II Kings, and the Prophets, all as separate books. He dedicates them to the church, requesting only that his two daughters may be allowed to chant, read and learn from them. He says that they may never be sold. He insists that the books 'must be used, as it is necessary, when it is necessary, and where it is necessary'. There is no clearer statement of the unchanging purpose of the Bible in Greek. Like the Jews with their Masoretic Bibles in Hebrew, members of the Greek Orthodox Church have been actively using Bibles in Greek since the first centuries AD, in their original languages.

40 opposite

This tenth-century New Testament was bound with its front cover lined with embroidered textile. Like a carpet page in a Hebrew Bible, it protects and ornaments the opening of the text
(LONDON, BL, ADD. MS. 28815)

3 | Giant Bibles of the Early Middle Ages

THE SCENE NOW SHIFTS to eleventh- and twelfth-century Europe. Bernard of Chartres (d. *c.*1130), teacher and philosopher, used to describe the theological authors of his own time as puny dwarfs, but he would add that even dwarfs could see further than their predecessors because they sat upon the shoulders of giants (Pl. 42). The eleventh and twelfth centuries represented a period of great intellectual and artistic renaissance in Western Europe. The so-called Dark Ages had lifted by the year 1000. The world did not end at the millennium, as some pessimists had confidently expected, and Europe entered a new period of relative prosperity and cultural self-confidence. It was strictly a renaissance, however, in that it relied on the giants of the past. The term 'Romanesque' is often used of the art and architecture of this period, because it reflected the ancient Roman style, although in many instances the new Romanesque buildings emerged as bigger and more innovative than their classical models.

The theological giants of the past, to whom Bernard of Chartres refers, were the great religious writers like Saint Jerome (*c.*342–420), translator of the Latin Bible, and others such as Saint Augustine (354–430) and Saint Gregory (*c.*540–604). Works of these irreproachable authors were brought back into prominence in the eleventh and twelfth centuries. Texts of Jerome, Augustine and Gregory were copied out into massive sets of big volumes. It is very striking to see how Romanesque librarians energetically set about restocking the shelves of their monasteries with books of the core texts of ancient Christian theology. These were often substantial manuscripts, generally larger and taller than texts by new authors such as Lanfranc or Abelard or Bernard of Chartres himself. The earlier works were often lengthier, and their importance was reflected in the

dierum · Conuerte nos dne ad te · et conuerte
mur · Innoua dies nros sicut a principio; Sed pro
iciens repulisti nos · iratus es contra nos uehement·
EXPLICIT HIEREMIAS PROPHA·

INCIPIT EZECHIHEL
PROPHA

ET FACTV EST

INCIPIT PF SIER PBRI
IN IEZECHIHELE PROPHAM·

Hiezechiel propha · cum ioachim rege iudae
captiuus ductus e in babilonem! ibiq; his q;
cum eo captiui ducti fuerant prophauit · poenitenti
bj qd adhucremis uaticinium sculpto aduersa
nis tradidissent · et uiderent adhuc urbem hierlm
stare · quam ille casuram ee p dixerat; Tricesimo
autem aetatis suae anno · et captiuitatis quinto
exor sui e ad concaptiuos loqui · Et eodem
tempore licet posterior, ie in chaldea hie
remias in iudea prophetauerunt · Sermo eius
nec satis disertus! nec admodum rusticus est!
Sed ex utroq; medie temperatus; sicut dos et
ipse sicut hieremias · principio uoluminis et
finem magnis habens obscuritatibj inuoluta·
Sed et uulgata eius editio · non multum dis
tat ab hebraico · Unde satis miror · quid cause ex
titerit · ut se eosdem in uniuersis libris habe
mus inter ptes · in aliis eadem · in aliis diuer
sa transtulerint · Legite igitur et hunc iuxta
translationem nram · qui a p cola scriptus est et
commata · manifestiorem sensum legentibj

mensis · cum essem in medio captiuor iuxta flu
men chobar · aperti sunt celi · et uidi uisiones · dei
in quinta mensis; ipse est annus quintus trans
migrationis regis ioachim · Factum e uerbum
dni ad hiezechiel filium buzi sacerdotem
in terra chaldeor iuxta flumen chobar · et facta
e super eum ibi manus dni · Et uidi et ecce uentus
turbinis ueniebat ab aquilone · et nubes ma
gna et ignis inuoluens! et splendor in circuitu
eius · et de medio eius quasi species electri de
de medio ignis! Et ex medio eius simi
litudo quattuor animalium · et hic aspectus
eor · similitudo hominis in eis · Et quattuor fa
cies uni · et quattuor penne uni! et pedes eor·
pedes recti · et planta pedis eor quasi planta pe
dis uituli · et scintille quasi aspectus eris can
dentis! Et manus hominis sub pennis eor
in quattuor partibj · Et facies et pennas per
quattuor partes habebant! iuncte erant
penne eor alterius ad alterum·; Non reuer
tebantur cum incederent! sed unum quodq;
ante faciem suam gradiebatur · Similitudo
autem uultus eor facies hominis · et facies leo
nis a dextris ipsor quattuor · facies autem bo
uis a sinistris ipsor quattuor! Et facies aquile
desuper ipsor quattuor · et facies eor et penne
eor extente desup; Due penne singulor iun
gebantur · et due tegebant corpora eor! et unu
queq; eor coram facie sua ambulabat · Ubi
erat impetus spus illuc gradiebantur! nec reuer
tebantur cum ambularent; Et similitudo
animalium · et aspectus eor · quasi car bonum

large and impressive format of the new manuscripts. In the visual imagination of the Middle Ages, size denoted status. Greater than even the Church Fathers, however, was the fundamental text of all Christianity, the Bible itself, the giant on whose shoulders every author sat. This was still the Latin Vulgate text, prepared and endorsed by Saint Jerome. From the mid-eleventh century until 1200 and beyond, the Latin Bible was reconfirmed as the greatest and consequently often as the largest of all books. This, then, is a chapter about status and giants reborn.

Big Bibles as such were not new. The great Carolingian biblical manuscripts from ninth-century Tours had been very substantial books, especially if they were pandects or single-volume Bibles comprising both the Old and New Testament together. The size of a Carolingian Bible, however, was more a consequence of the extent of the text than a deliberate symbol of importance and rank. The Christian Church in Europe underwent a movement of spiritual reform in the mid-eleventh century. The key figure in this was Hildebrand (*c.*1021–85), chaplain to Pope Gregory VI (1045–6), administrator of the papal see under Pope Leo IX (1048–54), archdeacon of the Roman Church under Pope Nicholas II (1058–61), chancellor of the Apostolic See under Alexander II (1061–73), and finally pope himself as Gregory VII, 1073–85. He is important in our story. As pope, Gregory VII was involved in the long controversy with the future Holy Roman Emperor, Henry IV, over the rights of the Church, culminating in the famous confrontation outside the town of Canossa in the winter of 1077, when the pope obliged the king to stand penitently in the snow. Even in politics, the balance of rank was extremely important. As reformer, Hildebrand emphasized a return to the spiritual life of the clergy. A crucial aspect of this reform was the affirmation of the Bible as a guide to religious life and as part of the cycle of daily worship in the community.

In the third quarter of the eleventh century, then, a new type of symbolic Latin Bible began to appear, probably from Rome. A very early example belonged to the Benedictine abbey of St Aurelius at Hirsau, in Württemberg in Germany (Munich, Clm. 13001, Pl. 41). It is inscribed 'Heinricus IIII rex dedit S. Aurelio', given to Saint Aurelius by Henry IV himself, king of Germany 1056–1106. He is called 'king' and so the gift doubtless dates from before his election as Holy Roman Emperor in 1084. This was the same Henry IV who contested the claims of the supremacy of the popes at Canossa. It may seem strange to begin our discussion of giant Bibles and papal reform with a manuscript presented by the pope's greatest ideological opponent, but Henry's relationship with the papacy constantly moved in and out of declared intimacy and staged antagonism. Diplomacy depended on symbolic gestures. Any book presented by Henry IV is likely to belong in the world of papal politics. The manuscript itself is of Italian origin, not German. It was doubtless made in Rome, presumably during a public truce between the donor and the papacy.

Another very similar giant Bible was acquired by Admont Abbey in southern Austria and is still in the library of the monastery there (Stiftsbibliothek, cod. C/D). A fourteenth-century inventory describes it as 'the whole Bible in two huge volumes which the founder Lord Gebehardus gave', identifying the donor as Gebhard (d. 1088), archbishop of Salzburg and founder of Admont in 1074. Archbishop Gebhard was a passionate adherent of the reforms of Gregory VII and was exiled to the papal court during the pope's dispute with Henry IV from 1076. He perhaps acquired the Bible in Rome before his return to Salzburg in 1086.

A third great Bible exported into northern Europe belonged to the cathedral of Geneva in Switzerland, and is now in the city library nearby (Bibliothèque Publique et Universitaire, ms. lat. 1, Pl. 43). At the end is a list of books, including this one, which Bishop Fredericus 'contributed from his own resources'. This is clearly Frederick, bishop of Geneva c.1031–c.1073/83. Again, to judge from its style, the manuscript was probably made in Rome and the bishop doubtless brought it back at his own expense from one of many visits to the papacy. Its illumination is very closely related to that of another giant Bible which is still in Italy at San Daniele del Fruili (Biblioteca Guarneriana, cod. 1–2). This manuscript, in turn, can probably be dated to not later than 1078 because it has an addition commemorating the death of an abbess Gerlenda in that year. Two other Bibles are perhaps to be associated with Cardinal Desiderius. One is the so-called Giant Bible of Monte Cassino (Monte Cassino, Archivio della Badia, cod. 515 AA), where Desiderius was abbot 1058–87. The second is the Bible of the church of Santa Cecilia in Trastevere in Rome (Vatican, cod. Barb. lat. 587), doubtless acquired during the office of Desiderius as cardinal priest of the

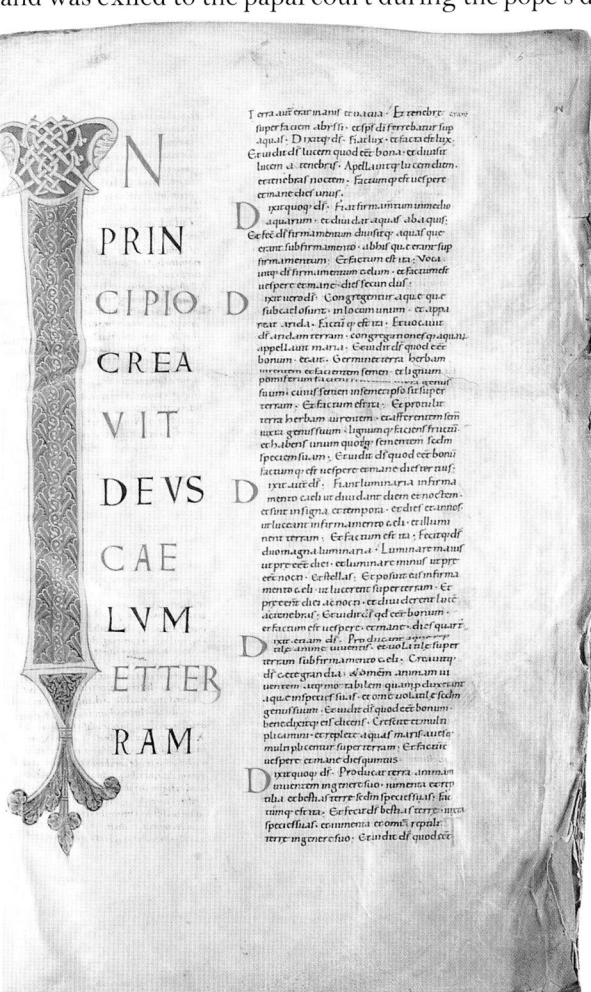

41 page 65

Henry IV, king of Germany 1056–1106, probably commissioned this giant Bible in Rome and gave it before 1084 to Hirsau Abbey in western Germany (MUNICH, BAYERISCHE STAATSBIBLIOTHEK, CLM. 13001)

42 opposite

This early thirteenth-century image of authors sitting on the shoulders of giants occurs in the stained-glass windows of Chartres Cathedral, where the Evangelists are shown on the shoulders of the great prophets of the Old Testament. Here Saint Matthew is seated on Isaiah

43

This enormous Bible was brought to Switzerland, probably from Rome, by Frederick, bishop of Geneva, before 1083 (GENEVA, BIBLIOTHÈQUE PUBLIQUE ET UNIVERSITAIRE, MS. LAT. 1)

44

*The giant Bible of St Florian
was probably given by Altman,
bishop of Passau, in the 1180s.
Unlike the Bibles of Hirsau
and Geneva, however, it was
probably made locally in
Austria*
(ST FLORIAN, STIFTS-
BIBLIOTHEK, COD. IX.1)

45 opposite

*The Lobbes Bible was copied
in Belgium by the scribe
Goderannus in 1084*
(TOURNAI, BIBLIOTHÈQUE DU
SÉMINAIRE, MS. 1)

church, held simultaneously with his abbacy of Monte Cassino from 1058. Desiderius was of the reforming party of Gregory VII, and after Gregory's death in 1085 he himself was elected pope as Victor III, 1086–7.

These early Italian manuscript Bibles, associated with the papal reforms of Gregory VII and his colleagues, are all large volumes, written in double columns in a great round rather archaic late Carolingian script. All the Bibles in the present chapter, including these, are of course in Latin, the common language of the clergy and religious administration across Europe. The copy which Henry IV gave to Hirsau is in a single volume, 275 leaves, 614 by 398 mm (just over 2 feet by 15½ inches). The Bible given to Admont by Archbishop Gebhard is in two volumes, 334 leaves altogether, 590 by 382 mm (23¼ by 15 inches). The one which Bishop Frederick brought back to Geneva is in a single volume, 423 leaves, 600 by 380 mm (almost 2 feet by 15 inches). It weighs 22 kilograms (48½ lbs). It was transferred to the city library with its own lectern, and it still requires two men to lift it. These are massive books, therefore, appropriate to the great status of their noble donors. The term 'giant' Bible is a relatively modern one, but is graphically very apt. Such manuscripts are sometimes called 'Atlantic' Bibles, not from the ocean but from Atlas, the mythological giant who held up the sky. The huge size of these new Bibles is their most notable feature. Their text evidently derives from those ninth-century Bibles edited by Alcuin and dispatched across Europe from the monasteries of Tours in the time of Charlemagne and his successors. One of these Tours Bibles was conveniently accessible in the eleventh century, the Bible of San Paolo fuori le Mura, still owned by the monastery of that name on the outskirts of Rome. It was certainly in Rome in the circle of the papal reformers during the eleventh century, for it includes an inserted oath of fealty to Gregory VII in 1080. It provides the link which leads us from the end of Chapter 1 into early Romanesque Italy.

The fashion for copying new large Bibles spread surprisingly quickly across Europe, well within the eleventh century. Several very early and vast Bible manuscripts were made for churches or monasteries in Tuscany, perhaps to be associated with Nicholas II and Alexander III who, before election to the papacy, had been respectively bishops of Florence (1045–59) and Lucca (1056–61).

Tuscan production of giant Bibles continues right through the eleventh and twelfth centuries. More striking is the new enthusiasm for production of huge Bibles north of the Alps. A splendid example, made probably in Austria, is the St Florian Bible (St Florian, Stiftsbibliothek, cod. XI.1, Pl. 44), a vast complete Bible in 358 leaves, 670 by 500 mm (26½ by 19½ inches). The Augustinian monastery of St Florian was founded by Altmann, bishop of Passau, in 1071. Altmann himself, like Gebhard of Salzburg, joined the papal cause in the controversy between Gregory VII and Henry IV and he was exiled to Italy. He returned to Austria in 1081, and presumably either gave the Bible then or commissioned its manufacture locally on the new Italian model.

Another intriguing glimpse of contemporary politics occurs in the one surviving volume (of two) of the Bible of Lobbes, a Benedictine house in Belgium in the ancient diocese of Cambrai (Tournai, Bibliothèque du Séminaire, ms. 1, Pl. 45). The manuscript is 495 by 325 mm (19½ by 12½ inches). The book is signed and dated by its scribe, Goderannus, in the year 1084. This is the earliest major Romanesque Bible with an exact date and the name of an identifiable scribe. The date is remarkably early in the history of giant Bibles. Gregory VII was still alive, and evidently Goderannus did not at all sympathize with the papal cause in the famous controversy with Henry IV. In a long colophon, Goderannus says that he offers to Saint Peter, patron of the abbey of Lobbes, this book on which he has worked for so long, and which he completed in 1084, while the emperor Henry had for three years been laying siege to Rome, where pope Gregory or Hildebrand was shut up in revolt, during the ninth year of Bishop Henry of Liège, the eighth of Bishop Gerard of Cambrai, and the sixth of Abbot Arnulph of Lobbes. Goderannus may have been unsympathetic to the papacy, but he was certainly up to date with current affairs. His line of communication with events in Rome may have brought an exemplar or very at least the idea of a giant Bible northwards.

Goderannus appears again some years later, writing a second giant Bible, even

46

*The scribe Goderannus
completed another giant Bible
in 1097, this time for Stavelot
Abbey. This long colophon at
the end of the book records his
effort in making the manuscript
over a period of four years*
(LONDON, BL, ADD. MS.
28106)

47 opposite above

*The Bible of Fécamp Abbey in
Normandy was made in the
time of Abbot Jean d'Alie, who
died in 1079. This is the opening of Leviticus*
(ROUEN, BIBLIOTHÈQUE
MUNICIPALE, MS. A.4)

48 opposite below

*This Bible was brought from
Normandy to Rochester
Cathedral after the Norman
Conquest of England. The
inscriptions here record the
Bible's contents and the dona-
tion of the book by Gundulf,
who was appointed bishop of
Rochester in 1077*
(SAN MARINO, HUNTINGTON
LIBRARY, HM. 62)

bigger, for the Benedictines of Stavelot
Abbey in the diocese of Liège, about 73
miles (118 km) east and slightly north
of Lobbes, towards the Rhineland. Both
volumes of the Stavelot Bible survive, a
total of 468 leaves, 581 by 390 mm (23
by 15½ inches) (London, BL, Add. MSS.
28106–7, Pl. 46). The second volume
is dated 1097. At the end of the first
volume Goderannus says he worked
with Brother Ernest as his helper and
colleague, by permission of the abbot of
Stavelot, that the volumes were written
one after the other with great effort and
were completed in almost four years,
including the writing, illumination and
binding, and that the work was finished
while Jerusalem was under attack. This
is another topical reference, alluding to
the First Crusade, proclaimed in 1095.
The implication in the colophons of
both the Bibles written by Goderannus,
one referring to the siege of Rome and
the other to that of Jerusalem, is that
the Bible is the safe and unchanging
rock of Christianity while even its
founding cities are under attack. The
name of Goderannus also occurs a third
time in a manuscript of ancient history,
not a Bible, made for Stavelot and
datable to not later than 1105 (Brussels,
BR, ms. II.1179). In that book he says
he copied the book and that Brother
Cuno made the parchment. There was
clearly serious monastic enterprise in
operation.

By the last quarter of the eleventh century giant Bibles were evidently being
made in some quantity in the region of Lorraine in north-eastern France and
across into the Rhineland. The scribe Ruotpertus, a monk, signed a giant Bible
for the abbey of Echternach in Luxembourg, commissioned by Abbot Reginbertus, who died in 1081 (Luxembourg, BN, ms. 264). The manuscript has 414
leaves, 600 by 400 mm (23½ by nearly 16 inches). Another Bible written in

Luxembourg well within the eleventh century belonged to the abbey of St-Hubert-des-Ardennes. It is in two volumes, now divided between Brussels and the Musée Archéologique in Namur (Brussels, BR, ms. II.1639, and Namur, Fonds de la Ville, ms.4). Together the volumes comprise a total of 525 leaves, 470 by 325 mm (18½ by 12¾ inches). It is contemporary with a similarly vast manuscript from St-Maximin in Trier, on the Rhine only a few miles to the east (formerly Phillipps MS. 400, still in private hands). This weighty volume comprises 438 leaves, 522 by 373 mm (20½ by 14½ inches). The library catalogue of Schaffhausen Abbey, near the waterfalls in the Rhine to the south of Trier, records a great Bible acquired by Abbot Sigefredus (1083–96): 'an incomparable Bible', the cataloguer called it, evidently intrigued by the format, 'all in a single volume'.

A similarly related group of giant Bibles seems to be clustered around the great monasteries of Normandy by the end of the eleventh century. One copy belonged to Fécamp Abbey, on the coast north of Le Havre, acquired for the monastery in the time of Abbot Jean d'Alie, who died in 1079 (now Rouen, Bibliothèque Municipale, ms. A.4, Pl. 47). Another was owned by the important abbey of Jumièges, on the Seine just upstream from Rouen, perhaps acquired during the rule of Abbot Robert, who died in 1072 (now Rouen, ms. A.6). This was the period of very great prosperity in Normandy following Duke William's conquest of England in 1066. One large two-volume Bible in Norman style came to England as a gift of Gundulf, a former monk at the abbeys of Bec and Caen in Normandy, who in 1077 was appointed bishop of Rochester. It is likely that he brought his Bible with him from Normandy. After a series of complicated adventures, the manuscript is now in California (San Marino, Huntington Library, HM. 62, Pl. 48). Another of similar date is Durham Cathedral MS. A.II.4 (Pl. 49), which has undergone a journey of a much simpler kind. It was demonstrably written at Bayeux in Normandy where the scribe's hand has been found in several cathedral manuscripts. It has a note that 'lord Willelmus the bishop gave [it] to Saint Cuthbert', patron saint of Durham Cathedral. This is the Norman bishop of Durham, William of St-Calais (1081–96), who was back in Normandy from 1088 to 1091. Evidently he brought the Bible across to England with him on his return and it has

49

*The Carilef Bible, or Bible of
Bishop William of St-Calais,
was written at Bayeux in
Normandy and was brought to
Durham, perhaps in 1091*
(DURHAM, CATHEDRAL
LIBRARY, MS. A.II.4)

50 opposite

*A great three-volume Bible was
commissioned by the abbot for
Engelberg Abbey in Switzerland. The frontispiece shows
Frowinus, abbot of Engelberg
c.1147–78, instructing the
scribe, Richene*
(ENGELBERG, STIFTS-
BIBLIOTHEK, COD. 5)

remained almost on the
same shelf ever since.

Here then, within 30 or 40
years at most, a new fashion
for large or very large one-
or two-volume Bibles, which
probably gained its impetus
in the reform movement in
the papal court in Rome, has
reached as far as Durham,
well over a thousand miles
to the north. It is, in fact, a
reversal of the route of the
Codex Amiatinus sent from
Northumberland as a gift
for the papal court some 500
years earlier (see above,
p. 33). Therefore this is an
appropriate point at which
to pause and to take stock of
how and why this new trend
had begun to take place.

Note how the eleventh-
and early twelfth-century
giant Bibles were often
given by bishops or abbots,
who evidently paid for them on their accounts. The chronicler Sigebert of
Gembloux (d.1112) records that Olbert, abbot of Gembloux 1012–48, was
inspired, like a second Philadelphus, to commission a Bible at his own expense,
comprising both Old and New Testaments in a single volume. The tactful
allusion is to the ancient king, Ptolemy Philadelphus, who ordered the translation of the Septuagint for the public library at Alexandria in the third century BC
(see above, p. 46). Some Romanesque donors of Bibles must have seemed patrons
on a truly princely scale. We have already encountered great gifts from Gebhard,
archbishop of Salzburg, Frederick, bishop of Geneva, Cardinal Desiderius,
Altman, bishop of Passau, Gundulf, bishop of Rochester, and William of St-
Calais, bishop of Durham. We could add others into the twelfth century, such as
Eberhard, archbishop of Salzburg (1147–64), who sent a giant Bible back to his
old abbey of Biburg in Bavaria (now Munich, Universitätsbibliothek, cod. 2° 28),
and Robert de Sigillo, bishop of London 1141-50, who similarly sent a two-
volume Bible to his own former monastery of Reading, where he had been a
monk 1135–41. Archbishop Samson de Mauvoisin of Rheims (d.1161) acquired

a Bible for the abbey of Igny; Archbishop Thomas Becket (d.1170) furnished one for the cathedral priory of Canterbury; the cathedral of Chartres received one from their bishop, John of Salisbury (d.1180); and Bishop Hugh du Puiset (d.1195) presented one to his cathedral priory of Durham. The fact that we know of the gifts at all is evidence that the recipients recorded and honoured the donors. The inscription in the Echternach Bible not only records Abbot Reginbertus (d.1081) as donor but actually describes him as 'author of this book',

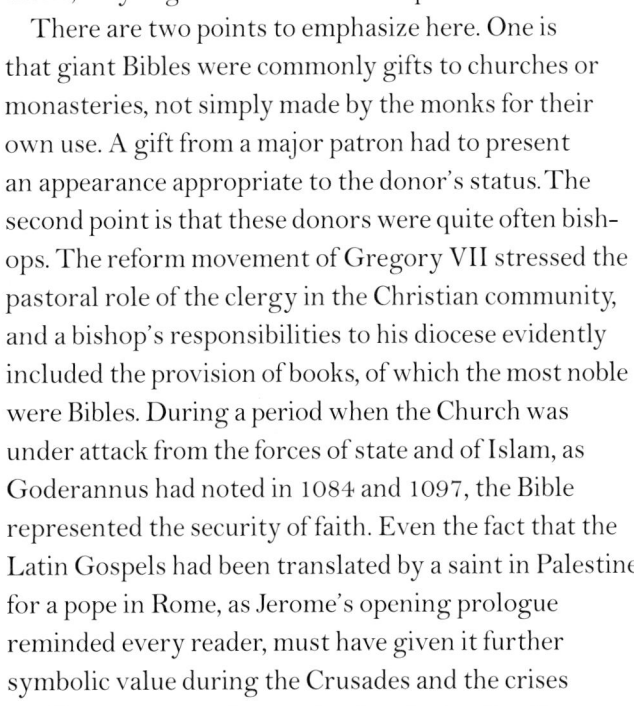

auctor, only begetter of the manuscript.

There are two points to emphasize here. One is that giant Bibles were commonly gifts to churches or monasteries, not simply made by the monks for their own use. A gift from a major patron had to present an appearance appropriate to the donor's status. The second point is that these donors were quite often bishops. The reform movement of Gregory VII stressed the pastoral role of the clergy in the Christian community, and a bishop's responsibilities to his diocese evidently included the provision of books, of which the most noble were Bibles. During a period when the Church was under attack from the forces of state and of Islam, as Goderannus had noted in 1084 and 1097, the Bible represented the security of faith. Even the fact that the Latin Gospels had been translated by a saint in Palestine for a pope in Rome, as Jerome's opening prologue reminded every reader, must have given it further symbolic value during the Crusades and the crises between empire and papacy. Romanesque culture valued ancient authority.

The practical purpose of early giant Bibles is much harder to document. We cannot necessarily assume that because a manuscript is big it must have been placed on a lectern for public reading, or that a large book would have been inappropriate for private study. Nonetheless, these are clearly books to be placed on display. They are books for public use. The Bible was a text which was read aloud in two places in a monastery, in the refectory during meals and in the chapel during the daily church services. For both uses, the text of the Bible was apportioned into daily readings, or 'lections'. Sometimes these readings are indicated in the Bibles themselves. The vast Dover Bible of about 1150 opens, before its prologue, with a detailed breakdown of how different portions of the Bible were to be read throughout the Church year, according to the Roman rite (Cambridge, Corpus Christi College, MS. 3, fol. 1r). A similar list of readings was added in the twelfth century into the Bible of Bishop Frederick of Geneva (Geneva, Bibliothèque Publique et Universitaire, ms. lat.1, fol.148v). The chronicle of the abbey of St-Pierre-le-Vif at Sens records how Abbot Arnold ordered a

*The vast Dover Bible was made
for public reading in the mid-
twelfth century. It was probably
written in Canterbury but was
sent for use at Dover Priory on
the coast of Kent*
(CAMBRIDGE, CORPUS
CHRISTI COLLEGE, MS. 4)

four-volume Old Testament in 1123. It details the contents. Volume I, the Penta-teuch, comprised the text read in the monastery between Quinquagesima Sunday to the middle of Lent. Volume II, with Joshua, Judges, Ruth and Jeremiah, comprised the text read from mid-Lent to Easter. Volume III comprised I–IV Kings and Chronicles. The chronicle does not say so, but this must have been for Easter to Pentecost, for Volume IV, with I–II Maccabees, Ezekiel, Daniel, the Minor Prophets and Isaiah, comprised the text read from Pentecost to Christ-mas. Further volumes, the account concludes, are still to be made. Here then, at very least, is a vast Bible in the 1120s which was specifically prepared in volumes which corresponded to the way that the texts might be used in church.

An intriguingly large number of very early giant Bibles do not include the Gospels. At first sight, this seems almost incredible. The Gospels are usually regarded as the most important part of the Scriptures. The text of the late eleventh-century Bible of St Maximin in Trier, for example, runs on directly from the Old Testament into Acts. Another is the Fécamp Bible in Rouen (Bibliothèque Municipale, ms. A.4), and a puzzled fourteenth-century annotator has added a note on fol. 304r, 'Here should follow the four books of the Evangel-ists completely lacking here'. The giant Bible of *c*.1100 from St-Amand omits both the Psalter and the Gospels (Valenciennes, Bibliothèque Municipale, mss. 9–11), and the medieval library catalogue of St-Amand describes it as containing all the Old and New Testament – 'except the Gospels and the Psalter' as its most distinguishing feature. The Gundulf Bible was perhaps originally conceived without a Gospel section, for there is no space for text between the Prophets and Acts in volume II and the Gospels occur instead misplaced after Chronicles at the end of the first volume. Furthermore the Gospels in that manuscript are written in much smaller writing than adjacent texts and the Psalms are in even smaller script again. It is as if the Psalms and Gospels were simply included as an after-thought. There is only one reasonable explanation. The omission from the Bible of the principal text of the New Testament and the Psalms from the Old Testa-ment must have been because these texts were already represented in the monastery in the form of Gospel Lectionaries, Evangeliaries and Psalters. These were service books. The observation is important. It suggests that the Bibles were complementary texts to liturgical manuscripts, perhaps kept together, and that their location might therefore have been the altar or sacristy rather than in the library or the cloister.

Even if giant Bibles were sometimes marked up with the beginnings and ends of the daily readings, this need not necessarily be evidence that these books were the very volumes used in services. Practical difficulties seem to make this unlikely. The script of eleventh-century Bibles (especially) is often quite small. One can prop up a manuscript like the Gundulf Bible and stand back: the script is written at about 4 lines to the inch and at a distance of more than about two feet the text is illegible. In a dark romanesque church, especially in winter or before sunrise, even a giant Bible would have been difficult to read publicly.

If the giant Bibles had a liturgical purpose, it was probably to act as a textual control for biblical readings in other volumes. A great monastery Bible provided a definitive model for any subsequent copies, most of which were liturgical. It was the arbiter for extracts transcribed into other books. Service books could be checked for accuracy against the authentic Bible. Especially if it could be associated with a bishop, the giant Bible was the authoritative exemplar for all other Bibles and biblical readings. There is good evidence that some surviving giant Bibles were used as exemplars for other copies, as one would expect. For instance, the St-Amand Bible of *c.*1100, just cited, was apparently the model for Douai, Bibliothèque Municipale ms. 1, a two-volume Bible written about 1125. The late eleventh-century Bible of William of St-Calais, also cited above, was probably the exemplar for Bishop Puiset's four-volume giant Bible written at Durham almost exactly a hundred years later (Durham Cathedral, MS. A.II.1). The Gundulf Bible has been marked up in a twelfth-century hand for re-copying. Instructions such as *non scribe*, 'do not write [this]', occur beside headings (e.g.,

volume II, fols. 194v, 199v, etc.) or *dimitte spacium*, 'leave a space' (fols. 199r, 199v, etc.). Someone evidently checked the manuscript carefully for use as a model. Perhaps this editor was Alexander, precentor of Rochester Cathedral, who in the twelfth century commissioned a three-volume Bible for the new library at Rochester and who copied its third volume himself, as recorded in the cathedral's catalogue of the very early thirteenth century. A giant Bible in any monastery or major church would provide a composite and authoritative quarry for any of the various uses of biblical texts in daily life, of which liturgy was one.

A very great giant Bible manuscript specifically prepared for use as a model exemplar is the Bible of Stephen Harding, abbot of Cîteaux 1109–34 (Dijon, Bibliothèque Municipale, mss. 12–15, Pl. 52). The manuscript is worth examining in some detail, for it contains an extraordinary account of how its text was prepared for use. The book is now in four volumes, but was originally made as two, 601 leaves altogether, 474 by 325 mm (18½ by nearly 13 inches). The original first volume ends with a colophon recording that the writing was finished in the year 1109 under the leadership of Stephen, second abbot of the monastery of Cîteaux. Stephen himself came from England and began his religious life at Sherborne Abbey in Dorset. He was one of the earliest recruits to the still tiny community of monks at Cîteaux in Burgundy, which he joined in 1098. The new Cistercians, as they came to be called, were dedicated to austerity and asceticism. Stephen became their prior and presumably in that capacity he began seeking out an appropriately uncontaminated Bible text for his monks, for the first volume of the manuscript was complete by the year he became abbot.

Stephen's account of his biblical enquiries follows the colophon (ms. 13, fol. 150v). He recounts that he sought out many manuscripts of the Bible (we know he had travelled in Italy) and had compared their texts. Since they all passed for the translation of the great Saint Jerome, Stephen says he was astonished to find them so different from each other. He refers to Jerome's prologue to Daniel which describes how Jerome had translated from Hebrew and Chaldean. Therefore Stephen himself went back to the Hebrew sources, and he made contact with the Jews in France, experts in Jewish script. He asked them, in French – the expression is *lingua romana*, the 'romance tongue' – about controversial passages and additions to the Latin text which, as the Jews confirmed to him, did not occur in the original Hebrew texts. Such interpolations are frequently found, Stephen reports, in the books of Kings. Therefore he deleted and scraped away from this present Bible every word which could not be confirmed as authentic by reference to the Hebrew Bible. Now Stephen's account becomes especially interesting. He implores all those who read this volume not to reinsert the deleted passages and he expressly forbids anyone to add anything to the manuscript, either in the text or the margin. Many pages of the manuscript itself have clear marks of erasure where passages have been excised, especially in the books of Kings, doubtless by Abbot Stephen himself.

The check against the Hebrew Bible, as then available in Jewish communities in France, could apply (of course) only to parts of the Old Testament. Marginal notes by Stephen Harding in the New Testament portions compare what he calls the 'most ancient' manuscripts, and the Greek text. Thus, for example, the manuscript underlines the standard Vulgate reading of the second part of Acts 10:6 ('he shall say to you what you should do') and says this phrase is not found in two of the oldest manuscripts and in many of the most truthful histories. Modern printed Bibles omit it too.

Such conscientious editing by reference to sources is extraordinary in the early twelfth century. Stephen was attempting to return to the pure text of the Vulgate as it would have been at the moment when Jerome finished his translation. He did not seek to go beyond that, and so, for example, did not delete the Apocrypha. Nonetheless, this is a remarkable attempt at textual criticism, and it is without parallel at the time. The idea that words of apparently biblical text could be pared away was breathtakingly new, and Stephen Harding feared (rightly, in fact) that later copyists would lack his bravery. Note that he consulted the Jews. Hebrew Bibles were actually more easily available in early twelfth-century France than the Greek scriptures. Stephen probably did not have Greek manuscripts at all, and he must have relied on Latin translations from Greek commentators. The Crusaders might have brought a few Byzantine books to France as curiosities or spoils of war, but probably almost no one could read them. There were, however, many Jews in France and England (Pl. 53). The two communities hardly mixed, except for purposes of trade and money-lending. Most Christians were frightened of Jews. In the twelfth century, several theologians in France, including Sigebert of Gembloux (d.1112), Peter Abelard (d.1142) and later Herbert of Bosham (d. c.1194), began to flirt with Hebrew, the language of heretics and God. It was a significant development to judge purity of the Bible by going back to ancient sources rather than confirming it by Church tradition. In essence what Stephen Harding presumably hoped to provide would have been a giant comprehensive Bible which would forever be the master exemplar for all subsequent Cistercian communities. As far as surviving Cistercian Bibles allow us to judge, Harding's Bible was never used as an exemplar, either for text or for copying its decoration. Perhaps it was simply too radical.

The extremely active foundation of new monasteries in the course of the twelfth century, including the Cistercians (who had rapidly set up over 300 abbeys by the mid-century), brought the need for great Bibles in huge numbers. It evidently became the fashion to have a monumental Bible at the heart of every library and church. From the second quarter of the twelfth century, very large numbers of giant Bibles were produced, all across Europe. They are one of the great phenomena of twelfth-century culture. They are often not only of great textual consistency (though never as pared down and austere as Stephen Harding's Bible) but they are also very often extremely handsomely written and lavishly illuminated. Very famous twelfth-century giant Bibles include the Pantheon Bible (Vatican, cod. Vat. lat. 12958), the Bury Bible (Cambridge, Corpus Christi College, MS. 2, Pls. 1 and 53–4), the Great Lambeth Bible (London, Lambeth Palace, MS. 3), the Parc Abbey Bible (London, BL, Add. MS. 14788), the Worms (or Frankenthal) Bible (BL, Harley MSS. 2803–4, Pl. 58), the Winchester Bible (Winchester Cathedral, MS. 17, Pl. 55), the Floreffe Bible (BL, Add. MSS. 17737–8), the Arnstein Bible (BL, Harley MSS. 2798–9), the Burgos Bible (Burgos, Biblioteca Provincial, cod. 846), the Manerius Bible (Paris, Bibliothèque de Ste.-Geneviève,

54

The Bury Bible was illumin-
ated by Master Hugo, who was
apparently an itinerant profes-
sional artist and metalworker
employed at Bury St Edmunds
in the 1130s and 1140s. The
illustration here shows Jeremiah
watching the siege of Jerusalem
(CAMBRIDGE, CORPUS
CHRISTI COLLEGE, MS. 2)

mss. 8–10, Pl. 60), the Pontigny Bible (fragments in Paris, BNF, ms. lat. 8823 and elsewhere), the Souvigny Bible (Moulins, Bibliothèque Municipale, ms. 1), the Capucins' Bible (Paris, BNF, mss. lat. 16743–6, Pl. 59), the Bible of Boulogne-sur-Mer (Boulogne, Bibliothèque Municipale, ms. 2), the Ansbach Bible (Erlangen, Universitätsbibliothek, Cod. 1 Perg, Pl. 61) and the vast *Codex Gigas* (Stockholm, Kungliga Biblioteket, MS. A.148, Pl. 57). These are exceptional examples but they are selected from very many dozens of surviving twelfth-century giant

Bibles scarcely inferior. They represent books from Italy, England, France, Flanders, Germany, Spain and Bohemia. They vary in their styles, of course, but are consistently manuscripts of the first quality. Nearly every one is magnificent. Each in its own way is a book of infinite luxury, handsomely designed and richly illuminated. No one can turn even a few parchment pages of one of the great Romanesque Bibles without being dazzled by the complexity of the designs, the quality of the materials used, the virtuosity of the painters' technique, and the finesse and astonishing effect of illumination on a vast scale. Monasteries and cathedrals must have competed to outdo each other in the luxury of their Bibles. The Bury and Winchester Bibles are among the greatest works of art ever produced in England. The Souvigny Bible can match them in France. These manuscripts stand among the supreme artefacts of mankind. Twelfth-century giant Bibles are not just particularly grand books, or the most beautiful Bibles of their time, but are among the most ambitious artistic enterprises surviving from the twelfth century in any medium, and they were made in very large numbers. That fact alone needs to be stated and emphasized in a history of Bibles.

These are whole Bibles, usually written in several consecutive volumes, with the Old and New Testaments following each other. This sense of comprehensiveness, all the books of the Bible together, is reflected in twelfth-century library catalogues. They frequently specify the text as the 'complete Bible', divided into such-and-such number of volumes. The earlier word *bibliotheca* is often used at this period, meaning both 'Bible' and 'library'. The Bible was a collection of texts, but by the first half of the twelfth century it had become an entity which was not only recognizable but which was considered an essential text for every church or monastery.

In the course of the twelfth century and later many monasteries seem to have felt the need of a second giant Bible for reading during meals. This comes in gradually. We know, for example, that the abbey of St-Amand in Flanders already had a giant Bible by about 1100 (Valenciennes, Bibliothèque Municipale, mss. 9–11, cited above). About sixty years later, the monk Sawalo copied another giant Bible for the same abbey of St-Amand (Valenciennes, mss. 1–5), which was described in the twelfth-century inventory there as the Bible to be 'read at table'. Similarly, the monks of Winchester evidently had two giant Bibles by the 1180s: the Winchester Bible itself and a second less elaborate copy described by a chronicler as the Bible 'to be used for reading during meals', probably to be identified with Oxford, Bodleian Library, MSS. Auct. E.inf. 1–2 (Pl. 56), which has been suitably marked up for reading aloud. Great Bibles which were new around 1100

must have seemed archaic and old-fashioned by the late twelfth century. A manuscript such as the four-volume Puiset Bible at Durham (Durham Cathedral, MS. A.II.1) was made *c.*1190 to replace the already archaic Carilef Bible of a hundred years earlier. By the fifteenth century, at the latest, the Carilef Bible was stored among the books used in the Durham refectory. The monks of Bury St Edmunds also seem to have downgraded their twelfth-century Bible into use in the refectory, perhaps when they acquired a newer Bible for the church around 1220. Large refectory Bibles were still being used when Gutenberg devised his printed Bible in the 1450s, as we shall see in Chapter 8 below. In the meantime, let us simply record the first occurrence of duplicate giant Bibles in the possession of monasteries by the mid-twelfth century.

Making any book as big as the entire Bible must have been a daunting undertaking, not started lightly. All books in Europe in the eleventh and twelfth centuries were made on parchment, and this was expensive and slow to prepare. A giant Bible used a great deal of parchment. Some monasteries certainly made their own: the scribe Goderannus worked with the monk Cuno who made the parchment at Stavelot. Other monasteries bought in parchment. Famous instances of the importation of parchment are recorded at Bury St Edmunds in

55 opposite

The Winchester Bible was painted between about 1160 and 1180, by a team of professional illuminators at Winchester Cathedral Priory. It was planned on almost unprecedented scale of luxury and elaboration, and was never finished (WINCHESTER CATHEDRAL, MS. 17)

56

A second Bible was made in Winchester in the later twelfth century. It is probably the copy referred to in a contemporary account as having been made 'to be used for reading during meals'. The initial here shows the opening of Daniel (OXFORD, BODLEIAN LIBRARY, MS. AUCT. E. INFRA 1)

Suffolk and at the abbey of San Isidoro in León in north-west Spain. The accounts
are worth repeating for both refer to parchment specifically for making giant
Bibles. The chronicle of Bury describes how Master Hugo, illuminator of the
Bury Bible in *c.*1135, was unable to find suitable parchment for the manuscript
locally and so he obtained some 'in Scottish parts'. It must have been purchased.
The colophon of the vast three-volume León Bible, written in 1162 (León,
Colegiata de San Isidoro, Cod. 1.3), recounts that parchment for this precious
work was obtained by one of the canons of San Isidoro from France by a sea journey of great effort and danger. The 622 leaves of the León Bible are up to 550 by
370 mm in size (21½ by 14½ inches). We do not know for certain the size of medieval pelts, but perhaps four leaves, or two bifolia, could be obtained from the skin
of one calf. If so, the hides of some 155 animals would have been needed for the
Léon Bible. That was a major investment even before the scribes began to write.

Let us remember again the vastness of the actual text of the whole Latin Bible.
The Winchester Bible is written with 54 lines to a column, two columns to a
page, over 461 double-sided leaves: if all the lines of text of this manuscript could
be measured end to end, they would stretch for a total distance of something over
11,000 metres (nearly seven miles). The sum, though whimsical, does illustrate
the huge effort which would be required to copy out an entire giant Bible.
Goderannus did it twice, and the second time in 1097 he recorded that it had
taken him and a colleague just on four years to make the whole Bible, including
the writing, illumination and binding (Pl. 46). Brother Heinrich, the scribe of a
two-volume Bible for the abbey of Bonne-Ésperance in Hainaut (Brussels, BR,
ms. II.2524), noted in a colophon that he had begun copying on 26 August 1132
and that he finished this work of great magnitude in July 1135, almost three
years later, except (he admits with the honesty of a monk) 'I did not work con-
tinuously, for I took breaks during time of fog'. This gives a charming insight
into conditions in an open-air cloister in medieval Belgium. Some scribes
must have worked on Bibles as an act of piety. The historian Ordericus Vitalis
(d. *c.*1142) tells a moral tale of a wicked monk who had committed every possible
sin but who also copied out a huge Bible. The monk died, the story goes on, and
he came to judgement. His sins were counted and were weighed against the exact
number of letters in every word in the Bible he had copied, and it was found that
there was one more letter in his Bible than the total of his sins, and so the monk
was given the benefit of the doubt. There was spiritual credit in copying a Bible.
The most giant of all Romanesque Bibles, the enormous *Codex Gigas* in Stockholm (Kungliga Bibli;oteket, MS. A.148, Pl. 57), was apparently copied by
'Hermannus the enclosed monk': presumably an anchorite, walled up in a cell,
could earn much merit and could pass the days not disagreeably copying a Bible.

Most scribes of giant Bibles, however, probably worked in small teams,
especially as the twelfth century advanced and the need for Bibles became ever
greater. We know this both from documentary references and from close

57 opposite

The enormous Codex Gigas,
*made in Bohemia in the late
twelfth century, was apparently
copied by an anchorite, a
solitary monk walled up inside
his cell*
(STOCKHOLM, KUNGLIGA
BIBLIOTEKET, MS. A.148)

examination of manuscripts. The Stavelot Bible was written by Goderannus assisted by Ernesto, monk of Stavelot. Verses in the Biburg Bible of 1147 (Munich, Universitätsbibliothek, cod. 2° 28) record that it was written out by three scribes: Ebrordus (a monk of Prüfening), Henricus (probably a monk of Biburg) and a third unnamed. Abbot Pontius of Cluny (1109–22) is similarly recorded as taking on three people to make a Bible for Cluny Abbey: Albert (a monk of Trier), Peter the librarian (*armarius*), and a certain Opizo. Examination of the script of the Worms (or Frankenthal) Bible in the British Library (Harley MSS. 2803–4, Pl. 58) shows that it was written by four scribes, of whom one wrote most of the book and another systematically corrected most of the text. Checking and correcting was an integral part of writing a Romanesque Bible. In the Weingarten Bible we have only the name of the corrector, Sator, but not of the scribe (New York, Morgan Library, M.11, fol. 23r). Note that in the Bibles from Stavelot, Biburg, and Cluny cited here, all the main scribes came from beyond the abbeys (from Lobbes, Prüfening and Trier, respectively) but were assisted in each case by a local monk of the commissioning abbey, in one case named as the librarian. It would be tempting to see Ernesto, Henricus, and Peter the librarian as correctors, or at least as internal monitors of the text.

Similarly, the provision of illumination became increasingly a task for craftsmen who were brought in from outside the commissioning monastery.

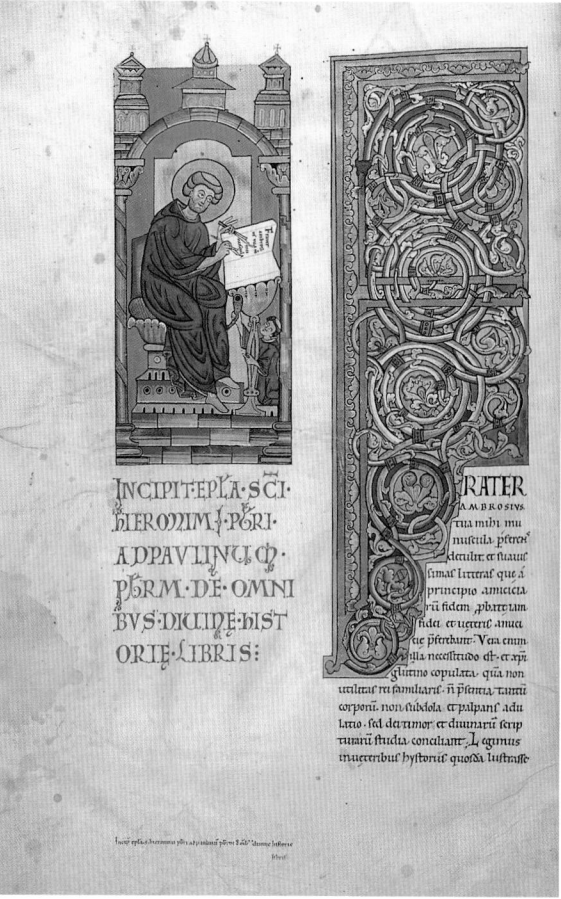

This touches on one of the most important topics in the history of twelfth-century art. We must not get side-tracked into the fascinating problem of when European artists began to become specialized and professional, earning their livings from painting, but the change is generally assumed to be have come about gradually between about 1100 and 1220. The great eleventh-century giant Bibles, with linear initials infilled with coloured ink, were doubtless often decorated by the scribes themselves. As the trend for elaborate illumina-tion increased, so other craftsmen were needed to supply it. Master Hugo, artist of the Bury Bible in the 1130s (Cambridge, Corpus Christi College, MS. 2), was certainly a profes-sional craftsman brought in to produce various enterprises for the abbey. The Bury chronicle records that Hugo also made bronze doors for the abbey church, a bell, a cross for the choir, and statues of the Virgin and Saint John. He was pre-sumably paid for his labour: the chronicle says that Hervey the sacrist, brother of Prior Talbot, himself 'found all the expenses' for the Bible. Master Hugo was probably an itinerant artist, and his hand has been tentatively recognized in a fragmentary wall painting in Canterbury Cathedral, where perhaps he moved on to later. The illuminators of the Winchester Bible seem also to have executed a cycle of wall paintings at Sigena in northern Catalonia. The late twelfth-century illuminator of the magnificent four-volume Capucins' Bible (Paris, BNF, mss. lat. 16743–6, Pl. 59) apparently also worked at St Albans in England in the time of Abbot Simon (1167–83) and probably at the abbey of St-Bertin, near St-Omer, and perhaps even painted a number of stained-glass panels formerly in the cathedral at Troyes. He must have travelled extensively in pursuit of work. Once artists customarily moved from place to place, doubtless carrying their pattern sheets and sketch books, so artistic styles and innovations could spread rapidly across Europe.

thu xpi fili dauid. fili abraham. A
braham genuit ysaac. Ysaac autem:
genuit iacob. Iacob autem: genuit iu
dam & fratres eius. Iudas autem: ge
nuit phares & zaram de thamar. Pha
res autem genuit esrom: esrom autem
genuit aram. aram autem genuit ami
nadab: aminadab autem genuit na
ason. Naason autem genuit salmon.
salmon autem genuit booz de rachab.
Booz autem genuit obed ex ruth: obed
autem genuit iesse. Iesse autem: genu
it dauid regem. Dauid autem rex genu
it salomonem: ex ea que fuit urie. Sa
lomon autem genuit roboam: roboa
autem genuit abiam. Abia autem
genuit asa: asa autem genuit iosa
phat. Iosaphat autem genuit ioram:
ioram autem genuit oziam. Ozias au
tem genuit ioatham: ioatham aute
genuit achaz. Achaz autem genuit
ezechiam: ezechias autem genuit ma
nassen. Manasses autem genuit amos:
amon autem genuit iosiam. Iosias
autem genuit iechoniam & fratres
eius in transmigratione babylonis.
Et post transmigratione babylonis:
iechonias genuit salathiel. Salathiel
autem genuit zorobabel: zorobabel
autem genuit abiud. Abiud autem

Doubtless scribes travelled too. One such professional and non-monastic scribe was Manerius, who in about 1180 copied a vast and magnificent three-volume Bible, probably for the abbey of St-Loup in Troyes (Paris, Bibl. de Ste-Geneviève, mss. 8–10, Pl. 60). Manerius himself, however, came from Canterbury in England. In a long colophon he tells us the names of his parents, Wimund and Liveva, his grandparents, Ulger and Elvera, his brothers, Ralph and Gerald, and so on, with vignettes of their characters, nostalgic reminiscences written a long way from home. His widowed mother (we know this from records in Canterbury) was still living there in 1165. There are very fine illuminated initials in Manerius's Bible. Little marginal marks beside many of them record a running total of the number of illuminated initials in each gathering of the book. This must be for purposes of payment, and the book was evidently commercially made. A Bible of such luxury and scale must always have been very costly.

For the final part of this chapter, therefore, we must address the difficulty which confronted any patron thinking of commissioning a giant Bible in the twelfth century – the problem of supply and cost. A giant Bible was by far the most extensive single manuscript-making project likely to be undertaken in the twelfth century. The materials and labour involved in making a great Bible must have been immense, especially as the work became increasingly undertaken by professional craftsmen who would expect a salary.

In the eleventh century, a great patron wanting a Bible for presentation probably simply commanded his local monastery to make him the book, perhaps furnishing the materials himself. The monetary cost of the labour would not have been relevant. A bishop or archbishop, such as Gebhard of Salzburg, Frederick of Geneva, Altmann of Passau or even William of St-Calais, all of whom we have encountered above within the eleventh century, would either have had clerical scribes in their own households or would have involved monasteries in their patronage. In return, a bishop could reward a monastery with favours. The abbey chronicle of St-Hubert-des-Ardennes records that Bishop Helinandus of Laon acquired a complete Bible from their monks in about 1082 for presentation by

The Manerius Bible was made in France, perhaps in Troyes, c.1180, by a scribe who identifies himself as coming from Canterbury in England. The initial for the opening of Exodus shows the finding of the baby Moses in the bullrushes
(PARIS, BIBLIOTHÈQUE DE STE-GENEVIÈVE, MS. 8)

Helinandus to Laon Cathedral, and that the monks supplied it in gratitude for
benefactions they had received from Laon in 1071 and 1082.

Kings and great secular lords probably always assumed the ability to appropriate Bibles for presentation to other monasteries. Leopold of Austria (1073–1136),
son-in-law of the Emperor Henry IV, needed a giant Bible for the abbey he was
refounding at Klosterneuburg. The agreement survives whereby he comman-
deered a three-volume Bible and a Missal from the Augustinians of St Nicholas
in Passau in 1136, offering the canons in return various land privileges and
exemption from customs duties on the Danube. That was probably regarded as
a fair exchange. A similar transaction is recorded of King Henry II of England
(1154–89). Between about 1180 and 1186, as we learn from the contemporary
life of Saint Hugh of Lincoln, which recounts the story, the king sought a great
Bible to present to the Carthusian priory of Witham. He heard that the monks
of Winchester had recently completed a giant Bible intended for their own use.
'The king was delighted', the chronicler recounts, 'and sending immediately for
the prior, asked for the Bible as a gift, promising that he would make it worth
their while to part with it, and thus secured it.' The monks of Winchester probably had little choice, but they gained royal favour in exchange. Some twenty-five
years later, in 1208, Henry's son, King John, acquired from the monks of Reading
Abbey the first volume of a Bible, presumably a large one. Again, the monks were
doubtless rewarded in some suitable fashion.

By about 1120, we begin to find traces of the commercial value of Bibles. This
is important, both in the history of Bibles and of the book trade. The chronicle of
St-Pierre-le-Vif at Sens records how Abbot Arnold in 1123 ordered immediate
excommunication for any person whatsoever who should allow the abbey's new
giant Bible to be sold or appropriated in any way outside the abbey's possession.
The fact that he legislated against the monks selling their Bible must reflect the
fear that they might be tempted do so. The anxiety about appropriation of the
book may suggest experience of the high-handedness of nobles or bishops.

By the mid-century, monasteries seeking giant Bibles needed very great
financial resources. No longer could a community of monks simply hope that a
kindly bishop or secular ruler would supply a Bible. There were now too many
monasteries; each monastery now seemed to require at least two Bibles; each
Bible was now far more extensively illuminated than had been customary fifty
years earlier; and the making of books was moving from the sphere of the unpaid
monk, working for spiritual merit, into that of secular scribes and painters who
were paid for their labour. It is a point worth making, especially in a history of
Bibles, that around 1140, for the first time, the Bible became a book which could
be commonly bought.

The giant Bible of Michaelbeuren Abbey in Austria (Michaelbeuren, Stiftsbibliothek, Cod. perg. 1) includes a contemporary note recording that it was actually
purchased by Abbot Walter (1161–90) for the sum of ten talents. To judge from

its archaic style of the second quarter of the century, the abbot may have bought it second-hand. Perhaps another monastery sold it. We even find early evidence of monasteries trading and dealing in Romanesque Bibles between themselves. The *Codex Gigas*, for example, was apparently pawned in the thirteenth century by the Benedictines of Podlazic to the Cistercian monastery of Sedlec, in the diocese of Prague, and was afterwards sold on by them to the nearby Benedictine monastery of Brevnev. A giant Bible of *c.*1140 (now Vienna, ÖNB, cod. n.s. 2701–2) had originally belonged to the Benedictines of Csatár in Hungary, but was later pawned through the agency of Master Wyd to a Jew named Farkas, and was sold on to the abbey of Admont in southern Austria.

Monasteries commissioning Bibles too needed to raise money to pay for them. The huge mid-twelfth-century illuminated Bible of Fleury Abbey (Orléans, Bibliothèque Municipale, ms. 13) was probably paid for out of an annual tax on the abbey's dependencies which Abbot Macarius had set up in 1147 specifically for the repair and purchase of books for his monastery. Sometimes there were fundraising campaigns. The Benedictine monks of St Gombert's abbey at Ansbach in Bavaria acquired a very fine illuminated giant Bible in the second half of the twelfth century (Erlangen, Universitätsbibliothek, Cod. 1 Perg, Pl. 61). It is a huge manuscript, 393 leaves, 670 by 460 mm (26½ by 18 inches), with eleven magnificent full-page miniatures, 26 half-page miniatures (either vertical or horizontal) and numerous historiated and illuminated initials. On the verso of the flyleaf is a very interesting inscription to the effect that the Holy Church should not be unmindful of the memory of the Lord – that is, that they need a Bible – and that it therefore seemed fitting to inscribe the names of those who furnished this book for the blessed Mary, mother of God, and for Saint Gombert, so that in this church their memory might be better known and be shown forever to readers of the manuscript. Then it lists contributions. The dean Gotebold (d.1195) gave one talent. Sigefrid gave three. Sigelous the leather-worker (*coriarius*) gave one, on condition that his anniversary be commemorated after his death. Various other citizens (unnamed) contributed five talents. Certain other faithful people (also unnamed) added two further talents. All this is recorded, in such words. The total comes to 12 talents, two more than Abbot Walter of Michaelbeuren paid for his second-hand copy.

An even more extensive and detailed record of fund-raising for a giant Bible survives in the great four-volume copy written and decorated for the monastery of San Vito in Pisa, begun on 6 October 1168 (Calci, Biblioteca dell'Archivio della Certosa, cod. 1, Pl. 62). In a long account in the fourth volume, the priest Gerardus explains that the project began when Mattilda Vecki (or Vecchi) presented 100 shillings in memory of her late husband Rainulf of San Vito, for the purchase of parchment to make a Bible. Gerardus says he used it to buy 240 sheets. This would be 5 pence a sheet, a point we will return to in a moment. Buying parchment, of course, was necessarily the initial expense. Once that was

61 opposite

The late twelfth-century Ansbach Bible was purchased by the monks of Ansbach Abbey from funds raised from local benefactors. The manuscript is richly illustrated throughout (ERLANGEN, UNIVERSITÄTS-BIBLIOTHEK, COD. 1 PERG.)

*The giant Bible of San Vito in
Pisa was begun in October
1168. It includes a detailed list
of all the expenses incurred in
making the book and the names
of the local citizens who contributed to its great cost. This
detail is from the opening of
Deuteronomy*
(CALCI, BIBLIOTECA
DELL'ARCHIVIO DELLA
CERTOSA, COD. 1)

done, Gerardus evidently set about raising funds for the rest of the work. He lists
in detail the names and sometimes occupations of over sixty people who made
contributions towards paying for the Bible, ranging from three pence, given by
Ebriacus, to 25 shillings given by Burnettus *faber* (the carpenter) and 32
shillings given by Mannus, son of Ciufettus, in memory of his mother Qualdrada.
It is a fascinating record, full of human interest. Many people gave sums for the
souls of relatives or friends who had died. Some returned several times. The
brothers Morico and Veckio, for example, gave 10 shillings for the soul of their

brother Ugolini and later came back with 2 shillings in memory of their sister Teodora. Vivianus de Carraria contributed 12 pence on his own account and another 12 pence for his friend Angelo. One man gave 5 shillings for the soul of Leo the doctor. Almost all the donors were laity, many evidently of quite humble rank. There was one priest, Gregorius, who gave 10 shillings for the soul of his cousin Sigismundus. A monk, Brumcardus, joined with his brothers Morcione and Marcolfus, to give 20 shillings for the soul of their late father Ugolinus de Pisa. Apparent occupations include two fisherman and two bakers. One fisherman was Petrus Vekius, who gave 12 pence, probably a relative of Mattilda Vecki whose bequest initiated the project. Perhaps the family money had all come from fishing. Altogether, including the contents of the collecting-box in the church, Gerardus apparently raised an additional 202 shillings and 2½ pence. With the 100 shillings from Mattilda, he now had just over £15.

The account then becomes slightly confusing. He says he paid £15 'and a little more' to one Master Vivianus, which sounds like the combined total being paid to the organiser of the work. However, he also gives a breakdown of the costs, which add up to just above the same total. Gerardus bought two further batches of parchment, spending 53½ shillings plus 4 shillings and 32 pence. At 5 pence a sheet, he ought now to have had 388 sheets. If each sheet was folded in two, he would have 776 leaves. The finished Bible, as it exists today, has 855 leaves, 560 by 380 mm (22 by 15 inches). Probably Gerardus got a slight discount for quantity.

Then he paid the scribe in two instalments. First he gave 97 shillings and then 10 shillings and 2 pence, naming the scribe as Albertus Vulterrensis. He was not apparently a monk, and doubtless came from Volterra, about 50 km (30 miles) south-east of Pisa. For the 855 leaves, the total Albertus was actually paid would be almost exactly 1½ pence a leaf, which was perhaps how the sum was done. Through the steward Benedictus, the scribe next received a further 7½ shillings to add big initials in gold and colours. These were probably text initials rather than miniatures. Andreas, nephew of the priest Gregorius, also received 9 shillings for supplying further initials. He was paid through the agency of Damian the prior. All this work evidently took place outside the monastery, for the priest Gregorius received the huge sum of 42 shillings and 4 pence 'when he brought back the quires': possibly he was the artist of the historiated initials, or more probably the abbey's representative correcting the text. Finally one Coloiannus received 12 shillings. He may have been the binder.

Here then, in 1168, a hundred years and not many miles from where we began this chapter in the papal court, a vast Bible is produced under entirely new circumstances. It is no longer a rare and symbolic gift of state but has become an essential item for even a small local monastery, now paid for by tradesmen of the town. They take pride in its completion. The Bible is no longer the monopoly of monks and clerics, working for no wages other than the accumulation of virtue, but has become a commercial book.

4 | Commentaries on the Bible

THE STORY SO FAR has looked at the Bible as an artefact. The Bible is a text which has been copied out and disseminated more often than any other in the history of the written word. Someone who had never heard of the Bible before might well ask what this book was all about, and why this collection of writings, more than any other, was perceived to be of such consuming interest. It is not possible or appropriate to summarize the text here. Tales from the Bible are still part of our folk culture. Most people, even now, know or can quickly discover that the Old Testament begins with an account of the creation of the world, and that it brings together the stories and customs of the Israelites in the ancient world, their special relationship to God, and their travels, wars, hymns of praise and predictions of a future Messiah. The New Testament comprises four parallel narratives of the life, death and resurrection of Jesus Christ, who lived in Palestine from approximately 4 BC to approximately 33 AD. He is shown as fulfilling the messianic prophecies and offering the possibility of spiritual salvation to all people. The New Testament continues with records of the early spread of Christianity in the time of Saint Paul, copies of letters of advice sent out to early Christian communities, and a strange visionary account of the anticipated end of the world.

It is relatively straightforward to read the Bible from end to end. Much of it comprises narrative. It covers an immense span of years and range of subjects. In all periods of history, however, people have questioned what the Bible actually means, and whether there are other meanings hidden behind the words. It contains many references to names and places unfamiliar to later readers. Even some narrative passages are very obscure and difficult to follow. The Bible is not only a composite text but is in its nature often very enigmatic, especially when

sup seruos di ancillas. idest sup centum uiginti credentium nomina. effusum iri in cenaculo sion. Qui centum uiginti ab uno usque ad quindecim paulatim. per incrementa surgentes. quindecim graduum numerum efficiunt. qui in psalterio mistice continetur. Ex tribus g generibus rethorum hec sumuntur principia. Et tres sunt argumentorum partes. ex quibus incipere solet omnis orator. Aut docabiles. aut beniuolos. aut attentos auditores debet efficere. hic g ypha recte a magnitudine cladis sumens principium eos q qui audituri erant uiolens ad penitentiam puocare. reddit intentos. admirans futurorum malum. ut considerantes uenture cladis aspritatem. oculis arripent penitentiam In hoc epha id circo nec reges nec tempora sunt prenotata. quia hisdem temporibus ac regibus quibus osee ppha tuit. Johel interpretatur incipiens. aut dni descensus tropologice. hoc e qd qui hostium di isciam di habent aperiam: recte incipit prophare.

ohel de tribu ruben. natus in agro bethoron ubi etiam in pace mortuus est atque sepultus.

Ieronis. fatuel ppheta pater iohel pphete. a septuaginta interpretibus batuel uocatur. Sz cum batuel in ebreo nichil omnino sonet: melius est ut legatur fatuel qd interpretatur ut apiens ds. Uni marco. effera quod e adapire. Febit iohel qui cum aplo poterat dicere. os nrm patet ad duos o.c. cor nrm dilatatum e. qui dicebat a domino. aperi os tuum. e.i.t. filius fatuel dicitur. i. dei. in cuius potestate e aperire os hois. y dilatare ipsum scm hominem donec ueniat ad pfectionem. huius g fatuel filius e iohel. idest incipiens. ut e deus. quia qui se incipientem cognoscit. p humilitatem crescere debet ut cum moyse audiat. Qui e misit me. i. uiis deus ad distinctionem eorum qui si sunt ue dii. Ad hunc g iohel recte factum e uerbum dni qd erat in principio. a. d uerbum factum non secundum

ER
BU

Ver-BU in pacis.

domini quod

Non quan

factum e

tum ad se. Incipiens ut e deus. Magnitudo ut apiet ds

ad iohel filium fatuel.

Audite hoc senes. & auribz

papite omnes habitatores

Senes idest iuniorum in domini infanciam reuer-tis. spituali intelligere misterie que dicuntur istuos habitat-terre. qui spen-trenis ponitur potestis audi-spiritualia. sal-auribz corpo-capite litterali sensum facit ypha exorditur quo ex magni-dine dicendo auditorem red-attentum. qui nec ubertati re-present. Residuu e.

ria nec in presenti etate talia dici contigisse. post exordiu sequitur na-

dealing with expressions of devotion or prophecy. There have been many differ-ent ways of understanding the text of the Bible; and we cannot begin to follow the history of the Bible itself without having some sense of how the text was interpreted and used at different periods of its history. The activity of explaining the Scriptures goes right back into biblical times. According to the New Testa-ment, Christ himself read and interpreted the ancient Law in the Temple; and the authors of the Gospels and the letters of Saint Paul quote prophecies from the Old Testament and apply them to specific events in the New. That itself is a form of biblical commentary. The preaching of a sermon or homily around a quotation from the Bible is a device established in the earliest years of Christian-ity and in essence has remained unchanged ever since. It is an ancient rhetorical method of teaching created in the classical period which survives in the pulpits of Christian churches throughout the modern world. A sermon is very often quite simply a spoken commentary on several sentences of the Bible. By the time of the conversion of the Roman Empire to Christianity, reading and attempting to explain the various parts of the Bible would have been a central part of Christian devotion, both in spoken sermons and in written form. Most early Christian writing is, to a greater or lesser extent, concerned with quoting and interpreting parts of the Bible.

Throughout the Middle Ages in Europe there were more biblical commen-taries than any other area of literary endeavour, and there were certainly more manuscripts of biblical commentaries in most medieval libraries than there were copies of the Bible itself. A large Carolingian or Romanesque monastery might perhaps have owned two or three Bibles or partial sets of biblical books, but it

63 previous page
The Gloss was a twelfth-century compilation of quota-tions from older commentaries on the Bible. This manuscript, written in France for Thomas Becket in the late 1160s, shows the opening of the book of Joel in large script, surrounded by an extract from the comment-ary of Saint Jerome in smaller script
(CAMBRIDGE, TRINITY COLLEGE, MS. B.3.11)

64
Almost half of the 229 remain-ing medieval manuscripts in the ancient library of Hereford Cathedral are commentaries or sermons on the Bible, but only six manuscripts are Bibles or parts of the Bible without commentaries

would have possessed many dozens of commentaries. A monk of the eleventh or twelfth century, for example, would probably not have gained most of his knowledge of the Scriptures from having looked at some giant monumental Bible but from listening to prescribed extracts from the Bible during church services and from reading and meditating afterwards on the sermons and commentaries of Augustine, Jerome, Gregory, Bede and others. More or less every word of any Scriptural text was incorporated into its commentary. A medieval reader who knew only the commentaries would through them have access to the words of the Bible; and before the twelfth century the way that the text of the Bible circulated most widely was in the fragmented but consecutive citations of a commentary.

The earliest Christian authors wrote mainly in Greek – we have traces of biblical commentaries by second-century writers such as Marcion and Melito of Sardis – but their works were not widely known, if at all, in the Western Europe of the Middle Ages. Fragile relics of biblical commentaries written by early Christians in the deserts of North Africa have been rediscovered in modern times and integrated into the history of biblical scholarship, but they did not travel down through the ages, like the works of Jerome and Augustine, for example, in the entourage of the Latin Bible. Some will reappear in the Chapter 12 below among the contributions made by the twentieth century to the history of the Bible.

Sometimes early interpretations of the Bible were controversial. While the theology and basic rules of Christianity were evolving and becoming crystallized during the first centuries, any author of that time stood the risk of having his opinions retrospectively reassessed as heretical, and having his texts suppressed and destroyed after his death. Some Greek writings of the early school of theology in Alexandria survived into the Middle Ages through Latin adaptations. Clement of Alexandria (*c*.150–*c*.215) and his successor, Origen (*c*.185–*c*.254), were both widely known in medieval Europe. Origen came under suspicion of heresy in the fifth century, and many of his texts were destroyed, including his commentaries on the Bible. Many of Origen's sermons on biblical texts, however, survived into Latin in the translations of Saint Jerome and Jerome's one-time friend and later opponent, Rufinus (*c*.345–410).

As Chapter 1 opened with Saint Jerome, so too Jerome was the first great writer in Latin to bring together the many strands of the early Christian biblical interpretation. He set in motion what has been since his time an unbroken tradition of writing and collecting commentaries on the Bible. Jerome wrote that in the course of a long life he had read a great many books, and in his commentary on Saint Matthew's Gospel he asserted that he had merely gathered up the flowers of other men's interpretations, including the works of Origen (in twenty-five volumes, he reported), Theophilus of Antioch, the martyr Hippolytus, Theodore of Heracleum, Apollonius of Laodicea, and Didymus the Blind. Such writers (except perhaps

Origen) were soon forgotten. Jerome transformed his sources and created the first staple texts of Latin biblical study.

In fact, almost the whole core of early Western Latin biblical commentary was assembled in the two hundred or so years between the time of Jerome and that of Saint Gregory the Great (*c*.540–604), roughly from the late fourth to the late sixth century. The great biblical commentators of this golden age are known as the 'patristic' authors, for they are regarded as the Church Fathers (*patres* in Latin). The term 'patristic' is sometimes loosely extended to incorporate Isidore of Seville (d.636) and by the thirteenth century Roger Bacon included even Bede (d.735) as a patristic writer.

Jerome wrote commentaries on the Psalms, Ecclesiastes, Isaiah (Pl. 65), Jeremiah, Ezekiel, Daniel, the Minor Prophets, the Gospel of Saint Matthew and some of the letters of Saint Paul. He also edited and rendered into Latin the earlier commentaries of Origen on the Song of Songs, Isaiah, Ezekiel, and the Gospel of Saint Luke; and he wrote groups of homilies (written sermons) on the Psalms and on each of the four Gospels. The massive industry of Jerome still amazes, 1,600 years later, and his books circulated extensively.

Jerome, studying in Bethlehem, was the contemporary of other great commentators in Latin working in Western Europe and in North Africa. He knew them all. One, whom Jerome praised as 'the trumpet of the Latins', was born in what is now France, Saint Hilary of Poitiers (*c*.315–67), who compiled commentaries on the Psalms and on the Gospel of Saint Matthew. Hilary's book on the Psalms, especially, was widely copied in the Middle Ages. Saint Ambrose (*c*.339–97) was born in Trier, son of the Praetorian prefect of Gaul, and was a Roman laywer and administrator in Lombardy before his appointment in 374 as Christian bishop of Milan. He wrote about twenty or so homiletic works on books of the Bible, about half of them on Genesis, including the *Hexameron*, on the six days of creation, and a commentary on the Gospel of Saint Luke. A well-known commentary on the letters of Saint Paul, also attributed to Ambrose throughout the Middle Ages, was later shown by Erasmus to have been the work of an unidentifiable contemporary of Ambrose instead. Its author is now inelegantly referred to as 'Ambrosiaster', a later downgrading which belies the text's influence in the Middle Ages when it circulated as by the master himself. Ambrose has a place in history too as the teacher and converter of Saint Augustine (354–430), one of the very greatest of all Christian writers and philosophers. Augustine was born at

Tagaste on the north coast of Africa and died not far away as bishop of Hippo Regius. He too knew and corresponded extensively with Jerome. It is worth remembering how many of these great saintly authors were personally acquainted, like the network of modern academics who meet up regularly at international conferences and exchange offprints by post. Augustine wrote commentaries on Genesis and the Psalms, especially (Pl. 66), and seven books on the Gospels, and shorter works on several letters of Saint Paul, including Romans and Galatians.

The second important generation of patristic writers is represented by two Italians, Cassiodorus (c.485–c.580), whose commentary on the Psalms was based on that of Augustine, and Saint Gregory the Great (c.540–604), pope from 590. Gregory wrote commentaries on Kings, Job, Ezekiel, and a series of forty homilies on the Gospels. We encountered Cassiodorus above (p. 32); we will return later to Saint Gregory. A quick survey of the end of the patristic period should probably encompass also a Spaniard and an Englishman, Saint Isidore of Seville (c.560–636) and the Venerable Bede (c.673– 735). Isidore wrote no full biblical commentaries as such but compiled biblical prefaces, and discussion questions on biblical passages, and put together the encyclopaedic *Etymologies*, which for a thousand years was the principal reference text for words and chronology in the Bible. Bede, a century later, was similarly fascinated by seeking chronology and facts of biblical history, and was author of commentaries and homilies on – among others – parts of Genesis, Exodus, Kings, the Song of Songs, the Gospels of Mark and Luke, Acts and the Apocalypse.

These, then, were the principal Fathers of the Latin Church whose biblical commentaries became the companion texts to the Bible. Note that the body of patristic writing was accumulative. Each new Bible commentary for several hundred years enlarged the existing corpus of texts, some of which overlapped in their coverage of books of the Bible and quoted from each other. The commentaries joined Bibles on the shelves. Patristic commentaries took on something of status of junior Bibles, as the central companion texts of Christianity, gradually acquiring antiquity and authority. The Middle Ages greatly respected the wisdom which came with age. A well-established authority was accorded an honoured status, whereas a new or original text was mistrusted.

We have seen a similar shift as the Vulgate gradually assumed acceptability and eventually authority. Even Bede in his commentary on Luke conferred credibility on his own work by citing by name the respected works of Jerome, Augustine, Ambrose and Gregory. The great Carolingian commentators did the same. There were many ninth-century compilers, popular writers like Claudius of Turin (d. *c*.830), Hamo of Auxerre (d. *c*.855), Rabanus Maurus (d.856) and Remigius of Auxerre (d.908), who all quarried extensively and mainly from patristic writers, consciously adding authority and credibility by virtue of copying from the old sources. They revelled in *florilegia* and anthologies, extracted from the old books; and scribes copied out the vast works of the Church Fathers over and over again.

By the twelfth century, Jerome, Ambrose, Augustine and Gregory were already regarded as the four Doctors of the Church, canonized saints almost on a level with the four Evangelists of the New Testament. The late twelfth-century library catalogue of the Benedictines of Burton-on-Trent in England described a three-volume *Psalterium secundum Augustinum*, a 'Psalter *according to* Augustine' (using the same phrasing as a few lines further down, 'the History of the English *according to* Bede'). It is as if Augustine actually wrote the Psalter. Saint Gregory is often shown in medieval art with the Holy Dove whispering directly into his ear, as if his writings were as divinely revealed as the Scriptures (Pl. 67).

It is remarkable how patristic Bible commentators fully came into their own from the ninth to the twelfth century, hundreds of years after the passing of the world for which the authors had written. Vast volumes of the Church Fathers became the standard works of the monasteries. To judge from surviving manuscripts, the greatest and most widely copied texts of all were Jerome on the twelve Minor Prophets, often in two volumes with Hosea to Michah and Nahum to Malachi respectively; Augustine on the Psalms, often in three volumes, divided into Psalms 1–50, 51–100 and 101–150 respectively; Augustine on John in one volume; and the thirty-five books of Gregory on Job, often in three volumes with books 1–10, 11–22 and 23–35 respectively. These are usually stout books, generally large in size. Other briefer texts, like Gregory on Ezekiel and on the Gospels and Bede on Luke, were sometimes bound up as part of big multiple volumes with other books. This handful of books (perhaps 'chestful' is more accurate)

67

Saint Gregory is often shown in medieval art with the Holy Dove dictating directly into his ear. This is a page from a late tenth-century manuscript made for the archbishop of Trier (TRIER, STADTBIBLIOTHEK, COD. 117/626)

68 opposite

Monks cutting up a tree, a detail from a manuscript of Gregory's Moralia *on the book of Job, written for the monastery of Cîteaux in 1111* (DIJON, BIBLIOTHÈQUE MUNICIPALE, MS. 173)

represented the core of biblical literature, and the texts were immensely widely read in early medieval Europe.

We get a shadowy sense too of the relative importance attached to such texts from the records of medieval library catalogues. Bibles are usually recorded first. This may sometimes simply be because Bible manuscripts were the biggest or most costly, but it is probably fair to see priority as some reflection of status. The library list of the abbey of St-Wandrille (*c*.787–806), for example, records books of the Bible first, followed immediately by two copies of Augustine on the Psalms. The list of Fontenelle Abbey (*c*.823–33), opens with an illuminated Bible followed by Augustine on Genesis. That of St-Riquier (831), starts with Bibles and then two copies of Jerome on Isaiah. The ninth-century St-Gall catalogue lists the Bibles and immediately next records Augustine on John. The eleventh-century catalogues of St-Vaast and Schaffhausen both open with Bibles followed by Gregory on Job. The Pfäffers catalogue of 1155 sandwiches its one-volume Bible between Augustine on John and Gregory on Job. One could cite very many other examples. The commentaries of Augustine and Gregory, especially, were such a fundamental part of the apparatus of the Bible in a medieval monastery that they can hardly be considered separately.

It is of little value to note the presence of such books all over Europe without some sense of what medieval readers would have learned about the Bible from studying the commentaries. We must therefore turn to what the great commentaries actually say. Patristic authors approached the Scriptures from two quite different directions. Both methods begin with the absolute assumption that the text of the Bible is complete, that it is not just a history book but the revealed Word of God himself, that God gave it to man for a specific purpose, and that every word is of equal importance. We must accept that all medieval commentators and readers took these assumptions for granted. To reach into the true meaning of the Bible text, one must look beneath the surface, and one could do so along two different planes. This is complicated. Let us therefore adopt a simple metaphor of the kind that would have helped and delighted a medieval reader. Imagine the whole Bible as a single tall tree growing from Genesis at its root right up to the New Testament Epistles and the Apocalypse at its very top. A medieval commentary, to sustain the metaphor, could open up the tree by cutting it in one of two directions, either vertically or horizontally. If one splits the tree vertically, one would follow the grain of the wood from one end to the other. If one saws the tree across horizontally, one would find all the layers of the wood, rings within rings. Now let us consider each of these directional cuts in turn.

Writers used the Bible to demonstrate the truth of Christianity. They searched the Old Testament for confirmation of fulfilment in the New. At the basic level, a commentary sought to prove that the incarnation of Christ and his death and resurrection were all foretold throughout the ancient scriptures. When Saint Augustine, on the brink of his conversion, consulted Saint Ambrose as to which book he should read to learn about Christianity, Ambrose recommended him not to the New Testament but to the book of Isaiah, 'since the prophet had predicted the Gospels and the calling of the gentiles'. The words of the Old Testament were studied in order to prove the truth of Christ. It is a technique of biblical analysis which depends on seeing the whole Bible from one end to the other as a complete entity. From the start to the finish of the Bible, every word is part of the same revealed truth. This itself tells us something about the sense of the Bible as a single timeless revelation, Jewish and Christian, all set in motion from the beginning of the world.

The linking of the Old and New Testaments goes beyond prophecy and fulfilment into seeing parallel stories which prefigure and echo each other. To take a simple example, the account of Joseph in the book of Genesis was interpreted as a prototype for the life of Christ, as Ambrose and others explained it, for Joseph was the good man sold into servitude for the salvation of others. Jerome, citing Origen, notes the obvious parallel between the selling of Joseph for a handful of silver (Genesis 37:28) and the account of Judas receiving payment for the betrayal of Christ (Matthew 26:15). Joab's pretended greeting of Abner before treacherously killing him (II Samuel 3:27) foreshadows the kiss with which Judas betrayed Christ in the Garden of Gethsemane (Matthew 26:49). The interconnection between Old and New Testaments works both forwards and backwards. For example, if Saint Peter can quote the Psalms to justify the expulsion of Judas from the apostles (Acts 1:20, citing Psalm 108:8 in

the Vulgate numbering), then Psalm 108:9 specifically refers to Judas, accurately prefigured before his time. That Psalm passage says 'let his children be fatherless and his wife a widow', and if we accept that prophecy is absolute, as we would have to, then from this reference alone and from nowhere in the New Testament, we can tell that Judas must have been married and had children. If a prophecy can be related unambiguously to its fulfilment, then every word of it must come literally true. 'It is less prophecy than history', said Cassiodorus of the Psalter, even when it refers to events set into what was still the future at the time it was written.

This technique of looking for events or phrases of the Old Testament which parallel those of the New Testament is known as 'typology' (from the Greek *tupoi*, meaning 'examples' or 'figures'). As a method of commenting on the Bible, it was especially popular in the early centuries of Christianity when it was still necessary to argue that Christ was indeed the long-prophesied Messiah. (It requires a leap from modern logic, for in order to argue that the New Testament is credible by citing its parallels with the Old, one must first accept that all the words in the New Testament are already true and independently reported.) Interest in typology explains why there were more early patristic commentaries on Old Testament books than on the Gospels. Commentators sought parallels not only in major narratives and prophecies but in individual phrases and even single words, uncritical of the fact that no part of the Latin Bible is in the original tongue. It shows little historical perspective and it judges all parts of the Bible as of equal value, irrespective of context. Typology remained popular throughout the Middle Ages and supplies much common imagery in medieval art, especially in books like the fourteenth-century *Speculum Humanae Salvationis* and the fifteenth-century woodcut books now called the *Biblia Pauperum*. We will return to these at the end of Chapter 6.

The second technique of medieval biblical commentary is that which, in the metaphor of the tree above, cuts horizontally across the grain. Every word and phrase of the Bible was seen as having several clearly-defined layers of meaning. The first level was the literal sense of the words: what actually happened historically in the Bible narrative. This was believed to be the least relevant. Some authors, such as Origen, were hardly interested in history at all. Whether or not Jonah was actually swallowed by a whale at some remote time in ancient history was of little practical importance to a monk in a cloister far from the sea and thousands of years and as many miles distant from Nineveh, but the symbolism of Jonah and the whale would be of enormous interest. Thus the second layer of meaning was the allegorical. The whale might be a symbol of the Devil, and its mouth a symbol of Hell, for example. Allegory could also be typological, for Jonah being disgorged by the whale after three days would be an obvious Old Testament symbol for the Gospel account of Christ descending into Hell and rising again on the third day (Pl. 69). That is an allegorical sense of the narrative of Jonah. Below this symbolism again, there was then a third level of meaning. This was the moral or tropological sense of the text. Tropology is concerned with behaviour or moral conduct. We may know that the whale represents Hell, but what does the story actually tell us about how we should live? This is the level of commentary to which Gregory peels back the layers of Scripture in his *Moralia* (as he calls it) on the book of Job – the levels of literal first, allegorical

69 opposite

Typology relates events of the Old Testament to their parallels in the life of Christ. Here, in a detail from a thirteenth-century Psalter, Jonah emerging from three days in the whale is paired with Christ rising up from three days in the tomb (LONDON, BL, ADD. MS. 54179)

second, and then practical third. Any verse or passage of the Bible could be profitably read at any of these three levels. Gregory in his commentary on Ezekiel says that in a single sentence of Scripture one person is nourished by the story alone, another may look for moral instruction, and yet another may seek for contemplative understanding through typology. There was sometimes, however, even a fourth level, deeper still than typology, called the 'anagogic'. This is the mystical or spiritual sense of the text. It tells of one's soul and its relationship to God. This is complicated, and we need not become too entangled in questions of spiritual meditation, except to acknowledge the fact that a devout medieval monk, reading the Bible verse by verse, would hope to come ever closer to a sense of mystical communion with God, and that any verse of Scripture might be a catalyst to bring the reader into a state of religious ecstasy.

Let us take an example of the three levels of Scripture from a source that would have been extremely familiar in the Middle Ages, the opening chapter of Gregory's *Moralia*. It begins by quoting exactly the first five verses of the book of Job. Gregory then goes through this text verse by verse, explaining the literal sense and setting the narrative in a historical context, such as (in commenting on verse 1) that the land of Hus where Job lived was a non-Jewish territory, and so Job was a man of God living among gentiles; and (commenting on verse 2) that Job had seven sons and three daughters and that, although having many children often leads to avarice (for all people naturally want to augment their wealth in order to leave property to their children), Job was unusual in being both an honest man and having many children; and so on. This is the literal sense of the text, the straightforward story, a bit pompous perhaps, but otherwise much like any modern biblical commentary. Then Gregory begins again with the allegorical sense of the same text. The word 'Job' in Hebrew (he says) means a man in sorrow; the word 'Hus' means a counsellor. Job in the land of Hus is to be understood as a symbol for sorrow living in wise counsel (as in Proverbs 8:12). Job had seven sons. Gregory revelled in number symbolism. Seven is formed of the sacred numbers of three and four added together. Since God rested on the seventh day, seven is the number of perfect unity, paralleled also by the Seven Gifts of the Holy Ghost which filled the twelve Apostles when they preached the Trinity (which is three) in the four corners of the earth. Seven is formed of three plus four, and twelve is formed of three times four, and so seven and twelve have the same symbolic value, and Job's seven sons are allegories of the apostles; and so on. It sounds to us rather contrived, but if one really accepts that every word was placed there by God in order to be decoded, then no interpretation can be too complicated. Then Gregory begins a third time. He works over the text once again, now seeking its moral sense. We have all lost paradise, like Job living among the gentiles, but the elect recognize their loss, as we should. Job's sons are the Seven Virtues and his daughters are faith, hope and charity, and Job lives with his ten children, who equal the Ten Commandments among which we should all live; and so on.

We should note several points about Gregory's *Moralia*. It originated in the daily lectures which Gregory had given to his monks on the book of Job and from the answers to questions they asked him (Pl. 70). Gregory lived in the late sixth century, when Rome was subject to constant raids from the barbarians. The Church was a refuge and a place of old-fashioned Latin culture, as the pagans were howling on the northern frontiers. Gregory wanted to give reassurance and comfort. It must have been easy for beleaguered Christians to identify with Job, a holy man who kept his faith and patience even among gentiles and when all fortune seemed to turn against him. So, later, monks in the cloister, aspiring to live as sombre men living in good counsel, took the text to heart. Gregory's *Moralia* is fundamentally a monastic text. Patience was a great virtue in monks. Reading a biblical commentary in a monastery was itself a spiritual exercise, interspersed with prayer and private meditation. The text is in conveniently short paragraphs, and one can pick it up at almost any point in the volume and read as long or as short a passage as one has time for. A monk would read the text to himself, doubtless aloud and probably quite slowly, and would then go over it again and again, more or less in the structure of the *Moralia*, considering each level of meaning. A monk would find spiritual benefit not just in the information he extracted from having read the text, but from the fact of spending time immersed in contemplating aspects of the Word of God.

This brings us back to a fundamental question. In reading a biblical commentary, a monastic reader was making use of the Bible. Conversely, in studying the Bible, a monastic reader would be more likely to have used a commentary, such as Augustine or Gregory, rather than a Bible itself. Any commentary quotes verses of the Bible extensively, and often many times. The question then is whether the reader necessarily always knew which words of the manuscript were taken exactly from the Bible, and which were a commentator's paraphrases or explanations, and indeed (if spiritual virtue is from pious rumination through and around the Scriptures) whether it really mattered to the reader at all. It is this last question which is so fascinating from the modern perspective.

Various techniques were used for distinguishing the actual words of the Holy Scriptures from those of a commentary. One practice was to write quotations from the Bible in coloured ink (Pls. 66, 71). The use of red ink in manuscripts for headings goes back to classical antiquity and continued right through the Middle Ages for directions and headings in liturgical manuscripts ('rubrics', from the red colour). Red ink was such a common feature of ancient and medieval book production that it cannot have been either expensive or difficult to write. Some

70

Gregory's Moralia *was the great monastic text. Here Gregory presents his book to a group of Benedictine monks and to a bishop. The manuscript dates from c.1140* (TOURS, BIBLIOTHÈQUE MUNICIPALE, MS. 321)

71

*As late as c.1200, the scribe of
this commentary on the Psalms
distinguished his biblical text
from its commentary by the use
of red ink*
(OSLO AND LONDON, THE
SCHØYEN COLLECTION, MS.
258)

72 opposite

*An early thirteenth-century
table of contents explains that
this book comprises two parts.
It opens with the Minor
Prophets, written in black,
without commentary. Then (it
says) the text begins again, and
in this second part the Bible
text is underlined in red to
distinguish it from Stephen
Langton's commentary, written
in black*
(CAMBRIDGE, CORPUS
CHRISTI COLLEGE, MS. 31)

early Greek theological manuscripts cite the words of the Scriptures in red. A sixth-century Greek manuscript of Saint Paul's Epistles uses red ink for those passages which Saint Paul himself quotes from the Old Testament (Paris, BNF, ms. Coislin 202). This must be partly because of a kind of typology, which we encountered above, relating Old Testament prophecies to New Testament texts. Probably from Greek practice, the use of red ink moved across into Latin manuscripts in the West. It was used especially (although not exclusively) for distinguishing the words of the Psalms in Psalter commentaries. One of the earliest surviving manuscripts of Saint Hilary's Latin commentary on the Psalms was written in northern Italy in the fifth century (Verona, Biblioteca Capitolare, cod.

XIII). It is a tall narrow book in two columns of uncial script, with the Psalm quotations written in pale red. The scribe signs the manuscript with his name as *antiquarius Eutalius*. His description of himself hints at a man who looked back to even earlier models. Manuscripts of Cassiodorus on the Psalms sometimes also have the words of the Psalms in red ink: a handsome early example is Durham Cathedral MS. B.II.30, of the mid-eighth century, where the first few words or even several lines of each extract from the Psalter are written in red.

Similarly, the commentaries of Saint Augustine on the Psalms sometimes also cite the Psalter in red ink, or at least they begin each quotation in red. The earliest example seems to be Autun, Bibliothèque Municipale, ms. 107, probably written in the Pyrenees in the sixth to seventh century. This manuscript indents all quotations from the Bible and opens every quotation from the Psalter in bright red. The practice of using red for the Psalms in manuscripts of Saint Augustine's commentaries was still relatively common in England around 1100. In some copies the practice of distinguishing the biblical text from its commentary begins with good intentions and trails away after a few pages. An agreeably engaging example is Würzburg Universitätsbibliothek, Cod. M.p.th.f.17, written in an Anglo-Saxon centre in Germany around 800. Its scribe started off with a passage from the Psalms in red, reverted to black for Augustine's commentary, then began again in red at the wrong point while still in Augustine's text, evidently realized he was muddled, and returned to black ink for the rest of the book regardless of whether the sentences were biblical or not. He, at least, realized he did not precisely know the words of the Bible from the commentary.

Another important way of indicating in manuscripts which passages were from the Bible was the litle device called the *diplē* (Pl. 73). This is a Greek word, meaning 'twice', and the term was used for the doubled-back V-shaped mark in Greek papyri for the opening of paragraphs. In his *Etymologies*, Isidore explains that by his time – the early seventh century – the *diplē* was employed by scribes of religious books to separate and to distinguish the words of Scripture from those of other texts. The *diplē* was in use in Latin manuscripts by the sixth century when it occurs in a copy of Jerome's commentary on the Psalms (Paris, BNF, ms. lat. 2235). The mark is found in various forms, like a sideways or upsidedown 'V' (resembling a number '7'), or an upright 'V' or 'Y' with a dot between its arms (this variant is probably only French), or a wedge-shaped mark, or a zig-zag shape rather like an 's' or a pair of 's's. The *diplē* was written in the margin of a manuscript immediately adjacent to the opening of any biblical quotation, and it was repeated in a vertical column down the margin beside each line as long as the quotation continued. The *diplē* has an unexpected survival into modern usage, for it forms the prototype of the modern inverted commas, or quotation marks.

It is easy to miss the use of the *diplē* in looking at manuscripts of biblical commentaries. It may resemble some fairy footprints down the margin, and one might not even realize that it was part of the text. Scribes evidently easily missed the *diplē* too in copying from an exemplar, and many manuscripts insert the marks extremely haphazardly. We can make a random comparison of two manuscripts of Jerome on Daniel, both in the British Library in London, Add. MS. 36668, written in the Rhineland in the first half of the ninth century, and Royal MS. 4.C.XI, written in southern England around 1100. Both ignored the *diplē* completely for the opening pages of commentary and then suddenly apply it for the first time from exactly the same point, Daniel 2:2 onwards, and then trail off again (Pl. 73). It would be intriguing to make a systematic record of scribes' application of the *diplē* in the margins of any patristic commentary on part of the Bible. Probably quite interesting textual families would emerge (and it could incidentally allow someone without too much Latin to make a useful contribution to the history of patristics). Of the twenty earliest recorded manuscripts of Augustine on the Psalms, all earlier than about the year 800, five of them use some kind of *diplē*, three use red ink for biblical quotations, two use larger script for biblical quotations, and ten employ no distinction whatsoever between Saint Augustine's prose and direct quotations from the Bible.

The conclusion, judging from manuscripts from (say) the seventh to the eleventh century, is that those who studied the Scriptures cared relatively little about which were actual words from the Bible and which were the interpretations of the commentators. The possible exception may be in the Psalms, which were sometimes distinguished by script or colour and sometimes in the ninth century were copied as full Psalters with glosses in the margins. In the early Middle Ages, God himself was generally approached through the mediation of saints. Similarly, the sacred Bible was mostly accessed through the reading of Jerome, Hilary, Ambrose, Augustine, Cassiodorus and Gregory, and through a whole series of other later compilers (including Bede) whose works are constructed mostly from citations of these half-dozen Church Fathers.

We must not simply dismiss this as negative. Firstly, by about the ninth century the Bible was already in an archaic language (Latin) and it concerned a civilization by then far away in place and time; some interpretation was needed (as it is today) to bridge the ages in order to understand even the literal meaning of the text. Secondly, the literal sense was regarded as less important than the deeper and necessarily concealed symbolic and mystical meaning, and even if one seeks no more than the moral sense, one needs a sympathetic guide to discover this interpretation beneath the words of the Bible. Thirdly, the Church Fathers themselves were holy men who had walked with God, and to join Saint Augustine, for example, on his journeys through the Pentateuch or the Psalms was a sure-footed way of stepping across sacred land. Fourthly, remember that the readers were mostly monks (or occasionally nuns). We have mentioned this before. We return to it now, for it is important. For almost five hundred years through the Dark Ages and the Carolingian empire, written learning was almost exclusively restricted to cloistered monks and nuns. A monk attempted to lead an entirely religious life. He heard the Scriptures in the liturgy, and he immersed himself in the Bible in the form of texts written about the Bible and nothing else. He had his whole life to soak himself in the Bible and every aspect of it. Reading, praying, meditating and ruminating on the infinite meanings of the Bible was almost the entire focus of a monk's intellectual activity throughout his whole life. In the end, according to Cassian (d.435), a monk can hope that even when he sleeps he will still be dreaming of hidden meanings in the Bible.

The monopoly of the monks began to be broken around 1100. We have crossed into the age of the twelfth-century renaissance, described in the previous chapter. Learning and literacy began to move from the cloister out into the city churches and into the spheres of courtly chivalry, commerce, law, and civil administration. Religion did not decline. On the contrary, this was a period of extremely active Christian renewal and recommitment, but it went in two directions. Religious life was no longer exclusively available within the walls of monasteries. The urban cathedrals, staffed by priests and canons, became increasingly important as centres of religious teaching and study. They looked out onto the secular world outside. Schools began to be founded, and centres of academic study grew up and evolved eventually into the first universities. Monasticism flourished at

the same time, and many new abbeys and priories were founded. The old Benedictine Order still drew many recruits and new religious orders were founded, including the Cistercians, Carthusians, Augustinians and others. More monasteries were built in Europe in the twelfth century than during any other comparable period of history. The difference, however, is that during the Dark Ages novice monks must often have joined monasteries to find rare islands of culture and civilization in an age and landscape of great bleakness, whereas from the twelfth century onwards they would more likely have joined in order to withdraw from increasingly prevalent sophistication and urban worldliness. Both are worthy motives but they make for a very different kind of monk.

It is this religious world independent of the monasteries which is of interest now. It brings us back to the use and interpretation of the Bible. Outside the cloister there evolved a new technique for studying the Scriptures. The Bible was still central to all scholarship but it started to be used rather differently. In the late eleventh century, primitive schools for theological training began to be set up in the precincts of the cathedrals of northern France, probably at Chartres and soon certainly at Laon, Auxerre and (by the second quarter of the twelfth century) in Paris. The Bible was their principal subject of study. They called it the Sacred Page, *sacra pagina* in Latin, and the teachers who lectured on it were known as Masters of the Sacred Page. Their classes were attended by those who planned to join the priesthood and also by clerks and others who sought careers in the increasingly bureaucratic royal and civil administration. A clerk was a kind of half-priest, in that he was committed to celibacy and religion but was not irrevocably ordained as a priest or professed as a monk. While a conventional monk read books about the Bible mainly in order to saturate himself totally in aspects of God, a scholar making a living in the secular world generally had less time and needed more information faster. Students used the Bible as their fundamental textbook, but they probably did not know every verse of the text as intimately as a monk who heard multiple readings from the Bible in the chapel and refectory of his monastery every single day of his life.

During the first half of the twelfth century, a convenient and innovative kind of Bible commentary came rapidly into fashion. It was disseminated into all parts of Europe from the French cathedral schools, especially from Laon and Paris. This was the biblical *Gloss*, sometimes called the *Glossa Ordinaria*. The principal compiler of the *Gloss* was probably Anselm of Laon (d.1117), with help from his younger brother Ralph (d.1133) and a collaborator from the schools in Auxerre, Gilbert the Universal (d.1134), who was famous for his universal learning and eventually retired as bishop of London. These three compilers did not pretend to write commentaries as such but merely to select quotations from wide reading among the traditional and recognized authorities, Jerome, Augustine, Gregory, and the others. Gilbert stated simply in his Gloss on the book of Lamentations that he had 'drunk from the fountains of the Fathers'. The earliest glossed books of the Bible were the Psalms and the letters of Saint Paul. These were in circulation by 1100. They were followed soon afterwards by the books of

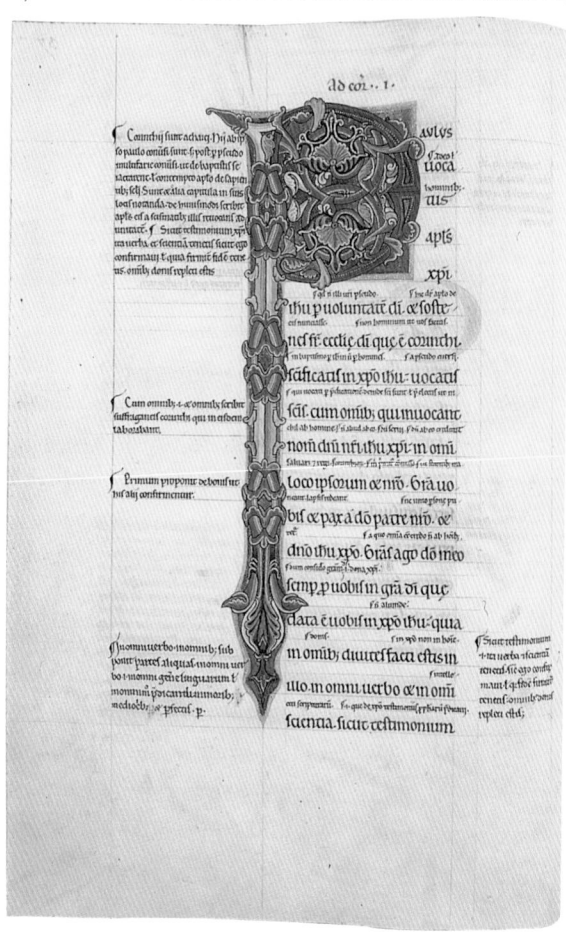

This is from one of the set of glossed books of the Bible brought to Clairvaux Abbey by Prince Henri, son of Louis VI, probably in 1146. The Bible text (this is the opening of I Corinthians) is in larger script in the centre; the Gloss is in smaller script on either side and between the lines (TROYES, BIBLIOTHÈQUE MUNICIPALE, MS. 512)

Job, the Song of Songs, the Gospels of Saints Matthew and John, and so on, book by book, until by about 1135 the entire Bible was available with a standard set of explanatory quotations (Pl. 75).

Glossed books of the Bible originally comprised slim volumes with a narrow central column containing the whole and unabridged text of one or more books of the Latin Bible. It is visually separate and distinctive and could not be confused with the commentary. In smaller script on either side of the central column and between the lines of the biblical text were arranged the short quotations from the recognized commentaries of the past. These were the glosses which gave their name to the compilation itself, the *Gloss* (usually spelled now with a capital 'G'). A reader could follow the central text and glance to the left or right to read briefly what this or that major commentator had said about each particular verse or passage of the Bible. Early manuscripts of the *Gloss* sometimes cite the original authorities by name, often abbreviated (such as *AU* for Augustine, *Cass* for Cassiodorus, *GR* for Gregory, and so on) and occasionally the level of interpretation, *AL* for 'allegorice' (the allegorical or typological meaning) or *MOR* for 'moraliter', the moral or tropological sense. Within a few years, scribes seldom bothered to include these symbols of authorship or level of meaning, for evidently the original sources of the glosses were no longer regarded as important. The new text, with its fixed selection of quotations on either side of the biblical narrative, was already accepted as an acknowledged Bible commentary in its own right, and it remained so for the rest of the Middle Ages.

By about 1170, the format of glossed books had grown larger and the arrangement of the pages had become much more elaborate. The blocks of Bible text and Gloss were integrated together on the page to form a single unit, like an elegant pattern of bricks, in which the Bible and its commentary were interlocked together. Sometimes the effect resembled a waterfall, in which the clearly recognizable column of Bible text flowed and tumbled down the page, running and jumping through the blocks of the Gloss. Nonetheless, the layout was designed so that there was never any possible ambiguity between the Bible text, written in large script, and the commentary in much smaller rounder writing. The books could be used two ways. One could pick up a glossed book and simply read the Bible narrative without the interpretation. Alternatively one could follow the commentary and, from time to time, check back across the page to the Bible text. The two texts were visually distinct but written in parallel.

The layout was so successful that it was adopted in the 1160s for the commentaries on the Psalms and the letters of Saint Paul which had been assembled by Peter Lombard (d.1160), religious encyclopedist and (briefly) bishop of Paris. These two books became known as the *Great Gloss*, or *Magna Glossatura* (Pl. 76). From about 1170 onwards we start to find evidence of wealthy patrons attempting to collect up complete sets of the Gloss on the whole Bible, inserting Peter Lombard's commentaries at the appropriate points in the sequence. A complete

76

In the Great Gloss of Peter Lombard, the commentary forms a clearly distinct block of script interlocked with the biblical text in large writing beside it. This manuscript of the Great Gloss on the Psalms was made in Paris not later than 1193
(PARIS, BNF, MS. LAT. 11565)

77 opposite

The Historia Scholastica *of Peter Comestor is an abridgement of the Bible, concentrating on the historical narratives of the Old and New Testaments. This manuscript dates from the late twelfth century*
(CAMBRIDGE, CORPUS CHRISTI COLLEGE, MS. 29)

set would run to something over twenty volumes. These are among the first books that seem to have been produced in any quantity by professional scribes, working on commission from private customers. One substantial run of matching books was evidently made in France, perhaps in Paris, for archbishop Thomas Becket before his return from exile to Canterbury, where he was martyred in 1170 (Pl.63). The contemporary chronicle refers to it as a *bibliotheca*, the word which means both library and Bible. Another set belonged to Master

Alexander (d. 1213), who already owned it by 1171 when he presented the volumes to Jumièges Abbey in Normandy. Ralph of Sarre, dean of Rheims (d. 1194), owned a set probably by 1176 when he seems to have presented them in twenty-four volumes to Christ Church Cathedral Priory in Canterbury. The benefaction was recorded at Canterbury, describing the books once again as a *bibliotheca* of the Old and New Testament. The books all included the unabridged text of the Bible as well as the Gloss, and so their owners regarded them primarily as Bibles. Many other wealthy scholars and prelates built up sets of glossed books of the Bible in the final quarter of the twelfth century, and the text was eventually used all across Europe. Manuscripts of the Bible *Gloss* became part of the fashionable furnishings in the households of successful clerics and churchmen in the early thirteenth century.

The fact that the text of the Bible became so graphically distinct in these books is a reflection of the new contemporary interest in the Bible as an unadulterated text. Readers considered the Bible without the accumulated clutter of centuries. The selected glosses are often quite literal in their interpretation, without excessive layers of allegory. Scholars in the city and cathedral schools began to reassess the Bible as a credible historical record, set in an authentic place and comprehensible chronology. Western Europeans had visited the Holy Land. The First Crusade was launched in 1095 and the second in 1147. The geographical setting of the Bible was brought almost within tangible reach for the first time since Jerome had lived there. The Parisian teacher, Hugh of St-Victor (d. 1142), emphasized the need to understand clearly the literal and historical sense of the Bible before attempting to proceed to the hidden allegory. We find twelfth-century readers returning to actual story recounted in the Bible. Still in Paris, Peter Comestor (d. *c.* 1179) compiled the *Historia Scholastica*, a reduction of the narratives of the

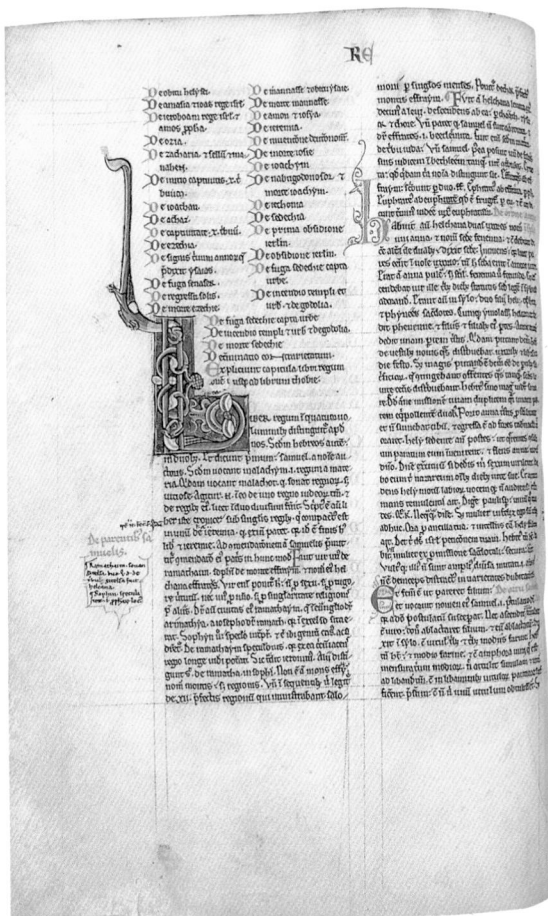

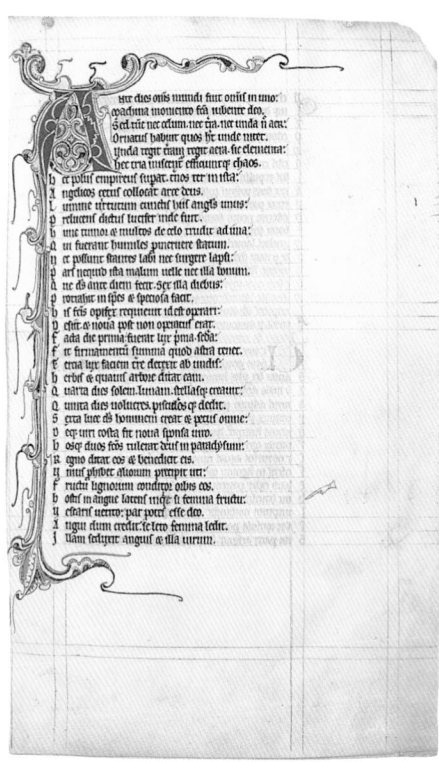

whole Bible into a condensed consecutive history (Pl. 77). He explains in the preface that he has traced the little stream of history (*rivulum hystoricum*, a charming phrase) which trickles from the cosmography of Moses to the Resurrection of Christ. The text incorporates allegorical explanations but it always begins from events rather than from symbols and words without context. Peter of Poitiers (d.1205) wrote a discursive chronicle, the *Genealogia Vitae Christi*, setting the Old Testament ancestry of Christ back to Adam and Eve within a framework which included datable events in authentic ancient history. Peter Riga (d.1209) rendered the historical narratives of the Bible into the *Aurora*, a kind of rolling doggerel poem, easy to memorize (Pl.78). The prologue to the *Aurora* praises at length the infinite depths of the Holy Bible and the value of scholarly study, but concludes 'if you seek to proceed more quickly in this discipline, you must begin with history. Although all theology is made up of four senses – historical, allegorical, tropological and anagogical – the first is the most worth knowing', Riga ends, 'for history is the foundation'. The guides to Bible history by Peter Comestor, Peter of Poitiers and Peter Riga all enjoyed enormous popularity and they survive in huge numbers of early manuscripts.

A major compilation of this period is the *Interpretation of Hebrew Names* (Pl.79). This began its life as a separate text but for almost 300 years it became attached to the end of Latin Bibles. It is a fascinating alphabetical list of just over 5,500 proper names which occur in the Latin Bible, some of great obscurity, with translations of what those names originally meant as words in Hebrew. This was useful both for a literal understanding of the text and also for application of allegory. For example, we referred above to the opening of Saint Gregory's *Moralia* on Job, in which Gregory explained that the name 'Job' meant 'a man in sorrow' in Hebrew and that 'Hus', where he lived, meant 'counsellor'. These names recur in the alphabetical *Interpretation*, explained as 'sorrow' and 'counsellor' respectively. Knowing those meanings allows the reader to understand the text as literally as a Jewish reader of the Bible could have done in Hebrew. There are several versions of the *Interpretation of Hebrew Names*. The longest and most common opens, '*Aaz*, apprehendens vel apprehensio; *Aad*, testificans vel testimonium …', and so on. This begins by telling that the name of Aaz, who merits only a brief mention in the Bible as the father of one of those who worked on the Temple of Jerusalem (Nehemiah 11:13), means in Hebrew 'taking hold' or 'seizing upon'; and that Aad, whose name is actually explained in Genesis 31:48, means 'bearing witness' or 'evidence'; and so on. Many are personal names, like Judith, for example, which means 'trusting' or 'glorifying'. Others are places. Bethlehem is 'house of bread', whereas Bethany is 'house of obedience'. Jerusalem means 'peace offering' or 'vision of peace', an interpretation which must have given a new level of meaning to many Bible readings and worrying contemporary reflection, for Jerusalem itself fell to Saladin in 1187.

The *Interpretation of Hebrew Names* is approximately alphabetical. It loses sequence on the second or third letters. It was not a new idea to explain biblical names by reference to the Hebrew, for Jerome had done the same. In fact most of the information in the *Interpretation* was derived from Jerome rather than from any actual knowledge of Hebrew. Its compilation dates from around 1180–1200, and it is commonly attributed to Stephen Langton (d.1228), though without any real foundation. It became extremely popular. It was of quick reference tool to simple allegory, and in that sense was a kind of alphabetical gloss. It provides an unexpected link between the Bible commentaries of this chapter and the one-volume Bibles of the thirteenth century, which form the subject of the next chapter. By about 1200, readers of glossed Bibles began to focus more and more on the Bible text itself, rather than the now quite separate marginal commentaries. A full glossed Bible ran to over 20 volumes. Instead of struggling with a vast series of weighty books, the commentary itself was dispensed with. Owners began to supplement their libraries with a new kind of book for easy reference – the Bible text alone. The alphabetical *Interpretation of Hebrew Names* was added to the end, as a separate text, and thus salvaged verbal allegory but relegated it to the back of the book. Thus the Bible without *Gloss* evolved from commentaries. The thirteenth-century catalogue of the library of Notre-Dame in Paris includes what was described as 'a complete Bible, without Gloss', doubtless what we would simply call a Bible.

ııııc õıu ıııĭıı ꞊ Aıııqııḭð ḟı ðeuḭ ı
ıꞇaıııꞇ ııoꞇ꞊ Auaꞇe eıɡo ðeȿpıeꞇ uııꞇ
ıı ııꞇıı. ꞇꞮoıı ȿuũ ııoꞮaıꞇꞮ ıꞇꞇꞇııı ıꞇꞇ
oıı. ꞇoıııɡȿꞮȿꞇꞇꞮ ꞻ ꞇuðaꞇ ꞻꞌĂbꞌoıııꞮꞮaıo
ꞌꞮıııꞇſ ꞻ ıꞮȿꞮıı Ꞷ꞊ oṭııııaꞮaııꞇ ıııðaꞇ ſð
Ɪoıı꞉ ðũ Ꞷuaṭu ðıſeꞇıꞇ ꞌꞬꞮſꞮeııⱥꞇ ꞱꞮ
ꞮꞮaꞮꞮeıı.ðꞮꞇꞮꞮðaꞇ ꞌ ꞇꞮuꞮꞮıı Ꞷuı ꞯeꞇꞮꞮꞇ
ııaɡıñı Ꞝ ðꞮ ꞇaṭꞮꞮıı ðꞇ ꞇaꞌbıꞮaeꞌſo ꞮaꞮꞾ
ıſꞇeꞮeııꞇꞇ ıııꞮꞮʃ ðꞮꞮo eꞇꞯꞇꞮꞮꞮ.fꞇ ꞮꞶꞇ ıı
ꞮꞮıı ꞯeaꞮꞮꞮ꞉ oꞬꞮeꞮaꞮꞮꞇ ꞮaꞇꞮꞮꞮꞮꞮꞇꞮaꞮꞇ
Ɪeꞇıı ꞻ ꞯꞇꞮꞮꞮꞮꞮꞮ ꞇeꞮ ꞮꞮꞇ ſı ꞇeʃpꞮꞇꞮaꞮꞮꞮ ıꞌ

5 Portable Bibles of the Thirteenth Century

MORE BIBLES SURVIVE from the thirteenth century than any other artefact, except perhaps coins and buildings. The coins are evidence of increasing prosperity and of urban commerce, and of efficient royal administration. The most famous buildings of thirteenth-century Europe are the great city churches and cathedrals. Very many hundreds of such buildings still stand, with their soaring pillars, pointed arches and vaulted ceilings, all made magical by dappled light from stained-glass windows in deep blue and red. This is the period of the earliest surviving secular music and vernacular literature in languages we can still recognize. The century saw the foundation of universities, and the bringing of scientific learning from the Near East. The term 'Gothic' was once applied critically to the thirteenth century, as if all this art and culture was brought by the barbaric Goths set upon destroying the civilization of Rome. We now use word 'Gothic' to represent an age of new beauty, innovation and light.

The difference between Latin Bibles of the twelfth and thirteenth centuries is considerable. If we laid on a table a Romanesque Bible of about 1170 and a Gothic Bible of 1270, they would hardly be recogizable as the same book. The Romanesque Bible is enormous, usually divided into several volumes. The early Gothic Bible is extremely small, smaller than many modern printed Bibles, sometimes no bigger than the palm of one's hand. Open the books up. The giant Bible is written in noble spacious script, proclaiming the majesty of its text displayed in a suitable size for reading from a lectern. Its letter forms are still rounded, like Romanesque arches. The thirteenth-century Bible is written in a minute script, as angular as gothic windows. The writing is densely blocked on the page and is so compact that it can encompass all parts of the Scriptures into a single unit, an entire Bible as one consecutive book in a single binding. The Romanesque Bible

dz magr. Dic ei ixc. noli me tangere. Nondum
eni ascendi ad prem meu. vade aut ad fres meos z
dic eis. Ascendo ad prem meu z prem urm. dm
meu z dm urm. Uenit maria magd. annucians
discipulis qa uidi dnm z hec dixit mi. Cu seo eet
esset uespa die illa una sabbatoz z fores eet clause ubi erant
discipli cogegati ppter metu iudeoz. uenit ihc z stetit in medio disciploz z dixit eis. pax uobis. Et cum
hoc dixisset ostendit eis manus z latus. Gauisi se-
zgo discipli uiso dno. Dixit ergo eis iterum. pax uobis. sicut misit me pater z ego mitto uos. hec cu dixisset
insufflauit z dixit eis. accipite spm scm quoz re-
miseritis peccata remittuntur eis z quoz retinueri-
tis retenta sunt. Thomas aut unus ex xii. qui dr didimus
non erat cu eis cu uenit ihc. Dixerunt g ei alii discipli. uidimus dnm. Ille aut dixit eis. nisi uidero in manibus
eius fixuram clauoz z mittam digitu meu in locum clauoz z mittam manu mea in latus eius non cre-
dam. Et post dies viii. iterum erant discipli eius intus z thomas cu eis. Uenit ihc ianuis clausis z stetit in medi-
o z dixit. pax uobis. Deinde dicit thome. Infer digitu
tuum huc z uide manus meas z affer manu tuam
z mitte in latus meu. z noli ee incredulus sed fide-
lis. Respondit thomas z dixit ei. dns meus z dns meus. Dicit
ei ihc. Quia uidisti me thoma credidisti. beati
qui non uiderunt z crediderunt. Multa quide z a-
lia signa fecit ihc in conspectu discipuloz suoz que
non sunt scripta in libro hoc. Hec aut scripta sunt ut credatis
qz ihc est xpc filius dei z ut credentes uitam ha-
beatis in nomine eius.

XXI.

Postea manifestauit se iterum ihc ad mare
tyberiadis. Manifestauit aut se sic. Erant simul
symon petrus z thomas qui dr didimus z na-
thanael qui erat a chana galilee z filii ze-
bedei z alii ex discipulis eius duo. Dicit eis symon
petrus. uado piscari. Dicunt ei. uenimus z nos tecum.
Exierunt z ascenderunt in nauim z illa nocte nichil
prendiderunt. Mane aut iam facto stetit ihc in litto-
re. Non tamen discipli cognouerunt qz ihc est. Dicit
ergo eis ihc. pueri nunquid pulmentarium habe-
tis. Responderunt ei. non. Dicit eis. mittite in dexteram nauigii
rete z inuenietis. Miserunt ergo z iam non
ualebant illud trahere a multitudine
piscium. Dicit ergo discipulus ille que diligebat ihc
petro. dns est. Symon ergo petrus cum audisset qa dns est tu-
nica succinxit se. erat enim nudus z misit se in
mare. Alii aut discipli nauigio uenerunt. non enim
longe erant a terra. sed quasi cubitis ducentis. trahentes
rete piscium. Ut ergo descenderunt in terram uiderunt
prunas positas z piscem superpositum z panem. Dicit
eis ihc. afferte de piscibus quos prendidistis nunc.
Ascendit symon petrus z traxit rete in terram plenum
magnis piscibus. cxliii. z cum tanti essent
non est scissum rete. Dicit eis ihc. uenite prandete.
Et nemo audebat discumbentium interrogare eu. tu
quis es. scientes qa dns est. Et uenit ihc
z accepit panem z dabat eis z piscem similiter.
Hoc iam tertio manifestatus est ihc discipulis
suis cum resurrexisset a mortuis. Cum ergo prandi-
ssent dicit symoni petro ihc. symon iohannis

diligis me plus his. Dicit ei. etiam dne tu scis
qa amo te. Dicit ei. pasce agnos meos. Dicit ei iterum.
symon iohannis diligis me. Ait illi. etiam dne tu
scis qa amo te. Dicit ei. pasce agnos meos. Dicit ei
tercio. symon iohannis amas me. Contristatus est petrus
qz dixit ei tercio. amas me. z dixit ei. dne tu omnia scis tu scis qa amo te. Dicit ei. pasce oues meas. Amen
amen dico tibi. cum esses iunior cingebas te z ambulabas
ubi uolebas. cum aut senueris extendes manus tuas z a-
lius te cinget z ducet te quo tu non uis. hoc aut dixit sig-
nificans qua morte esset clarificaturus dnm. z hec cum dixisset dicit ei. sequere me. Conuersus petrus uidit illum
discipulum quem diligebat ihc sequentem. qui z
recubuit in cena super pectus eius z dixit. dne quis est
qui tradet te. hunc ergo cum uidisset petrus dixit
ihc. dne hic aut quid. Dicit ei ihc. Sic eum
uolo manere donec ueniam quid ad te. tu me
sequere. Exiuit ergo sermo iste inter fres qd discipulus
ille non moritur. z non dixit ei ihc qz non moritur
sed sic eum uolo manere donec ueniam. quid ad
te. Hic est discipulus ille qui testimonium perhibet de
hiis z scripsit hec. z scimus qa uerum est testimonium eius.
Sunt aut z alia multa que fecit ihc. que si scribantur per
singula. nec ipsum arbitror mundum capere eos
qui scribendi sunt libros. — incipit prologus ad romanos se in
Romani sunt in
partibus ytalie. hii preuenti sunt
falsis apostolis z sub nomine dni nri iesu xpi in legem z prophetas erant
inducti. hos reuocat apostolus ad ue-
ram z ad euangelicam fidem scribens eis a co-
rintho. — incipit epistola ad romanos.

Paulus seruus ihu xpi uocatus
apostolus segregatus in euangelium
dei. quod ante promiserat per
prophetas suos in scripturis sanctis de
filio suo qui factus est ei ex semine
dauid. secundum carnem. qui predestinatus
est filius dei in uirtute secundum spm san-
ctificationis ex resurrectione mortuorum iesu xpi dni nri. per quem accepimus gratiam z apostolatum ad obediendum fidei. in omnibus
gentibus pro nomine eius. in quibus estis z uos uoca-
ti ihu xpi. omnibus qui sunt rome dilectis
dei uocatis sanctis. Gratia uobis z pax a deo pa-
tre nostro z dno ihu xpo. Primum quidem
gratias ago deo meo per ihm xpm pro omnibus uobis. quia fides uestra annunciatur in uni-
uerso mundo. testis enim mihi est deus cui seruio
in spu meo in euangelio filii eius quod si-
ne intermissione memoriam uestri facio
semper. in orationibus meis obsecrans si-
quo modo tandem aliquando prosperum iter ha-
beam in uoluntate dei ueniendi ad
uos. Desidero enim uidere uos ut aliquid
impartiar uobis gratie spiritalis ad confirmandos uos. id
est simul consolari in uobis per eam que inuicem
est fidem uestram atque meam. Nolo aut
uos ignorare fratres quod sepe proposui ue-
nire ad uos. z prohibitus sum usque ad

116

Portable
Bibles
of the
Thirteenth
Century

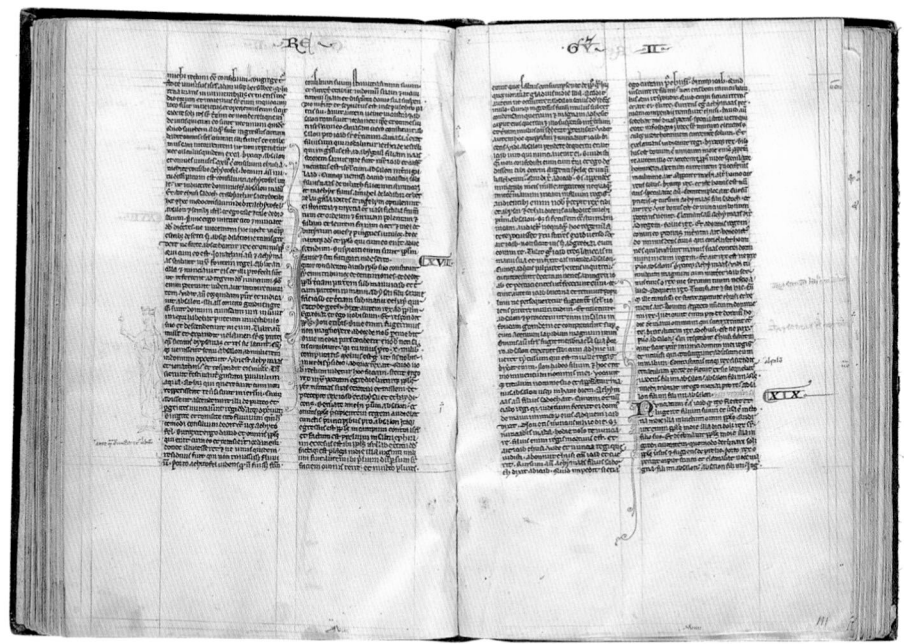

80 previous page

This Paris Bible is dated 1236. It is filled with aids to the reader, to make it usable and searchable. It has running-titles, chapter numbers, leaf numbers (a great rarity at this date), subject headings in the margins and cross-references to other books of the Bible (PARIS, BNF, MS. LAT. 36)

81

Thirteenth-century Latin Bibles were made remarkably small, in two columns of tiny script, with headings and red and blue chapter numbers. This is a characteristic Bible made in France around 1250. Each page is 233 by 156 mm (8¾ by 6 inches) (OSLO AND LONDON, THE SCHØYEN COLLECTION, MS.115)

82 opposite

In the late twelfth century, Bible manuscripts began to diminish in size. This one-volume Bible, probably made not later than 1183, measures 315 by 205 mm (12½ by 8 inches), and is significantly smaller than the giant Bibles discussed in chapter 3 above but still larger than a Bible of the thirteenth century (CAMBRIDGE, CORPUS CHRISTI COLLEGE, MS. 48)

is written on huge sheets of parchment which crackle as you turn the pages. The thirteenth-century Bible is on parchment so white and thin that it looks like tissue paper, almost weightless and so delicate that it is quite easy to turn two pages at once without noticing. Compare the decoration. The twelfth-century Bible may well have several full-page paintings and each of its texts opens with a great illuminated initial letter which extends far across the page, often filled with symbolic pictures which could be up to a quarter of the size of the page or even more. The thirteenth-century Bible has no more than tiny illustrated initials at the start of each text, so small that it may require a magnifying glass to see little biblical dramas unfolding in the space of a fingernail. Look then for further ornament. On the many pages between one spectacular initial and another, the twelfth-century Bible is austere, comprising columns of black or brown, like solid pillars of text. The thirteenth-century book looks festive in comparison, gaily decked out with bright red or blue chapter initials with tall waving banners of penwork in the contrasting colour. There are headings in red and blue running right across the tops of the pages like ropes of flags in alternating colours, and even the text is pebble-dashed in red. Start comparing the text. The words are those of the same Latin Vulgate of Saint Jerome, but the order of the books is quite different. Supplementary texts have been added, and others have disappeared, like the Canon Tables for the Gospels. The prologues have been elevated almost to the status of miniature books of the Bible, each beginning with its own illuminated initial. Added at the end is the new alphabetical *Interpretation of Hebrew Names*, which we encountered at the end of the last chapter. This became such a standard feature of the thirteenth century Bible that one might

117

Portable
Bibles
of the
Thirteenth
Century

easily mistake it for one of the books of Scripture. Finally, close the books up and put them away again. The massive volumes of the Romanesque Bible are heavy and the books are difficult to shelve, except by heaving them in sideways. The thirteenth-century Bible can be lifted with one hand and it sits easily on the shelf like any modern book.

Then compare that thirteenth-century Bible with a modern printed edition of the Bible. In all essentials, they look virtually identical. The weight, size, shape, thin paper, initials (but usually no big pictures), chapter numbers, running-titles, concordances of names, even (often) two columns of text, and especially the order of the books from Genesis to Revelation, one text, are all, even now, virtually unchanged. The hundred years between about 1170 and 1270 produced a form and a format for the Bible which transformed it more dramatically than at any century since the invention of the codex, and the Bible creation of that time is still with us. Most of this development took place in France.

This change is unambiguous and unmistakable. It came about in two principal steps. It began with the gradual physical changes to the Bible format which occurred in northern France between about 1170 and about 1230. In the second stage, from about 1240 onwards, the new Bible exploded in popularity and was disseminated across Europe. We will need to follow each step with great care. To plot the changes and to account for them is fascinating but complicated, for much depends on a mass of small details which evolved in parallel and finally coalesced into the creation of a new form of Bible. We must proceed slowly, for we need to be sure of what actually happened before we can hope to explain it.

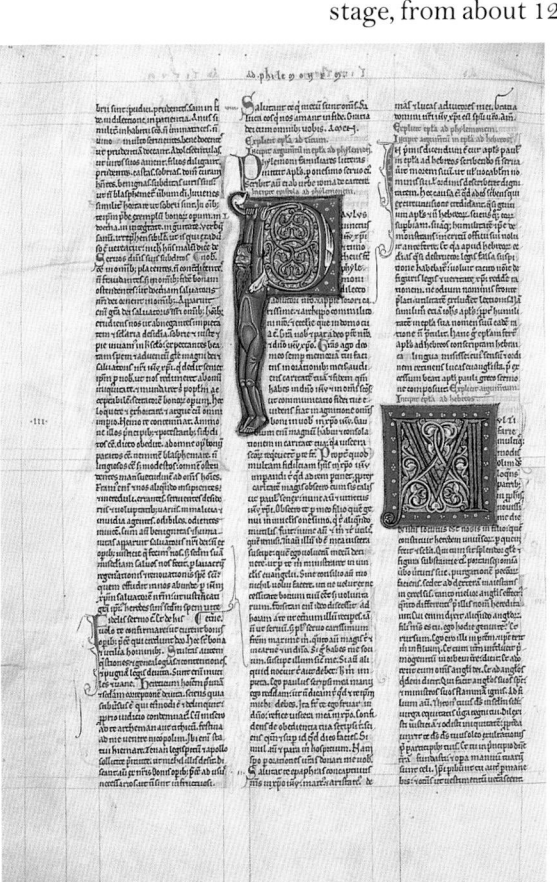

Let us begin with the shape and the structure of the Bible. The developments of the late twelfth and early thirteenth century can be summarized under four headings. These are (1) the size of the pages gets smaller; (2) the Bible goes into a single volume according to a standardized order of books; (3) supplementary texts are added, principally the alphabetical *Interpretation of Hebrew Names* and a fixed set of prologues; and (4) the text is divided and marked up into numbered chapters. Let us consider these one by one.

The gradually diminishing page-size of Bibles began around 1160. It happened very slowly. One Bible of relatively small dimensions from the third quarter of the twelfth century was apparently made for the abbey of La Trinité in Vendôme (Paris, Bibliothèque de la Chambre des Députés, ms. 2). It measures 320 by 220 mm (about 12½ by 8¾ inches). Another, slightly later, made for St Albans Abbey in the time of Simon, abbot there 1167–83, is 315 by 205 mm

118

Portable
Bibles
of the
Thirteenth
Century

(12½ by 8 inches; Cambridge, Corpus Christi College, MS. 48, Pl. 82). These manuscripts were both made as part of groups of the new glossed books and other texts disseminated from the French schools, like the textbooks of Hugh of St-Victor and Peter Lombard. In the last chapter we saw how sets of biblical books with the Gloss began to circulate around 1140. Eventually these sets began to be supplemented by copies of the Bible without Gloss. Thomas Becket (d.1170), for example, owned a separate Bible among his glossed books. It is noticeable that as the glossed biblical books got larger in dimensions in the second half of the century, so the matching Bibles got smaller. The glossed books grew and the Bibles diminished until they matched each other in size, which happened around 1180, and then each kept on growing and diminishing respectively. By about 1200, glossed books were commonly around 300 mm tall (12 inches) and many Bibles were decreasing to perhaps 250 mm tall (10 inches). By 1240, glossed books of the Bible have often grown further to 350 mm (14 inches) while one-volume Bibles have sometimes shrunk to 200 mm (8 inches).

Long lists of statistics are distracting in a narrative account such as this, but let us see a few actual examples of diminishing Bibles, manuscripts of *c.*1200 at 335 by 230 mm (13¼ by 9 inches, Windsor, Eton College MS. 26); *c.*1210 at 217 by 152 mm (8½ by 6 inches, Paris, Bibliothèque de Ste-Geneviève, ms. 1185); *c.*1215 at 210 by 140 mm (8¼ by 5½ inches, London, BL, Add. MS. 15452); and *c.*1225 at 160 by 110mm (6¼ by 4¼ inches, Paris, BNF, ms. lat. 16267, Pl. 83). To judge from their illumination, all these manuscripts were probably made in Paris. The decreasing size of Bibles became one of the features of the books which contemporaries noticed and commented on. One was called 'small and good' when it was given to Newenham

Abbey in Devon in the 1240s. Another was described in a thirteenth-century inscription as 'small and portable' (*parva portatoria*): the book itself, Lille, Biblio- thèque Municipale, ms. 7, is 211 by 152 mm (8¼ by 6 inches), not exactly pocket- sized but certainly portable.

The script too became smaller as the format of the books gradually reduced between the end of the twelfth century and the second quarter of the thirteenth. This too helped to achieve volumes of manageable thickness. In fact, another curious transposition took place with glossed books. Looking backwards for a moment, a typical glossed book of the Bible of around 1180 would have its central Biblical text written in a large, bold, rather old-fashioned hand and its gloss on either side in a new highly abbreviated and small script. This minute glossing script was recognized as ideal for small-format Bibles, and it was taken across from its use as medium for a commentary into that of the new Bibles them- selves. A script which started out as a glossing hand was thus adopted for the Bible. Scribes evidently attempted to write smaller and smaller. Gothic script lends itself to extreme compression, helped by the increasing use of abbreviations. A tiny thirteenth-century Bible in the Free Library of Philadelphia, for example, is copied with 55 lines to the page and no fewer than 20 lines to the inch – hardly more than a millimetre a line (MS. 39). It is difficult to imagine how any script could be executed so small, unless it was done with a magnifying lens. Primitive magnifying glasses were invented in the mid-thirteenth century. The size of the script of Bibles is sometimes mentioned in the second quarter of the thirteenth century, for it was evidently a novelty. When Cardinal Guala Bicchieri returned to Italy from Paris and bequeathed his library to the abbey of San Andrea in Vercelli on his death in 1227, one book was described as 'a very costly small Bible in Parisian letter'. The beneficiaries had noted the size of the book and its script, which they associated with Paris. Four years later, we find monks in Brittany encountering a new Bible and observing the smallness of the writing, for when Master Adam, treasurer of Rheims, gave a Bible to Paimpont Abbey in 1231, the donation contract described it as 'a certain Bible in minute script'. By 1247–8 Glastonbury Abbey already had what the cataloguer there described as seven copies of 'the complete Bible in small script'.

This brings us to the second parallel development. These were all complete Bibles. That is remarkable when we compare most of the biblical manuscripts of the previous 1,200 years of Christianity. In earlier chapters we have encountered the occasional all-encompassing 'pandect', some vast whole copy of the Bible in one gigantic book made for some exceptional and usually symbolic purpose. Examples were cited on pp. 33 and 37–8, but these were rarities. Most biblical manuscripts in general use had until now been separate volumes, or sets of vol- umes, each part comprising a few portions of the whole Bible at most, for example the Pentateuch or the Major Prophets or the New Testament Epistles. Between about 1170 and about 1210, all the various components of the biblical corpus

83 opposite
By about 1225, Bibles had been reduced in size to an easily portable format. The plate here is shown life-size (PARIS, BNF, MS. LAT. 16267)

120

Portable
Bibles
of the
Thirteenth
Century

were brought together between two covers into a single book, and (more importantly) from that moment onwards this became the norm.

Already in the twelfth century, as we saw in the last chapter, scholars were re-
addressing the question of the biblical canon and were attempting to make up sets
of volumes to furnish a complete and definitive Bible. It is quite an interesting
philosophical development to want to set physical perimeters to the extent of the
Word of God, and to seek to separate the ancient Bible itself from its subsequent
commentaries. Multiple volumes, however, could be shelved in any order. Once
the whole Bible was to be copied as one book, then the exact order of its parts
mattered greatly.

The one-volume Paris Bibles of the thirteenth century would generally
comprise:

1   The Octateuch (Genesis, Exodus, Leviticus, Numbers, Deuteronomy,
     Joshua, Judges and Ruth).
2   I–IV Kings (I–II Samuel and I–II Kings in a modern Bible).
3   I–II Chronicles, followed by the short apocryphal Prayer of Manasses.
4   I Ezra; II Ezra (Nehemiah in a modern Bible); III Ezra (II Ezra in a
     modern Bible).
5   Tobit; Judith; Esther; Job.
6   Psalms.
7   The Sapiential Books (or Books of Solomon – Proverbs, Ecclesiastes,
     Song of Songs, Wisdom and Ecclesiasticus).
8   The Major Prophets (Isaiah, Jeremiah [and Lamentations], Baruch
     [and the apocryphal Epistle of Jeremiah as Baruch chapter 6], Ezekiel
     and Daniel).
9   The Minor Prophets (Hosea, Joel, Amos, Obadiah, Jonah, Micah,
     Nahum, Habakkuk, Zephaniah, Haggai, Zechariah and Malachi).
10   I–II Maccabees.
11   The Gospels (Matthew, Mark, Luke and John).
12   The Epistles of Saint Paul (Romans, I–II Corinthians, Galatians,
     Ephesians, Philippians, Colossians, I–II Thessalonians, I–II Timothy,
     Titus, Philemon, and Hebrews).
13   Acts.
14   The Catholic Epistles (or Canonical Epistles – James, I–II Peter,
     I–III John, Jude).
15   The Apocalypse (Revelation in a modern Bible).

As a sequence for the books of the Bible, this may seem to us quite normal.
That is because it is so similar to what we know today. Minor variants from the
modern contents include the insertion of the Prayer of Manasses after II
Chronicles, the inclusion of III Ezra but not IV Ezra, and the positioning of Acts

121

Portable
Bibles
of the
Thirteenth
Century

between the two sets of Epistles. In fact, much of this order was actually quite new in the early thirteenth century. The placing of the books of Chronicles after Kings looks familiar and logical, for these are almost consecutive narratives of the rulers and wars of ancient Israel, but this is not the order of the Hebrew Bible (even now) and we would not expect to encounter Kings and Chronicles together in the twelfth century. In the Winchester Bible of about 1160, for example, I–II Chronicles, Job, Tobit, Esther and I–II Ezra are placed together between the Sapiential Books and Maccabees, and instead the Major and Minor Prophets are between Kings and Psalms (Winchester Cathedral, MS. 17). In the late twelfth-century Capucins' Bible, I–II Chronicles follow Ruth, but Ezra and Kings are between the Psalms and the Sapiential Books (Paris, BNF, mss. lat. 16743–6).

The expression 'Paris Bible' is often used to refer to the revised order of texts of the early thirteenth century. The term was used in the Middle Ages. Let us adopt it here, but cautiously, for it implies rather more of an authorized promulgation by the university of Paris than was actually the case. The thirteenth-century Paris order apparently first evolved as a matter of convenience rather than of any deliberate publication. Very briefly, it follows the Greek tradition rather than the Hebrew. Many earlier attempts to revise the sequence of books, like that undertaken by Stephen Harding for Cîteaux Abbey, had opted for the Hebrew order which divides the text into Prophets and Hagiographa, and thus widely separates Kings and Chronicles, for example (above pp. 76–7). The Paris text can be explained in the context of the new biblical commentaries, discussed in the previous chapter, which emphasized the need to separate history from prophecy, and to understand first of all the historical events of the Old Testament before proceeding to allegory (pp. 111–12). Classes taught in the schools of Paris doubtless followed this order in their study of the books of the Bible. Therefore, the narratives of ancient history – Genesis, Exodus, Kings, Chronicles, etc.– are placed into a chronological sequence before turning to the more timeless books of praise and prophecy.

The common sense of this sequence baffled many scribes and owners of Bibles in the thirteenth century. They evidently struggled to comprehend the logic of the order and to bring their manuscripts into line. Many Bibles of the first half of the thirteenth century show at least some evidence of uncertainty, especially if they were copied outside Paris. The books of Ezra and parts of Esther and Daniel caused terrible worry for scribes, and these sections of these books frequently occur crammed onto pages at the end of the Old or New Testaments with despairing notes as to where they should have been put. Lists of the order of the books of the Bible were very often added in thirteenth-century Bibles. They become a very common feature of the flyleaves at either end of Bibles. Readers did not understand the new order by intuition and went to great effort to try to comprehend and use it. London, BL, Harley MS. 1748 is a good

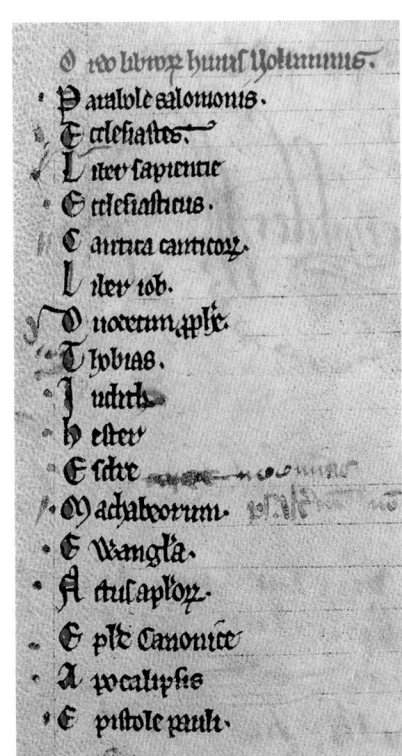

84
Scribes of Bibles in the early thirteenth century struggled despairingly with the order of biblical books. This list from the second volume of a two-volume Bible of c.1220 shows only a partial revision of the order
(PRIVATE COLLECTION)

122

Portable
Bibles
of the
Thirteenth
Century

85

A note is inserted into this Bible of about 1230 between the end of Malachi and the opening of the Psalms. It says that, according to the new arrangement of the books of the Bible, the books of Maccabees should be at the end of the Old Testament and that the Psalter should now precede the books of Solomon (LONDON, BL, HARLEY MS. 1748)

86 opposite

Prologues were systematically inserted at the beginning of each book of the Bible, supplementing the old prologues of Saint Jerome. The prologue to the Apocalypse was taken from the work of the French theologian Gilbert de la Porrée (d.1154), French theologian (PRIVATE COLLECTION)

example of an English Bible of about 1230. It was originally written according to what its contemporary annotator calls the 'old Paris order'. It has long notes to bring it in conformity with the new order (Pl. 85). These include annotations such as that Maccabees should have been the last book of the Old Testament, following Malachi, and that the Psalms should precede the Books of Solomon, 'according to the new order of the books of the Bible' (fol. 260v) or that the Epistles of Paul should follow the Gospels and that Acts should come between the Catholic Epistles and the Apocalypse, again – not quite rightly this time – 'according to the new order' (fol. 305r). Readers understood that the order was new and they wanted to adopt the new system. This is almost the only moment in the history of the Bible when textual novelty appeared to be a virtue rather than a hindrance.

The Parisian sequence of the books is a very visible development. It is much more difficult to document textual corrections associated with these new Bibles. Historians sometimes refer to the Paris Bible as an 'edition', as if the Latin text itself was actually collated and republished in a revised version. There seems to be no obvious evidence for this in the manuscripts. In 1236, the Dominican General Chapter promulgated the use of a *Correctorium* or *Correctiones Bibliae* in Paris for use in emending Bibles, which sounds like a list of textual improvements. The title is misleading. The *Correctiones* are, in fact, little more than a list of relatively minor variants of specific words, as they occur in different manuscripts of the Bible. It offers no advice as to which is a superior reading. This is very typical of thirteenth-century scholarship. Like many petty bureaucrats today, biblical scholars felt inhibited from making decisions on their own authority. Even the great commentator, Stephen Langton (d.1228), revelled in suggesting possible alternative readings for words in the Bible, either by comparing manuscripts or by logical deduction, but he refused to decide in favour of one or the other. Leaving one's options open is fundamental to medieval scholastic methodology. We often see this reflected in manuscript Bibles of the period. MS. 25 at Eton College, for

123

Portable
Bibles
of the
Thirteenth
Century

example, has some alternative words marked in red with the letters 'h', 'g' or 'a'. A note explains that these letters indicate readings found in the Hebrew, the Greek, or in unspecified ancient sources (*antiqui*). The writer of the note presumably did not himself know any ancient language beyond Latin, and had probably taken his variant readings from Jerome or some other biblical commentator. In many manuscripts, a choice of readings is added in the margin, each introduced by the word *vel* – *either* this *or* that. Thus, for instance, emendations have been carefully added to London, BL, Add. MS. 40006, at least as far as fol. 108r, where the annotator made a note to himself that his corrections have reached Judges 9:8. To take an example, he suggests two possible readings for Genesis 3:23, 'And the Lord God sent him from paradise …' (this is Adam being banished from the Garden of Eden). The manuscript reads *Emisit eum*. Jerome, according to our annotator, writes *Emisitque* and the Septuagint, he notes, reads *Et emisit*. He may have known the Septuagint from the Latin translation of Origen's commentary on Genesis. The difference is negligible and the meaning is identical; the corrector, however, prefers not to opt for one alternative or the other.

In the last chapter, we looked at the origin of the alphabetical list of proper nouns in the Bible, known as the *Interpretation of Hebrew Names*. This is grafted on to the end of the Bible text, after the Apocalypse, and it becomes a standard feature of Bibles from about 1230 onwards. In Paris, BNF, ms. lat. 36, this text is accompanied by a preface explaining the semantic difficulties in transliterating Hebrew script, and hoping that this effort may contribute to the conversion of the Jews to Christianity. The preface is dated 1234 (fol. 355v). The usual version of the *Interpretation of Hebrew Names* opens, '*Aaz apprehendens …*'; a shorter version sometimes found in England begins, '*Aaron mons fortis …*' In a sense, the *Interpretation* too offers alternative readings, for it introduces two choices for understanding a single word. One can read a Hebrew name literally, as a proper noun for person or place, or as a translated word or phrase.

At about this time, the prologues were standardized. Many books of the Latin Bible traditionally opened with short prefaces about the text or its author, often extracted from the writings of Saint Jerome. In the first third of the thirteenth century these were made consistent throughout the new one-volume Bibles. Some were eliminated, and others were added, including (for example) a new prologue to the book of Apocalypse taken from the works of Gilbert de la Porrée (d. 1154; Pl. 86). A typical Bible made in Paris around 1250 would have a set of 64 prologues, including several that were quite new. The prologues

124

Portable
Bibles
of the
Thirteenth
Century

rapidly became so intimately linked to their texts that they gave the appearance of being part of the Bible itself. The illusion went both ways. The opening four verses of Saint Luke's Gospel, beginning '*Quoniam quidem ...*', were often written as if they were a medieval prologue to a Gospel which began '*Fuit in diebus ...*' (Luke 1:5). Verses 1–4 are, in fact, authentically biblical.

One of the most enduring developments of the early thirteenth century was the introduction of standard chapter numbers throughout the Bible. We still use these. There was nothing especially new about dividing the Scriptures into manageable passages, either for reference or liturgical reading, and we find numbers assigned to such sections in Greek Bibles as early as the fourth or fifth century. The ancient use of Canon Tables in Gospel Books depends on being able to cite numbered references to parallel chapters of the text. There are also *Capitula* lists, as they called them, in many large Carolingian and Romanesque Bibles, listing the headings for numbered sections throughout each book of the Bible. However, these were erratic and inconsistent from one manuscript to the next. The chapters of Romanesque Bibles were often short and impractical. Exodus, for example, was sometimes divided into upwards of 130 little sections (it now has 40 chapters) and even Saint Mark's Gospel commonly had nearly 50 chapters (it now contains 16).

The need for standardized chapter numbers arose from commentaries in the late twelfth century. An early patristic author, writing for monks, could hope that his readers would know their Bible well enough to recognize and locate any passage by the citation of a few words of text. Those who lectured on the Bible in the early universities must have learned by experience that they could not necessarily expect so much from their students. Peter the Chanter (d. 1197), one of the first generation of teachers of theology in Paris, used chapter references in his biblical commentaries but according to a numbering scheme of his own. His successor, Stephen Langton, often used a system so similar to that in modern Bibles that it has generally been supposed that Langton himself may have devised the chapter numbers which became such a feature of thirteenth-century Bibles. They occur in their modern form, for example, in a manuscript of Stephen Langton's commentary on the Minor Prophets dated 1203 (Troyes, Bibliothèque Municipale, ms. 1046). In several manuscripts the numbering of the chapters is actually ascribed to Stephen Langton, either by name or as the archbishop of Canterbury, to which post he was nominated in 1207 (e.g., Oxford, Magdalen College, MS. 168, fol. 51r, and Paris, BNF, ms. lat. 14417, fol. 125r). Certainly the establishment of a recognized system of chapter numbers for every book of the Bible must have evolved in the classrooms of Paris in the first quarter of the thirteenth century.

Chapter numbers caught the imagination of readers and scribes of Bibles from about the 1220s onwards. The idea spread rapidly across Europe. Old Bibles were marked up according to the new chapter numeration. New copies of the Bible were transcribed with the chapter divisions in place. In the first half of the century,

125

Portable
Bibles
of the
Thirteenth
Century

one chapter might well run on into the next in the middle of a line. The chapter number would then be written in the margin, opposite its opening (Pl. 87). One would expect this in the 1230s, for example. Sometimes scribes found the numbers difficult to apply, and these marginal numbers can show several layers of despairing emendations and repositioning. Once the new chapter numbers were accepted, the old *capitula* lists and Canon Tables disappeared, for their references no longer matched. By about 1240, the chapter breaks had

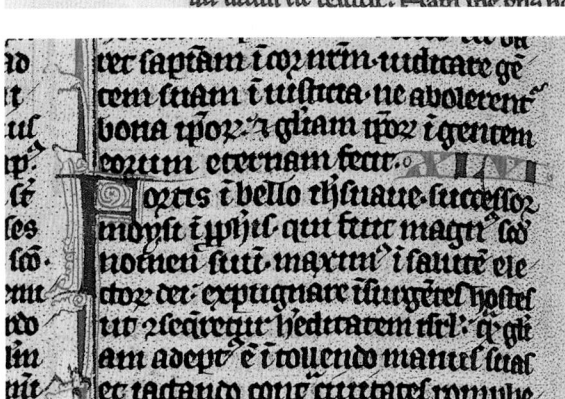

87, 88

The modern system of chapter numbers was introduced in the first half of the thirteenth century. Both illustrations here show the opening of Sirach 46. In the first, c.1220, a small initial is inserted into the middle of the line and the number is placed in the margin. By c.1270, in the second plate, there is a clear paragraph break between the chapters, and the initial and number are inset into the text
(PRIVATE COLLECTIONS)

generally settled into those we know today. They became very visible in Bibles. Scribes began opening each new chapter at the beginning of a line (Pl. 88). It thus became easy to allow space for a large chapter initial and to indent the chapter number itself into the block of text. These were usually written in roman numerals in alternately red and blue letters.

Similar trails of red and blue letters appeared across the upper margins of thirteenth-century Bibles. These are the running-titles. They give the name of the book of the Bible across the opening, half the word on the left-hand page and half on the right (Pl. 89). Running-titles are extremely convenient for locating one's place in a manuscript Bible. Anyone in the mid-thirteenth century opening a Bible at random could recognize immediately, from the coloured pennant headings, which book they were in and at which chapter number. The Bible dated 1236, cited above (Paris, BNF, ms. lat. 36), goes a stage further. It actually has original leaf numbers in red ink throughout, an extraordinary rarity and refinement at such an early date (Pl. 80). A medieval note

89 below

This detail from Pl. 80 above shows the left half of a running-title 'AD RO', continuing 'MANOS' on the facing page, showing the text to be from the Epistle to the Romans

126

Portable
Bibles
of the
Thirteenth
Century

ZACHA

127

Portable
Bibles
of the
Thirteenth
Century

128

Portable
Bibles
of the
Thirteenth
Century

at the beginning draws attention to them, observing that they make it easier for the reader to find whatever page he seeks. In fact, leaf numbers were not necessary once all the other devices were in place, and most medieval Bibles are not paginated.

The one component of the Bible which was not altered in the early thirteenth century was the book of Psalms. It escaped the whole process of redesigning. The 150 Psalms in a thirteenth-century Bible were never numbered, and they would be cited instead from their opening words. Some of these titles are still in common use, such as the name *Venite* for Psalm 94 (95 in the numbering of the Authorized Version). There are no running-titles along the top of the pages of the Psalms in a Paris Bible. The upper margins are simply left blank for the duration of those pages in the Bible. Instead there is colour in the body of the text, for the opening capitals of each sentence in the Psalms are usually painted with alternately red and blue initials. In other books of the thirteenth-century Bible, the verses are not indicated, except perhaps with a splash of red paint on each opening capital (Pl. 91).

The design of the Psalms is so visibly different from that of other books of the Bible that there must be some reason why they were exempted from the new

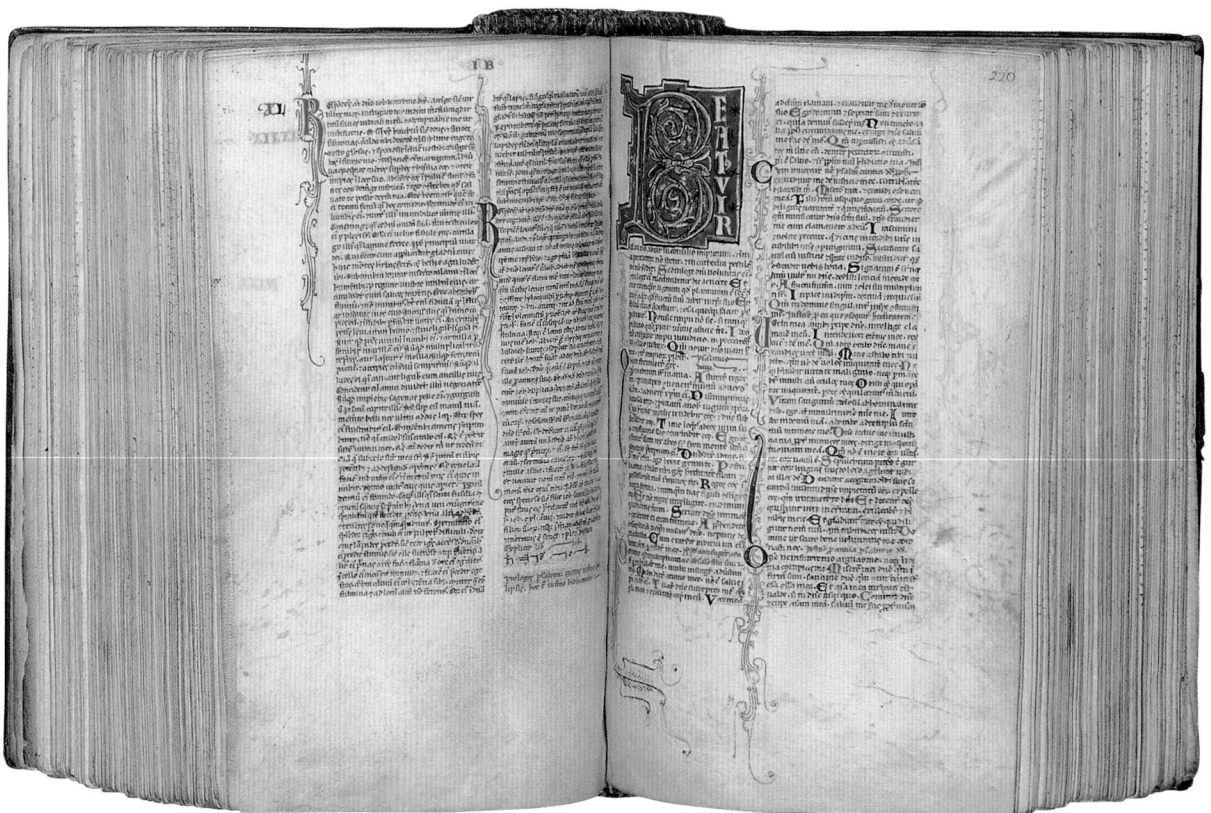

129

Portable
Bibles
of the
Thirteenth
Century

reforms. The Psalms were always an exceptional text in the canon of the medieval Bible, for the Psalter also circulated independently as a liturgical book. It might be that the original copies of the Bible which were first used to mark up the chapter numbers did not include the Psalms. Quite a number of Bibles do indeed omit the Psalms altogether, especially copies made in England. An early instance is the one-volume copy made for Simon, abbot of St Albans 1167–83, cited above (Cambridge, Corpus Christi College, MS. 48). Thirteenth-century examples, among many, include London, BL, Royal MS. 1.A.III and Harley MSS. 1034, 1661 and 1287, and Oxford, Bodleian Library, MSS. Auct. D.5.6, Auct. D.5.18 and Rawl. G.8, all of which were written in England. Perhaps Stephen Langton, who was English, or some other scholar in his circle, designed the new Bible from a copy without the Psalms. If so, this would suggest that there was once a single master prototype of the new page design which then became the exemplar for other copies. Subsequent scribes adopted the new Paris Bible with such respect for the authority of their exemplars that they left the Psalms unmodernized, exactly as they found them. The Psalter remained the exception in all thirteenth-century Bibles.

The Psalter apart, the Bible had become by the mid-1230s a book which was undoubtedly very easy to use. It had evolved into a reference work prepared for convenient consultation. All the devices which it adopted were part of a great late twelfth-century trend towards making texts accessible. This was not limited to France. Scribes of books in the late twelfth and early thirteenth centuries were preoccupied with methods of ordering and arranging information so that it could be consulted rapidly and easily. A logical sequence of texts, numbered chapters, alphabetical concordances, tables of contents, running-titles, and so on, were all features common to very many books of the period, especially texts associated with the teaching of the schools. The standard student textbooks of law and theology, the *Decretum* of Gratian and the *Sentences* of Peter Lombard respectively, use many similar devices to enable those books to be readily consulted. The Bible certainly kept up with the latest developments in book design in the first quarter of the thirteenth century, but it was not unique in its adoption of a format which made it easy to use.

The editorial role of the masters of the schools in Paris at this period is still extremely elusive. Much of what had happened to the Paris Bible had evolved from the use of commentaries, which had themselves emanated from the early schools of theology. That seems clear. The phantom of Master Stephen Langton hovers constantly around the process of adapting the Bible into its new format, but his proven participation is always just out of sight. Common sense links the developments with Paris but absolute evidence is still hard to find.

Let us therefore look at Paris as a city in the early thirteenth century. It had a population of perhaps upwards of 50,000 in 1200, rising rapidly. It had probably exceeded 150,000 by the mid-thirteenth century. Paris was the seat of the royal

90 pages 126–7

This is a characteristic manuscript Bible illuminated in Paris c.1260. It measures 157 by 107 mm (6¼ by 4½ inches). The initials here mark the openings of the books of Haggai and Zechariah (PRIVATE COLLECTION)

91 opposite

The Psalms were always a special case in thirteenth-century Bibles. They begin here on the right. There are no running-titles or psalm numbers. Instead each verse is marked by a coloured initial (PRIVATE COLLECTION)

130

Portable
Bibles
of the
Thirteenth
Century

administration, and the new Gothic cathedral of Notre-Dame was probably the richest in France. However, we must not exaggerate the organization of the university of Paris at the beginning of the thirteenth century, or imagine that there was some kind of sophisticated corporate faculty of theology in any modern sense. There was still hardly more than a clustering of masters offering private lectures and classes in the vicinity of the cathedral of Notre-Dame and of the houses of Augustinian canons, especially those of St-Victor and Ste-Geneviève. The schools were only one aspect of the dominance of Paris as the largest and most prosperous city in northern Europe. Visiting clerics, royal officials, bishops and papal legates, lawyers, merchants and knights must all have mingled with students jostling up and down the narrow Rue Neuve Notre-Dame between the royal palaces and the cathedral on the Ile de la Cité. It was in this street, directly opposite the west door of Notre-Dame, that the earliest fixed bookshops seem to have opened for business in the early decades of the thirteenth century. From what we can judge from books which can be ascribed to such enterprises, the one-volume Bible was an early commodity which was offered for sale.

Surviving manuscripts of all kinds can be attributed to book painters in Paris in the first quarter of the thirteenth century. Art historians assign them by the style of their illumination to several different 'workshops', however imprecise this word must be. We cannot know whether or not the products of a particular workshop are necessarily the same as those of any specific bookseller. Nonetheless we can sense from the stylistic grouping of manuscripts that the book trade in Paris was supplying a wide market, not only scholars attending the schools. Products of one workshop, probably active around 1210–20, include five Bibles, a luxury manuscript on astronomy, a collection of medical texts, a long set of glossed books of the Bible, and a treatise in French on good government. Surviving manuscripts from another workshop of about 1215–25 include about a dozen Bibles, several glossed books, a Missal, a monastic Lectionary and a Psalter. The nature of such books suggests that the early Paris book trade was furnishing books as much to the Church and court as it was to the schools. In fact, no surviving Bibles of the early thirteenth century have evidence of ownership by students or teaching masters. Where the patrons can be identified, they were canons, bishops, cardinals and other men of substance. We have already referred to Bibles owned by Cardinal Guala Bicchieri (d. 1227) and in 1231 by Adam, treasurer of Rheims Cathedral. Troyes, Bibliothèque Municipale, ms. 577, a product of the first workshop summarized above, belonged to Garnier de Rochefort, bishop of Langres (d. 1226 or soon after). These are probably characteristic purchasers of one-volume Bibles in the first third of the thirteenth century in Paris.

The evolution of the thirteenth-century Bible might very easily have stopped around 1230. By that date, it had become a single volume, generally approximately 250 mm by 215 mm. (10 by 8½ inches), and its text was ordered and numbered. Its arrangement was neither more nor less sophisticated than that of many other

131

Portable
Bibles
of the
Thirteenth
Century

excellently constructed reference books of that time. It was evidently possible to commission copies from professional scribes in Paris. Manuscripts of the one-volume Bible were evidently acquired by wealthy patrons in Paris and were carried home to other countries. The new Paris format was admired and imitated. That, to repeat, might have been the end of the story, except for one thing. This was the advent of the friars. The arrival of Dominicans and Franciscans in Paris transformed the Bible yet again. The friars seized upon the Paris Bible and brought it into a level of refinement and popularity which put it far ahead of any other text of the thirteenth century.

The Orders of friars are a development of the thirteenth century. Friars resembled monks except that they did not live in communities. They travelled from place to place, like the apostles, preaching the Word of God and usually relying for sustenance on the charity of faithful Christians. They renounced all material possessions. The two principal orders of friars at this period were the Dominicans and Franciscans. The former were established by Saint Dominic (d.1221), with emphasis on scholarship and an especial mission to avert heresy. They are also known as the Order of Preachers or Black Friars. The Franciscans, or Order of Friars Minor, or Grey Friars, were founded by Saint Francis of Assisi (d.1226), and stressed personal piety and simplicity of faith. Both orders had public preaching at the heart of their activities (Pl. 92). The Dominicans set up schools in Paris in 1229 and the Franciscans in 1231. By 1230, the Dominicans were training their friars within the faculty of theology in Paris.

The new one-volume Paris Bible was an ideal book for the friars. Already in 1220, Pope Honorius III was referring to the Dominicans as students of the Holy Scriptures in Paris. It was natural that they should turn to the format of the Bible available locally. They grasped its value as if they had invented it. The Paris Bible suited the friars for four fundamental reasons: it was portable, it was definitive, it was searchable, and it was available commercially. Because of the friars, each of these features became a universal and enduring characteristic of Bibles. Let us take all four points in turn.

The friars travelled. There was probably no part of Europe where they had not preached by the mid-thirteenth century. By the end of the century, they had been as far as China and north Africa. Very small books were essential to anyone who carried all he possessed in his pockets. Medieval friars' books, especially those of the Franciscans, are easily recognizable now simply by their size. Little books of sermons, manuals of confession, breviaries, and so forth, became smaller and more compact in the thirteenth century to suit the convenience of travelling friars. The Bible had already gone from a set of multiple folio volumes in 1160 to a single square quarto around 1230. It might fit in the saddle bag of a bishop but hardly into the folds of a friar's habit. In the time of the friars, then, the Paris Bible was transformed into a pocket-book.

The script became minute, written probably with the quill of a very small bird,

92

The friars were preachers. This late fourteenth-century image of Saint Francis shows him preaching with a Cross and a Bible (PRIVATE COLLECTION)

132

Portable
Bibles
of the
Thirteenth
Century

sharpened to the finest possible point. Contractions and abbreviations became more extreme than at any other period in the history of European script. Hardly a word of a mid-thirteenth-century Bible is written in full, without some contraction. Around 1240, the pages of Bibles start to become astonishingly small, and a complete Bible of the 1250s can slip easily into a modern pocket. Scribes economized on the bulk of the book by using parchment of quite unprecedented thinness. A thirteenth-century Bible might have 500 or so leaves and yet be no thicker than many paperbacks today. The term 'uterine' parchment is sometimes used (and is a medieval term), referring to the exceptionally thin and silky skin that could be obtained from the pelt of an aborted or still-born calf. It must have been an expression of quality rather than of literal origin, for it was made in huge quantities, especially in Paris and Bologna. It may have been prepared by splitting the thickness of the skin into more than one layer, or it may simply be the result of scraping the skin over and over again to achieve a writing surface which was as thin and weightless as modern tissue but opaque and white. The uterine parchment of the thirteenth century was perfectly suited to making diminutive manuscripts compressing all of the Bible within a single volume.

The obvious model for the size of the pocket-Bible was the breviary, the essential hand-held service book of any cleric, including the friars. The very word 'breviary' derives from its small size, and a breviary was often called a *portiforium* in medieval Latin, a portable book. A list of a private library in Liège in 1269 includes two items described as being *manuale*, the Bible and the breviary, a pair of hand-sized books. Some friars' Bibles include abbreviated missals, so that they served a double purpose for their owners, both liturgical and biblical. A good many tiny Bibles of the thirteenth century incorporate liturgical Calendars

93

*Friars' Bibles sometimes
included Calendars. This
example must have belonged to
a Dominican because the feast
of Saint Dominic is singled out
in red ink as a double feast on 5
August*
(PRIVATE COLLECTION)

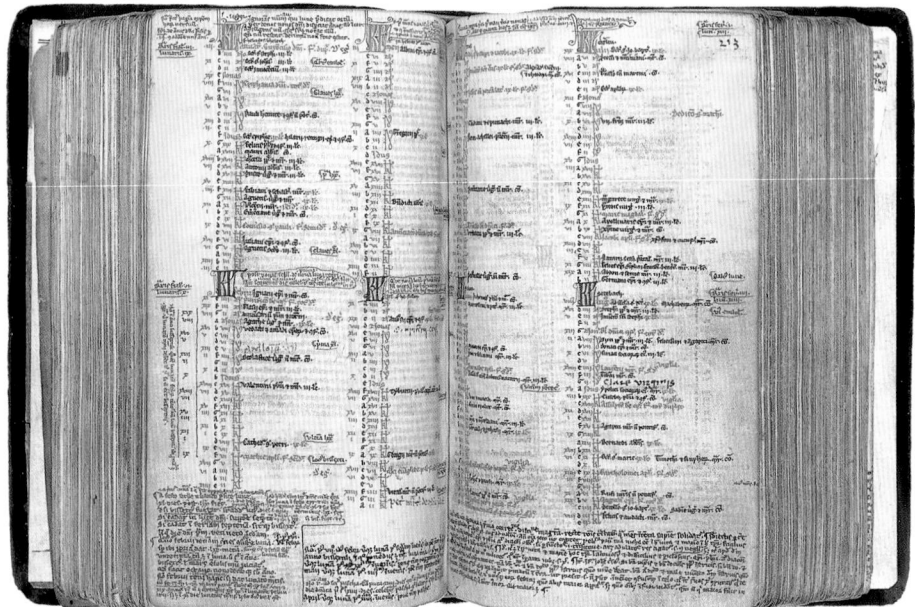

133

Portable
Bibles
of the
Thirteenth
Century

(Pl. 93). This too would bring them into line with breviaries and missals. The helpfulness of any Calendar now is that we can see what saints were accorded special honour by the manuscript's owner, and we can tell that almost every Calendar in a thirteenth-century Bible is either Dominican or Franciscan. The wandering life of the friars is dramatically reflected in the portability of their Bibles.

The second reason why the Paris Bible appealed to the friars was that it was definitive. This was especially relevant to the Dominicans, who were founded to stand against heresy. Gregory IX charged them in 1233 with the rooting out of the Albigenses, the heretical movement is south-west France which denied the literal truth of much of the Bible, especially the Old Testament. The Bible of the 1230s had brought all of established Scripture into one book. The friars immediately saw its value as a symbol, a physical three-dimensional object which represented and enclosed the totality of the Word of God. It was the Dominicans who introduced the *Correctiones*, not exactly corrections (as we have seen) but an attempt to bring comprehensiveness and consistency. Europe was facing internal heresy for the first time. The friars' response was a book, the Bible, which defined authority. They must have travelled with it, shown and shaken it, and doubtless thumped their pulpits with it. This brought the definition of the Scriptures as a single and sacred entity into almost every village of Europe, and that legacy is still with us.

The third aspect of the Paris Bible, which the friars adopted joyfully as their own, was that the text was searchable. We have seen how the original apparatus of chapter numbers and headings arose out of classroom study of the Bible. It was easy to seek and cite references from the Paris Bible, and the friars added new techniques for searching the Bible for words and subjects. Standardized chapter numbers were a prerequisite for such techniques. The Dominicans in the convent of St-Jacques in Paris under the supervision of Hugh of St-Cher (d.1263) devised a vast verbal concordance of the Bible which was apparently in use by 1239. Each word is referred to a biblical book and chapter number, and each chapter was then notionally subdivided into seven, indicated alphabetically by the letters 'a' to 'g'. The Dominicans had produced two further versions of their concordance by the 1280s. A very similar dictionary of subjects was undertaken probably by the Franciscans, the *Concordantiae Morales Bibliorum*, compiled about 1240. It too uses the chapter numbers of the Paris Bible and an alphabetical subdivision within the chapters. It was not actually necessary to insert these alphabetical letters into manuscript Bibles themselves, for one can mentally divide the chapters into fractions of text, but it was essential to use Bibles with consistent chapter numbers.

The friars searched their Bibles for preaching. All medieval sermons are based on biblical readings and quotations. Sermon themes are often jotted on the fly-leaves and in the margins of thirteenth-century Bibles. Frequently Bibles include

134

Portable
Bibles
of the
Thirteenth
Century

added lists of readings for each Sunday or feast day, indicated by book and chapter references and the opening couple of words of each day's reading. The reading would often be the subject of a sermon. Sometimes one can guess from these lists alone whether or not the Bible belonged to a friar. For example, a little thirteenth-century Bible is now owned by Appleby Magna parish church in Leicestershire. It has tables of readings for a small number of feast days including that of Saint Francis. The owner must have been Franciscan. Furthermore, he lists suitable readings for preaching to specific audiences, including 'to masters and scholars' and 'to poor people'. This sets the scene for his preaching to audiences of the widest range of backgrounds. The friar would doubtless actually preach in the vernacular language, but he would prepare his sources from the Latin Bible. If he could locate suitable passages, the friar could preach on any topic. If he could cite actual chapter numbers (and late medieval sermons do), then he brought credibility and authority to his sermon. A monk preaching to his convent or a priest to a learned audience might reasonably expect his listeners to recognize the source of biblical quotations. A friar, however, standing in the marketplace and preach-

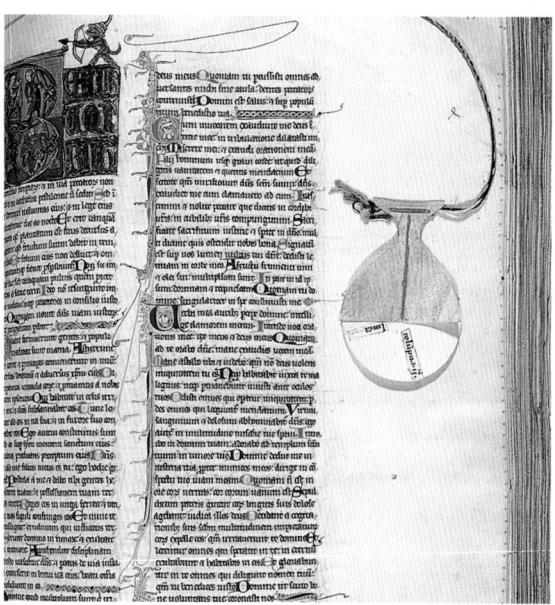

ing to poor people, needed to invoke Scripture by something more than general allusion. Doorstep evangelists do the same today, urgently piling one scriptural citation upon another, with a rattle of chapter and verse numbers. The thirteenth-century friars used chapter numbers for their own use, and in their preaching they broadcast the usefulness of the numbers across Europe. Anyone in their audience who knew the Bible but could not match the friars in the quick citation of chapters would immediately be at a disadvantage. It is easy to envisage how Paris chapter numbers were therefore speedily implemented everywhere.

By the mid-thirteenth century there were Dominican and Franciscan convents in every major town of Europe. The convents acted as administrative centres for the friars. If rules were adhered to, each preaching friar needed a Bible, and so copies would have been required in their thousands. The friars were not organized or trained as scribes. In the late 1220s, when the friars discovered the merits of the Paris Bible, they must have been attracted not only by the fact that it was potentially portable, definitive and searchable, but also by its commercial avail-

ability. This was one of those happy coincidences of timing. We have noted that
the early professional workshops of Paris included one-volume Bibles among
their wares in the first quarter of the century. By about 1230, there were many
professional booksellers or stationers (as they came to be called). The patronage
of the wealthy laity and of the newly organized university of Paris now supported
a considerable industry in the copying and decorating of books. By the middle
third of the century, there were more than a dozen recognizable workshops of
manuscript illuminators in Paris. All of them produced Bibles, among many
other books. For the first time in the Middle Ages, Bibles could thus actually be
bought in considerable numbers. The friars supported this trade vigorously
and helped transform it further. There is a certain irony that the Orders which
renounced all worldly possessions probably furnished a good part of the regular
income of many secular workshops. Several stationers opened in the rue St-
Jacques on the left bank in Paris, in the same street as the Dominican convent.
The Franciscan constitutions of 1338 decreed that each of their students in Paris
should simply be assigned a Bible up to the value of 300 *livres*, or should be given
the equivalent sum to buy one.

Technically, the friars' Bibles were the always property of their Orders and
were lent to each friar for the duration of his life. They were forbidden to sell
them except by express permission of their house or provincial prior. Inscriptions
in manuscripts adopt the formula '*Ad usum …*' such-and-such, meaning that it
was assigned to the use but not the ownership of a particular friar. Many Bibles
must have been bought for distribution. Some must have been made in workshops
in the big cities to be issued to friars through their provincial convents. We find
Bibles which are surely Parisian in origin with inscriptions of friars from as far
away as Scandinavia and Bohemia. Many Bibles were produced in Italy too, where
secular booksellers were also becoming established. In 1242, the Dominicans on
Majorca employed a professional scribe, Fulchetus, to copy a Bible for them. In
the contract, which was witnessed by Martin the parchment-maker, the friars
agreed to pay his fee of 200 Majorcan *livres* and to give him board and lodging
while he was working. The island of Majorca, of course, was remote from any
convenient stationer or bookseller. Even there, nevertheless, the friars were
depending on professional help.

Friars were not the only customers for portable Bibles but they must have been
the principal means for disseminating everything that the Paris Bible represented.
In the hands of the friars, portability, definitiveness and searchability became
universal features of the Bible. Sometimes the friars evidently traded in Bibles,
despite many prohibitions. In 1240, the Dominican Chapter General in Bologna
deprived Friar Bartolomeo of his Bible because of the irregular way he obtained
it, and he was committed to performing penance. One thirteenth-century Bible
(Brussels, BR, ms. 4911), has a contemporary note that its owner, one Master P.,
bought it with his own money from a preacher, apparently a Dominican friar

135

Portable
Bibles
of the
Thirteenth
Century

136

Portable
Bibles
of the
Thirteenth
Century

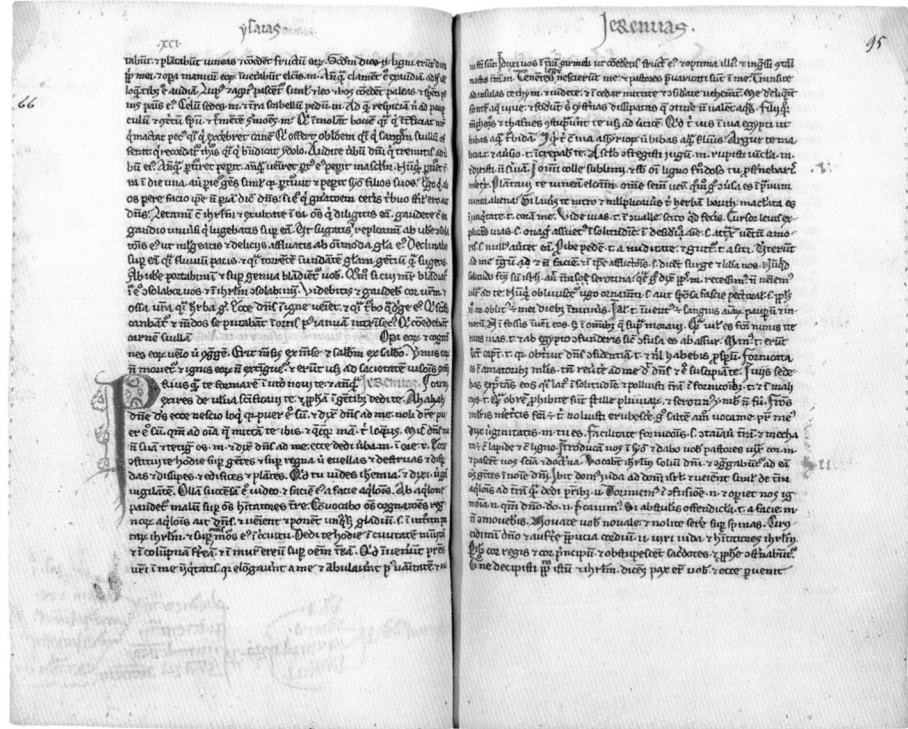

95

*This thirteenth-century Bible
includes a note that its owner
bought it with his own money
from an unnamed Dominican
friar and then bequeathed it to
a Brother Guillelmus*
(BRUSSELS, BIBLIOTHÈQUE
ROYALE, MS. 4911)

96 opposite

*Not all thirteenth-century
Bibles were made in France.
There are good examples from
north-eastern Italy, especially
from Bologna, Padua and
Venice. This dates from
c.1250–75*
(PRIVATE COLLECTION)

(Pl. 95). By one means or another, many Bibles which had once belonged to friars found their way into general circulation.

Let us come now to a central point of this chapter. These little portable Bibles are often referred to as university Bibles. It is commonly claimed that their small format was convenient for students carrying the books to their classes. There is not the slightest evidence that this happened. Students of theology certainly studied the Bible in class, spending four years on the subject, but the manuscripts they used during lectures would have been of separate books of the Bible, with the Gloss. Copies of glossed biblical books are often crammed with student notes. Biblical commentaries of various kinds were also read and discussed in class. The tiny one-volume Bibles were too small for annotation in the lecture room, and there is no space for notes between the lines. The supposed convenience of portability was of no advantage to a student, who probably had no considerable journey from lodgings to lecture. Compared with the needs of a travelling friar, a student of theology had nothing to gain from a book of diminutive size. On the contrary, books of law were certainly studied and annotated in the classrooms of Bologna and these are usually volumes of vast dimensions, with ample margins for notes.

Secondly, it is often asserted that the one-volume Bibles were copied in Paris on the *pecia* method. This was the famous system whereby stationers who were endorsed by the university would lend out disbound numbered sections of official exemplars to be copied by students or scribes working for the university market. The Bible does not appear on the official *pecia* lists circulated by the university authorities in the late thirteenth century. Three extant copies of the Bible, however, are generally said to be have been transcribed from university *peciae*. They are Paris, BNF, mss. lat. 28, 9381 and 14238. If these are indeed *pecia* copies, then they would furnish some evidence that the university was authorizing the distribution of Paris Bibles for student use. In fact, not one of these three manuscripts appears to have any connection with *pecia* copying. All three differ from each other. Marginal numbers refer to chapters, not *peciae*. Lat.9381 does not even remotely correspond to the new arrangement of texts and prologues and it is without chapter numbers. It is not the Paris text at all. An inscription at the end of lat. 14238 might have been misread as referring to 30 *peciae* but, in fact, it is a value, 'Ista byblia precii triginta francorum …', the price of 30 shillings, and it records that the large Bible was a gift to the abbey of St-Victor from Jean Auchier, procurator and counsellor to the king. It is in no sense a student's or stationer's copy. All three supposed *pecia* copies must be eliminated as red herrings. The Paris Bible was not a *pecia* book; and thus it was not a set text in the university.

Thirdly, it is commonly assumed that there must be a connection between the size and importance of the faculty of theology in Paris and the huge number of Bibles attributable to Paris in the thirteenth century. This is to miss the obvious point. The second largest centre for making one-volume manuscript Bibles was Bologna. There are many hundreds of late thirteenth-century portable Bibles with illumination which can be ascribed to workshops in Bologna, far more than from anywhere else in Italy. However, there was no faculty of theology at the University of Bologna until 1364. What Paris and Bologna had in common was not the teaching of the Bible within the universities but

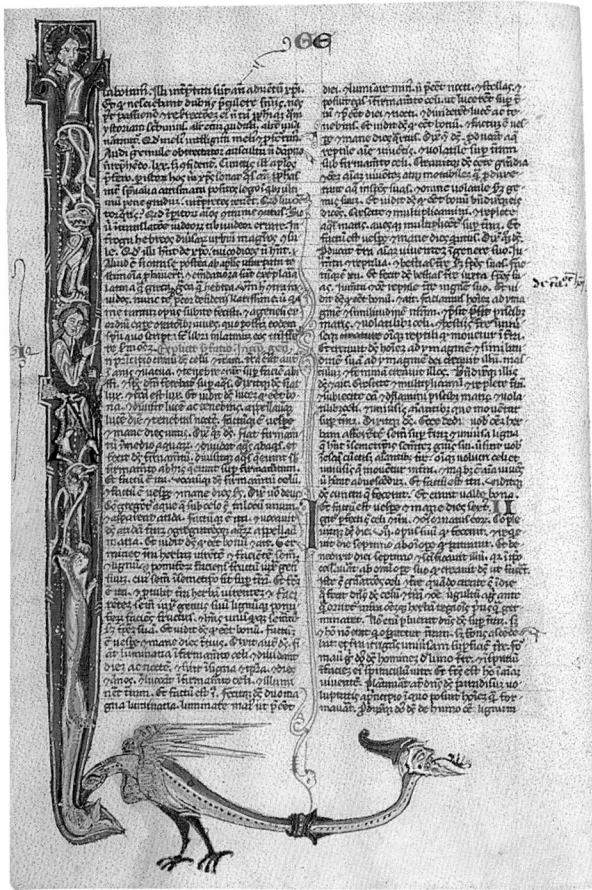

137

Portable
Bibles
of the
Thirteenth
Century

138

Portable
Bibles
of the
Thirteenth
Century

the presence of the two largest Dominican houses in Europe. Once again, we return to the friars.

Finally, a quotation from the *Opus Minus* of Roger Bacon is often invoked to suggest the involvement of the university in promulgating the Paris text. In 1267, Bacon recalled that about forty years earlier many theologians of Paris had collaborated with the booksellers in supplying the most corrupt exemplars for the new text of the Bible, what he calls the *exemplar Parisiense.* This would take us back to about 1227. This date, in other words, is almost exactly at the moment when the friars first adopted the Paris Bible as their own. Roger Bacon (*c.*1214–*c.*1292) was himself a friar, writing in the Franciscan convent in Paris. In fact, he was probably quite right in his recollection. The masters of theology had some unclear role in devising the one-volume Paris Bible but their concern was not with revising the text but with restructuring the format. The redesigned Bible was indeed disseminated by the booksellers. They were independent of the university; Bacon disapproves of this and describes them disdainfully as uneducated and married men (i.e. laymen). That may well be a fair statement, and the dates tally. This is the crucial point. It was the friars who salvaged and promoted the Bible in the late 1220s, not the university. The thirteenth-century Paris Bible owes its success to the Dominicans and the Franciscans, after about 1227.

Of course we cannot say that thirteenth-century Bibles were never used by students at the universities of Paris, Oxford, Bologna or elsewhere. The library of the Sorbonne in 1338 had about 40 one-volume Bibles, including one bought from money raised by the sale of a breviary bequeathed by Pierre de Ausone. Probably most of them were thirteenth-century copies. Little Latin Bibles were made in extraordinary quantities in the thirteenth century, especially in France but also in large numbers in Italy and England. Inspired by the friars, countless people must have bought portable Bibles in the third quarter of the century. The text was in Latin, which restricted its readership to those who had received some education. Some must have been students; others were monks, clerks, royal officials, local nobility, administrators of estates, and so on. The one-volume Bible, in order and divided into numbered chapters, impressed itself on the consciousness of people who had never owned books before. Paris Bibles and their imitations were made and sold in such large numbers that almost no other copies ever needed to be made again in the Middle Ages, for they were constantly resold from one generation to the next. Very many hundreds (possibly thousands) still exist. Even now, thirteenth-century Bibles are so common that they have never once disappeared completely from the antiquarian book market.

There are very many references to thirteenth-century Bibles being still available on the market in the fifteenth century and still being acquired for actual use, especially by monasteries and parish churches. They occur in all parts of Europe. The further they are from Paris, the more impressive the statistics. As background to Chapter 7 below, then, let us conclude with a few examples from

English sources. Margaret, duchess of Clarence (d.1439), the king's aunt, gave money to purchase a Bible for the Bridgettine monastery at Syon near London around 1430. One might expect that a royal donor would have bought a new book: on the contrary, the manuscript is a little volume of the mid-thirteenth century, with the Paris corrections inserted (London, BL, Add. MS. 40006). Richard

139

Portable
Bibles
of the
Thirteenth
Century

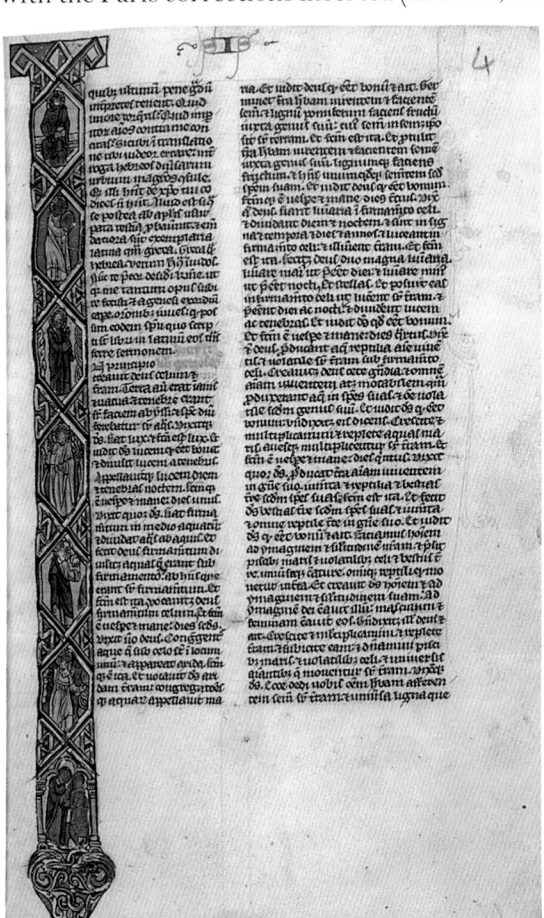

Pede, dean of Hereford 1463–80, bought a thirteenth-century Bible in Hereford for £3 6s. 8d., a considerable sum for a second-hand book (Eton College, MS. 179). Another was bought in 1473 for 20 shillings (still no small sum) from Thomas Hunt, bookseller and publisher in Oxford, and was given that year to St Augustine's Abbey in Canterbury (Oxford, Bodleian Library, MS. Burney 11). Some were regarded as so precious that they were required to be chained. A thirteenth-century Bible was given to Bredgar Church by the vicar who died in 1474 on the condition that it should be chained in the church and read by the brothers of the church 'whene it plese hem' (London, Lambeth Palace, MS. 1362, Pl. 97). Another was given to Buckingham parish church by John Rudyng (d.1481) to be chained in the church for the use of the chaplains who may want to study it. It still belongs to the church there. A final example was given to the parish church of St Martin in Coney Street in York as late as 1510, to be chained in the choir there forever. It survived the Reformation. The church itself was destroyed in an air raid in April 1942, but the indestructible little manuscript Bible still exists, a monument to the extraordinary creation and production of Bibles in the thirteenth century. It is now MS. XVI.D.13 in York Minster Library.

6 | Bible Picture Books

MOST LATE MEDIEVAL Bibles did not have pictures as we
might expect them now in a modern illustrated book. Instead, many had illuminated initials enclosing miniatures. Each of the individual books in manuscript
Bibles usually opened with a large initial, and within the shape of this initial was
often a small picture. This might be a representation of the author of that book –
King David with his harp, for example, or Saint Paul preaching – or it might be a
distinctive image from a particular book, such as Jonah and the whale or Daniel
in the lions' den. These little pictures would help a user of the Bible to locate and
recognize a specific text. A reader of the Bible could skim through the pages looking for the opening initial. The subject would act as a visual key to identifying the
particular book. These were not strictly illustrations of the Bible text in a modern
sense. They were more like visual mnemonics, to help find, use and remember the
location of each book. The pictures frequently relate simply to the opening words
of text, not to the subject of the whole book. The book of Judges in a thirteenth-
century Bible, for instance, is often marked by an initial showing the death of
Joshua. The first sentence of Judges opens 'Now after the death of Joshua it came
to pass …', and so on, after which Joshua is never mentioned again. However, the
picture would remind the reader that here was the opening of the familiar text of
Judges which began with that verse. Sometimes the subjects chosen do not appear
in the Bible at all, such as the common picture for the opening of the book of Isaiah.
The initial often shows Isaiah being sawn in half. The horrible and apocryphal
martyrdom of the prophet does not occur in the book of Isaiah or anywhere else in
the Bible. It was, however, a striking and unforgettable image which would have
been familiar to a medieval reader as a symbol for Isaiah and so he or she would
easily recognize the opening of the book which Isaiah had written.

uali dauit ueniens i castra cum offerre uellet que attulerat. audito clamore acierum que
ad pugnam parate erant dimittit omnia ad sarcinas ostorum sub manu custodis τ ipse
appetano uadit ad locum preliz ~

Qualiter cum Dauit uenisst ad locum certaminis. et ille gigas more solito exploraret. atqȝ ois
ISrl cum ualde timeret. unus dixit qȝ quicuqȝ illu posst excedere. rex et filiam suam cu diuiciis
multis daret. atqȝ cum et oem domu patris sui immunem faceret a tributo. qo audiens Dauit.
et de conditionibȝ ill diligenter interrogans: cum omnia dioiasȝ contempsit illum gigantem τ
de uictoria a se habere optimam spem ostendit. k fratres cu sui grauiter increpuerunt.

Even though most thirteenth- and fourteenth-century Bibles did not have pictures beyond small initials like this, there was certainly no lack of biblical illustration in other manuscripts. This is the period of what is probably the most beautiful and complex biblical imagery ever produced. This chapter will include some of the most famous and spectacular of all illuminated manuscripts. They are not strictly Bibles but books of Bible stories. Sometimes they are called 'Picture Bibles'. These volumes are something between Bibles and biblical commentaries. They were not texts for the saddlebags of poor mendicant friars but were made for the religious education and delight of a new class of wealthy and educated laity. They are books of great grandeur and costliness. Some were made for the private chapels and chambers of royal families. Probably the best-known type of medieval Picture Bible is the text commonly called the *Biblia Pauperum*, or 'Bible of the Poor'. The title is a relatively modern one and seldom has a name been so entirely inappropriate. Most of the books we are about to consider must have been seen only by some of the very wealthiest people in Europe. The fourteenth-century Holkham Bible Picture Book, by no means the grandest of these books, opens with a drawing of the manuscript's editor instructing the scribe and saying to him in Anglo-Norman, 'Do the work well and neatly, for it will be shown to rich people' (London, BL, Add. MS. 47682, fol. 1r). The patronage of rich people and their interest in the Bible becomes the theme of the present chapter.

The first manuscripts made in any quantity for private use by wealthy laity were Psalters. The Psalms, of course, were part of the Bible, but medieval Psalters were used primarily as liturgical texts, for reading like prayer-books, and so they mostly fall outside the scope of this survey. Nonetheless, Psalters provide the immediate and perhaps unexpected background for picture Bibles. We can step back and watch the gradual evolution of cycles of illustrations in medieval Psalters from the late eighth century. An early example of what was probably a privately owned Psalter is in Montpellier (Faculté de Médecine, ms. 409). It was perhaps copied at the abbey of Mondsee in southeast Germany but it was evidently commissioned by a noble or royal patron, perhaps Rotrude (d.810), daughter of

Charlemagne. It opens with two full-page miniatures of figures standing beneath

arches. The first is David, with a musical instrument. The second is Christ, holding a book (Pl. 99). David is appropriate, as the author of the Psalter, and even in the Gospels Christ identified himself as the subject of prophecies in the Psalms (Luke 24:44). Saint Matthew's Gospel opens with a genealogy connecting David to Jesus Christ.

The intellectual link between the ancient Psalms and the New Testament was very important in the Middle Ages. The Psalms were a principal ingredient of monastic liturgy, Jewish hymns redirected into Christian use. Allusions to Christ were discovered in many Psalms. From the ninth century onwards, the more luxurious manuscripts of the Psalter often opened with illustrations which associated the author of the Psalms with aspects of the life of Christ. These were not depictions of the text of the Psalter as such, but become cycles of free-standing pictures, grouped together, reflecting independently the balancing of the Old Testament and the New. By the twelfth century, it was the custom to incorporate these clusters of full-page miniatures into the beginning of a Psalter, as a distinct unit, sandwiched between the Calendar and the first psalm. Some cycles of pictures are entirely from the New Testament. Others open with scenes of the Creation and the expulsion from the Garden of Eden from the very beginning of Genesis. These images might then be paired with miniatures of the Crucifixion and Last Judgement, showing the fall and the salvation of mankind. Other Psalters focus more directly on the life of David, defeating Goliath, for example, and then echo this in scenes from the life of Christ, who overcame the Devil. There is a certain sense in which the New Testament illustrations in Psalters are depictions of prophecy being fulfilled. There is an anonymous ninth-century text which was then believed to be the work of Alcuin. It says of the Psalter, 'In the Psalms you will find, if you examine them intently and can reach to a full spiritual understanding of them, the Incarnation, the Passion, Resurrection and Ascension of the Divine Word and also the judgement to come as well as the prophecy of the general resurrection.' Those New Testament subjects are, almost exactly, the themes depicted in Romanesque Psalters.

In some very expensive Romanesque manuscript Psalters, the number of these inserted pictures was increased in range to include illustrations of all Old Testament history up until the time of King David, writer of the Psalms. Then the cycle begins all over again, from the Annunciation and the birth of Christ right through to the Resurrection, Ascension and Last Judgement. It is as if David is placed in context by showing events which preceded him back to the beginning of the world, and Christ is placed in context by depicting events from his incarnation until the end of the world. Psalter illustrations jump from the time of David to that of Christ, passing over nearly a thousand years of Old Testament history. Sometimes the Psalms and the Gospels are bridged by a Jesse tree. Jesse was the father of King David. He is often shown lying asleep with his

St come set fit en demeuraest le veel pur aorar.

St come moyses pecore lestable?

100

The Psalter of Ingeborg, queen of France, was illuminated c.1195. It opens with 51 full-page pictures. This shows the worship of the golden calf and the anger of Moses
(CHANTILLY, MUSÉE CONDÉ, MS. 9)

101 opposite

The full-page pictures once in an English twelfth-century Psalter take the story of the Old Testament as far as the coronation of King David, and then they leap, by way of a Jesse tree, to illustrations of the birth of Christ
(NEW YORK, PIERPONT MORGAN LIBRARY, M. 724)

descendants from David to Jesus in the branches of a tree growing upwards from his loins. An example is New York, Pierpont Morgan Library M. 724 (Pl. 101). This is a single sheet but was originally one of a series of prefatory miniatures which prefixed a grand Psalter illuminated in Canterbury about 1150. It consists of rows of little pictures. The previous page must have begun with the Creation. The surviving leaf opens with Old Testament stories from the finding of the baby Moses in the bulrushes to the death of Goliath, with David being offered the crown of Judah and entering Jerusalem as king. At that point the narrative sequence stops and there is a Jesse tree. The pictures then jump to the Visitation, the birth of John the Baptist, and so on, in the life of Christ. Another example, also English work of about the same date, is the Winchester Psalter (London, BL, Cotton MS. Nero C.IV). It opens with a cycle of pictures from the Expulsion from Eden to the anointing of David by Samuel. Then it moves immediately to the New Testament, from the birth of Christ to the Last Judgement. The picture cycle has no text, except the simplest of marginal captions, in French.

The very grandest of these Psalter cycles are French, and royal. One of the most spectacular is the Ingeborg Psalter at Chantilly (Musée Condé, ms. 9, Pl. 100). This is certainly a manuscript of royal quality, made for Ingeborg (1176–1236), the enigmatic and tragic Danish princess whom the French king, Philip Augustus, married in 1193. He then immediately repudiated her, apparently after a wedding night which proved a great disappointment for one or both parties. Ingeborg was forced into matrimonial litigation with the king, who was eventually obliged by the pope to readmit her as his wife, though he kept her safely in prison until 1213. Her magnificent Psalter must have been made quite soon after her ill-fated wedding, perhaps around 1195. It is prefixed by a cycle of 51 full-page miniatures, each usually with two pictures to a page. They illustrate the Old Testament from Abraham to the Jesse tree, and then they begin with the New Testament from the Annunciation to the Last Judgement. Again, there is no text, except for short captions in burnished gold, in French. Queen Ingeborg herself did not know French (one of many factors which contributed to her unhappiness in France). The pictures in her Psalter would only be usable if she knew the Bible stories already and recognized their subjects.

A similar series of pictures occurs at the beginning of another royal Psalter, almost as grand. This is the copy made for Blanche of Castile (1188–1252), daughter-in-law of Philip Augustus. She was the daughter of Alfonso IX of

Castile, married as a child in 1200 to Prince Louis, who inherited the French throne in 1223 as Louis VIII. Their eldest surviving son became Louis IX (king 1226–70), Saint Louis of France. Blanche's Psalter is now Paris, Bibliothèque de l'Arsenal, ms. 1186 (Pl. 102). It opens with a sequence of 22 full-page compositions, mostly divided into two pictures each. The first shows an astronomer and a scribe. The following seven show scenes from the Old Testament, from the Creation to the Jesse Tree. Then the cycle begins with pictures from the New Testament, from the Annunciation onwards. As in the Ingeborg Psalter, the pictures presuppose that the queen already knew the texts which they illustrate. According to a medieval tradition, it was from this very Psalter that Saint Louis was taught to read by his mother and, if so, they must have looked at the picture cycle together. Saint Louis's own Psalter also survives (Paris, BNF, ms. lat. 10525). It opens with an almost unbelievable cycle of 78 full-page miniatures, all of them from the Old Testament, beginning with Cain and Abel, the sons of Adam, and concluding with King Saul, in the time of David.

It is against the background of these Psalter pictures that we have to consider the four quite extraordinary surviving manuscripts of the thirteenth-century *Bible Moralisée*. The name is not a contemporary one, but it refers to the Bible with a tropological or moral interpretation. We encountered this term in the chapter on Bible commentaries (pp. 101–2): the moral sense of Scripture tells us how every verse of the text can be interpreted to show a mirror for behaviour in our own time. The manuscripts of the *Bible Moralisée* show not only these moral parallels but also typological links between events in the Old and New Testaments, as we shall see in a moment. They are primarily famous simply as picture books.

Setting aside a number of much later variants, the *Bible Moralisée* is represented by four manuscripts, all assumed to have been made in Paris between about 1220 and 1240. They are: (1), in a single volume, Vienna, ÖNB, cod. 2554; (2), in a single volume, Vienna, ÖNB, cod. 1179; (3), in three volumes, Toledo cathedral treasury, with the final 8 leaves detached and now in New York, Pierpont Morgan Library, M. 240; and (4), in three volumes, now dispersed (a) Oxford, Bodleian Library, MS. Bodley 270b, (b) Paris, BNF, ms. lat. 11560, and (c) London, BL, Harley MSS. 1526–7. The order here probably represents the sequence in which these great books were illuminated, the earliest being ÖNB, cod. 2554 (Pl. 105). These are all vast volumes, each with many thousands of Bible pictures, eight to a page, in roundels like stained-glass windows (a comparison which may be closer than mere simile). The latest set, divided between Oxford, Paris and London, has well over 13,000 miniatures. There is no text, as such, though all pictures have captions, either in French or Latin. The miniatures illustrate scenes from the Bible, mostly the Old Testament. Each roundel is one of a pair. The upper picture is a biblical scene. The picture below it represents its typological or tropological interpretation. In other words, these are picture-book commentaries on the Bible, depicting (usually) an Old Testament incident and its corresponding parallel in the New Testament or in the life of the thirteenth century. The scale and richness of these enormous books is breathtaking. They are huge folio volumes. Like the pictures in Psalter cycles, the pictures are on every second opening, leaving the versos blank, an extravagance which doubles the thickness of the books. The pages are vibrant with colour and encrusted with

burnished gold. These are no everyday manuscripts. The first was probably made for Blanche of Castile. The second Vienna manuscript ends with a miniature of a king apparently commissioning an illuminator. This may be Louis VIII. The Morgan fragment (once at the end of the Toledo volume) concludes with a magnificent miniature of a king and a queen evidently supervising a cleric who is instructing an illuminator who can be seen actually sketching out the pages of a *Bible Moralisée* (Pl. 103). The king is probably Louis IX. One way or another, these must all have been royal commissions.

These are books without earlier precedent. Therefore the comparison with Psalter illustrations is a valuable one, and may actually show us what inspired the *Bible Moralisée*. The royal Psalter cycles too are made up of page after page of multiple images of Bible scenes, with the very slightest of captions in French or Latin. They too frequently focus on the early parts of the Old Testament and on the Last Judgement. The oldest of the *Bibles Moralisées*, ÖNB, cod. 2554, covers precisely the text of Psalter cycles, from the Creation to the life of King David and no further. The second Vienna copy adds a few further short Old Testament books, such as Job, Tobit and Judith, and then jumps to the Apocalypse. The idea of Psalter pictures is that they should echo the relationship between the Old Testament and its fulfilment in the life of Christ and the teachings of the Christian Church. The *Bible Moralisée* does exactly the same, but by bringing the miniatures into literal juxtaposition with their counterparts.

Stylistically too, the pages of the *Bible Moralisée* resemble giant Psalter miniatures. A good parallel is Manchester, John Rylands University Library, MS. Lat. 22 (Pl. 104), a Psalter which was owned by the French royal family by the fourteenth century. It must have been illuminated in Paris around 1220, and may be by the same artists as ÖNB, cod. 2554. It certainly originates from the same period and place. Its full-page miniatures are composed in patterns very close to those of the *Bibles Moralisées*, with eight roundels of biblical scenes on each page, and brief marginal captions naming their subjects.

104

The design of the Bible Moralisée *illustrations closely resembles that of pictures inserted at the beginning of Psalters, such as in this manuscript, illuminated in Paris c.1220. The marginal captions describe the illustrations* (MANCHESTER, JOHN RYLANDS UNIVERSITY LIBRARY, MS. LAT. 22)

We must return to the history of Psalters for a moment to see what happens in the thirteenth century. With the great increase in lay ownership of books from around 1200, personal Psalters became more and more sophisticated. Supplementary components were grafted onto each end. They not only incorporated cycles of typological pictures at the beginning of each volume, but they also concluded with texts of prayers and readings for private meditation in honour of the Virgin Mary. Each supplementary section became longer and more complex, the illustrative cycles expanding at the beginning of the Psalter and the devotional offices at the end. Around 1250, the final section had become so extensive that it fell away to become a distinct text in its own right. It developed into what is now called the Book of Hours, a text for private devotion. Let us suppose that the preliminary clusters of Psalter illustrations did the same. The ultimate embodiment of a cycle of Psalter pictures separated off from its parent would have to be a *Bible Moralisée*. Beyond expanding a Psalter into unmanageable size, there is no other logical direction in which the pictures could evolve.

Let us take one page of a *Bible Moralisée*, selected almost at random, to show how the symbolism works. The sample is Vienna, ÖNB, cod. 2554, fol. 37r (Pl. 105). It illustrates scenes in the life of Saul, soon after his coronation as king of Israel (I Kings 12–14, I Samuel in a modern Bible). Four scenes are from the Bible and four are from their allegorical parallels. At the top left, the prophet Samuel rebukes the sons of Israel for their foolishness in wanting any king but God, and they bow their heads in agreement (I Kings 12:1–5). Immediately below, Christ holds out a manuscript before a group of Jews, who similarly bow before him. This is, incidentally, a good illustration of a medieval manuscript in its soft leather or textile wrapper, known as a 'chemise' binding; and it shows medieval Jews in caricature, ugly men with big noses and pointed hats, characteristic anti-Semitism which often occurs in the *Bibles Moralisées*. The caption explains that, as Samuel rebuked the children of Israel, so Christ rebuked the Jews for wanting any ruler other than God.

105

This page from the first Vienna Bible Moralisée *shows scenes from the life of King Saul with allegorical parallels. As in the Psalter shown in Pl. 104, the adjacent captions explain the pictures. The manuscript probably dates from the early 1220s* (VIENNA, ÖNB, COD. 2254)

The narrative moves to the top right. It shows the Israelites going down to the camp of the heathen Philistines with iron, which is beaten on the forge into swords and axes for the sons of Israel (I Kings 13:19–20). Below, the miniature draws an interesting contemporary moralizing parallel. It says that as the Israelites went to the land of the heathens to have weapons made, so today wicked students leave the study of the Gospel and go instead to Bologna to study law and the decretals and thus they come away with what will destroy them. This is one of the very rare contemporary and datable references in the *Bible Moralisée*. It alludes, of course, to the students of the Bible at the university of Paris. In 1219, the schools of civil law in Paris were closed, and thenceforth ambitious or worldly students began to travel to the rival schools of Bologna to equip themselves with the dangerous weapons of secular law. It must have been a familiar enough problem to be recognizable to any reader of the *Bible Moralisée*. The miniature shows students abandoning the Gospels on a table and turning with their purses to teachers and a scribe writing law books. The next Bible picture is the third from the top on the left. It illustrates King Saul stepping forwards to encourage his troops, telling them not to eat or drink until the day's battle is done (I Kings 14:24). The image below, in the lower left-hand corner of the page, shows a medieval king and a bishop similarly addressing a group of knights. The caption says that good princes and prelates should encourage Christians not to enjoy the pleasures of the world until they have defeated the devil. The final biblical picture is the third down on the right. It depicts the bloodthirsty battle described in I Kings 14:27–31, with Jonathan licking honeycomb off a rod, thereby disobeying his father's order not to eat until the battle was won. Below, the miniature shows a battle in the contemporary setting of the medieval Crusades. In fact, the captions here refer to the Philistines of the Bible as 'sarazins', the Saracens, a parallel very vivid to Saint Louis, for example, the crusading king who eventually died on the Crusades in 1270. The caption compares the Christians, who totally defeat the enemies of God, with Jonathan, who in this context represents those who ignore the commandments of Jesus Christ and enjoy sweet pleasures instead. The defectors are feasting on the left and apparently gathering up gold coins, spoils of the Crusades.

This page of ancient Bible history is thus filled with references to the contexts in which the manuscript itself was used – the world of ambitious students in Paris, Jews in medieval France, the public duties of kings, and the virtue of the Crusades. That tells us something about the presumed patronage of the manuscript in the court of the kings of France and also about the use of Bible history in the thirteenth century as a justification for contemporary politics. This particular page perhaps has an unusually high 'moralized' content. Other miniatures in the *Bible Moralisée* are more strictly typological, and refer across to similar episodes or parallels in the New Testament. Thus Samuel's acknowledgement of Saul as king (I Kings 10:1) signified Christ's acceptance of Caesar as ruler over the Jews (Matthew 22:21). The scene of David concealed in a cave (I Kings 24:4–5) prefigured Christ enclosed in the womb of the Virgin. David's hunger in the desert of Paran (I Kings 25:1) represented the fasting of Christ in the wilderness (Matthew 4:2). The eventual defeat of Saul by the Philistines (I Kings 31:1–3) signified the killing of the Jews by the Antichrist at the end of the world (Apocalypse 20:9, etc.).

There are no specific references to biblical books or chapters in the *Bible Moralisée*. The summary captions are at best no more than paraphrases. To use the manuscripts at all, one would need to know the Bible text very well, or to have someone well-informed who could explain the captions and their parallels. Perhaps that process of explaining was a function of the books, as the example of Blanche of Castile teaching her son with an illustrated Psalter suggests, and there is no doubt that dramatic images of swashbuckling biblical history would impress themselves on the memory of the person receiving instruction.

The most extreme example of a biblical picture-book constructed with no text at all is the so-called Shah Abbas Bible (New York, Pierpont Morgan Library M. 638, with some leaves elsewhere, Pl. 98). The frustrations of trying to use the manuscript without a text became apparent several times in its long and dramatic history. It is a volume of large but not enormous size, with only 46 leaves, 390 mm by 304 mm (about 15 by 12 inches). It consists entirely of pictures and, like the prototypes in Psalter cycles, the Shah Abbas Bible has Old Testament illustrations from the Creation to the life of King David and no further. It is one of the most beautiful and elegant Gothic manuscripts in existence. The quality and richness of the book suggest that it may well have been commissioned by Saint Louis himself, probably around 1250. Each of its pages comprises between two and four pictures, usually set beneath arches with medieval architectural rooftops above. Backgrounds of each compartment are in blue, red or burnished gold. The pictures comprise dramatic and chivalric scenes from the Bible, many of them concerning conflicts between the Israelites and their enemies. It includes some 35 illustrations of military engagements and battles, filled with knights, horses, banners and the clash of arms. The *Bible Moralisée* relates such Old Testament events to the contemporary Crusades and, if this metaphor was generally known, the Shah Abbas Bible too reflects the theme of Christian knights battling with the Saracens. This is consistent with the assumption that it was made under the court patronage of Saint Louis, king of France.

There survives a story of one illustrated manuscript Bible which concerns Saint Louis. There is no evidence that the tale relates specifically to the Shah Abbas Bible, but it may provide a context for a similar kind of biblical picture

106

In 1253 Louis IX sent Friar William of Rubruck on a mission to Mangu Khan, and he gave him a Bible to show to the Mongol king. This initial shows the delegation setting off on their journey (CAMBRIDGE, CORPUS CHRISTI COLLEGE, MS. 66A)

book. In 1253–4, Louis sent an embassy of Franciscan friars and others to the Mongols in the Far East with the hope of persuading them to join the Crusades against the Muslims. The leader of the party, Friar William of Rubruck, compiled a detailed report for the king (Pl. 106). He mentions that the queen had given him a Psalter and the king had entrusted him with a Bible to display at the Mongol court. He was able to show the Bible twice to Mangu Khan, grandson of Ghengis and brother of Kublai Khan. On the first occasion, the king 'had a good look at it', and at their second audience 'he made a diligent inquiry as to the meaning of the pictures'. It sounds like a book with notable illustrations, not merely a Bible with initials. The chivalric theme of a manuscript like the Shah Abbas Bible would have been suitable on such an embassy. In the event, William of Rubruck reported that he was obliged to leave the queen's Psalter behind as a gift to the Mongol court. He evidently brought the royal picture Bible back to Europe.

By the late thirteenth century, the Shah Abbas Bible was apparently already unusable without captions, or else its owners then no longer required a Bible whose purpose was to instruct and to provoke inquiry. Latin captions were therefore filled in around its margins in a neat italianate hand. The script is consistent with southern Italy or even the crusading kingdom in the Holy Land. Very similar script occurs in a French translation of the Old Testament, written in Acre in 1280–1 (Paris, BNF, ms. nouv. acq. fr. 1404). It is worth noting that William of Rubruck became lector in theology in Acre on his return from the orient.

In the seventeenth century, the Shah Abbas Bible was certainly sent to the East with the express purpose of attracting converts. It was donated in 1604 by the cardinal bishop of Cracow to the pope's mission of Carmelite friars to Shah Abbas the Great, king of Persia 1587–1628, to whom the manuscript was presented in January 1608. The parallel with the story of Mangu Khan is so close that one wonders if some tradition or lost inscription had suggested the

appropriateness of sending this particular 350-year-old illuminated manuscript as a gift. The friars reported that Shah Abbas looked closely at the book, asked about it, and passed it to his chamberlain so that an expert Mullah could insert 'the meaning of the pictures' in Persian captions. This is the very same phrase as was used of Mangu Khan in 1253. The picture titles furnished for Shah Abbas are still there,

exotic oriental writing around so European a book. Even still, the book continued to provoke interest in the subjects of its pictures. It seems to have fallen afterwards into the possession of a Jewish community, perhaps in Egypt. Once again, captions were added, this time in Hebrew around the Persian around the Latin around the margins of a book which had been designed to have no captions at all.

The lack of any detailed text in these mid-thirteenth-century Bible picture cycles is worth emphasizing, for it suggests that those who commissioned or used such books had a very good knowledge of the Bible itself. We must assume the same in regard to stained-glass windows of the thirteenth century, which often depict typological parallels quite as complicated as anything in a *Bible*

Moralisée. The bright little roundels in the glass of the Sainte-Chapelle in Paris, for example, built by Saint Louis in about 1245, soar far above the sight of the viewer. Any brief captions are quite invisible from the floor, and yet the contemporaries of Saint Louis were evidently expected to recognize biblical subjects and their parallels from the images alone.

The relationship between pictures in manuscripts and those of other media can be seen too in a strange little book known as the Eton Roundels (Windsor, Eton College, MS. 177). It is English work of about 1260–70. It comprises twelve pages of pictures looking so like Gothic stained-glass windows that it has been suggested that it might have been a glazier's model book (very unlikely, in fact). Each page has five complete roundels and two half-roundels at the sides. Two pages are from the Old Testament, and ten pages are typological. The subjects are almost identical to those which we know from medieval descriptions were once around the walls of the chapter house of Worcester Cathedral Priory. We cannot know if one copies the other, or whether both depend on some third source. An interesting development is that the captions in the manuscript are quite explicit in identifying the subjects shown and they give full biblical references, including chapter numbers. A reader could look them up. We can take fol. 5v as an example of the Eton Roundels (Pl. 108). In the centre is a roundel of the Three Maries arriving at the Holy Sepulchre on Easter morning to find the Tomb empty. At the upper left is Jonah being cast up out of the mouth of the whale, referring us to Jonah chapter 2. The caption around the edge equates the emergence of Jonah from the whale with the resurrection of Christ from the Tomb. At the upper right is a lion breathing on its cub. This is an unusual subject in a biblical context. The identification of Christ with a lion cub goes back to Genesis 49:9, but the subject here is actually from the Bestiary, the well-known book on animals which was so popular in twelfth- and thirteenth-century England. According to the Bestiary, lion cubs are born dead. After three days, the father lion breathes on the cubs and they come to life. The parallel with the Resurrection is so obvious that an example from natural history has assumed a place among images from Old Testament. At the lower left are two standing figures. One is Job, predicting that in his flesh he will see God his saviour (Job 19:26). The other is Jonah again, saying that God will raise up his life (Jonah 2:7). In the lower right is an empty city guarded by four soldiers, like those who kept night watch over the Sepulchre. The caption equates Christ's empty tomb with the city of Gaza, left empty by the departure of Samson in Judges 16:2–3.

The Eton Roundels are actually bound up with an illustrated Apocalypse, and the two texts have probably been together since they were made. The Apocalypse is one of the strangest books of the Bible. Richly illustrated Apocalypses of various kinds were popular in the middle to late thirteenth century, especially in England. Approximately 80 manuscripts survive, many of them very grand copies. To judge from the evident expense of such books, they were often made for bishops and noble families. One, Oxford, Bodleian Library, MS. Douce 180, was illuminated for Edward I and his wife, Eleanor of Castile, some time before his accession to the throne in 1272. Another, Cambridge, Corpus Christi College, MS. 20, belonged to the Countess of Huntingdon, who gave it to St Augustine's Abbey in Canterbury (Pl. 109). The format of Apocalypses is fairly standard. Most have about a hundred miniatures, taken from Saint John's extraordinarily surrealistic vision of the end of the world. In the hands of a good artist, the subjects lend themselves to dazzling and often terrifying images. In most Apocalypses, the miniatures are in rectangles across the width of the page, with an

109 opposite
The Apocalypse is attributed to Saint John. In the opening miniature of an English Apocalypse the evangelist is shown with Christ at the Last Supper and later being sent in exile to the island of Patmos, where an angel reveals to him a vision of the end of the world (CAMBRIDGE, CORPUS CHRISTI COLLEGE, MS. 20)

accompanying text written below in two columns. There is great variety in these texts, however, both in language and content. About half are in Latin and about half in French (or Anglo-Norman), sometimes in verse. Most give the biblical text, in full or in summary, often citing chapter numbers, and the majority of copies follow this with some version or extract from the commentary on the Apocalypse by the ninth-century monk, Berengaudus of Ferrières. Perhaps we should not regard these as Bible picture books, for they concern only a small part of the Bible, taken in isolation and without cross-references. Nonetheless, they are manuscripts of great beauty.

We can illustrate the Apocalypse by looking at a page from one of the most magnificent of its manuscripts, the so-called Trinity Apocalypse (Cambridge, Trinity College, MS. R.16.2, fol. 14r, Pl. 110). Most of the page is taken up with a large square compartment with pictures on two tiers. On the upper level is a rather fat dragon with a red body and seven heads spewing water out of one of its mouths into a hole in the ground. Beside this, an angel is fitting a pair of wings onto a woman who is then able to fly through the sky. On the lower level, she sits under a tree and is given bread and a chalice by the same angel. To the right, little figures of knights and clerics attack the fat dragon with a wide range of medieval weapons, including a cross-bow, a hatchet and long-sword. The noblewoman in the extreme left-hand corner occurs several times in this manuscript, and she may have been the original patron of the book, possibly Eleanor of Provence, wife of Henry III of England. The whole atmosphere here resembles a romance of chivalry. These are like figures from some adventure of knights and a magic dragon.

The text below brings us right back to the Bible. The first paragraph is a translation of Apocalypse 12:13–17 into Anglo-Norman French. The great dragon of the Apocalypse has just been defeated in battle by Saint Michael and his angels and has been cast down from the heavens onto the earth. It pursues the woman clothed with the sun, whom God had placed in a safe refuge for 1,260 days (Apocalypse 12:6), and it attempts to wash her away with a flood. But an angel gives her the wings of eagles, and the earth swallows up the flood. Therefore the dragon turns instead to fighting the righteous people of the earth. It would not be difficult to interpret this in terms of Christian allegory. The commentary explains that this is Satan thrown down from Heaven, pursuing the Holy Church. The angel is Christ. The wings he brings are the Old and New Testaments, and he nourishes her in the wilderness with his Sacraments. When Satan can no longer attack the Church by persecution, he turns on the multitude. This is not an especially deep interpretation. The text has no intellectual subtleties and none of the fashionable typology of the time.

It is not difficult, however, to understand how the Apocalypse seemed relevant in the thirteenth century. The 1,260 days of refuge were seen as pointing unambiguously to the year 1260 for the imminent end of the world. There was great activity in making Apocalypse manuscripts in the 1250s, as the date came closer. The stability of Europe seemed to be under threat. The Muslims and Mongols were advancing on the eastern front and the Cathars and other heretics were gathering strength in the south-west. In the mid-thirteenth century it was easy to believe that Satan had indeed turned on the Church in preparation for Armageddon. Rather as the *Bibles Moralisées* related biblical events to parallels in the 1220s, so these Apocalypses seemed to be speaking directly to the mid-thirteenth century. In the event, however, the world did not end in 1260, and Apocalypses slipped easily into the realms of romance and of books made for the diversion of aristocrats. Several quite grand Apocalypse manuscripts were left unfinished, as if some of the urgency had been lost, including Paris, BNF, ms. lat. 10474, Oxford, Bodleian Library, MS. Douce 180, and London, BL, Add. MS. 42555. As an immediately practical book, the illustrated Apocalypse was out of date. It hardly survived beyond 1300.

110 opposite

The mid-thirteenth-century Trinity Apocalypse was perhaps made for Eleanor of Provence, queen of Henry III of England. This picture shows the dragon pursuing the woman clothed with the sun and fighting with the righteous people of the earth (CAMBRIDGE, TRINITY COLLEGE, MS. R.16.2)

Puis ke li dragun uit ke il fu iete en tere, il pur
siwi la feme ke enfaunta le masle, e deus ele
de un graunt egle sunt dunes a la feme ke ole uo
last en desert lui, u ole est nurrie par un tens, e par
plusurs tens, e par demi tens, de la fate al serpent.
E la serpente mist hors de sa buche apres la feme
ewe ausi cum un fluine, ke il la feist estre tret del flu
ine, e la tere aida a la feme, e la tere ouera sa buche
e transglura le fluine ke le dragun mist hors de sa
buche. E le dragun curete a tuinte la feme, a la fe
re bataile od les autres de sa semente, ki gardent les
comaundemenz deu, e unt le testmoine ihu.

Puis ke li diable uit ke il aueit pdu graunt mul
titudine des eluz, e enclot de deus les destruies del
quens des reproues, il pursiwi la feme co est seinte
eglise, kar il enuia les empereurs de roume e tute la
multitudine del manuel a pursiwere le poeple deu.
Ple egle poum entendre est. Deus eles sunt deus testa
mens. Deus eles sunt dones a seinte eglise, co sunt deus
testamens, ke ole eschapet le diable, e ke ole munte

al pais celestre ple aprise de eus. Il apele tut pais desert,
si cum nostre seignur dist en le euuangile, kaunt il dist
sai auet lasse nonaunte nof owailes en le desert e auet
ale quere une ke aueit erre. Il apele le hu de seinte eglise
cest pais, si cul dira en le iugement. Les beneis mun
pere ueneis, e receueis le regne ke est aparie auus de
la nesaunce del munde. P un tens, e plusurs tens e
demi tens, le tens de la passiun ihu est, treske a la fin
del munde est signifie. Le fluine de ewe sunt charneus
desirs. Kaunt li diable ueit ke seinte eglise ne pot estre
abatue par psecutiuns, mes crestre e estre fermee, il
enuei la multitudine de charneus desirs, ke il la sa
ce estre trete par eus. Nus poum entendre les reprouel
ple tere, ki furent receuurs des charneus desirs. Enuis po
um entendre par meimes la tere est, u pla buche de la tere n
poi entedre la pouste de cist. La tere aida a la feme co est
cist, seinte eglise. Il ouerr le sen de sarmsencor de, e sa pou
re esteint del tur enuir le fluine de uices. Les autres de la
semence de seinte eglise sunt les eluz, ki sunt a nestre en la
fin del munde, od les queus autreist se combatera.

By that time, Bible picture books were becoming more intellectual, and they began to move slowly down the social scale from kings and prelates to the lower nobility and monks. The captions and texts became fuller, and explained the Bible stories more graphically. There is no reason to suppose that owners of manuscripts knew their Bibles less well than they had in the 1240s. On the contrary, those little portable Bibles were very widely available by the late thirteenth century, and the precise citation of biblical passages suggests that readers would expect to look up the references in their own Bibles. Quotations from the Bible, whether in words or in pictures, cite their sources. Pictures without captions become increasingly rare. Cycles of untitled full-page biblical miniatures began to disappear from Psalters. One of the final great illustrated Psalters is the Peterborough Psalter in Brussels, completed sometime before 1318 (Bibliothèque Royale, mss. 9961–2). On groups of leaves interspersed throughout the Psalms are 109 typological miniatures, up to four to a page, of which 71 are from the Old Testament and 38 are their New Testament parallels. A new development in the history of Psalters is that every miniature in this manuscript has quite detailed captions and verses explaining the typology. That would not have been considered necessary a century earlier.

A major text of the early fourteenth century was the *Biblia Pauperum*. The name is very misleading, for it implies that this was simply a book for poor people, or at best for beginners or children. The text is especially well-known now from the crudely printed fifteenth-century blockbook editions, which fascinated collectors in the nineteenth century, hoping that these were older than the Gutenberg Bible. The general naïvety of primitive blockbook printing strengthens the impression that the *Biblia Pauperum* must be some kind of amateur text. Nothing could be further from reality. It is one of the most intellectually sophisticated of medieval biblical commentaries, combining text and image to a remarkable degree. It survives in over 80 manuscripts, about the same number as Apocalypses, but over a much wider period and geographical span. There are manuscripts of the *Biblia Pauperum* from Germany, France, Italy, England and elsewhere. Only a few of these have no illustrations, and it is in an unillustrated manuscript of 1398 that we first encounter the title 'Byblia pauperum' in a colophon (Munich, Clm. 12717). Perhaps a copy without pictures could have been a poor man's copy, although most manuscripts of the *Biblia Pauperum* were undoubtedly costly and precious.

The author of the *Biblia Pauperum* has never been satisfactorily identified. The elaborately constructed theology seems to point to thirteenth-century France, perhaps to a Dominican house. The earliest surviving manuscripts of the *Biblia Pauperum* are all German or Austrian, from around 1300. The text circulated very widely in central Europe in the first half of the fourteenth century. When the medieval owners can be identified, most were monasteries rather than private individuals. There are extant copies which belonged to the abbeys of Benedictbeuren, St Florian, Mallersdorf, Tegernsee, Wessobrunn, the Dominicans in

Regensburg, St Peter's in Erfurt, and so on. It might be that copies from secure monastic libraries are simply those that happened to survive, and perhaps there were as many or more which were privately owned and were used until they fell apart. A good many copies are attested only by fragments, including the oldest, a group of eight leaves made probably in Regensburg, *c.*1300 (Munich, Clm. 23425).

In its standard form, the *Biblia Pauperum* consists of 40 elaborate pictures. These are either arranged two to a page, one above the other, or, in the fifteenth century, as 20 double openings, with a full-page picture on each side. Each design shows two scenes from the Old Testament, mostly (though not exclusively) from the Pentateuch or the Books of Kings, like Psalter miniatures. Captions often record the names of the characters above their heads. Long paraphrases from the Bible tell the stories, giving the appropriate biblical reference and explaining their symbolic parallels. Running vertically through the middle of these Old Testament pictures are scenes from the life of Christ and the Virgin Mary. These begin with the Annunciation and include the infancy and ministry of Christ, with his Passion and Resurrection, the Ascension, Pentecost, the Coronation of the Virgin and, finally, the Last Judgement and the admission of good souls into Paradise. Around the central pictures are four little figures from the Old Testament again, usually King David and three prophets, each holding a quotation from a Psalm or other text which that author had written. As before, references to the Bible are given in full. In the spaces between all these pictures and captions are strange cryptic verses, as obscure or as ambiguous as horoscopes. Each part of each design relates to others. The prophecies refer to the scenes which are being fulfilled in the central pictures. Events and actions of the Old Testament are paralleled by those of the New. Spiritual themes link all images together, often at several levels of interpretation. Opposites are neatly composed and balanced. Pictures are constructed to form visual echoes across the pages. The text includes sacred puns and word play. Even across pairs of compositions there is a common theme, each linked in some way to the previous composition and in some different way to the one which follows. The text alone is not sufficient to comprehend the extent of the comparisons and contrasts across the breadth of the Scriptures, and so biblical sources and their chapter numbers are recorded. This cannot have been a book which was in any way a substitute for the Bible itself. On the contrary, the reader would need access to one of the new Bibles, divided into chapters, in order to study each page of text.

Once more, let us take a single example of an image from the *Biblia Pauperum* to show, even briefly, the complexity of the subject (Pl. 111). The fourteenth composition in the series shows in the centre of the page the Entry of Christ into Jerusalem, on a donkey, watched by a crowd of people (Matthew 21: 8–11). On the left, David enters Jerusalem with the head of Goliath, to the cheers of women (I Kings 18:6, I Samuel in a modern Bible). On the right, Elisha enters Jericho,

heralded by young boys (IV Kings 2:15, II Kings in a modern Bible). Christ is
both king and prophet, David and Elisha. Jerusalem is a symbol of Heaven; the
crowd accompanying Christ is not just women or boys, but all people. Jerusalem
is also the Christian Church: it receives Christ as king, but will kill him. David
here quotes from Psalm 149:2 here, 'Let the children of Syon rejoice in their king';
Solomon cites his own Song of Songs 3:11, exhorting the daughters of Syon to
see their king with a golden diadem. Christ, the king of kings, however, is as a
pauper, riding bare-headed on a donkey. Isaiah appears with Zechariah, with

quotations from Isaiah 62:11 and Zechariah 9:9, on the rejoicing of Syon when their king comes, humble and on a donkey. This animal had first appeared in the *Biblia Pauperum* carrying Christ as a baby into Egypt to escape death from Herod; now it carries him into Jerusalem where he will be crucified by the Jews. All four prophecies refer to the children of Syon, who are literally the Jews. The verse across the page states that the hymn of the good Jews praises Christ. Syon, however, also denotes the Church; Christians praise Christ as king. This adds a liturgical level to the image. The symbolism is infinite, and we have hardly begun.

To judge from the early manuscripts of the *Biblia Pauperum*, the focus was originally on the Old Testament pictures and prophecies of the text. These were painted in large format and filled most of the pages. The New Testament pictures are in small roundels, like the *Bible Moralisée* and similar thirteenth-century books, and appear almost as if they were superimposed in the centre of the pages. The figures are much smaller in scale. In some manuscripts they appear like discs connected to a ribbon which runs from one page to the next. The same convention was used in medieval family trees, and in the illustrated *Genealogia Vitae Christi* of Peter of Poitiers (Pl. 112). The chain of the life of Christ running through the Old Testament is the visual theme of the *Biblia Pauperum*.

In later manuscripts of the text, the pictures from the New Testament are increased in relative size, and they take their central place in the arrangement of the pages. From the layout of the woodcut editions (Pl. 114), one might assume at first glance that the text was a pictorial life of Christ and the Virgin Mary, supplemented by prophecies. It is a subtle shift but an interesting one. From the thirteenth century onwards, the cult of the Virgin Mary assumed an ever greater importance. This was exemplified most famously by the popularity of Books of Hours, the most widely circulated book of the fifteenth century. A Book of

111 opposite

Many copies of the Biblia Pauperum *were made in Germany and Austria in the first half of the fourteenth century. This page shows the symbolism associated with the Entry into Jerusalem and the Last Supper* (MUNICH, BAYERISCHE STAATSBIBLIOTHEK, CLM. 4523)

112

The Genealogia Vitae Christi *of Peter of Poitiers links major figures of the Old Testament with their descendants in the New and relates them, by patterns of interconnecting branches, with people in secular history, such as Julius Caesar, shown here* (CAMBRIDGE, CORPUS CHRISTI COLLEGE, MS. 83)

Hours was a religious text for recitation by the laity. Its principal component
was the Hours of the Virgin Mary, a collection of devotions to be read in private
at each of the eight canonical 'hours' of the day, from Matins to Compline
(Pl. 113). A good part of the Hours of the Virgin consists of Psalms and readings
from the book of Job, the Song of Songs and other parts of the Old Testament. Its
well-known cycles of pictures, however, usually follow the life of the Virgin Mary
from the Annunciation to her coronation in Heaven and the Passion of Christ
from the Betrayal to the Entombment. Even by stretching the definition, we
cannot define the Book of Hours as a Bible picture book, although it contains
pictures which are mostly of biblical subjects. It is worth noting, however, that
the subjects of the miniatures in Books of Hours correspond with almost identical sequences in the *Biblia Pauperum*. Both texts were extremely widely known
in the late Middle Ages. Both were presumably used for devotional contempla-
tion. A major function of the pictures in the *Biblia Pauperum* must have been to
help the reader to memorize the text and to conjure the pages in his or her mind
when the book itself was no longer present. Doubtless, then, the miniatures in
the same reader's Book of Hours would trigger the recollection on typological
knowledge learned from the *Biblia Pauperum*. This introduces us to a function of
art which is profoundly medieval in spirit.

The original purpose of the *Biblia Pauperum* is still obscure. It was primarily
for those who knew their Bible well. It would certainly have been useful in

writing sermons, or in marshalling arguments against heresy. The Cathars and other religious protestors, condemned by the Church as heretical fanatics, emphasized the Gospels to the exclusion of the rest of Scripture. The *Biblia Pauperum* is reassuringly comprehensive in reasserting the value of the Old Testament and indeed it emphasizes its authenticity by arguing backwards from the Gospel story. Used in conjunction with a Bible, the *Biblia Pauperum* provides a virtual concordance or index of orthodox medieval theology.

The *Biblia Pauperum* is often associated or even confused with a somewhat similar text, the *Speculum Humanae Salvationis*. Its title, 'the mirror of human salvation', promises rather more than it actually delivers. Like the *Biblia Pauperum*, it is divided into 40 compositions or, as the text calls them, 'chapters'. In the best copies, each of these has four illustrations, usually spread across the upper half of each double opening in the manuscript, making a total of 160 pictures. It was even more widely circulated than the *Biblia Pauperum* and over 200 manuscripts have been recorded, many of them fifteenth-century. Several manuscripts assert that the text was composed in 1324, which is credible, and the author may have been Ludolf of Saxony (d.1378), at that time a Carthusian monk in Strassburg. Unlike the *Biblia Pauperum*, the *Speculum* has pictures from religious legend as well as from the Bible itself. The text is in rhyming verse. This, like the use of pictures, is a mnemonic device to help the reader to memorize the text by heart. It was written in Latin, but was later translated into German, Dutch, Middle English, French and even Czech. The pictures stand above columns of text, without the elaborate mixing of words and images which is so distinctive of the *Biblia Pauperum*. Each column alternates between a picture from the New Testament (or the legends associated with the Virgin Mary) and its Old Testament parallel. Like the *Bible Moralisée*, each scene has a

113 opposite
The illustrations in Books of Hours, like those of the Biblia Pauperum, *follow scenes in the life of the Virgin and the Passion of Christ. This, the standard picture for Sext, shows the Magi and the shepherds coming to worship the new-born Christ in Bethlehem* (LONDON, VICTORIA AND ALBERT MUSEUM, SALTING COLLECTION NO. 1222)

114
The Biblia Pauperum *was printed several times as a block-book in the Rhineland and the Netherlands. This edition probably dates from c.1465* (BRITISH LIBRARY)

single pair. Unlike the *Bible Moralisée*, the New Testament picture comes first. The long text explains the typology in rather long-winded style. It is certainly a book with very many Bible pictures but it is not strictly a Bible picture book. It is quite usable with no pictures at all, and something over half its surviving manuscripts are unillustrated. The *Speculum Humanae Salvationis*, therefore, falls slightly outside our central theme.

The pictures from the *Biblia Pauperum* and from illustrated manuscripts of the *Speculum* had a huge influence in the spread of biblical imagery across Europe. They were copied from one manuscript to another, and then from these manuscripts into other contexts. Single pictures reappear with the same compositions adapted into manuscripts of many kinds. We find their images repeated in other media. They reappear in the late medieval stained-glass windows of King's College chapel, Cambridge. Elements of the pictures were often repeated in wall paintings, misericords, ivories and tapestries, for example, and they are echoed in the settings and themes of medieval religious drama. It is a point worth noting that while complete Bible manuscripts themselves were seldom illustrated, images from Bible picture books were everywhere.

The final manifestation of biblical pictures brings us to a medium which would have been inconceivable when the *Bible Moralisée* and the Shah Abbas Bible were copied and illuminated. The illustrated Apocalypse, the *Biblia Pauperum* and the *Speculum Humanae Salvationis* were all revived or preserved in the mid-fifteenth century as printed blockbooks (Pls. 114–15). These are fascinating and enigmatic books, which fall somewhere between manuscripts and early printing. They are texts reproduced by xylography, the technique of printing a text from a wood block on which all the text and associated pictures had been carved in reverse. It differs from movable type, in that each entire page is stamped from a single unit. The Apocalypse was the first of the biblical texts reproduced in the form of a blockbook, probably printed in the Netherlands in the early 1450s. Block-books are notoriously difficult to date and localize, and whether the oldest examples first appeared before or after the Gutenberg Bible is a matter of hotly debated honour among historians of book production. Within a year or so either way, they were contemporaneous. The majority of blockbooks were apparently produced in the Netherlands and the Rhineland during the third quarter of the fifteenth century. They are all on paper, not parchment. Compared with printing from metal type, the ink usually looks thin and brown. The technical difficulty of carving every composition by hand confers a crude and homely flavour to the pages of blockbooks. Because of the deep indentations which the block makes into the paper, a blockbook can usually only be printed on one side of a sheet. A bound blockbook therefore, by coincidence, resembles the *Bible Moralisée* and the Shah Abbas Bible, in that every second opening is blank.

In fact, blockbooks take us back to several features of thirteenth-century picture Bibles. The blockbook Apocalypse is based directly on the long-obsolete

115

The illustrated Apocalypse made an unexpected revival as a printed blockbook in the third quarter of the fifteenth century (PRIVATE COLLECTION)

Anglo-Norman tradition which was so popular when the end of the world was expected in 1260. It must have seemed very archaic by the fifteenth century. There were several versions of the block-book *Biblia Pauperum*, also a two-hundred-year-old text. It became the most widely circulated of the blockbooks. Other biblical texts similarly reproduced included the *Cantica Canticorum*, an emblematic commentary on the Song of Songs, and an action-filled picture text called the *Historia David*. This is an illustrated life of King David abridged from the Books of Kings. This reverts to the subjects in early Psalter cycles and to the theme of thirteenth-century Bible history books, like the Shah Abbas Bible.

Most blockbooks are slim publications, with no more than about 50 leaves. Probably they were originally intended to be collected together and bound up into single multiple volumes, so that the owners could assemble their own picture books with different combinations of biblical texts. Occasionally they survive with several blockbook components all bound together in their original bindings. Other blockbook texts extend beyond biblical themes towards popular magic and the occult. There are blockbooks on palmistry, the Antichrist and on the art of dying. In this rather unsettling context, the old Bible picture texts enjoyed a sudden and unexpected blossoming in the third quarter of the fifteenth century. By about 1480 they had disappeared. Northern Europe on the brink of the Reformation had no time for thirteenth-century typology.

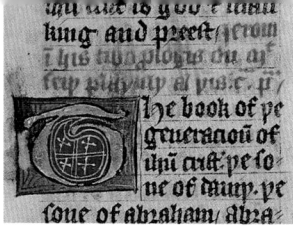

7 | English Wycliffite Bibles

IN THE FOURTEENTH and fifteenth centuries, the Bible continued to be copied and used in Latin. Most surviving Bibles of the late Middle Ages conform to the standard Latin text and the arrangement of books devised in thirteenth-century Paris. Portions of the text were sometimes translated into everyday languages, such as French or German, but generally such versions attracted little attention from readers and were not widely copied. Most people, if they had been taught to read at all, seemed content to use the Bible in Latin. The supreme exception to this was in England. Wycliffite translations are probably the most notorious Bibles of the late Middle Ages. Even now, Wycliffite Bibles enjoy an extraordinary status. Over hundreds of years they have acquired a charisma and aura of sanctity, bordering on relic-veneration, which is unique among Bible manuscripts of the Middle Ages. Wycliffite Bibles are translations of all or parts of the Scriptures into the English language. The text was prepared in two principal stages in the late fourteenth century by a group of Oxford academics associated with the controversial theologian, John Wycliffe (c.1330–84). For a short period, the translations were benignly tolerated by the establishment. By around 1400, they were strongly suspected of being heretical. In 1407–9, the Wycliffite translations of the Bible were outlawed by the archbishop of Canterbury and, as so often happens when books are banned, they took on a furtive glamour. For the next 125 years, it was illegal to make or own any Wycliffite Bible in England without special licence, and anyone caught in possession of a copy could in theory be tried for heresy and burnt to death. Many people found using Bibles in English were indeed executed, often with great cruelty. After the Reformation of the sixteenth century, the archaic Wycliffite Bibles became in retrospect symbols for the right of the common man and woman to read the Bible in their own language.

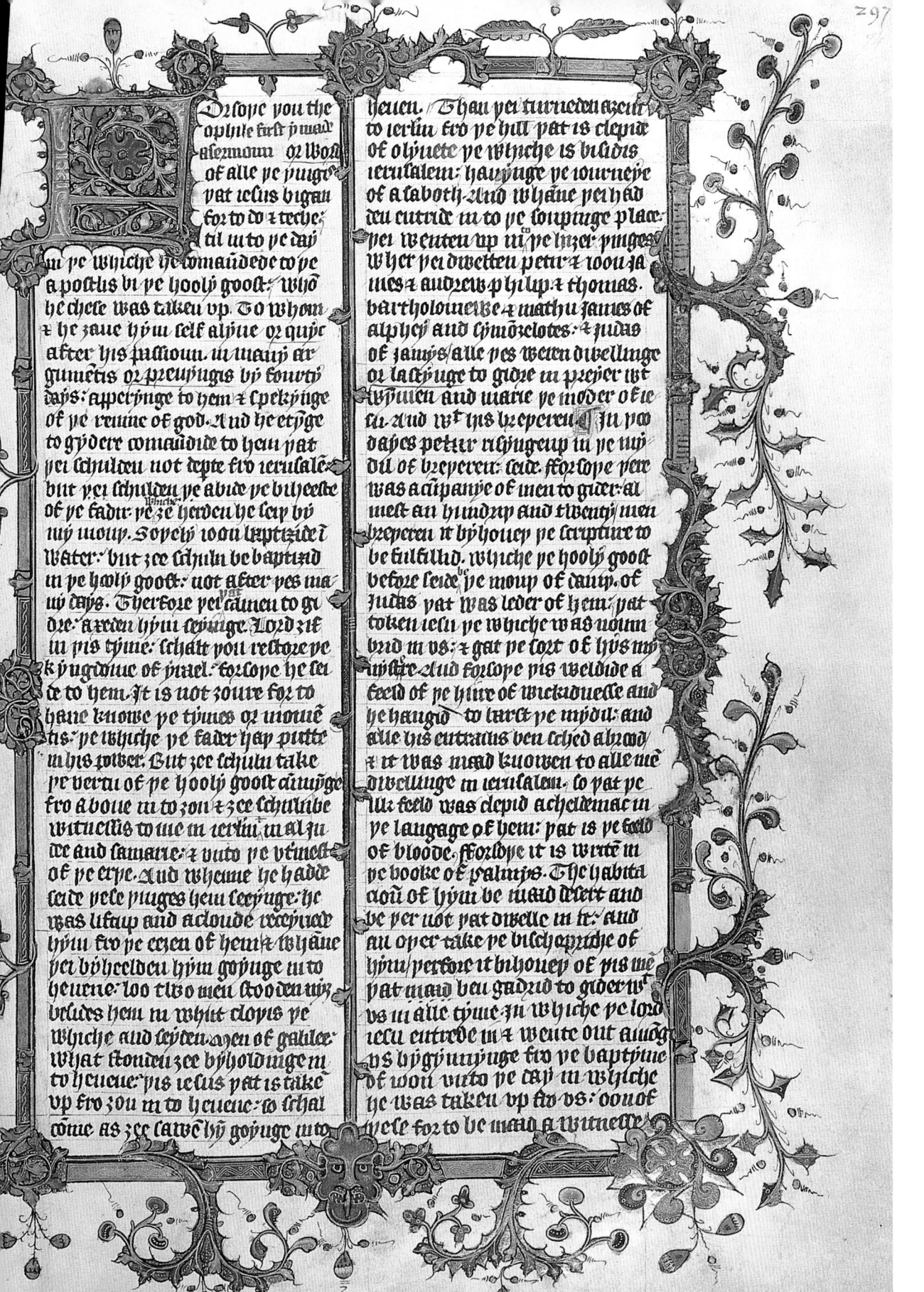

Or sope you the
opistle first þ maid
a sermoun or worst
of alle þe þingis
þat Iesus bigan
for to do ⁊ teche:
til into þe day
in þe whiche he comaundede to þe
apostlis bi þe hooly goost: who
he chese was taken up. To whom
⁊ he ʒaue hym self alyue or quyc
after his passioun in many ar
gumentis or preuyngis by fourty
days: apperinge to hem ⁊ spekynge
of þe reume of god. And he etynge
to gydere comaundide to hem þat
þei schulden not depte fro ierusalem
but þei schulden þe abide þe biheeste
of þe fadir þe ʒe herden he seiþ by
my mouþ. Sopely Ioon baptizide i
water: but ʒee schuln be baptized
in þe hooly goost: not after þes ma
ny days. Therfore þei camen to gi
dre: axeden hym seyinge. Lord ʒif
in þis tyme: schalt þou restore þe
kyngdome of israel. forsope he sei
de to hem. It is not ʒoure for to
haue knowe þe tymes or momen
tis: þe whiche þe fadir haþ putte
in his power. But ʒee schuln take
þe vertu of þe hooly goost cumynge
fro aboue in to ʒou ⁊ ʒee schulnbe
witnessis to me in ierlm in al iu
de and samarie: ⁊ vnto þe vtmest
of þe erþe. And whanne he hadde
seide þese þingis hem seyynge: he
was lifup and a cloude receyued
hym fro þe eʒen of hem ⁊ whanne
þei byheelden hym goþinge in to
heuene: loo two men stoden niʒ
beside hem in whiit cloþis þe
whiche and seyden aʒen of galilee:
what stonden ʒee byholdinge in
to heuene: þis iesus þat is take
up fro ʒou in to heuene: so schal
come as ʒee sawe hym goþinge in to

heuen. Than þei turneden aʒein
to ierlm fro þe hill þat is clepid
of olyuete þe whiche is bisidis
ierusalem: hauyinge þe iourneye
of a saboth. And whane þei had
den entride in to þe soupinge place
þei wenten up in þe hiʒer þingis
Wher þei dwelten petir ⁊ ioon ia
mes ⁊ andrew philip ⁊ thomas
bartholomewe ⁊ mathu iames of
alphey and symon zelotes: ⁊ iudas
of iamys alle þes weren dwellinge
or lastynge to gidre in preyer wt
wymmen and marie þe moder of ie
su and wt his breþeren. In þo
dayes petir risyngeup in þe myd
dil of breþeren: seide. ffor sope þere
was a cumpanye of men to gider: al
mest an hundrip and twenti men
breþeren it byhoueþ þe scripture to
be fulfillid. whiche þe hooly goost
before seide: þe mouþ of dauiþ: of
iudas þat was leder of hem: þat
token iesu þe whiche was noumn
brid in vs: ⁊ gat þe sort of þis my
nystre. And forsope þis weldide a
feeld of þe hyre of wickidnesse and
he hangid to brast þe mydil: and
alle his entrailis ben sched abrood
⁊ it was maad knowen to alle men
dwellinge in ierusalem. so þat þe
ilk feeld was clepid acheldemac in
þe langage of hem: þat is þe feeld
of bloode. fforsoþe it is write in
þe booke of psalmys. The habita
cioun of hym be maad deserte and
be þer not þat dwelle in it: and
an oþer take þe bischopriche of
hym. þerfore it bihoueþ of þis men
þat maad ben gadrid to gidre wt
vs in alle tyme: in whiche þe lord
iesu entride in ⁊ wente out amonge
vs by gynnynge fro þe baptyme
of ioon vnto þe day in whiche
he was taken up fro vs: oon of
þese for to be maad a witnesse

Despite this, medieval Wycliffite Bibles are not especially rare, even now. Something like 250 copies have been recorded, far more than any other text in the Middle English language. Compare this with about 180 extant copies of the next most common text, the so-called Brut chronicle of England, or 64 copies and fragments of Chaucer's *Canterbury Tales*, or single copies only of texts as famous as the *Book of Margery Kempe* or Malory's *Morte d'Arthur*. Furthermore, Wycliffite Bibles are often handsomely written, usually on parchment, and frequently illuminated. It seems at first difficult to equate such multiplicity and opulence with an illegal and underground text, furtively copied for simple God-fearing labourers who used it in secret.

John Wycliffe was primarily an Oxford University theologian and philosopher. He was a fellow of Merton College in 1356, was for a short period Master of Balliol College, and lived mostly at Queen's College from 1363 until the early 1380s (Pl. 117). He gave lectures in English as well as Latin. Rejecting the extravagant metaphysics of medieval university teaching, Wycliffe returned to the text of the Bible as a direct guide to religion and human government. According to his reading of the text, authority in religious matters should derive from spiritual grace rather than from any human appointment. Therefore he challenged the automatic right of the medieval Church to legislate in the affairs of the world, and he maintained that all people were answerable solely to God and not necessarily to any intermediate authority, whether appointed by Church or state. This was an astonishing claim from a university teacher and a priest. It

116 previous page
A great two-volume Wycliffite Bible was made for Thomas of Woodstock (1355–97), son of Edward III, before possession of such books became a capital offence
(LONDON, BL, EGERTON MS. 618)

117
Queen's College in Oxford was founded in 1341 and became a place of study for John Wycliffe and his followers in the later fourteenth century. The medieval buildings are shown on the left in this engraving by David Loggan of 1675

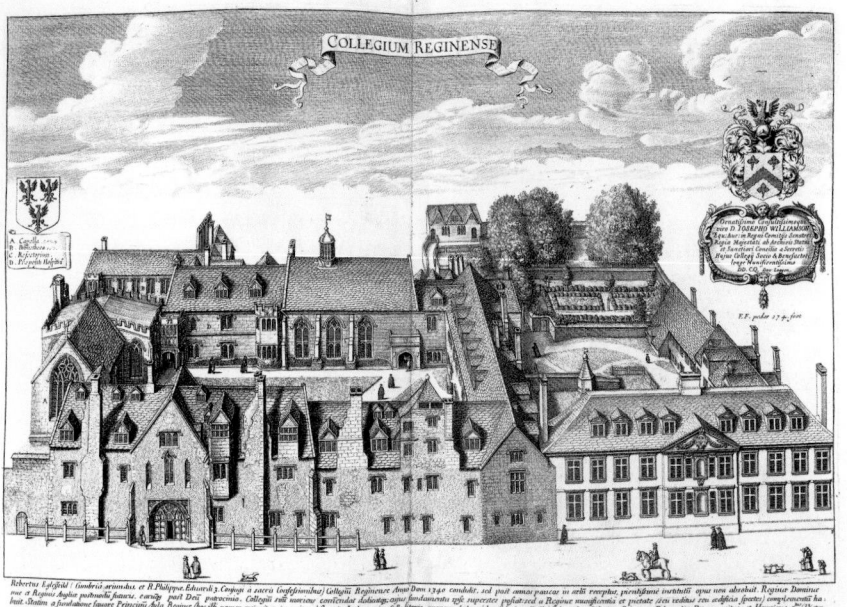

was interpreted as a call to revolution, or anarchy. By the 1370s, Wycliffe's views were arousing serious alarm among the authorities, but he began to draw around him in Oxford a small group of zealous followers, including Nicholas Hereford, Philip Repington and John Purvey. In 1382, citing the Bible, he questioned the Church's doctrine that the bread and wine at the Communion were literally transformed during the Mass into the actual body and blood of Christ. That was too much. On 21 May that year, the archbishop of Canterbury summoned a council or synod at the Blackfriars convent in London to condemn 24 points of Wycliffe's teaching as heretical. An earthquake occurred during the meeting of the council, seen afterwards by the Wycliffite followers as a supernatural portent. They called it the 'Earthquake Synod'. After being judged guilty, John Wycliffe himself withdrew from Oxford to the village of Lutterworth in Leicestershire (where he had technically been rector since 1374) and died there two years later.

118

There are no contemporary portraits of Wycliffe. This is an engraving made in 1649

The possibility of putting the text of the Bible into the English language was certainly central and logical in Wycliffe's teaching. Linguistically, England was unusual among the countries of medieval Europe, in that it used three languages. These were Latin, French and English. Their hierarchy was vertical, not geographical. As elsewhere, Latin was the language of literacy and education, and the Latin Bible would have been as clearly understood by clerics and scholars in England, for example, as anywhere in continental Europe. For everyday speech, however, there were two further languages. The aristocracy mostly still used French, or the English dialect of it known as Anglo-Norman. The peasants and commercial tradesmen, however, spoke Middle English. The illustrated Apocalypses of the thirteenth century were in Anglo-Norman and their orthodoxy was never doubted, since they could only be read by the nobility and upper ranks of society. In France, translations of books of the Bible into French were quite acceptable, for they were rapidly adopted and endorsed by the court as texts for aristocratic reading. If Wycliffe had rendered the Bible into French, it would never have been controversial.

By the late fourteenth century, however, Anglo-Norman was already in decline. John Wycliffe was almost contemporary with Geoffrey Chaucer (d.1400) and John Gower (d.1408), whose writings in Middle English first lifted the language into literary respectability. In the 1380s, however, it had not yet transcended the social barriers. By questioning the innate authority of the ruling establishment, Wycliffe was already suspected of stirring revolution. This was a period of great social unrest in England. It culminated in the Peasants' Revolt of 1381, when mobs of frustrated labourers marched on London. The instigators invoked the politics of Wycliffe in justification. English was the language of peasants. In proposing that the Bible should be translated, therefore, Wycliffe was touching on issues of class prejudice which still confound society in England but which were then of exceptional sensitivity.

The term 'Wycliffite Bible' is often used. Others call it the 'Lollard Bible', taking its name from the movement of religious dissent which followed from the teaching of Wycliffe. The word 'Lollard' is said to derive from the Dutch for a person who mumbles. The Lollards were the adherents of the radical theology of Wycliffe, famous in their time (apparently) for their constant mumbling of phrases of Scripture in support of their campaign. There is no agreement among historians as to whether or not Wycliffe himself had an active part in translating the Bible. There is quite good evidence that he was credited with the translation in the late Middle Ages, but we must balance two historical trends. One is the medieval passion for dogmatically linking texts with the names of famous authors. The other is the modern mania for downgrading the personal achievements of popular heroes of the past. It seems certain that the first version of the Bible translation of the 1380s was undertaken at very least in Wycliffe's immediate circle in Oxford and with his endorsement.

There are two extremely early and famous manuscripts of the Wycliffite translation of the Old Testament into English. Both of these, by different routes, are now in the Bodleian Library in Oxford. They are large and heavy volumes, one bound in green velvet and one in red. The first is MS. Bodley 959. This is a rough manuscript, full of corrections and alterations. The second is MS. Douce 369, a tidier book but no great beauty. For many years, it was supposed that Bodley 959 was actually Wycliffe's autograph manuscript. Douce 369 was certainly copied directly from it, for its text takes account of some of the many textual improvements of its model but not all of them, and so the exemplar was still being improved after a clean copy had been taken.

It will be necessary to consider these two books very closely, for they will bring us eventually to an important conclusion. Bodley 959 follows the order of the Paris Bible as far as the apocryphal book of Baruch among the major prophets and it suddenly breaks off at the foot of the recto of its last leaf, fol. 332r, in the middle of a sentence in Baruch 3:19–20, '… on hem risen / the yunge' (Pl. 119). The verso of that leaf is blank. This is such a strange place to stop that it has been romantically suggested that Wycliffe and his disciples were actually translating this very verse when the summons arrived from the Blackfriars Synod in May 1382, and that they leapt from their task in mid-sentence. In fact, the book cannot be in Wycliffe's hand, or not entirely, for it is the work of at least four scribes, and meticulous examination of scribal errors has led its editors to the conclusion that it was copied (hastily, no doubt) from a text already in English. Therefore they were not translating but transcribing when they reached Baruch 3:20 and suddenly stopped.

Now compare Douce 369. It is made up of two manuscripts bound together, and we are concerned only with the first part, fols. 1–250, of the late fourteenth century. Remarkably, it too goes precisely as far as Baruch 3:20 and then stops at the very same word '… yunge', towards the top of the second column on fol. 250r (Pl. 120). Then a different hand has added a line in Latin, *Explicit translacom' Nicholay de herford*, 'Here ends the rendering of Nicholas of Hereford'. The rest of the page is blank. It shows that when this fair copy was transcribed from Bodley 959, the ultimate original was no longer present, for the Douce copyist could not add a single word beyond his exemplar. He simply stops writing and records that the translator up to this point was Nicholas Hereford, Wycliffe's disciple and colleague from Queen's College, Oxford.

The most unexpected feature of Douce 369, which seems not to have been noticed until now, is that the manuscript itself is not actually

120

A copy of MS. Bodley 959 was made soon afterwards, and breaks off at exactly the same verse, marked here with the name of Nicholas Hereford. The manuscript was probably made in Rome, during the imprisonment of Nicholas there, 1382–5
(OXFORD, BODLEIAN LIBRARY, MS. DOUCE 369)

English, but is almost certainly Italian in origin. Its parchment is smooth and shiny on the flesh side and flecked brown on the hair side, in the manner of southern Europe. The painted and penwork initials are continental, with the rather orange red pigment and blue penwork with a turquoise tinge, which are both characteristic of Italy. The design of the ornament is entirely Italian, not of great quality, and is consistent with the late fourteenth century. Only the language is English: every other feature of the book points to Italy. It comes as a surprise to learn that one of the primary manuscripts of the most influential Middle English text was apparently not made in England at all.

There is only one easy explanation, so disarmingly simple that it is probably right. Nicholas Hereford was indicted by the Blackfriars Synod in May 1382 and was excommunicated for heresy on 1 July. Instead of attempting to answer the charges in London, he appealed to the pope and set off for Rome, doubtless with a dossier of quickly assembled manuscripts in order to vindicate the orthodoxy of the Oxford Wycliffites. He must have taken Bodley 959 with him. He may even have had it copied rapidly that summer for that very purpose. It would be needed to demonstrate to Urban VI that the primitive translation was extremely literal and exact, precisely from the Vulgate. Perhaps he even deliberately stopped in the opening pages of Baruch. Consider this: the order and selection of the biblical books in Bodley 959 corresponds exactly that of the thirteenth-century Paris Bible, sanctioned by the Dominicans, papal champions in the war on heresy. Bodley 959 furnishes all proof Nicholas Hereford would have needed. Once his Bible located Chronicles in the right place after Kings (and it does), and once the major prophets were put in the new Paris sequence following the books of Solomon (and they are), and once these prophets can be shown to include the much-disputed Baruch immediately after Jeremiah (where it appears), then the whole of the rest of the Bible automatically falls into order. One would, in theory, only need to transcribe a manuscript of the Old Testament as far as the beginning of Baruch, in order to prove that the text was the orthodox version sanctioned by Paris. Anything less would have been suspect; anything more would have been superfluous.

The pope was unconvinced. Nicholas Hereford was sent to prison in Rome and he remained incarcerated, evidently in relatively mild conditions, until his release by papal amnesty, almost three years later, probably in July 1385. During that time, he must have had Douce 369 copied. That explains its Italian parchment and decoration. It is the work of three scribes. Sir Frederic Madden claimed in 1850 that the third hand was that of the final scribe of Bodley 959, and this assertion has never been challenged. If this is true, then the scribe can only be Hereford himself. In fact, the hands are probably not identical. The added colophon, naming Nicholas Hereford, may be by the last scribe of Bodley 959 and is almost certainly by the hand who added corrections and chapter numbers into the Douce book. That seems to point to Hereford. There was, in fact, a long tradition of copying manuscripts in Italian prisons, especially debtors' prisons, where it was a common way of raising money. The three scribes of Douce 369 may be any companions or staff with whom Hereford had travelled, or his fellow inmates. The decorated initials, at least, were added by an Italian.

We therefore now have a probable date for the translation of the Bible into English, much of which was ready in draft form by the time Nicholas Hereford left England in the late summer of 1382. His claim to be the translator is made more secure by the likelihood that the colophon is autograph. He returned to England in 1385, with both copies. From that moment, then, his text could be married up with the work of other translators for the second half of the Bible and released for copying by professional scribes. An early transcript must be Cambridge University Library, MS. Ee.1.10, which has a note inserted exactly at Baruch 3:19–20, 'Here endith the translacioun of N, and now bigynneth the translacioun of J & of othere men' (Pl. 121). This seems to confirm the accepted involvement of Nicholas Hereford in the part which he took to Rome, and it accepts that the residue was a collaboration between several translators, perhaps during Hereford's absence. 'J' may be John Wycliffe, who died in 1384, or his secretary at Lutterworth, John Purvey. A professional 'parchemyner', William Smith, who was charged with heresy in Leicester in 1392, claimed to have been copying Bibles in English for eight years. This too would take us back to the mid-1380s, when Nicholas Hereford returned from Rome.

For a brief period, it looked as though this first Wycliffite translation might have received the endorsement of the English royal family. If that had happened, its future patronage could have been quite different. Wycliffe himself had served on diplomatic embassies for John of Gaunt (1340–99), fourth son of Edward III, an association which may have saved his life at the time of the Blackfriars Synod. A magnificent two-volume Wycliffite Bible belonged to John of Gaunt's youngest brother, Thomas of Woodstock (1355–97). It is now London, BL, Egerton MSS. 617–18. It is written in two columns with illuminated bar borders surrounding the opening of every book (Pl. 116). The royal duke's arms are on the first page. A second large and noble copy of the Wycliffite Old Testament belonged to John of Gaunt's grandson, Thomas of Lancaster (c.1388–1421), brother of Henry V. It is now Wolfenbüttel, Herzog-

121

After the return of Nicholas Hereford to England, further copies were made, including this, which, at Baruch 3:20, towards the lower right, records the end of N's translation and the beginning of J's (CAMBRIDGE, UNIVERSITY LIBRARY, MS. EE.1.10)

August-Bibliothek, Cod. Guelf. Aug.A.2, illuminated with the arms and motto of Thomas, evidently before he was created duke of Clarence in 1412 (Pl. 122).

These two ducal manuscripts were expensively illuminated, probably in London. They look more like romances of chivalry than Bibles. The Egerton manuscript was described among the books seized from Thomas of Woodstock after his execution for treason in 1397. This list opens with a *Roman de la Rose*, valued at 6s. 8d. The English Bible comes second, described as being in two great volumes covered with red leather, valued at 40 shillings. The list continues with books of Livy, Merlin, Lancelot, romances of Troy, and so on, all books of aristocratic entertainment rather than of spiritual piety. In such a context, the Wycliffite Bible might have received the respectability of texts such as Giyart des Moulin's French translation of the *Historia Scholastica* of Peter Comestor. This big book of Bible stories circulated in French under the name of *Bible Historiale* and it was much appreciated in the court of France. It had crossed the border into literature.

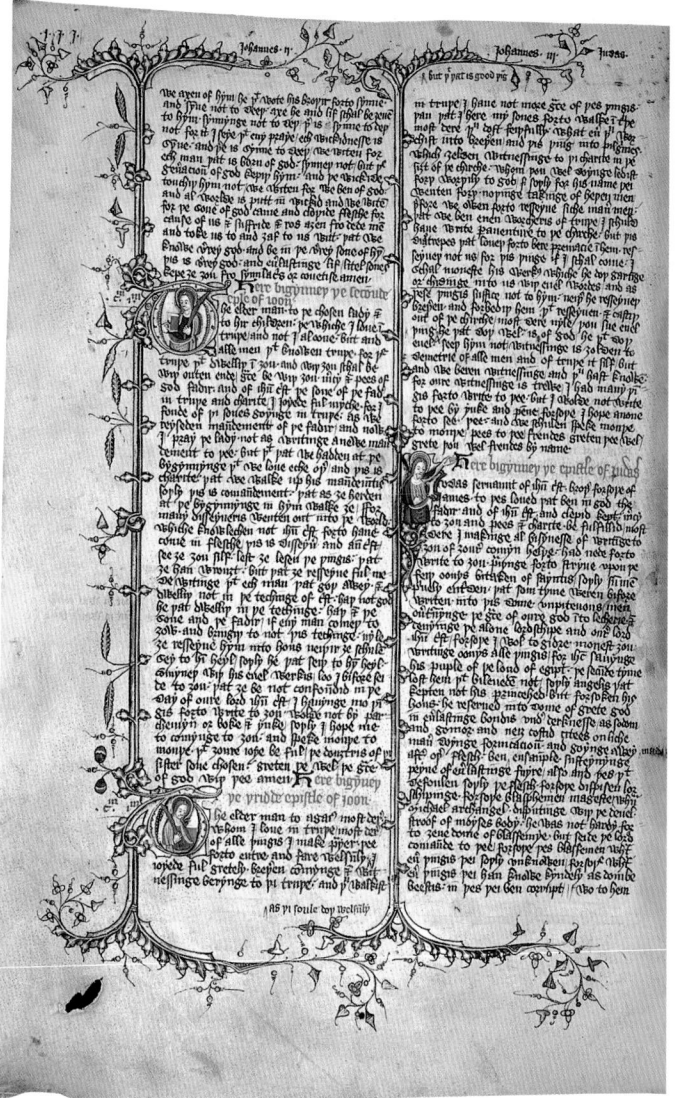

The Wycliffite translation of the Bible by Nicholas Hereford and his collaborators was not literary at all. The text is extremely literal, generally offering little more than substitution of English equivalents for the Latin text in virtually the same word order. It is almost like a string of glosses, as if every word had a translation written above it. This may have been part of a deliberate attempt to represent the text exactly as in the Vulgate, without any possible suspicion that it had been tampered with or adapted in any way. Nicholas Hereford had obviously believed that he could present the uncontroversial nature of the text to the pope.

The result, of course, was a version that was remarkably orthodox and yet often grotesquely inelegant and sometimes actually incomprehensible. One would have to know the Latin text quite well, or to have a copy beside one, in order to understand the meaning fully.

Some time in the early to mid-1390s, the text of the Wycliffite Bible was completely revised. This was not the work of Nicholas Hereford, who recanted his Lollardy around 1391 and became a respectable priest and eventually lived to an honourable old age as a Carthusian monk in Coventry. The revision is commonly and credibly attributed to Wycliffe's personal assistant, John Purvey (*c*.1353–*c*.1428), though there is no real evidence of his authorship other than reasonable conjecture. Purvey is sometimes described as the *librarius lollardorum*, an engaging epithet, 'book-supplier of the Lollards'.

The editor of this revision (Purvey or not) wrote an extremely long Prologue to his version of the Old Testament. The Prologue fills some 60 pages of small print in the massive edition in which it was first published in 1850. It is enormously long and discursive. Much of it is made up of a summary of each of the books of the Old Testament and an assessment of their relative value as history or allegory. The editor confidently departs from the Paris text where this seems justified, and (for example) he explains that he rejects the book of Baruch altogether as uncanonical, since it is not found in the Hebrew Bible. Nicholas Hereford, as we saw above, included it scrupulously in order to emphasize to the pope the conventionality and uncontroversial nature of the project.

The final chapter of the Prologue concerns his method of revising the English text (Pl. 123). This is a very detailed and early statement of the difficulties of translating from one language into another. The author alludes to himself as 'a symple creature' who, with fellows and helpers, gathered as many old Bibles as possible. He found, as did Saint Jerome (who makes a similar remark in his own prologue to the Vulgate), that they all differed greatly from each other. He suggests that the common Latin Bible itself would merit correction, even more than the 'English bible late translatid'. This must be a reference to Nicholas Hereford's version of the 1380s. However, he continues, a literal word by word translation of any Latin text will never furnish idiomatic English, for the grammatical constructions and word order of Latin are different. He gives many actual examples. One of these is *Dominum formidabunt adversarii eius* (I Kings 2:10, I Samuel 2:10 in a modern Bible). This sentence is actually translated in the earlier Wycliffite version as 'The Lord shulen drede the adversaries of hym', which thus emerges as the exact opposite of the meaning in Latin. The revised Wycliffite text rearranges the word order into English usage, so that it reads 'Adversaries of the Lord shulen drede hym.'

He divides the labour of a translator into four stages. First of all, he tells that he collected manuscripts of the text in Latin. Then he judged the validity and merits of each book of the Bible, using works of the Church fathers, the Gloss on the Bible, 'and speciali Lire on the elde testament'. This is the commentary on the Old Testament by Nicholas of Lyra (*c*.1270–1340), who knew Hebrew. The Wycliffite scholars often graciously acknowledge Nicholas of Lyra, despite the

122 opposite

Several very grand manuscripts of the Wycliffite Bible were made around 1400. This copy belonged before 1412 to Thomas of Lancaster, son of Henry IV (WOLFENBÜTTEL, HERZOG-AUGUST-BIBLIOTHEK, COD. GUELF. AUG.A.2)

123

The Prologue to the revised Wycliffite Bible discusses the difficulties of translation. The detail here says that Jerome translated into Latin, which was the everyday language of the time, 'as englische is comyn langage to oure peple' (CAMBRIDGE, CORPUS CHRISTI COLLEGE, MS. 147)

fact that he was a Franciscan and the friars and Lollards were bitter opponents. The third stage in translating, according to our editor, was with dictionaries of grammar in order to understand exactly any obscure passages. The final step was to produce a fluent translation, judging each sentence as a whole, and to have this text constantly revised and polished by his colleagues.

The author of the Prologue makes a number of gratuitously unkind generalizations about proud and ignorant priests, and he urges the use of his translation by 'symple men of wit'. This revised English Bible was directed at a very much wider and less learned public than the professional or even royal audiences of the earlier text. In the 1390s and early 1400s, Lollardy was on the increase. There had never been significant heresy in England and the authorities did not know how to respond. It is as difficult today as it was then to judge whether the Lollards were primarily concerned with religious piety (which might have been acceptable) or with the overthrow of social order (which most certainly was not). There are early references to the prosecution of Lollards, not specifically for owning translations of the Bible but for challenging the authority of the Church. An example is William Thorpe, a Lollard priest and former member of Wycliffe's circle in Oxford, who was brought before Archbishop Arundel in 1407. He was charged with preaching without a licence and with advocating insubordination to legitimate authority. His Psalter, presumably in English, was impounded. The archbishop told him he should not have it back, 'nor none other book', until he recanted his heresy.

Although the Prologue of the revised Wycliffite Bible commends it to the use of common people and Lollards, the text seems to have moved quite quickly into the repertoire of the regular book trade, with a clientele decidedly above the rank of peasantry. The inflammatory Prologue occurs in only nine surviving copies, out of about 70 which include parts of the Old Testament. It was probably judged to be inappropriately political. The general style of early Wycliffite Bibles suggests that the text was already being sold commercially within the first decade of the fifteenth century. One copy, Oxford, Bodleian Library, MS. Fairfax 2, was dated 1408 on its last leaf, fol. 385r. Buyers of such manuscripts might well have been sympathetic to the reforms advocated by Wycliffe but they were not necessarily practising Lollards. There is, for example, a contemporary reference to a copy of the Gospels in English which was acquired by the chaplain of Redcliffe Church in Bristol in 1404. Nonetheless, Wycliffite Bibles were symbolic of a deeply unsettling trend of modernity and unorthodoxy. They became increasingly associated with fears of religious dissent, free thinking and social rebellion.

In late 1407, Archbishop Arundel summoned a committee of clergy in Oxford to draw up a series of thirteen Constitutions on the new Lollard heresy. The text was promulgated in 1409. Much of it was concerned with tighter controls on preaching without proper licence and on teaching controversial theology in the universities. Clause 7 directly concerns Wycliffite Bibles. It forbids the translation of any biblical text into any written form of English. It prohibits absolutely the reading of any such manuscripts made in or since the time of John Wycliffe or any that might be prepared in the future, in whole or part, in public or in private, unless the translation had been approved by the local diocese. Anyone who infringed this clause (the Constitutions stated) would be excommunicated and then charged with inciting heresy. This was no empty threat, since heresy under English law was punishable by death.

After the promulgation of Arundel's Constitutions in 1409, therefore, possession of any Bible translation became illegal, unless the text was older than the time of Wycliffe. This would have been a difficult ruling to enforce, since dating of manuscripts was never easy. No Wycliffite Bible manuscript is exactly dated later than 1409, for that would be to invite prosecution. Oxford, Bodleian Library, MS. Fairfax 2, cited above, was originally dated by its scribe in the 'eer of the lord M.CCCC. & viii', 1408, just before the publication of Arundel's decree: the final 'C' has been carefully erased, presumably so that the book appeared to have been made in 1308, which would make it legal after all. Cambridge, Magdalene College, Pepys MS. 15, was once dated, perhaps in 1406 (or 1416, Pl. 124). The original date has been heavily erased and overwritten and it is no longer recoverable. That too was probably to eliminate incriminating evidence. A Wycliffite New Testament in Manchester (Rylands Library, MS. Eng. 80), purports to be dated 1343, before the time of Wycliffe: the date is a medieval

124

This Wycliffite New Testament of the early fifteenth century was once dated, but the date has been erased to avoid prosecution for possession of a recent translation (CAMBRIDGE, MAGDALENE COLLEGE, PEPYS MS. 15)

fabrication, for the manuscript was made in the mid-fifteenth century, probably in or near 1448, to judge from its tables for finding Easter.

It is not clear what Archbishop Arundel intended by the clause that no Bible translation was permitted unless it had been authorized by the diocese. There may be an echo of this ruling in another Wycliffite New Testament in Manchester, John Rylands University Library, MS. Eng.77. It has a medieval note that it was bought for £4 6s. 8d., and that it was 'overseen and read by Doctor Thomas Ebbrall and Doctor Yve'. These must Dr. Thomas Eborall (d.1471), master of Whittington College, London, 1444–64, and his successor, William Ive (d.1486), Oxford graduates of unquestioned orthodoxy. Perhaps the owner hoped to allay suspicion by invoking their names.

No copy of the Wycliffite Bible contains evidence that any bishop had officially sanctioned it for use. Many manuscripts of another Middle English text, Nicholas Love's *Meditations on the Blessed Life of Jesus Christ*, proudly invoke the special licence which their author had obtained from Archbishop Arundel to quote the Scriptures in English. We must assume by the complete absence of any such statements in Bibles that formal consent was seldom, if ever, given. In 1431, John Stafford, then bishop of Bath and Wells, issued a general mandate that no part of the Scriptures in English was permitted in his diocese. There is no option to obtain a licence. Stafford became Lord Chancellor in 1432 and archbishop of Canterbury in 1443, and it is likely that Wycliffite Bibles were never again officially tolerated.

Let us now return to the manuscripts. Despite everything, very large numbers of Wycliffite Bibles still survive. Some must have been furtively written and kept hidden from sight. Most of the manuscripts, however, are handsome and well-made books, and do not appear to be amateur productions. An example of a thoroughly professional-looking Wycliffite New Testament is Oxford, Bodleian Library, MS. Bodley 183 (Pl. 125), illuminated around 1420. It forms a virtual twin with Bodleian Library, MS. Fairfax 11 (Pl. 126), and the two books were certainly written by the same scribe and were apparently decorated by the same illuminator. Both books, in turn, are strikingly similar to MS. Bodley 665, which is much smaller but comprises an identical text and is very probably by the same scribe again. Two books might be coincidence. Three begins to sound like a commercial production line. Such books must have been expensive and were probably disseminated through the London book trade. In 1429, one Nicholas Belward of Norfolk confessed to having bought a Wycliffite New Testament in London for 4 marks and 40 pence (£2 16s. 8d.). He was probably related to Richard Belward, of Earsham, Norfolk, who was charged with Lollardy in 1424 and admitted that 'a certain parchment-maker brings him all the books containing that doctrine from London'. Note the occupation of parchment-maker. This was a trade within the professional book trade but was a step aside from mainstream bookselling, as if (perhaps) the supply of Wycliffite texts was through the back door rather than

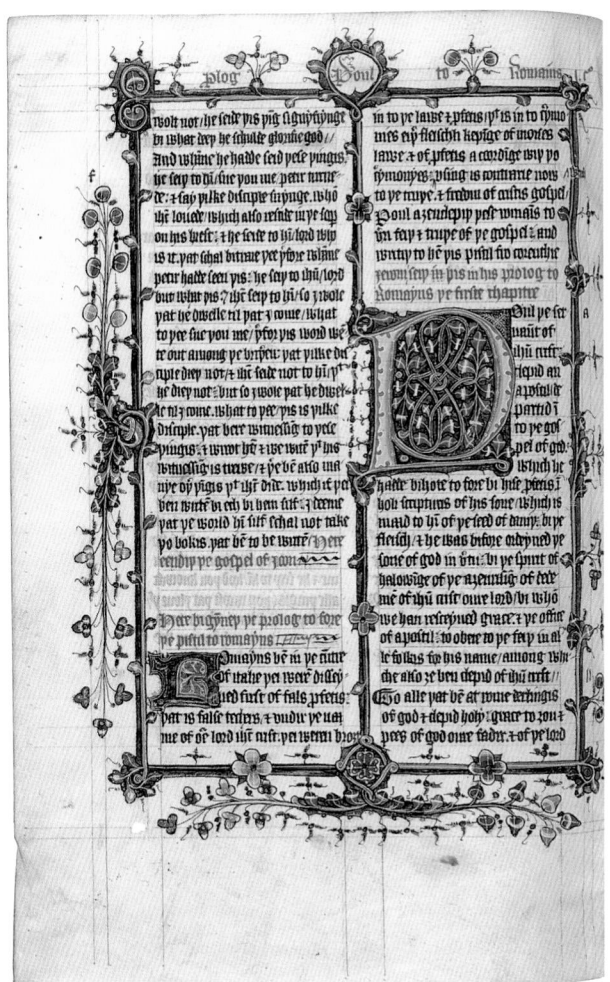

125, 126

By about 1420, Wycliffite Bibles were being commercially produced in London. These two copies of the New Testament were written by the same scribe and apparently decorated by the same illuminator, doubtless for different customers
(OXFORD, BODLEIAN LIBRARY, MSS. BODLEY 183 AND FAIRFAX 11)

over the front counter. William Smith, cited above for his confession of copying Wycliffite Bibles in 1392, gave his occupation as 'parchemyner'. A parchment-maker was among those who helped the Lollard, Sir John Oldcastle, escape from the Tower of London in 1414.

Parchment was important in making Wycliffite Bibles. A primary observation about the surviving manuscripts is that virtually every single copy is written on parchment. This is curious, for parchment was always much more expensive than paper. A very high percentage of other Middle English texts were being made on paper by the fifteenth century. The consistency with which Wycliffite Bibles are on parchment is therefore notable. New College, Oxford, MS. 320, a Wycliffite Psalter, is apparently the only medieval exception, written around 1500 or even later. It might be argued that parchment was safer for any Wycliffite book, for it is very difficult to burn; but so were the heretics themselves and incombustibility saved no one's life. Nor was it true that other Bibles were always on parchment. Many Bibles were being written in continental Europe in the fifteenth century, in the vernacular as well as in Latin, and probably the majority were copied on paper. About three out of four copies of the Gutenberg Bible, for example, were made on paper. The only other fifteenth-century texts which were invariably copied on parchment were personal Books of Hours. We will return to this observation in a few moments.

Two chapters ago, we saw the creation of the thirteenth-century Paris Bible as a physical entity. Its very precise shape, format and textual structure endured right through the late Middle Ages into the period of printing, and it is more or less still with us today. The one-volume comprehensive Bible, promoted by the friars, came to embody the very definition of 'the Bible'. Its many components were in a fixed order, it was always written in two columns in a script which was recognizably biblical, it had running-titles throughout (except in the Psalms), it included the *Interpretation of Hebrew Names*, and so on. It was a single entity. It was simultaneously a timeless religious concept and an unvarying physical book. As an artefact it would have been identifiable by anyone in Europe, whether they could read it or not. The specific format, in short, represented the Bible.

Looked at from that perspective, Wycliffite manuscripts of the Scriptures are hardly Bibles at all. They vary immensely in size, shape and format. Their text is inconsistent, and is no more structured than in Bibles of the eleventh century, for example. Only about 20 copies, of about 250, comprise the whole Bible. About a hundred are made up of the New Testament on its own. Just under 30 consist of the Gospels alone, and almost as many (24 manuscripts) comprise the New Testament Epistles on their own. We will return to this point too. A bewilderingly large number of the residue of Wycliffite biblical manuscripts include odd little selections of books, often in an order which has no obvious precedent. Furthermore, many of the manuscripts do not look like Bibles in the physical sense which we have just defined. A very early copy of the unrevised version of Nicholas Hereford (Oxford, Bodleian Library, MS. Douce 370), written around 1400, resembles a traditional medieval Paris Bible. That was almost the last example. By the first quarter of the fifteenth century, Wycliffite Bibles had taken on a different physical identity. The whole page layout is different, sometimes in one column, and many of the old features of the thirteenth-century Bible are absent, including most obviously the *Interpretation of Hebrew Names*. The script of Wycliffite Bibles varies greatly from one copy to another, but if one had to seek for parallels they would be probably found in Breviaries and Books of Hours rather than in Bibles or biblical commentaries.

The next unexpected feature of Wycliffite Bibles is how liturgical they are. Some include Calendars of saints' days, in Latin, like a standard prayer book. An extremely large number of copies are marked up to show the translations of readings used in the Latin Mass. This is a consistent feature of Wycliffite Bibles. They open or conclude with long and detailed tables in English itemizing the readings from the Bible for use during public church services throughout the year, according to the established Use of Sarum. They describe this as a 'rule' or a 'kalendar' to recognize readings from the Old Testament and (especially) the Gospels and the Epistles. The lections are exactly those 'that ben redde in the chirche bi al the yeer', or 'stondying by ordir, as thei ben redde in the messebuk, after the use of Salsbury'. They are thus very conventional and orthodox. The tables list the opening and closing words of each lection, in English, with the chapter number of the Bible and a letter between 'a' and 'g'. These letters are inserted in the margins of the majority of Wycliffite Bibles, even those with no explanatory tables, dividing each chapter into up to seven sub-sections (Pl. 127). In form, they resemble the alphabetical symbols devised for the Dominican concordance of words of the Bible produced by the convent of St-Jacques in Paris in the thirteenth century, except that there is no Wycliffite word concordance and their use here is exclusively to locate whole readings for use at Mass. Occasionally, as in London, BL, Add. MS. 15580, full headings for readings are marked in the margins. This is doubtless one reason why Wycliffite Gospels and Epistles are so common – not necessarily because of Lollard devotion to these texts, but because these two sections of the Bible are the sources for the standard readings at Mass. Several Wycliffite manuscripts comprise only the liturgical readings, in full but extracted out of context, as in a Lectionary. Examples of a comprehensive set of Old Testament readings for the weekday Masses are in Oxford, Bodleian

127

The text of Wycliffite Gospel Books was often marked up with little letters of the alphabet, from 'a' to 'g', corresponding to tables of the readings used at Mass. A letter 'a' is in the lower right-hand margin here, beside I Timothy 2:1
(PRIVATE COLLECTION)

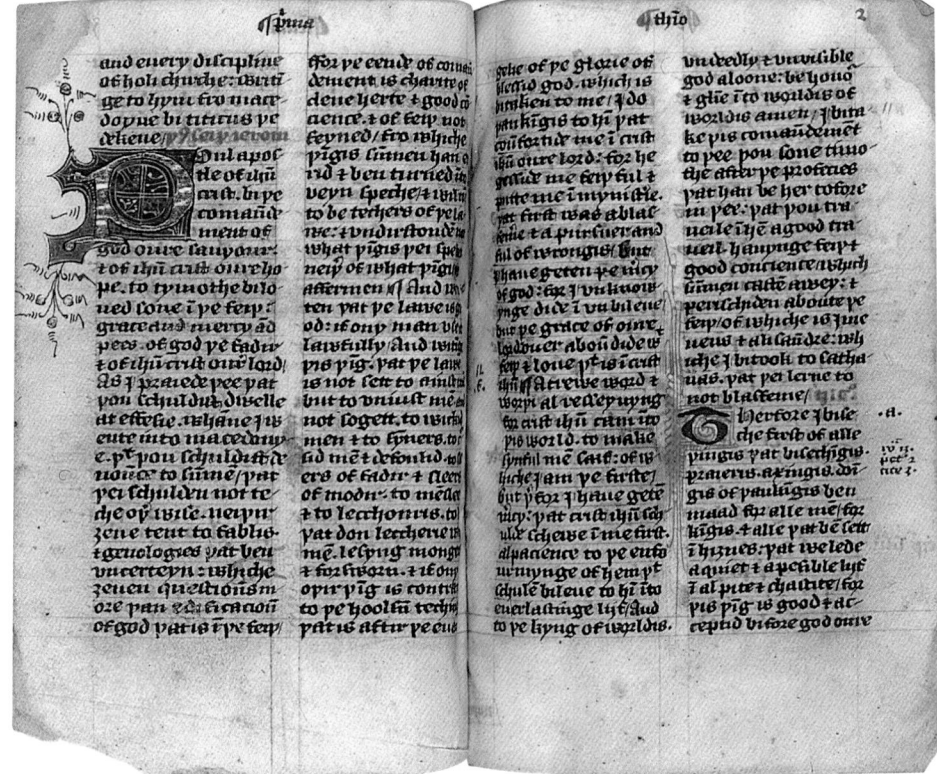

Library, MS. Fairfax 11, fols. 226v-266r, while examples of the New Testament readings for the Sunday Masses are in London, BL, Harley MSS. 1029 and 1710.

The emphasis on readings for the Mass is at variance with the Lollards' widely proclaimed rejection of the authority and ceremonies of the established Church. Wycliffite Bibles are completely orthodox and conventional in their liturgical aspect. The Mass was the most sacramental and priestly of church services. The lists of days for celebrating Mass include all the commemorations of the establishment, with the readings for the feasts of saintly bishops and popes, and Masses for good weather, success in battles, pilgrimages, weddings, and so on. One Wycliffite New Testament, London, BL, Harley MS. 272, opens with a prayer for use of which, it asserts, the pope has granted 80,000 years' indulgence. This is far from the world of revolutionary Protestantism.

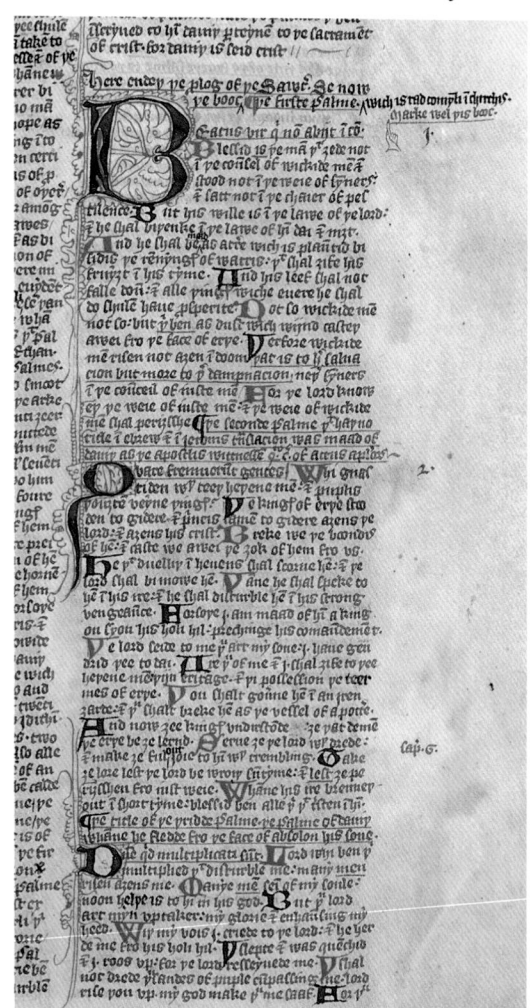

Similarly, the Psalms in Wycliffite Bibles are usually constructed more like a liturgical Psalter than as an ordinary book of the Bible. Headings refer to the text as 'the sauter, which is red comounli in the chirche'. The Psalter in a Wycliffite Bible has running-titles, which it would not in a Latin Paris Bible. The Wycliffite Psalms often conclude with the canticles, including those which are non-biblical, like the Athanasian Creed, 'the which Attanasy a doctor of greke made' (as it is described in Bodleian Library, MS. Fairfax 2). In the liturgy, the Psalms are not numbered but are referred to by their opening words in Latin. These titles are almost always copied into the Psalters of Wycliffite Bibles. The Latin names were so familiar in the fifteenth century that the individual Psalms were no longer identifiable once their opening words had been translated into English, changing the opening initial. In MS. Fairfax 2, just cited, the large decorated letters for the opening of each Psalm preserve the original Latin initials, which could be matched from the liturgy. Thus it uses 'B' for Psalm 1 (*Beatus vir*), 'Q' for Psalm 2 (*Quare fremuerunt*), 'D' for Psalm 3 (*Domine quid multiplicati*), and so on, even though these opening words had been made obsolete by translation (Pl. 128). This suggests that the Wycliffite Psalms were not simply being read in English but were used by people who already knew the names of the Psalms in Latin.

Church Psalters in the Middle Ages were often illustrated, especially at each of the seven liturgical divisions of the text. Readers of a Latin Psalter would customarily recognize each section of the book by the presence of a picture. The Lollards, at least from 1395, were deeply opposed to the use of images in manuscripts. The owner of a Wycliffite Psalter, London, BL, Arundel MS. 104, evidently found it difficult to comprehend without the standard repertoire of illumination. He or she cut up two splendid illustrated manuscripts and pasted selected initials into the margins of the Wycliffite Psalms (fols. 350r, 353r, 354r, 364v, 372v, with offsets of very many others now lost). One of these pillaged books was a Psalter commentary by Peter Lombard, with high-quality miniatures, c.1220. The other was a Psalter of c.1370 (Pl. 129). What is interesting is that although the subjects of the added miniatures are randomly applied, the

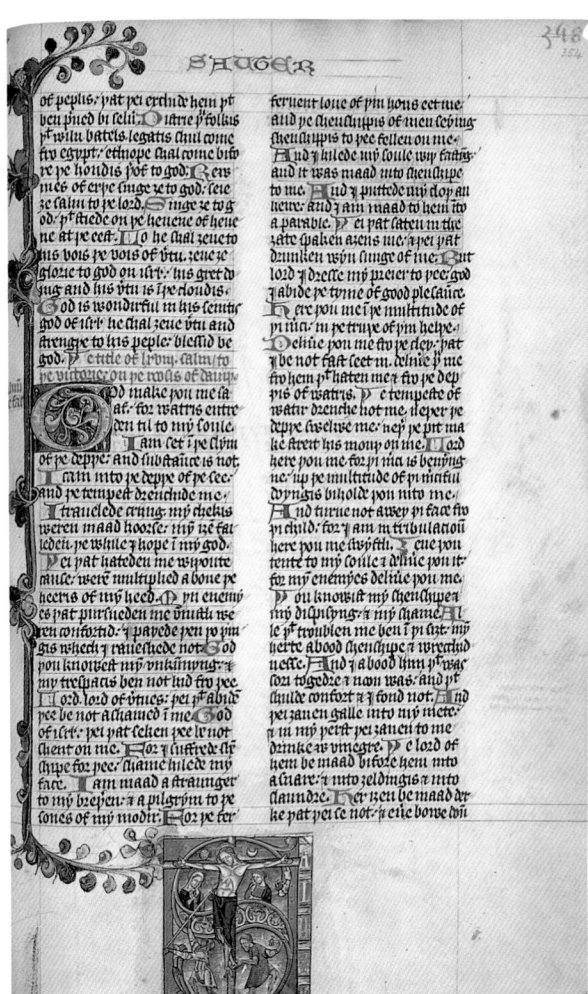

initials selected correspond with what would have been the opening letters of the Latin text. The owner had been unable to use the book without the traditional liturgical apparatus in place.

How, then, were Wycliffite Bibles actually used? We have noted the choice of texts, the flexible size and thickness of the books, the consistent use of parchment, the script, the divisions of text and the very common cross-references to the orthodox Mass. All these have parallels with common books of private devotion, like personal Psalters and Books of Hours in the fifteenth century. Such features begin within the first quarter of the fifteenth century, as Wycliffite Bibles already began to diverge from Lollardy. Let us take one final example of a complete Wycliffite Bible in use. Oxford, Bodleian Library, MS. Bodley 277, is one of the grandest of copies, as one might expect, for it belonged to the saintly Henry VI (king of England 1422–71), who gave it to the Charterhouse in London. By any interpretation, this is far removed from suspicion of common Lollardy. Chapters of the text were originally divided with the Wycliffite letters, 'a' to 'g' so that passages could be matched with a table for readings at Mass. The Carthusians, however, took it further. They marked the manuscript up in the margins throughout with readings from other uses of the Bible in their monastery, mostly in the refectory (Pl. 130) and once for the Psalms in the choir (Pl. 131). Each reference notes the beginning of a reading and then the number of leaves over which it extends. Several instances compare this length with the equivalent reading in another Latin manuscript of the same text (e.g., fol. 18r, 3 leaves in English, 10½ in the other, or fol. 159r, 3 leaves in the English, 9 in the Latin text). They were obviously using two texts of the Bible together, the Latin of the daily monastic use and the English of the translation. They cannot actually have sung the Psalms in English in the choir. The Carthusians were a highly orthodox but contemplative order. They doubtless still performed their public readings in the refectory and

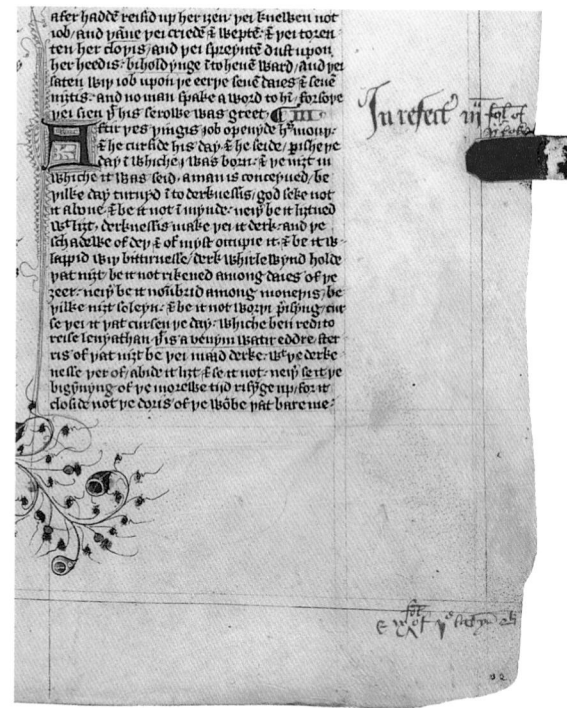

chapel in Latin, but they seem to have marked up their Wycliffite translation in order to be able to read and meditate on the parallel text in English.

Let us suppose that many private owners of ordinary Wycliffite Bibles did the same. Like Books of Hours, these were frequently texts of private devotion. Lay attendance at Mass became much more common in the fifteenth century than ever before. Even a laymen without the slightest Lollard tendencies might have difficulty following the readings in Latin. To use a Bible in English was illegal, but to concentrate on the meaning of the Latin text was an accepted act of piety. This is an extremely delicate point of argument. The true Bible, in the mind of the devout, was still a Latin text. Even a monk, meditating on the words of the Bible, might let his thoughts slip into English without committing heresy. To a fifteenth-century layman, an English parallel version might seem like no more than a sustained gloss or mirror to the original, to help focus devotion by increasing understanding of the sacred Latin text. This is the crucial point. Most owners of what we call Wycliffite Bibles would probably not have thought of them as Bibles at all, or as especially Wycliffite. The books did not look like Bibles or function like Bibles. The Bible was an identifiable entity, a Latin text. These were instead a layman's guide to what was in the Bible. It is a subtle but crucial distinction. Oxford, Queen's College MS. 369, a Wycliffite Gospel Book,

130, 131

This manuscript was given by Henry VI to the Charterhouse in London. It is marked opposite Job 3 with a Latin rubric to the effect that the text is read in the abbey refectory and that the passage fills 3 pages in the English translation and 9 in the text in Latin. The place is marked by a contemporary leather tab on the edge of the page. The Psalms (opposite) are marked with Latin titles. A note at the upper right records that this is the text sung in the choir (OXFORD, BODLEIAN LIBRARY, MS. BODLEY 277)

concludes, '… here is the endynge of alle the gospelles *as thei stonden in the bible*'. It is as if this was a text which was not actually the Bible, but resembles what is in the Bible.

Now we can understand the outrage aroused by the Lollards. They treated these books as if they were actually Bibles. They accorded them the veneration which should have been reserved for the real Bible, the text in Latin. That seemed like blasphemy. It was as heretical and impious as the pretence by unqualified Lollard preachers that they were ordained priests. The Wycliffites introduced a parallel reality in which the world was turned upside down, and books in English were said to be Bibles. This was completely unacceptable, and was punishable by death.

There is no shortage of tales of committed Lollards who were arrested for heresy and who were found to be in possession of Wycliffite Bibles. Many confessed to reading the text aloud in secret meetings. The most detailed records of heresy trials survive from the very end of the fifteenth century and the beginning of the sixteenth. Five Lollards were burned at the stake in London in 1496 with their manuscripts tied around their necks. Very many others were charged with Lollard heresy, including Thomas Watts, Christopher Shoemaker, James

132

This Wycliffite New Testament was perhaps the actual manuscript described in the trial of Richard Hunne in 1514, charged with heresy and possession of a Bible in English (PRIVATE COLLECTION)

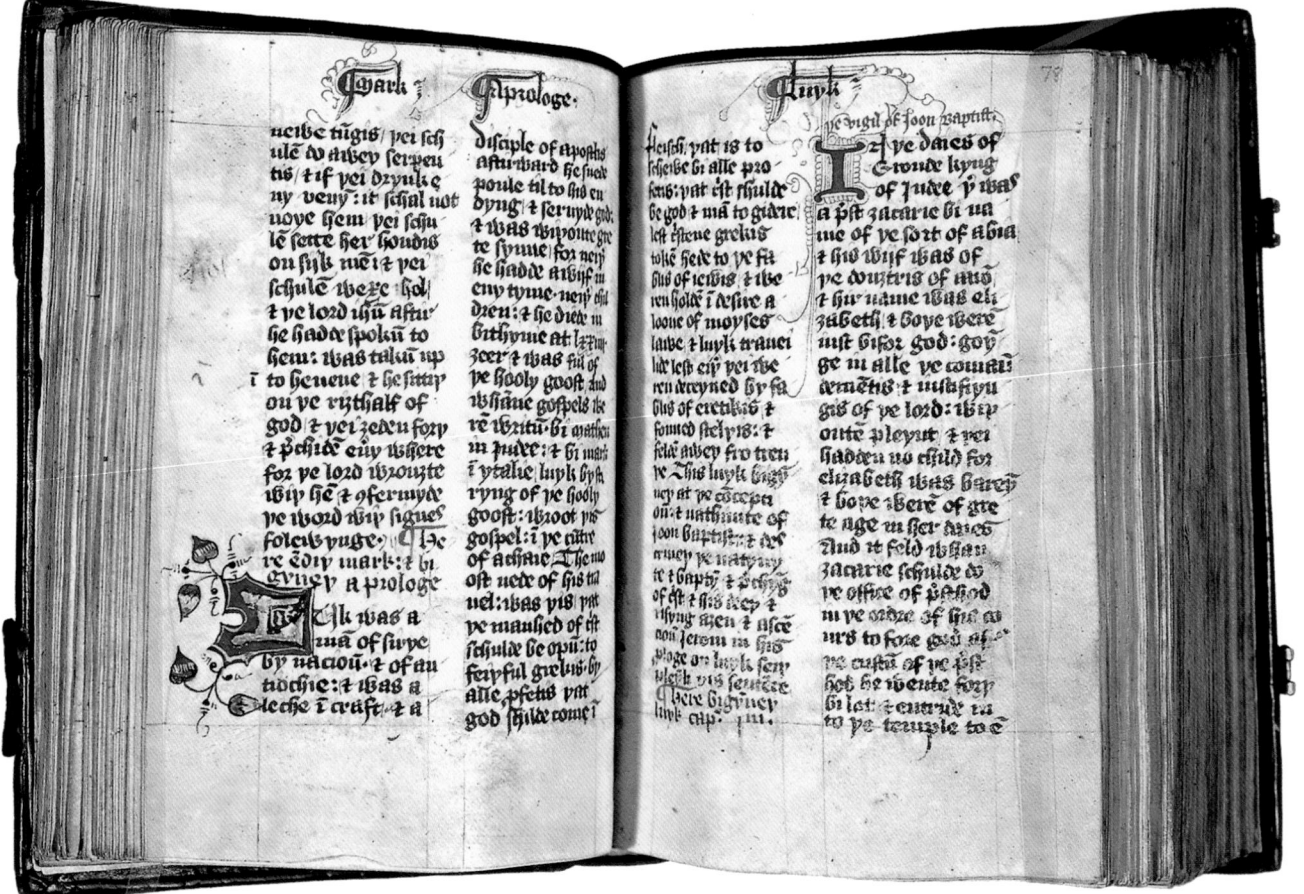

Brewster, William Sweeting, John Southwick, Nicholas Durdant, John and Joan Barret, John Butler, Thomas Geffrey, Richard Hunne, and so on, among countless others, all of whom owned Wycliffite Bibles (Pl. 132). Most died as martyrs, usually by being burned alive. Some of their deaths are chronicled in John Foxe's *Book of Martyrs* (1563), the battle roll of the English Reformation. The details of Lollard trials make heart-rending reading, for these were often people of humble backgrounds and limited education. James Brewster was a carpenter in Colchester and claimed (perhaps quite truthfully) that he was not even able to read the 'little book of Scripture in English … almost worn for age', which was found in his possession. He was executed, all the same, in 1511. We can never doubt the extraordinary courage and religious conviction of those who gave their lives for their beliefs. However, most Lollards were prosecuted for practising heresy, of which owning a Wycliffite Bible would have simply been one further piece of corroborative evidence. Where Bibles are mentioned in trials, this is usually in the context of giving public readings. Lollards who seemed to be aping priests were sentenced without mercy, but simple possession alone would probably not bring a conviction.

Something of a realistic approach was described by Sir Thomas More (1478–1535), who, as lawyer, sheriff and later Lord Chancellor, had often attended heresy trials for the prosecution. In his lengthy book, *A Dialogue Concerning Heresies* (1529), More asserted that Bibles in the English language were not at all rare. If copies were found in the possession of heretics, he said, they would certainly be seized. If they were infiltrated with heretical doctrines, they would be destroyed. Many others, according to More, might be quite well known to the local bishop and such manuscripts would be 'left in ley mennys handys & womens', if these lay owners were 'good & catholyke folke' and if they used the text devoutly and soberly. Thomas More implies that this was common policy. The Church turned a blind eye to respectable middle-class owners, with no taint of Lollardy, who used English Bibles for private piety. It is inconceivable that upwards of 250 copies could have survived if every manuscript had been at daily risk from the heresy police. We know that the authorities were capable of extreme thoroughness in searching out and burning books, for a number of mainstream Lollard texts do not survive in a single English copy. Bibles in English did not suffer that fate. Despite the fact that Wycliffite Bibles have since the Reformation become holy symbols of the struggle for freedom, probably most extant copies belonged to uncontroversial owners who were regular attendants at Mass.

Quite often, a Wycliffite Bible must have been almost the only book in an owner's household. They were sometimes used like Books of Hours for recording historical anniversaries. Oxford, Bodleian Library, MS. Rawl. C.259 includes notes commemorating a great storm in 1361 and the arrival of the Black Death in London in 1348, a date already a century old but never to be forgotten. Another, Cambridge, Magdalene College, Pepys MS. 15, includes not only the anniversary of the Black Death and other natural events, but also 'the erthe grone' in 1382. This may be a subtle Lollard reference, masquerading as meteorology, for this was the famous earthquake which occurred during the Blackfriars Synod, called to condemn the heresy of John Wycliffe and his followers in May 1382. One manuscript includes an inscription apparently signed by Richard III, as duke of Gloucester, 'A vous me ly, Gloucestre' (New York Public Library, MS. 67). It is commonly asserted that the book belonged to Richard himself (Pl. 133). On the contrary, the manuscript was presumably being used as an autograph book. It was a common custom, which probably originated in the court of Burgundy, that

133

The owner of this Wycliffite manuscript was evidently acquainted with Richard of Gloucester before his coronation as Richard III in 1483, for the royal duke signed his name in the book
(NEW YORK PUBLIC LIBRARY, MS. 67)

134 opposite

As soon as the Reformation began, ownership of Wycliffite manuscripts became a matter of pride. This fifteenth-century Wycliffite Gospel book was bound with the arms of Sir Heneage Finch (d.1631), Speaker of the House of Commons
(DUNEDIN, PUBLIC LIBRARY, REED MS. 6)

a great prince or high aristocrat who visited a private house would be asked to write a suitable inscription in some precious book, often a Book of Hours. There are at least three other examples of Richard III doing this, in books he certainly did not own. The interest for us is that it furnishes evidence that this manuscript, a Wycliffite New Testament, was its owner's most valuable book and he or she was prepared to bring it out when the king's brother came to visit.

In 1538, as the English Reformation reached its height, it finally became legal to translate and to print the Bible in English. The reasons leading to this will emerge in Chapter 9. The Great Bible of Henry VIII was published in 1539. Immediately, Wycliffite Bibles emerged from hiding in huge numbers. Sixteenth-century ownership inscriptions are as common as those of the fifteenth century are rare. The status of the treasured Wycliffite Bible as the most precious book in the household was exonerated. At once owners began using them for recording identifiable family anniversaries. John Tey, of Essex, started recording the births of his children in a Wycliffite Bible in 1543 (London, Lambeth Palace, MS. 25). Sir Henry Gate began doing the same in a Wycliffite New Testament in 1544 (Dublin, Trinity College, MS. A.1.10). It is improbable that these books were bought second-hand in the early 1540s. To have assumed the status of family record book, they must already have been their owners' most carefully preserved possessions for generations. Their custodians were probably not Lollards – just careful.

re oſtenſa deſcribit:ut ſicut i
o canonis id ē libri geneſe
ptibile principiū pnotat: ir
ttuptibilis finis p virginē
ſi redderet dicens . Ego l
o:inioū et finis. Qic eſt iot

8 | The Gutenberg Bible

IN A POPULAR SURVEY at the end of the year 1999, a British national newspaper reached the conclusion that the person who had made the single most outstanding contribution to civilization in the second millennium was the inventor, Johann Gutenberg (*c.*1400–68). He discovered and perfected the art of printing in the Western alphabet. For the first time in Europe, it became possible to multiply written words in infinite quantity and in identical copies. The principal key to Gutenberg's invention was the use of movable type. Let us explain. Within the first half of the fifteenth century, pictures and short lines of writing were sometimes reproduced by inking whole blocks of wood carved in reverse and then by stamping these blocks onto sheets of paper. We encountered some such primitive publications at the end of Chapter 6 above. The obvious disadvantage in printing a whole book by such a method is that every page has to be painstakingly cut into a new and separate piece of wood, letter by letter, line after line, all in scrupulous mirror image. One error or slip of the chisel would render the whole block invalid. Every page would take very many hours to prepare: it would be far quicker and more accurate simply to copy the text as a manuscript. Gutenberg, however, devised a system of casting separate pieces of metal type for versions of each of the 26 letters of the alphabet. These individual letters were mass-produced mechanically. The printer could rapidly assemble these loose letters into any sequence to spell out a piece of text, lock them into place, and then print from them. When sufficient numbers of copies had been run off, the metal letters would then be released again and could be subsequently reassembled into some other text, using the same pieces of type over and over again. That, in essence, is the invention attributed to Gutenberg.

Although he certainly experimented with a number of little texts, the book on

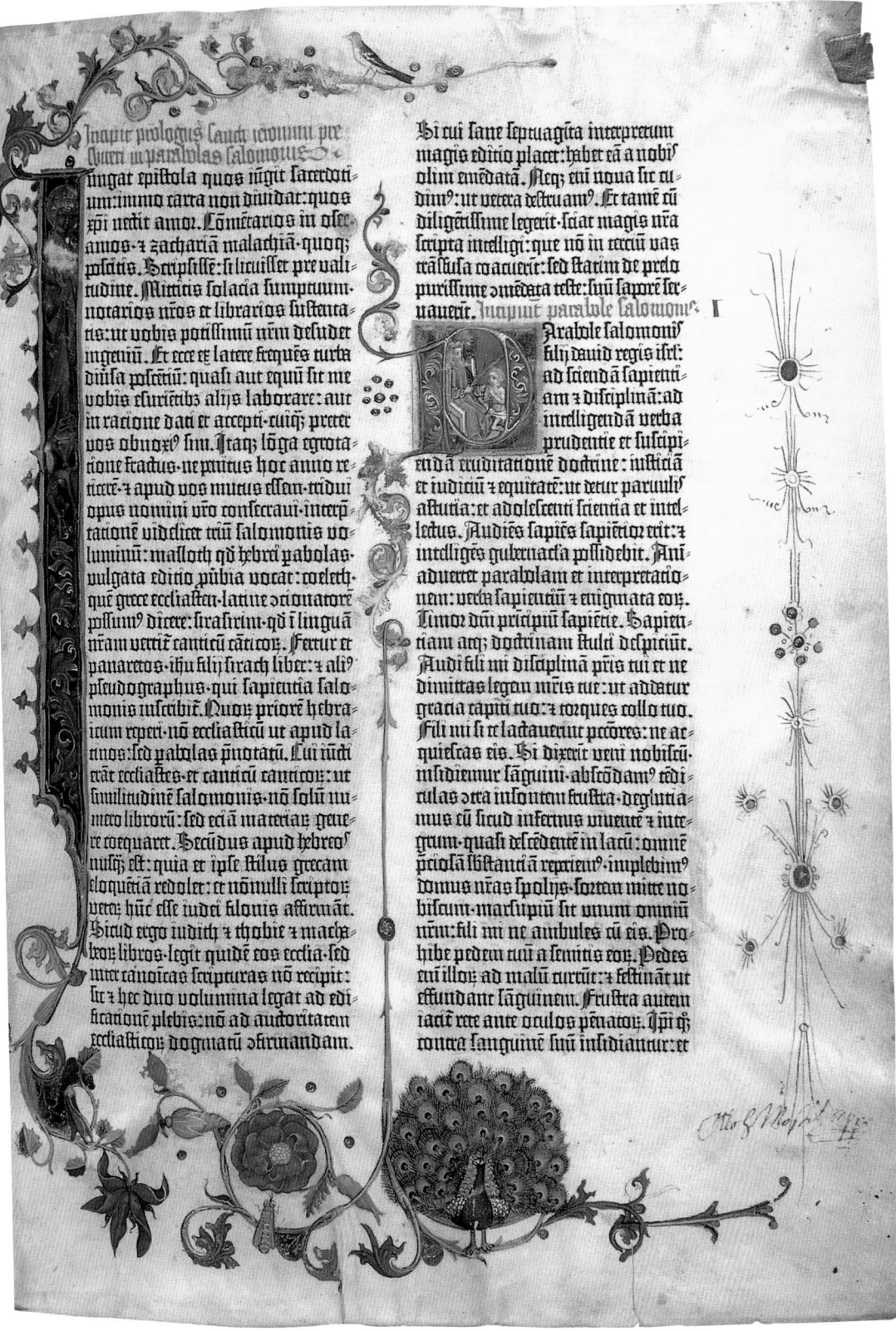

Iungat epistola quos iungit sacerdotium: immo carta non diuidat: quos xpi nectit amor. Commentarios in osee amos et zachariam malachiam quoque poscitis. Scripsissem si licuisset pre valitudine. Mittitis solacia sumptuum notarios nostros et librarios sustentaretis: ut vobis potissimum nostrum desudet ingenium. Et ecce ex latere frequens turba diuisa poscentium: quasi aut equum sit me vobis esurientibus aliis laborare: aut in ratione dati et accepti cuiquam preter vos obnoxius sim. Itaque longa egrotatione fractus: ne penitus hoc anno reticerem et apud vos mutus essem: triduo opus nomini vestro consecraui: interpretatione videlicet trium salomonis voluminum: masloth quod hebrei parabolas vulgata editio prouerbia vocat: coeleth quem grece ecclesiasten latine contionatorem possumus dicere: sirasirim quod in linguam nostram vertitur canticum canticorum. Fertur et panaretos ihu filii sirach liber: et alius pseudographus qui sapientia salomonis inscribitur. Quorum priorem hebraicum reperi non ecclesiasticum ut apud latinos sed parabolas prenotatum. Cui iuncti erant ecclesiastes et canticum canticorum: ut similitudinem salomonis non solum numero librorum sed etiam materiarum genere coequaret. Secundus apud hebreos nusquam est: quia et ipse stilus grecam eloquentiam redolet: et nonnulli scriptorum veterum hunc esse iudei filonis affirmant. Sicut ergo iudith et thobie et machabeorum libros legit quidem eos ecclesia: sed inter canonicas scripturas non recipit: sic et hec duo volumina legat ad edificationem plebis: non ad auctoritatem ecclesiasticorum dogmatum confirmandam.

Si cui sane septuaginta interpretum magis editio placet: habet eam a nobis olim emendatam. Neque enim noua sic cudimus: ut vetera destruamus. Et tamen cum diligentissime legerit: sciat magis nostra scripta intelligi: que non in tercium vas transfusa coacuerint: sed statim de prelo purissime commendata testem sui saporem seruauerint. Incipit parabole salomonis.

Parabole salomonis filii dauid regis israhel: ad sciendam sapientiam et disciplinam: ad intelligenda verba prudentie et suscipiendam eruditionem doctrine: iustitiam et iudicium et equitatem: ut detur paruulis astutia: et adolescenti scientia et intellectus. Audiens sapiens sapientior erit: et intelligens gubernacula possidebit. Animaduertet parabolam et interpretationem: verba sapientium et enigmata eorum. Timor domini principium sapientie. Sapientiam atque doctrinam stulti despiciunt. Audi fili mi disciplinam patris tui et ne dimittas legem matris tue: ut addatur gratia capiti tuo et torques collo tuo. Fili mi si te lactauerint peccatores: ne acquiescas eis. Si dixerint veni nobiscum insidiemur sanguini: abscondamus tendiculas contra insontem frustra: deglutiamus eum sicut infernus viuentem et integrum quasi descendentem in lacum: omnem preciosam substantiam reperiemus: implebimus domus nostras spoliis: sortem mitte nobiscum: marsupium sit unum omnium nostrum: fili mi ne ambules cum eis. Prohibe pedem tuum a semitis eorum. Pedes enim illorum ad malum currunt: et festinant ut effundant sanguinem. Frustra autem iacitur rete ante oculos pennatorum. Ipsi quoque contra sanguinem suum insidiantur: et

which Gutenberg's fame depends is the Latin Bible. It is of some relevance in our story that the Bible was the first substantial book ever printed in Europe. The Gutenberg Bible, as it is popularly called, is probably the most famous printed book in the world. It is also one of the most valuable books in existence. Some bibliographers, anxious to affect scholarly disdain for hero worship, refer to it as the '42-line Bible', from the number of printed lines in each column of text. Others, more erudite still, commonly abbreviate this to 'B42'. The Gutenberg Bible—let us revert to the easier name – was printed in Mainz, in western Germany, around 1453–5. It is a large format Latin Bible, complete and in two volumes. Perhaps about 180 copies were made (the exact figure is open to dispute, as we will see), and about 50 of these original copies still survive, a remarkably high number.

We can begin with two pieces of documentary evidence which mention Gutenberg by name. One dates from almost fifty years after the printed Bible was finished; and the other refers to events more than a decade before it was begun. It is from little clues like these than we can begin to move inwards towards the production of the Gutenberg Bible itself.

A world history published in 1499 in Cologne, about 75 miles (120 kilometres)

down-river from Mainz, recounts that Ulrich Zel, a local printer, used to recall that the first printed book was a Latin Bible, produced in Mainz by one Johann Gutenberg. Ulrich Zel could well have known Gutenberg personally, for he probably learned his craft in Mainz in the early 1460s, and he was printing in Cologne by at least 1464, well within Gutenberg's lifetime. His memories are likely to be credible. Zel recollected that this first Bible was printed in a large typeface 'such as that now used for the printing of Missals'. This phrase is crucial, for the Gutenberg Bible itself includes no obvious clue as to its date or printer, but it is one of only two fifteenth-century Bibles printed in a Gothic liturgical type, like that appropriate for Missals. The other edition of the Bible in similar type, also evidently very early, is known as the '36-line Bible' or 'B36', by analogy with the 42-line Bible. Because of a number of clumsy misreadings in the text of B36, it is evident that its typesetters actually copied it from the B42 edition. Therefore, of the two Missal-type printed Bibles of the fifteenth century, the earlier has to be B42. That is more or less how it was discovered in the eighteenth century that the 42-line Bible has to be the edition which Ulrich Zel remembered as the first work of Johann Gutenberg.

136 opposite

The city of Mainz, on the Rhine river, as shown in the world chronicle of Hartman Schedel printed in Nuremberg in 1493

137

No contemporary picture of Gutenberg survives. This is an imaginary portrait published in 1584

There are a number of relatively slight contemporary documents which mention Gutenberg by name, mostly administrative records concerning law suits or taxation. He was Johann Gensfleisch zum Gutenberg. He was born in Mainz, but from the early 1430s until about 1444 he was evidently living in Strassburg. (The city was then on the German side of the border; when it became part of France the spelling changed to 'Strasbourg'.) There is a fascinating and much-debated document of 1439. It survives in a transcript and shows Gutenberg to have been involved at that time in another speculative invention which evidently included some kind of press. The record concerns the failure of an enterprise in which Gutenberg and three partners had planned to mass-produce mirrors (*Spiegeln*), which they intended to sell during a forthcoming pilgrimage to Aachen. Evidently, a great deal of money had been invested. Many things went wrong, including the misjudging of the date of the pilgrimage (1440 instead of 1439) and the death of one of the partners. The equipment for making the mirrors, over which the legal quarrel took place, apparently included a mechanical stamping process.

Some historians of books have hoped that this enigmatic enterprise of 1439 might have been a primitive experiment in printing, even suggesting that the 'mirrors' could be the 'mirror of human salvation', the blockbook *Speculum Humanae Salvationis*, or *Spiegel der menschlichen Seligkeit* in German, which we encountered earlier (pp.163-4). In fact, they clearly do refer to actual mirrors, probably stamped or inset into impressed metal borders. The pilgrimage to Aachen took place every seven years. On such occasions, the relics of the town were displayed to pilgrims outside the cathedral. They included some amazing treasures, such as (apparently) the actual nightgown the Virgin Mary had worn in the stable in Bethlehem when she gave birth to Jesus and the original swaddling bands in which she wrapped the newborn baby, made from Joseph's stockings. Relics so astonishing were greatly admired. One day in the early 1490s (admittedly later than Gutenberg but within the fifteenth century), 142,000 pilgrims were counted entering the city gates of Aachen in a single day of the pilgrimage. Such enormous numbers could not hope to touch or hardly even to see the relics. Therefore, the custom was for pilgrims to buy little convex

mirrors which they would hold up before the relics of Aachen. The reflection captured some of the spiritual presence of the holy relics, and happy pilgrims returned home with these mirrors pinned to their hats, knowing that they carried absorbed light from the actual relics (Pl. 138).

Whether or not Gutenberg actually sold any of his pilgrim mirrors, the reference tells us several things about the man. The enterprise involved mass production by a complicated mechanical process. It required greater financial capital than the inventor was able or willing to invest, but it had the potential for enormous profit. The partners had a very specific market in mind, a religious one, and the whole scheme depended on evolving an inexpensive means of supplying and exploiting that market.

Gutenberg was back in Mainz by October 1448. It is impossible and pointless to try to guess when he first conceived the idea of mass-producing the Bible by a mechanical process. It is often assumed that he invented printing and then looked about for a major text to publish by this new technique and that he opted for the Bible. It could as well be the other way round. Gutenberg had grasped the unlimited potential for selling pilgrim mirrors in Aachen and he then set about perfecting a method of reproducing them, and perhaps he perceived a market for Bibles and pondered how to supply them in large numbers. A record of 1455, which we will come to in a few moments, suggests that Gutenberg had taken out two financial loans for some vast and confidential enterprise in 1450 and 1452. It is apparent that these concerned his audacious plan to create a lectern Bible by machinery.

By the middle of the fifteenth century, lectern Bibles were returning to fashion, especially in northern Europe. For 300 years the giant biblical volumes of the twelfth century had been put aside in favour of the little hand-held manuscript Bibles invented in thirteenth-century Paris. Now the monasteries began to look back with nostalgia on their Romanesque pasts. Many of the ancient monasteries in western Germany joined movements of reform and renewal. They were all still Catholic, for this was still a hundred years before the Protestant Reformation. One of the most prominent programmes of revival was associated with the abbey of Bursfeld, which established a network of Benedictine houses dedicated to re-commitment. They all emphasized the central role of the uncontaminated Bible in the religious life. There is some case for suggesting that Gutenberg may have

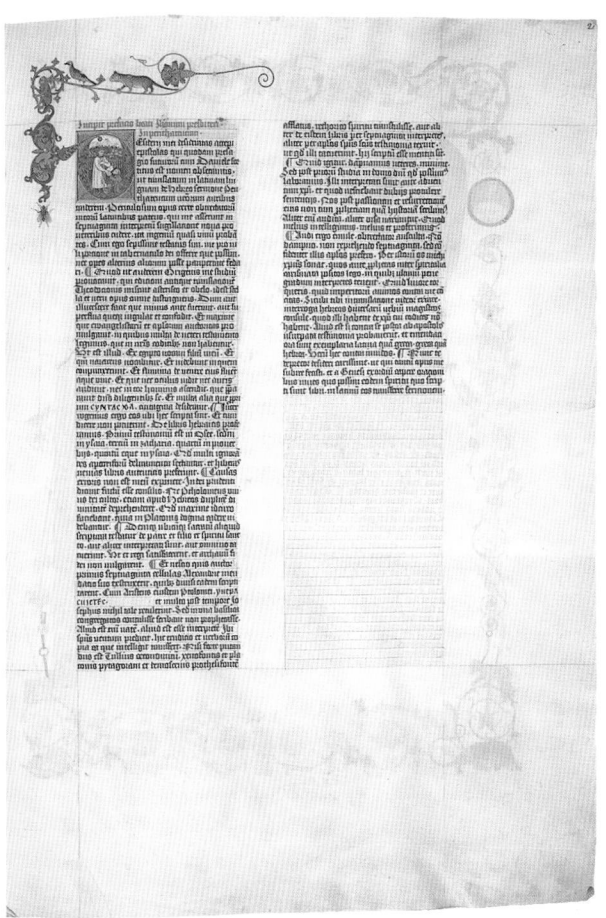

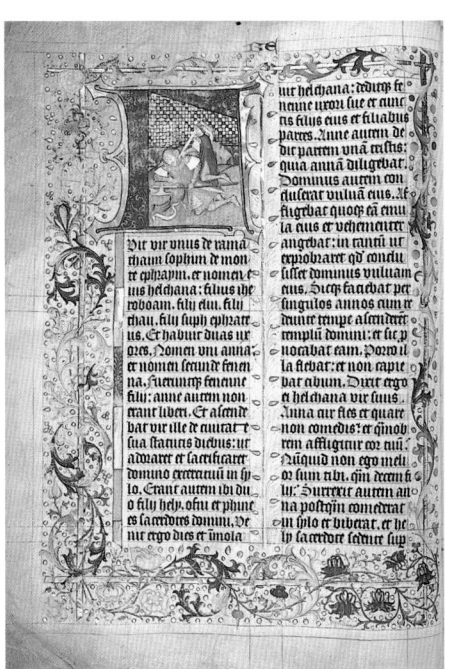

been personally acquainted with Nicholas of Cusa (1401–64), the philosopher and papal legate to Germany, who was a passionate advocate of the monastic reforms. If so, Nicholas of Cusa might himself have suggested the righteousness of mass-producing Bibles which would have the virtue of identical texts. It is probably more likely, however, that Gutenberg looked into the commercial realities of the Rhineland and the Netherlands and perceived a limitless market for lectern Bibles.

There are a number of major surviving manuscript Bibles in large format from almost exactly the period of the Gutenberg Bible. One of the most celebrated is the so-called Giant Bible of Mainz, written in two volumes between April 1452 and July 1453 (Washington, Library of Congress, MS. 8, Pl. 139). It belonged to Mainz Cathedral by the sixteenth century, and may have been made locally. To judge from contemporary notes, the Butzbach Bible was certainly made in Mainz in 1452–4 (Giessen, Universitätsbibliothek, cod. 653). It was written for the Augustinian chapter of Butzbach and was finished in September 1454. Another, from slightly further afield, is a vast set completed for the abbot of St Lawrence near Liège in 1456 (Brussels, BR, mss. 9158–67). The colophon records that those who contributed to its enormous cost would be indelibly inscribed in the Book of Life. In the summer of 1462, Hermann Droem, dean of Utrecht, commissioned a vast six-volume manuscript Bible for the Brothers of the Common Life in Zwolle. It cost him 500 gold florins. It is now Utrecht, Bibliotheek der Rijksuniversiteit, MS. 31 (Pl. 140). Such books were extremely expensive, and the fact that private donors were prepared to invest large sums of money in them would easily suggest a potential profit for anyone who could make such books less expensively.

We should not assume that a fifteenth-century lectern Bible was primarily for reading during church services, as in Protestant churches after the Reformation. On the contrary, the extracts from the Bible which were required for reading during the Catholic liturgy were usually arranged in a separate volume called a Lectionary. Public readings of the Bible, however, took place on many occasions outside the church. These included the reading of passages in the chapter houses and refectories of monasteries and, probably more often than we might at first imagine, in private households of devout laity.

Of the established religious orders, the Carthusians remained especially strong in the fifteenth century. They had a rigorous programme of reading the Bible aloud during meals. A very large number of northern European large-scale manuscript Bibles copied during the lifetime of Gutenberg were, in fact, made for Carthusian houses, and are carefully marked up for reading in the refectory. Examples include a four-volume Bible made for the Carthusians in Utrecht, *c.*1398–1403 (Brussels, BR, mss. 106–7 and 204–5). Another Carthusian copy, similarly marked up, is Brussels, BR, mss. 49 and 201–3). From the cross references in Oxford, Bodleian Library, MS. Bodley 277 (cited above, p.184), we know that the London Carthusian house had a lectern Bible for use in their refectory around 1430. In 1424 (or in 1454, the date is ambiguous) the Carthusians of Nuremberg acquired a fourteenth-century lectern Bible in four volumes and they marked it up in that year with accents for refectory reading (Erlangen, Universitätsbibliothek, Cod. 7 Perg). Another was commissioned for the Carthusians of La Chapelle at Hérinnes-lez-Enghien, south-west of Brussels, apparently in 1457 (again the date is slightly unclear; the manuscript is now in Malmesbury Parish Church, England). All these include a sequence of readings described as *in refectorio*.

Other north European monasteries in the fifteenth century evidently returned to their shelves and pulled out the old Romanesque lectern Bibles and blew off the dust of the previous 300 years. A surprisingly large number of eleventh- and twelfth-century lectern Bibles show evidence of rebinding and repair in the fifteenth century. Missing leaves were replaced in the fifteenth century in the giant Bible of St Maximin in Trier, for example (Phillipps MS. 400, still in private hands), the Gladbach Bible (Cologne, Historisches Archiv, W.277, I–II), and in the second volume of the Dover Bible (Cambridge, Corpus Christi College, MS. 4). Perhaps these were adapted to refectory use. The famous twelfth-century Bible of Bury St Edmunds was referred to in the fifteenth century as *magna biblia refectorii*, 'the great Refectory Bible', a use it would perhaps not have had when it was new. As late as 1633, the Augustinian canons of Corsendoncq in Belgium described their three-volume manuscript Bible as *Biblia Sacra Refectoralia*. If every religious house in Europe seemed to want a refectory Bible in the fifteenth century, it is no wonder that Gutenberg formed a vision of a potential market quite as attractive to his fellow investors as that for pilgrim mirrors in Aachen.

Around 1450, another factor began to affect the political and religious life of Europe. Apocalyptic rumours arrived from the eastern Mediterranean of the relentless advance of the Turks on the outposts of Christendom. The extraordinary possibility that Christianity itself was under threat caused extreme alarm. Throughout history, nations have frequently resorted to the reassurance of their Bibles during times when their religious security seemed most under challenge. The ancient eastern Christian capital of Constantinople fell to Mehmet II on 29

May 1453. The news spread across Europe with extraordinary speed. By this date, work on preparing the Gutenberg Bible must have been considerably advanced. Someone involved with the process may have realized that a renewed anxiety in Germany about the advance of the forces of the Antichrist could only help potential sales of the very orthodox Latin Bible. More than that, the functioning press offered a perfectly timed opportunity for mass sales of another religious commodity with a market as vast as that for pilgrim mirrors in Aachen. These were indulgences. With these we return to the printing press in Mainz.

An indulgence is really a fund-raising certificate. From time to time, the late medieval Church would give permission to an appropriate agent to collect money from the general public for a charitable or religious cause. In exchange, the donor would receive a document recording the purpose of the contribution and promising that, if the gift was made out of piety, he or she would be entitled to confess their sins and to receive forgiveness from God. The printing press was ideal for making such documents, for identical copies were needed in huge qualities. Gutenberg's press printed at least four editions of indulgences for raising funds for the war against the Turks and for the defence of the Christians in Cyprus (Pl. 141). These were printed for intended use during the years 1454 and 1455, and they include words in the same printed type as was being used for the printing of the Gutenberg Bible. The press also printed a quirky little 6-leaf pamphlet known as the *Türkenkalendar*, a verse text warning of the imminent danger from

141

Among the first productions of Gutenberg's printing press were certificates of indulgence, acknowledging funds for the defence of Chistendom against the Muslims. This example was sold on 13 April 1455 (NEW YORK, PIERPONT MORGAN LIBRARY)

the Turks. It includes Calendar material and prognostications for the forthcoming year, 1455, and the earliest printed New Year's greeting (*Eijn gut selig nuwe jar*). It is assumed therefore to have been printed before the end of the year 1454. These, then, are the oldest datable examples of printing with movable type, and they must have been made in Mainz at the same time as the Gutenberg Bible was being printed. Whether they were printed on the same press or in a separate shop (there is some evidence for both possibilities), this highly topical anti-Turkish propaganda was certainly an enterprise which must be attributed to Gutenberg.

Each indulgence is printed with a blank space for the precise date, so that the collector of alms could fill in the date by hand when he issued the document. The earliest surviving copy of a Gutenberg indulgence with its date actually completed like this was issued on 22 October 1454. By chance (probably), this was during the meeting of a conference of noblemen in Frankfurt, 15–28 October 1454, called for the express purpose of rallying public support for a military campaign against the Turks. Johann Gutenberg (or one of his immediate colleagues) also attended the conference, and he publicly exhibited there samples of the Gutenberg Bible, apparently for sale.

Now we have our first documentary sighting of the Gutenberg Bible. It comes from a letter written by Enea Silvio de' Piccolomini (1405–64, afterwards Pope Pius II, 1458–64). Enea Silvio was at that time chancellor to the Holy Roman Emperor (Pl. 142). He gave the opening address at the conference in Frankfurt. The following year, in February 1455, Enea Silvio attended another similar anti-Turkish conference in Wiener Neustadt and, after this second meeting, he wrote in March 1455 to the Spanish cardinal, Juan de Carvajal, following up an earlier letter (now lost) about having seen specimen sheets of the Gutenberg Bible. It was in Frankfurt, he reported, that he was shown the examples of the Bible by 'that miraculous man' (*viro illo mirabili*, perhaps Gutenberg himself). They were not whole Bibles but gatherings from various different biblical books. The writing was beautiful and most correct and, Enea Silvio noted, Cardinal Carvajal would be able to read it effortlessly, without glasses. Several people said that 158 copies were done, and others said that there were 180 copies. If he had known of the cardinal's interest, he continues, he would have bought a copy for him. Some quires were brought to show the emperor in Wiener Neustadt. Enea Silvio says he will try to have a copy for sale sent to him so that he can acquire it, but he fears this will not be possible, both because of the distance and because buyers are said to have been found for every copy, even before the books were finished.

There is much information in this brief reference. We learn that one man, regarded as a worker of wonders, was actually present during the imperial conference on the Turkish threat. Gutenberg's participation in supplying indulgences may have brought the occasion to his attention, or *vice versa*. It is notable that Gutenberg's first apparent exhibition of his miraculous Bible took place in a gathering of nobles and princes of the Church who has assembled because they were alarmed that the Christianity of Europe was under threat. He was soliciting customers in this context. That is one clue as to Gutenberg's perceived market for his book. Evidently by October 1454 the whole Bible was not yet ready, but enough separate gatherings were available to demonstrate the work to full effect. Between then and March 1455, when Enea Silvio wrote his letter, the edition was fully subscribed, even before it was finished. No price is mentioned but evidently Enea Silvio considered it well within the budget of his correspondent. The unbound samples shown to the Emperor Frederick III at Wiener Neustadt were presumably brought to the conference there in February 1455. Therefore we may guess that the whole book was still not completed by then, and that Gutenberg was again attending an anti-Turkish congress, soliciting buyers among the delegates. On this occasion, presumably, he announced that the edition was sold out. We need not regard it as strange that Gutenberg Bibles could be ordered before they were completed, because, after all, most manuscripts were commissioned before they were made. It was the normal way of buying books.

The printing of the Bible was probably brought to conclusion during the course of 1455. The most famous document concerning Gutenberg and his press was drawn up on 6 November 1455. It concerns the recovery of a loan by Johann Fust, evidently Gutenberg's principal partner in the project. Fust asked for the return of 2,020 *gulden*, representing two loans to Gutenberg of 800 *gulden* each, plus interest. From the sums and the rate of interest stated, these loans must have been made in 1450 and 1452. The first of these was secured against the collateral of Gutenberg's equipment. The second loan, according to Gutenberg's evidence, was simply a profit-sharing partnership in 'the work of the books'. The court decision was that Gutenberg would have to pay back the first sum, with interest, and any part of the second sum not invested in the joint project.

There is no clear evidence that the negotiations between Fust and Gutenberg in November 1455 were necessarily hostile. The fact that the dissolution of the partnership is expressed as a lawsuit may be no more than a reflection of the large sums involved. The Bible was presumably finished and the profits were at least calculable. The traditional view is that Gutenberg had been almost bankrupted by the printing of the Bible and was unable to pay back what was required of him. It is also possible that it was by his own choice, or by friendly agreement with Fust, that Gutenberg exercised the collateral and made over his printing press to Johann Fust instead of paying money.

One can imagine that in late 1455 and even early 1456, the printed gatherings of the Gutenberg Bible were assembled into complete sets and were dispatched across Europe to the customers who had ordered them. They would need to be decorated and bound by hand before they could be used. One copy now in the Bibliothèque Nationale de France in Paris has two notes added by a cleric of the church of St Stephen in Mainz, recording that he finished rubricating and binding volume II of the Bible on 15 August 1456, and that he completed volume I a week later, on 24 August 1456 (Pl. 143). By that date, at the absolute latest, the entire Bible existed as a printed book.

Having followed the isolated pieces of historical evidence for Gutenberg and his publication, let us now turn to the Gutenberg Bibles themselves. About fifty copies still survive, now scattered among the rare book libraries and treasuries of the world, as far from Mainz as Tokyo and Austin, Texas. There are quite a large number of fragments and single leaves of others. Gutenberg Bibles have been subjected to an enormous amount of extremely close examination. A great deal of information about the production of the Bible can be deduced from a mass of little clues in the books themselves. From this we can then look back again over the few datable documents and we can eventually fill in many gaps in the story.

The Gutenberg Bible is a folio-sized book, about 405 by 295 mm (16 by 11½ inches). It is in two volumes, the first with 324 leaves of text and the second with 319 leaves of text. It is thus a large book, much bigger than the friars' Bibles of the thirteenth century but moderate in comparison with those giant Bibles of

143

This defective final leaf of a Gutenberg Bible in Paris records the completion of its rubrication on the feast of Saint Bartholomew (24 August) 1456 (PARIS, BNF)

eleventh- and twelfth-century Italy. It comprises the normal Latin Vulgate in the

order made standard in thirteenth-century Paris, as tabulated above (p.120), and
it is quite possible that the exemplar was actually a thirteenth-century manuscript. The Gutenberg text was set into type with great care, so far as can be
judged. Occasional misreadings of abbreviations in setting the text suggest that
the exemplar may have been of much smaller size that the spacious Gutenberg
Bible itself. Scholars who have compared large fifteenth-century manuscript
Bibles from the Rhineland have never found a copy similar enough to show any
textual affiliations. The principal divergence between the Gutenberg Bible and
most late medieval manuscripts is that it includes all four books of Ezra instead
of the three which are normal in the Paris text. IV Ezra (called II Esdras in Latin)
was always a debated text, and is not extant in any Greek Bible. It occurs in
volume I of the Gutenberg Bible, fols. 247r–260r.

The Gutenberg Bible includes the standard medieval prologues, except those
for each of the Minor Prophets, which are omitted, and it is divided into chapters
in what was by then the normal manner. This is worth recording, simply because
the Gutenberg Bible itself rapidly became the principal exemplar for nearly all
other printed Bibles, and the features that entered its textual and physical repertoire in the early 1450s became immortalized for generations. The Gutenberg
Bible does not include the alphabetical *Interpretation of Hebrew Names* at the end.
This omission was unusual enough in the fifteenth century to attract notice at the
time. The Carthusians of Erfurt owned a Gutenberg Bible by the 1470s, probably
the copy now at Eton College, and the contemporary catalogue description of it
in the monastery library remarked on the absence of the *Interpretation*. Perhaps
even because they happened not to be present in the Gutenberg Bible, this section
rapidly evaporated from all copies of the Latin Bible after that time.

The print of the Gutenberg Bible is, of course, in columns of 42 lines, or mostly
so (we will come back to this point). The typeface, as was noted in 1499, resembles
the formal black-letter script of Missals and other substantial liturgical books.
There is an ingenious theory that Gutenberg made his type with the original
intention of printing a Missal, but no trace of any such Missal is known. A good
Gothic script was equally appropriate for a lectern Bible. Enea Silvio commented
on the beauty and clarity of the script in 1455. It is a very upright and compressed
Gothic type, with a crispness and density on the page which is of remarkable
elegance. Scientific analysis of the ink shows unusually high levels of lead and
copper, which may explain the deep and shiny black finish to the print in the
Gutenberg Bible. The type is not especially large, and is much smaller than the
script of many manuscript Bibles of the period. It is, however, eminently practical
for public reading. With normal eyesight, the Gutenberg Bible is perfectly legible
at about three feet. One feature of the text suggests that it was deliberately
designed for reading aloud. Numbers are always written in words and never in
their equivalent roman digits, as they often were in the portable manuscript

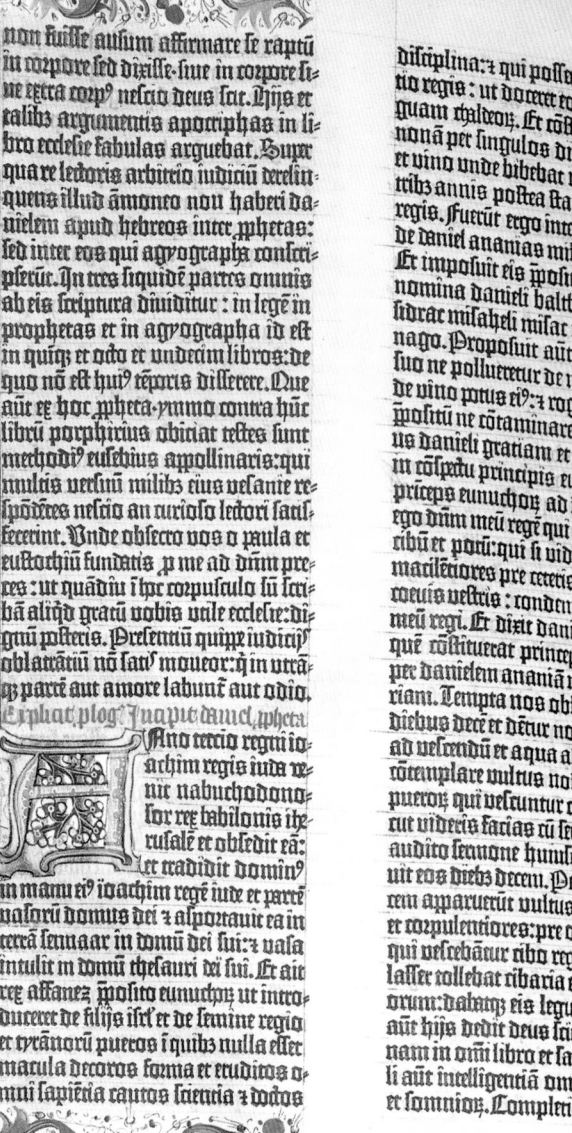

non fuiſſe auſum affirmare ſe raptū
in corpore ſed dixiſſe·ſiue in corpore ſi
ue extra corp⁹ neſcio deus ſcit. Hijs et
talibꝫ argumentis apocriphas in li
bro eccleſie fabulas arguebat. Sup̃
qua re lectoris arbitrio iudiciū derelin
quens illud āmoneo non haberi da
nielem apud hebreos inter ꝓphetas:
ſed inter eos qui agyographa conſcri
pſerūt. Jn tres ſiquidē partes omnis
ab eis ſcriptura diuiditur: in lege in
prophetas et in agyographa id eſt
in quinꝫ et octo et undecim libros: de
quo nō eſt hui⁹ tēporis diſſerere. Que
aūt ex hoc ꝓpheta·ymmo contra hūc
librū porphirius obiciat teſtes ſunt
methodi⁹ euſebius appollinaris: qui
multis verſuū milibꝫ eius veſanie re
ſpōdentes neſcio an curioſo lectori ſatis
fecerint. Unde obſecro vos o paula et
euſtochiū fundatis·ꝓ me ad dūm pre
ces: ut quādiu ī ipſe corpuſculo ſū ſcri
bā aliquid gratū vobis vtile eccleſie: di
gnū poſteris. Preſentiū quippe iudiciis
oblatratiū nō ſatis⁹ moueor: q̄ in utra
ꝗ partē aut amore labūt aut odio.

Explicit plog⁹ Jncipit daniel ꝓpheta

Anno tercio regni io
achim regis iuda ve
nit nabuchodono
ſor rex babilonis ieꝝ
ruſalē et obſedit eā:
et tradidit dominus
in manu ei⁹ ioachim regē iude et parte
vaſorū domus dei et aſpoꝛtauit ea in
terrā ſennaar in domū dei ſui: et vaſa
intulit in domū theſauri dei ſui. Et ait
rex aſſanez ſpoſito eunuchoꝛ ut intro
duceret de filijs iſrl et de ſemine regio
et tyrānorū pueros i quibꝫ nulla eſſet
macula decoros forma et eruditos o-
mni ſapientia cautos ſcientia et doctos

diſciplina: et qui poſſent ſtare in pala
tio regis: ut doceret eos litteras et lin
guam chaldeoꝝ. Et cōſtituit eis rex an-
nonā per ſingulos dies de cibis ſuis
et vino unde bibebat ipſe: ut enutriti
tribꝫ annis poſtea ſtarent in cōſpectu
regis. Fuerūt ergo inter eos de filijs iude daniel ananias miſahel et azarias.
Et impoſuit eis ꝓpoſitus eunuchoꝛ
nomina danieli balthazar: anani-
ſidrac miſaheli miſac et azarie abd-
nago. Propoſuit aūt daniel in corde
ſuo ne pollueretur de menſa regis neqꝫ
de vino potus ei⁹: et rogauit eunuchoꝝ
ꝓpoſitū ne cōtaminaretur. Dedit aūt de
us danieli gratiam et miſericordiam
in cōſpectu principis eunuchoꝝ. Et ait
princeps eunuchoꝝ ad danielē. Timeo
ego dūm meū regē qui cōſtituit vobis
cibū et potū: qui ſi viderit vultus vro-
marſilentiores pre ceteris adoleſcentib⁹
coeuis veſtris: condemnabitis capud
meū regi. Et dixit daniel ad malaſſar
quē cōſtituerat princeps eunuchoꝝ ſu-
pꝛ danielem ananiā miſahelē et aza-
riam. Tempta nos obſecro ſeruos tuos
diebus decem et dentur nobis legumina
ad veſcendū et aqua ad bibendum:
et contemplare vultus noſtros et vultus
pueroꝝ qui veſcuntur cibo regio: et ſicut
videris facias cum ſeruis tuis. Qui
audito ſermone huiuſcemodi temptaui
it eos diebus decem. Poſt dies aūt de-
rem apparuerunt vultus eorū meliores
et corpulentiores: pre omnibus pueris
qui veſcebātur cibo regio. Porro malaſſar tollebat cibaria et vinū potus e-
orum: dabatqꝫ eis legumina. Pueris
aūt hijs dedit deus ſcientiā et diſcipli-
nam in omni libro et ſapientia: dani-
li aūt intelligentiā omniū viſionum
et ſomnioꝝ. Completis itaqꝫ diebus

post quos dixerat rex ut introduceret
tur:introduxit eos ſposit9 eunuchoꝛu
in conſpectu nabuchodonoſoꝛ. Cunq;
locut9 fuiſſet rex : nõ ſunt inuenta ta
les de vniuerſis ut daniel ananias mi
ſahel z azarias. Et ſteterut in conſpe
ctu regis:et omne verbum ſapientie z
intellect9 quod ſciſcitatus eſt ab eis
inuenit in eis decuplum ſuper cunctos
ariolos et magos qui erant in vni
uerſo regno eius. Fuit autem daniel
uſq; ad annu primu cyri regis. (cap ij.)
In anno ſecundo regni nabuchodonoſoꝛ
uidit nabuchodonoſoꝛ ſomniu:et cõ
territus eſt ſpirit9 eius:et ſomniu eius
fugit ab eo. Precepit aut rex ut conuo
carentur arioli et magi et malefici et
chaldei:ut indicaret regi ſomnia ſua.
Qui cu veniſſent ſteterut corã rege : et
dixit ad eos rex. Vidi ſomniu : z men
te confuſus ignoro quid viderim. Re
ſponderutq; chaldei regi ſiriace . Rex
in ſempiternu viue. Dic ſomniu tuu
ſuis:et inpretatõe eius indicabim9.
Et reſpõdens rex ait chaldeis. Sermo
receſſit a me. Niſi indicaueritis michi
ſomniu et coniecturã ei9 peribitis vos:
et domus veſtre publicabunt. Si aut
ſomniu et coniectura ei9 narraueritis
premiã z dona et honore multu acci
pietis a me. Somniu igitur et inpre
tatõe eius indicate michi. Reſpõde
runt ſecudo atq; dixerut. Rex ſomniu
dicat ſeruis ſuis:z interpretatõe ei9
indicabim9. Reſpõdit rex z ait. Certe
noui q; temp9 redimitis:ſcientes q; re
ceſſit a me ſermo. Si ergo ſomniu
nõ indicaueritis michi vna eſt de vo
bis ſentetia : q̃d inpretatõe qq; fal
lacem et deceptione plenã cõpoſueritis
ut loquamini michi donec tempus pre
tranſeat. Somniu itaq; dicite michi:

ut ſciam q; inpretatõe quoq; eius
veram loquamini. Reſpõdentes ergo
chaldei corã rege dixerut. Nõ eſt homo
ſup terrã:qui ſermonem tuu rex poſſit
implere : ſed neq; regum quiſquã ma
gnus et potens verbu huiuſcemodi ſci
ſcitatur ab omni ariolo z mago z chal
deo. Sermo eni que tu queris rex gra
uis eſt : nec reperietur quiſquã qui in
dicet illu in conſpectu regis exceptis diis
quoru nõ eſt conuerſatio cu hoibus.
Quo audito : rex in furore et in ira ma
gna precepit ut perirent omnes ſapien
tes babilonis. Et egreſſa ſententia:ſa
pientes interficiebãtur : querebanturq;
daniel et ſocij eius ut perirent. Tuc da
niel requiſiuit de lege atq; ſententia ab
arioch principe militie regis:qui egreſ
ſus fuerat ad interficiendos ſapientes
babilonis. Et interrogauit eum qui a
rege poteſtatem acceperat:quã ob cau
ſam tã crudelis ſententia a facie regis
eſſet egreſſa. Cu ergo rem indicaſſet a
rioch danieli:daniel ingreſſus rogauit
regem ut tempus daret ſibi ad ſolutione
indicandã regi. Et ingreſſus eſt domu
ſuã:ananiæq; et miſaheli et azarie ſo
cijs ſuis indicauit negociu ut quereret
miſericordiã a facie dei celi ſuper ſacra
mento iſto:et non perirent daniel et ſocij
eius cu ceteris ſapientibus babilonis.
Tunc danieli miſteriu p viſione noctis
reuelatu eſt. Et daniel benedixit deo celi
z locutus ait. Sit nomen domini benedi
ctum a ſeculo et uſq; in ſeculu:quia ſa
pientia et fortitudo eius ſunt : et ipſe
mutat tempora et etates. Tranſfert re
gna atq; conſtituit : dat ſapientiam
ſapientibus : et ſcientiã intelligentibus di
ſciplinã. Ipſe reuelat pfunda et abſcõ
dita:z nouit in tenebris conſtituta:et
lux cu eo eſt. Tibi deus patru noſtroru

Bibles of the friars. Thus, for example, Genesis 5:26 records that Methuselah lived for 782 years after the birth of Lamech. Any reader whose native language was not Latin (which means every person in Europe by the fifteenth century) might well falter over rendering 'DCCLXXXII' unhesitatingly in public, but anyone could read aloud the words 'septingentis octoginta duobus' printed in full in the Gutenberg Bible (volume I, fol. 7r). There are thousands of examples of this. The consistency shows it to have been editorial policy; and the policy shows that Gutenberg probably originally had an institutional market in mind.

It is not absolutely certain how Gutenberg made the individual pieces of metal type which he assembled into words and sentences for printing. Most printers until the nineteenth century initially prepared hard metal punches for each letter of the alphabet, engraved in reverse. They would strike these with a hammer into a copper base, to produce a deeply indented letter shape. A lead alloy was then melted and poured into this reusable copper mould, and by this means unlimited numbers of identical pieces of soft metal type could be produced at great speed. That was certainly the standard method of type-casting from at least the 1470s. Very close examination of the type in the Gutenberg Bible, however, reveals very small discrepancies between letterforms which one would have expected to have

been identical. It may be that Gutenberg pressed his letter punches into very fine wet sand, rather than into copper. By this more primitive method he could only have cast one piece of metal type at a time, for the sand mould is destroyed each time it is used. The technique of sand casting was well established among metal workers in Gutenberg's time, and perhaps he had himself employed it for the pilgrim mirrors. The use of sand moulds might explain how Gutenberg created combinations of letters and contractions, for he could have pressed out complex moulds by building up shapes from multiple small elements as required. Although the Gutenberg Bible was certainly printed from separate pieces of reusable type, the compactness of the writing looks much more like the effect of a hand-written page than a row of detached letters.

It is often asserted that the Gutenberg Bible was made to resemble a medieval manuscript. Of course no one would have thought of it like that. It was made to look like a book, and all books in Europe at that time were what we would now call manuscripts. Probably the most visible difference between any manuscript of the Middle Ages and later printed books is that the majority of manuscripts are in more than one colour. Even the most humble of medieval books include headings in red and initials perhaps in red and blue. Many are dazzlingly polychrome or filled with gold. Most printed books, even now, are black and white. Colour was a casualty of printing. Gutenberg would have assumed automatically that his Bible would need headings in red, at the very least. A number of pages which must have been printed very early on in the work on the Gutenberg Bible do actually have headings printed in red ink, but clearly this proved technically very difficult or unrealistically time-consuming. Instead, the typographers began to leave spaces for headings to be completed by hand. This is not really very different from

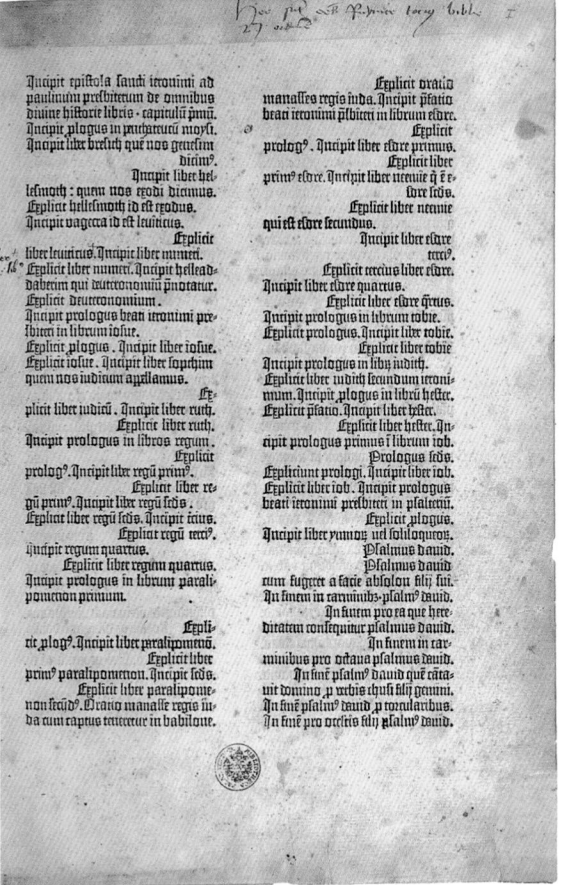

leaving a blank space in a printed indulgence for an added date. The coloured headings for each book and prologue, however, were an inflexible part of the apparatus of any usable Bible. Gutenberg therefore printed an 8-page supplement to the Bible with a long list of all the required headings, one after the other in sequence, so that the rubricators could copy them into the appropriate spaces of the Bible. These strange-looking lists survive bound into only two extant copies of the Gutenberg Bible, resembling those old-fashioned sheets of jam labels made to be cut up (Pl. 146). It is not clear whether the Bibles were

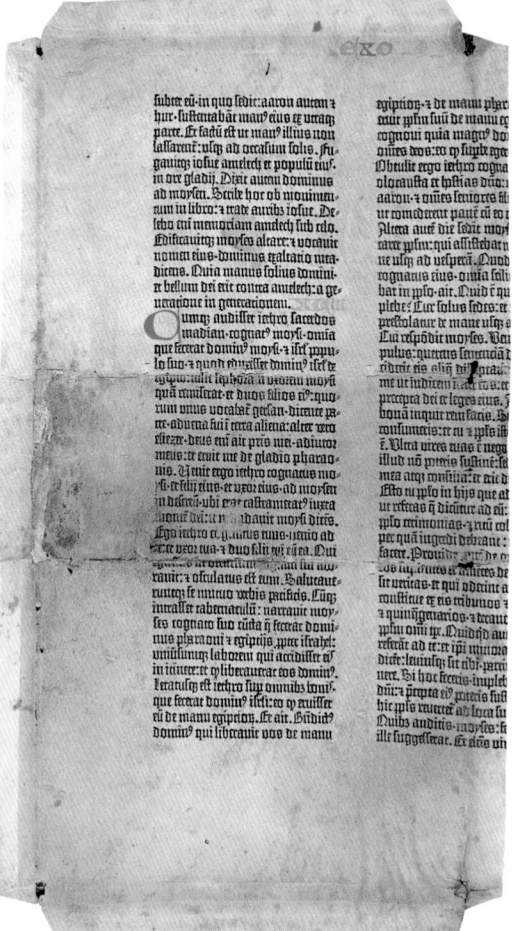

standardly issued with lists of headings as an integral part of the book (in which case the owners of the 48 other Gutenberg Bibles must admit that their copies are bibliographically defective), or whether the lists were perhaps available on loan. The Leipzig vellum copy of the Gutenberg Bible has the same guide words for the headings handwritten in a minute cursive hand in the lower margins of the pages where they were required. Presumably that copy, at least, was published without any integral supplement of headings.

Although Gutenberg must have originally hoped to print the headings in red ink, there is no evidence that he ever planned that coloured initials would be printed, either at the start of texts or for the running-titles across the tops of the pages. From the beginning it was intended to have these added by hand after the text was complete. Spaces were indented into the columns of text for the supply of initials. The sizes varied according to the relative importance of the opening of text. Thus, for example, on fol. 1r of the first volume a rectangular space 6 lines high was left at the top left of the first column for the insertion of a large initial 'F' for the general prologue to the whole Bible (Pl. 148). In the right-hand column of the same page a 2-line space was left for an initial 'Q' at the beginning of Chapter 2; on fol. 1v, further 2-line spaces were left for the opening of Chapters 3 and 4; and so on. On fol. 4v a larger, 4-line, space was left for a 'D' at the opening of the prologue to the Pentateuch. No space is allowed for the opening initial of Genesis on fol. 5r, because the Latin Bible opens with the letter 'I' (*In principio creavit* ...) and a tall 'I' was customarily painted in the margin right up against the adjacent block of text (Pl. 153).

There is no allowance for pictures in the Gutenberg Bible. This is unusual enough to be worth mentioning. By the fifteenth century, some large manuscript Bibles had miniatures as wide as the columns of text and most had opening initials which were large enough to enclose illustrations. There are no spaces between the books of the Bible in Gutenberg's scheme, and the sizes of even the largest initials were hardly big enough for pictures. There is one theory that Gutenberg might have intended to include engravings of birds and animals in the margins of the Bible but no evidence supports it. On the contrary, the Gutenberg Bible is an austere book. It was not devised as a luxury Bible, at least not when compared with many Netherlandish or Rhenish manuscript copies of the period.

Buyers of the Gutenberg Bible were offered one optional concession to luxury. Some copies were printed on parchment and some on paper. Probably about a quarter of the edition was originally to be on parchment. A buyer could choose. This was the first time in the history of book production that an identical book was available in two versions, and Gutenberg could not accurately anticipate which would prove more saleable. The parchment copies must have been much more expensive. They would also have been bulkier and considerably heavier. A paper copy of the Gutenberg Bible, with its binding, weighs about 30 lbs (approximately 13.5 kilograms) whereas the same book on parchment weighs about 50 lbs (approximately 22.5 kilograms).

The printers' investment in sheets of parchment and bales of paper would have been considerable. A complete Gutenberg Bible comprises 643 leaves, or approximately 322 bifolia. Medieval farm animals were smaller than their modern descendants and so we cannot be quite certain how large an area of parchment could be obtained from a single calf skin. Assuming that two pairs of leaves could be obtained from a single pelt (which is likely but not certain), every copy of the Gutenberg Bible printed on parchment would have required the skins of about 160 animals. A projected run of about 25 copies, for example, would have required nearly 4,000 skins. Paper was needed in even larger quantities. It was imported in bales from Piedmont. The initial purchase of paper for printing the Gutenberg Bible comprised sheets with a maker's watermark showing a bull's head. This observation (seemingly unimportant) will become significant in what is about to follow. It is likely that Gutenberg made an initial purchase of seven bales of paper and that he assumed this would suffice for the edition. A bale comprised ten reams of paper; each ream would furnish 500 bifolia. Seven bales would thus provide 35,000 pairs of leaves, which, allowing for experiments, proofs and waste sheets, is consistent with about a hundred copies on paper being originally planned.

It appears that the typesetters divided the copy for the Gutenberg Bible between them and began working on four different sections of the text more or less simultaneously. The first set the opening pages of the Bible (volume I, from fol. 1r). While he or she was doing this, a second person began setting up the type for the text from the opening of I Kings (volume I, from fol. 129r). At almost the same time, a third typesetter started on the Books of Solomon at the opening of the second volume of the Bible (volume II, from fol. 1r). The fourth person began

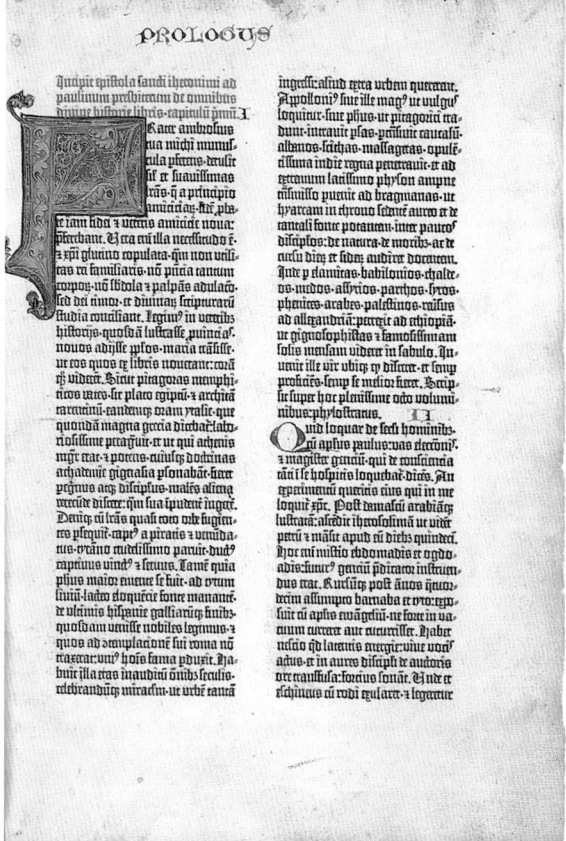

148

*The first pages of each volume
of the Gutenberg Bible were
originally set with 40 lines to
the column. This is the opening
of Volume I*
(MANCHESTER, JOHN RYLANDS
UNIVERSITY LIBRARY)

with I Maccabees (volume II, from fol. 162r). These four main campaigns of production may mean that there were four presses in the printing shop, or they may represent no more than four desks preparing pages of type for a single press. As the pages were set and locked into place, so the workmen began to print off what they hoped would be a sufficient number of sheets for the edition. To begin with, the typesetters arranged their pages with only 40 lines of print to a column (Pl. 148). While the early pages were being printed there was a change of plan to compress the blocks of text into a tighter and more economical page layout. Fols. 1r–5r of volume I are set with 40 lines; folio 5v is set with 41 lines; thereafter the text follows the standard pattern of 42 lines. Similarly, fols. 129r–132r of volume I are set with 40 lines; from fol. 133r onwards, the Bible has 42 lines again. When a decision was made to increase the number of lines, the first typesetter was evidently nine pages into his task, the second was seven pages into his apportioned section, but the third and fourth had not yet begun printing.

Thereafter, the printers worked on these four different units of the book, page by page, setting the text, running off sheets, and stacking up the printed leaves to await the completion of the whole Bible. Probably they initially printed about 100 to 110 copies of each page on paper and about 25 on parchment. Each page was printed as a separate operation, and of course each leaf had to be printed on both sides. This work continued until they had printed volume I, fols. 1r–32r (Genesis 1:1 to Exodus 8:18), volume I, fols. 129r–158v (I Kings 1:1 to II Kings 21:20), volume II, fols. 1r–16r (Proverbs, Ecclesiastes and Song of Songs to 5:1), and volume II, fol. 162r only (I Maccabees 1:1 to 1:25). Then another halt was called. There was a further change of plan. A decision was taken at this point to increase the print-run significantly. From those four places in the text, therefore, they started printing about 130 to 140 copies of each page on paper and up to

about 40 on parchment.

We cannot know for certain the reason for this decision. Gutenberg probably found that he was able to sell more copies than he had originally expected. Orders were coming in steadily while the Bible was being printed. The parchment copies were evidently selling signifi-cantly better than the printers had calculated. The print-run of paper copies was increased by around 30 per cent but that of the more expensive copies on parchment was increased by about 65 per cent. Perhaps Gutenberg's participation in the con-gress in Frankfurt in October 1454 showed him that there were more private customers than he had anticipated. Institutions, buying out of community funds, might opt for the cheaper paper editions, but wealthy individuals might well prefer the more luxurious copies. Enea Silvio's reference to the display of samples in Frankfurt tells us that buyers there were subscribing avidly in 1454, and that Cardinal Carvajal contemplated buying a copy personally.

The increase in the print-run can be calculated from a simple fact. Of course, the type had by then been redistributed for the 155 pages which had already been printed. These pages therefore had to be reset into type and printed again in order to make up the difference between the original total and the number now required. We find this in the Gutenberg Bibles themselves. At each of the expected four sections of the Bible, leaves are extant in two versions, the first and the reset second impressions. The text is identical but has been carefully set up again in type so that the end of each reprinted section matches up exactly with where the first printing had ended. The second settings all use 42 lines to a page, not the 40 with which the typesetters began their first run. Rather fewer abbrevi-ations are therefore used in the second settings of these pages. To give a couple of simple examples, the word *deus* in Genesis 1:29 was printed as *de⁹* in the first printing of fol. 5r of volume I, but in full, *deus,* in the second. A few words later,

150, 151

The slightly different settings of the text of Genesis 1:29 can be seen in details from the John Rylands copy, which has 40 lines to the page, and the Grenville copy in the British Library, which is set with 42 lines (MANCHESTER, JOHN RYLANDS UNIVERSITY LIBRARY, AND LONDON, BL)

habent was abbreviated to *hn̄t* in the first setting but expanded slightly to *habēt* in the second (Pls. 150–1). When the sheets of the Gutenberg Bibles were eventually bound up, no regard was taken as to whether the quires happened to be of the first or second impressions. Extant copies of the Bible show wide variation in combining elements of the two printings.

It is by recording the ratio of the first to second settings in these reprinted leaves in surviving copies that one can estimate the relative increase in the size of the whole edition during the printing process.

At this point, the evidence of the paper supplements the picture. The original purchase of seven bales of paper with bull's head watermarks cannot have proved sufficient for the enlarged edition. It is likely that two more bales were bought, with watermarks showing variations on a bunch of grapes. This would furnish about 10,000 more bifolia, or enough paper for about another 30 copies. It should have sufficed but, in the event, even this was inadequate. A final bale of paper must have been purchased, with a watermark of an ox. One can watch these new stocks of paper gradually being introduced into the Gutenberg Bible as the printing progressed through the each of the four simultaneous campaigns in the book.

Let us remind ourselves of Enea Silvio's report that some people said that 158 copies were being made while others said the total was to be 180. Perhaps this represented a two-stage increase which was actually under discussion in October 1454. Let us suppose, for example, that the original budget had been for 125 copies (about 100 paper and 25 parchment). Two more bales of paper and an unmeasurable quantity of parchment might bring the intermediate totals to 158 copies (say, 130 paper and 28 parchment). A further bale of paper and more parchment again might bring the eventual print-run to 180 copies (say, 140 paper and 40 parchment). Such totals are at least credible, and are consistent with what Enea Silvio was told during a late stage of the printing.

The technical perfection of the Gutenberg Bible is often remarked upon, but we should remind ourselves too of Gutenberg's extraordinary achievement in actually finishing the project. At times it must have seemed too vast to pursue. It must have taken unimaginable effort with little certainty of ever completing the task. By the time the last page was eventually printed, there would have been well over 100,000 Bible pages stacked up in Gutenberg's shop. Collating them into complete and ordered sets must have been a further immense task. Even with all possible care, several copies were found to be still lacking the occasional sheet.

Yet again, therefore, more supply leaves had to be reset in type and printed off for a third time. There are thus some leaves of the Gutenberg Bible which exist in three different variants, including (for example) the opening leaf of Genesis. The textual differences are slight and are mostly in the use of abbreviations. As a final example, a sentence in Genesis 1:2 in the first (40-line) printing is typeset as *et tenebre erāt sup facie abissi*. In the second (42-line) printing, it appears as *& tenebre erant sup facie abissi* (Pl. 153). In a third printing, represented (for example) by supply leaves in the paper copy of the Gutenberg Bible in the Pierpont Morgan Library, it is printed as *& tenebre erāt super facie abissi*.

Although the great virtue of the printing process is that every copy is supposedly identical, there are, of course, many small differences between surviving copies of the Gutenberg Bible. Human error was not avoided. For example, in the copy in the Württembergische Landesbibliothek in Stuttgart, the text of volume II, fol. 279v, appears in duplicate on fol. 272v, instead of the text which should have been there. Some copies show evidence of errors detected at the last minute in the printing shop. There is a copy of volume I in Keio University Library in Tokyo. For some reason, fol. 134 was cancelled and substituted by a single leaf evidently printed specially to replace a fault which must have been noticed before the book was sent for binding. Small variants like this are very common. The possible different states and substitutions of many leaves in the Bible mean that probably no two copies of the Gutenberg Bible are absolutely identical in every respect. In that sense, all copies of the Gutenberg Bible resemble scrupulously copied manuscripts, with all the little quirks of individuality common to any work of craftsmanship.

There is one aspect of Gutenberg Bibles which makes copies appear strikingly different from each other. This is the decoration supplied by hand. When the 180 or so copies of the Bible were dispatched from the printing shop in Mainz, probably in 1455–6, they still required headings and large initials. The decoration was inserted by or on behalf of the purchaser of each Bible. If it was possible to guess when or where each copy was decorated, then we would have a good picture of where the Gutenberg Bible was distributed and who its original customers may have been.

First of all, no surviving Gutenberg Bible is undecorated. However, there is no reason to assume that decoration was necessarily added immediately on publication. The paper copy in the Bibliothèque Nationale, as mentioned above, was decorated and bound by a cleric of the church of St Stephen in Mainz, Heinrich Cremer, in August 1456. To judge from what can be deduced about the printing of the Bible, that was easily within the first year of its completion. The decoration of two other copies, however, is dated 1461, five years later. These are the parchment copy in the Universitätsbibliothek in Leipzig and the copy in Munich, which were probably painted in Erfurt and Bavaria respectively, beyond the Rhineland but not too far distant from Mainz.

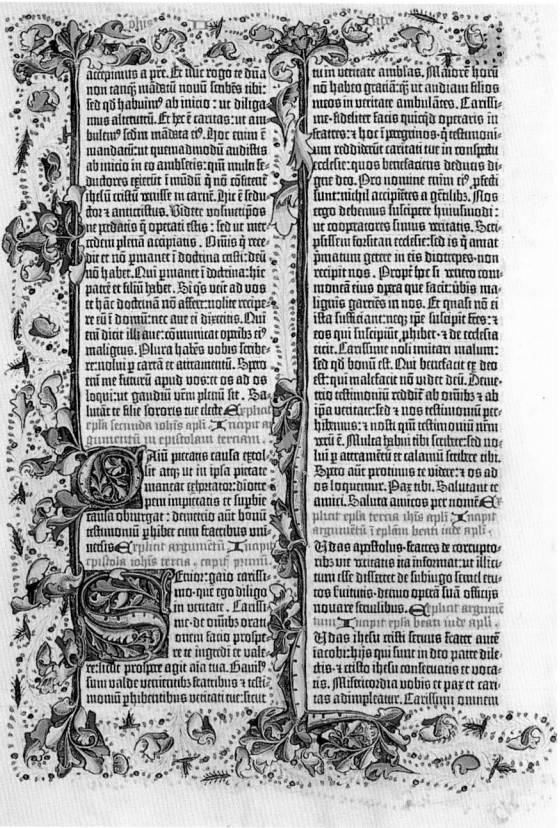

About a dozen copies of
the Gutenberg Bible have
illumination which can be
attributed stylistically to
Mainz, or its region. These
were doubtless sold locally.
At least three others seem
to have been illuminated in
a single workshop in Erfurt,
and two probably in Leipzig.
Others are attributable by
their decoration to Trier,
Lübeck, Augsburg, and
perhaps to Frankfurt, Strassburg and northern Austria,
all suggesting a plausible
market among the commer-
cial towns of the German
empire. Others, more in-
triguingly, were decorated
outside Germany. Most of
those illuminated furthest
from Mainz are Gutenberg Bibles printed on parchment. This may be chance or
it may mean that the more expensive copies had some kind of wider appeal or
were promoted more vigorously. The parchment copies in the Deutsches Buch-
museum in Leipzig and in the Pierpont Morgan Library in New York were both
illuminated in Bruges (Pl. 144). The copy in Lambeth Palace Library in London
and a single leaf from another copy, now in the British Library, were both illuminated in England, probably in London (Pl. 152). Both are on parchment. Only one
copy seems to have been decorated in Italy, the parchment copy acquired by the
Vatican Library with the Barberini collection. It is just possible that Cardinal
Carvajal acquired one after all, and that this is it (Pl. 153).

We suggested above that Gutenberg might originally have envisaged a need
for lectern Bibles in monasteries. We noted that the Carthusian Order, especially,
appeared to have a need for refectory Bibles. To judge from apparent sales in
Mainz itself, he was perhaps right in his assessment of his local market. One of
the copies with Mainz illumination, now in the Niedersächsische Staats- und
Universitätsbibliothek in Göttingen, is marked up for public reading and must
have belonged at least to a religious community of some kind. It has a contemporary note, for example, in volume II, fol. 134r, *hic continuetur in refectorio*, 'this
is to be continued in the refectory'. At least one Gutenberg Bible belonged to
the Carthusian monastery in Mainz. They owned the paper copy now in the

Genesis

In principio creauit deus celü et terram. Terra autem erat inanis et vacua:⁊ tenebre erant sup faciè abissi: et spiritus dñi ferebatur super aquas. Dixitq; deus. Fiat lux. Et facta è lux. Et vidit deus lucem ⱷ esset bona: et diuisit lucem a tenebris·appellauitq; lucem diem ⁊ tenebras noctem. Factu ⱷ est vespere ⁊ mane dies vnus. Dixit quoq; deus. Fiat firmamentü in medio aquaru: et diuidat aquas ab aquis. Et fecit deus firmamentü: diuisitq; aquas que erant sub firmamento ab hijs que erant super firmamentum:⁊ factum est ita. Vocauitq; deus firmamentü celü:⁊ factum est vespere et mane dies secundus. Dixit vero deus. Congregentur aque que sub celo sunt in locum vnü et appareat arida. Et factum est ita. Et vocauit deus aridam terram:cögregationesq; aquaꝛ appellauit maria. Et vidit deus ⱷ esset bonü· et ait. Germinet terra herbä virentem et facientem semen: et lignü pomiferü faciens fructum iuxta genus suü: cuius semen in semetipso sit super terram. Et factum est ita. Et protulit terra herbam virentem et facientem semen iuxta genus suü:lignüq; faciens fructü et habes vnüquodq; sementem secdm specie sua. Et vidit deus ⱷ esset bonü: et factü è vespere et mane dies tercius. Dixitq; aut deus. Fiant luminaria in firmaméto celi · ⁊ diuidät diem ac nocte:⁊ sint in signa ⁊ tepora·⁊ dies ⁊ annos: ut luceät in firmaméto celi et illuminét terrä. Et factü est ita. Fecitq; deus duo luminaria magna:luminare maius ut pesset diei et luminare min⁹ ut pesset nocti:⁊ stellas·⁊ posuit eas in firmaméto celi ut lucerent sup terrä: et

pessent diei ac nocti:⁊ diuiderét lucem ac tenebras. Et vidit de⁹ ⱷ esset bonü: et factü è vespere et mane dies quart⁹. Dixit etiam deus. Producant aque reptile anime viuentis et volatile sup terram: sub firmaméto celi. Creauitq; deus cete grandia·et omné animä viuentem atq; motabilem quä produxerant aque in species suas:⁊ omne volatile secundü genus suü. Et vidit deus ⱷ esset bonü: benedixitq; ei dicens. Crescite et multiplicamini·et replete aquas maris : auesq; multiplicentur super terram. Et factü è vespere ⁊ mane dies quitus. Dixit quoq; deus. Producat terra animä viuentem in genere suo:iumenta ⁊ reptilia·⁊ bestias terre secundü species suas. Factü è ita. Et fecit deus bestias terre iuxta species suas:iumenta ⁊ omne reptile terre in genere suo. Et vidit deus ⱷ esset bonü: et ait. Faciam⁹ hominem ad ymagine ⁊ similitudiné nosträ·⁊ psit piscib; maris·⁊ volatilib; celi·⁊ bestijs vniuseq; terre: omniq; reptili qd mouet i terra. Et creauit deus hominem ad ymagine et similitudiné suam: ad ymaginem dei creauit illü:masculü et feminä creauit eos. Benedixitq; illis deus· et ait. Crescite et multiplicamini ⁊ replete terram· et subicite eam:⁊ dominamini piscibus maris·⁊ volatilibus celi:⁊ vniuersis animätibus que mouentur sup terrä. Dixitq; deus. Ecce dedi vobis omné herbam afferentem semen sup terram et vniusa ligna que habet i semetipis sementé generis sui:ut sint vobis i esca·⁊ cüctis aiantibus terre·omniq; volucri celi ⁊ vniuersis ⱷ mouetur in terra·et i quibus è anima viuens:ut habeät ad vescendü. Et factum est ita. Viditq; deus cuncta que fecerat: et erät valde bona.

Hofbibliothek in Aschaffenburg and, according to an eighteenth-century note, the same monastery was also the source of the parchment copy now in the British Library. It seems that Gutenberg's local Carthusian house may have bought two copies, one on paper, one on parchment.

Beyond speculation about copies such as these, it is difficult to point to other Gutenberg Bibles which were obviously bought on publication by monasteries. The fact that many extant copies were indeed in the possession of religious houses by the seventeenth or eighteenth century may well explain their survival, but the Bibles may easily have been given into the custody of monastic libraries long after the book was printed. The copy in the Widener Library at Harvard University was given to the Bridgettines in Soest, near Amersfort, by Hans Vlyeger, canon of Utrecht, in March 1471. Until then it was privately owned. The copy in the Nationalbibliothek in Vienna was given in 1530 to a nun in the Dominican convent of Maria-Steinach, with the hope that the recipient would pray for the donor and for Benedict Wegmacher (d. 1490), who had apparently been the previous owner of the book. He had been priest and chamberlain of Archduke Sigismund of Tirol (d. 1494). The suggestion from Enea Silvio is that private buyers were securing Gutenberg Bibles. The need to increase the print-run of parchment copies seems consistent with this. Probably Gutenberg anticipated selling copies to monasteries and probably most buyers were private individuals.

We began with a quotation from Ulrich Zel who remembered the distinctive fact that the Gutenberg Bible was printed in a typeface which resembled that used in Missals. A Missal is a book for public display and institutional use. Only one other fifteenth-century Bible was printed in a Missal type, the so-called 36-line Bible, probably printed in Bamberg around 1460. That too must have been envisaged as a book for monastic or institutional use, and this time it was evidently a failure as a commercial enterprise. The print-run must have been small; very few copies survive. Even by 1460 it must have been apparent that the future lay not in printed Bibles for public use but for private owners, who had no need for Missal type.

In the meantime, back in Mainz, the press founded by Gutenberg continued in the hands of Johann Fust, who had taken control of the printing equipment in November 1455. By 1457, Fust was publishing books in his own name, in partnership with a younger man, Peter Schoeffer, who had apparently once been a scribe

154

This Gutenberg Bible was probably decorated locally in Mainz and was evidently used in a religious house for reading aloud during meals (GÖTTINGEN, NIEDERSÄCHSISCHE STAATS- UND UNIVERSITÄTSBIBLIOTHEK)

and had probably worked on the Gutenberg Bible. In about 1457, Schoeffer married Fust's daughter, Christina. They had four sons, three of whom also became printers. With the passing of time (and the loyal imagination of Schoeffer's descendants), some people believed that Fust himself had invented printing. A further corruption of the legend confused the name of Fust with that of Faust, and it has sometimes been asserted that Johann Fust was the model for the mad genius who had sold his soul to the Devil. It is worth observing, in passing, that Gutenberg avoided any imputation that printing was actually achieved by magic or that it interfered in any heretical way with the natural world. Perhaps the production of a Bible as his first great project gave him reputable credentials, and the Bible's evident success must have greatly helped the prestige of the printing press. Fust died in Paris in 1466, bequeathing the press to Schoeffer. Gutenberg lived on, receiving a pension from the archbishop of Mainz, and died probably in February 1468.

The Bible has remained in print continually since the 1450s. There were no fewer than 80 further editions of the Latin Bible in the fifteenth century alone, and more than a dozen editions of the Latin text with accompanying commentaries. Almost every one owes its text ultimately to the Gutenberg Bible. The text printed in Mainz in 1453–5 became the ancestor of all but two of the fifteenth-century printed editions of the Latin Bible (the exceptions are two rare Italian Bibles of the mid-1470s). Sometimes a copy of the Gutenberg Bible must been the actual model for the typesetters of later editions, such as the 36-line Bible of around 1460 and the smaller Bible printed by Fust and Schoeffer in Mainz in 1462. The Gutenberg Bible in Cambridge University Library is marked up with corrections and page breaks which suggest that it was the very copy used for typesetting the Eggestein edition of the Latin Bible printed in Strassburg in 1470 (Pl. 155). Subsequent editions copied each other. The big liturgical type and graceful Gothic elegance of the Gutenberg Bible were transformed into smaller Bibles for private use, but the text of the Gutenberg Bible endured for centuries.

155
The text of the Gutenberg Bible was used for typesetting other printed Bibles of the fifteenth century. This copy was evidently used for the printing of an edition in Strassburg in 1470 (CAMBRIDGE UNIVERSITY LIBRARY)

| Bibles of the Protestant Reformation

THE SIXTEENTH CENTURY is the period of the domestication of the Bible in Europe. For almost a thousand years it had been written in a language which many people did not easily understand, and copies of the Bible had belonged mainly to churches, religious institutions and the great houses of wealthy people. It was never deliberately kept from the reach of ordinary or poor people but medieval Bibles had necessarily been expensive and remote. Even the Gutenberg Bible was a patrician book. During the course of the sixteenth century the Bible was brought into the hands of the ploughman, to use a favourite image of the period. Between about 1520 and 1550, it entered the households of men and women at all levels of society, in the everyday languages of the time. Within a century of Johann Gutenberg's invention of movable type, the printed Bible reached countless thousands of people who had never before owned or even turned the pages of any book. It was read fervidly and universally, and it became an intimate possession of daily lives. The importance of the Bible for the development of literacy and language in the sixteenth century can hardly be overstated.

The translation of the Bible into contemporary languages was primarily a feature of Protestantism. This movement towards separation from the authority of the papacy had already started by the time of the Wycliffites in the late fourteenth century, as we saw in Chapter 7. It was brought to a crisis on a European scale by Martin Luther (1483–1546), who drew up his famous manifesto of 95 theses in Wittenberg in Germany in 1517. Luther publicly denied the supremacy of the popes and the necessity of priests to mediate between God and man. He exalted the Bible as the sole authority in matters of religion. The controversy evolved rapidly into a widening schism between the new and popularist

tages jnn einer wolck feulen/das er fie den rechten weg füret/vnd des
nachts jnn einer fewr feulen/das er jnen leuchtet/zu wandeln tag vnd
nacht/die wolckfeule vnd fewrfeule weich nimer von dem volck.

XIIII.

Vnd der HERR redet mit Mofe / vnd fprach / Rede mit
den kindern Ifrael/vnd fprich/das fie fich rumb lencken
vnd jr gezelt auffschlahen gegen dem tal Diroth / zwi=
fchen Migdol vnd dem Meer/gegen Baal Zephon/vnd
dafelbs gegen vber das gezelt auffschlahen ans meer/
Denn Pharao wird fagen von den kindern Ifrael / Sie
wiffen nicht wo aus im lande/die wüften hat fie beschloffen/vnd ich
wil fein hertz verftocken/das er jnen nach jage/vnd wil am Pharao/
vnd an all feiner macht ehre einlegen / vnd die Egypter follen jnnen
werden/das ich der HERR bin/Vnd fie thetten alfo.

Vnd da es dem König jnn Egypten ward angefagt/das das volck
war geflohen / ward fein hertz verwandelt vnd feiner knecht gege

Protestantism, originally in northern Europe, and the increasingly dogmatic and conservative Church of Rome, centred in the Mediterranean. The bitter rift is not yet healed, five hundred years later. Luther became the first champion of what in effect was an independent branch of Christianity. Luther's own translation of the Bible into ordinary German will form an important part of the present chapter.

By chance rather than intention, the Protestants were extremely fortunate in their timing. In adopting the vernacular Bible as a public symbol of reform, they took advantage of current research by Catholic scholars into the original texts of the Old and New Testaments. Protestants made translations which were not based on the medieval Latin Vulgate but on newly edited texts of the Bible in Greek and Hebrew. This is extremely important. Their direct sources were the languages in which the Bible was originally written. Reformation translations of the Bible thus proclaimed with some reason that their revolutionary texts, even though translated, were actually purer and more authentic than the current version in the Latin of Saint Jerome. It was a stroke of strategic genius. As the battle lines between the Protestants and Catholics became more inflexible, the Catholic camp was reluctantly forced backwards into defending the authenticity of the Vulgate. In the light of recent humanistic scholarship, that position was indefensible. The new and radical form of Protestant Christianity found its cause allied to a Bible text which was older than the Church of Rome. This, as much as any other factor, conferred legitimacy on Protestantism. Let us see how it came about.

During the Italian Renaissance of the fifteenth century, the humanist scholars joyfully rediscovered the Latin and Greek texts of the ancient civilizations. They attempted to construct accurate texts by collecting and comparing the oldest manuscripts they could find. The history of scientific textual criticism goes back to the classical studies of the Renaissance. The period marks a vast change in mental attitude towards distant antiquity. Once scholars began examining classical texts with a new spirit of inquiry, it was inevitable that eventually the Vulgate text of the Bible should also come into consideration, for it was the best-known of all ancient Latin texts. Although not strictly classical in the purest sense, Saint Jerome's translation of the Bible was by far the most extensive piece of Latin prose surviving from the late Roman Empire. Lorenzo Valla (1407–57) was one of the first of the humanist scholars to focus on the Bible as a Latin text and to question the transmission of this and other documents from the early Christian Church. His *Collatio Novi Testamenti*, written in the 1440s, is a fascinating verse-by-verse comparison of the Latin Vulgate of Saint Jerome with a selection of Greek manuscripts of the New Testament in Valla's possession. Although in theory Greek manuscripts of the Bible had probably always been available in southern Italy and the eastern Mediterranean, no one had ever systematically attempted the comparison before. The variants that Valla found were not great (perhaps even disappointingly slight) and mostly they comprise inconsistencies in the tenses of verbs, or the inclusion or omission of single words which do not affect the overall meaning of a phrase. Nonetheless, the importance of Valla's collation is that, in the privacy of a scholar's study, he was willing to test the sacred words of the Latin Bible against the Greek from which Saint Jerome had originally made his translation a thousand years earlier.

Hebrew manuscripts of the Scriptures were also relatively common in the Renaissance, even if they were unintelligible to many Christian scholars (Pl. 26). Jewish communities flourished in fifteenth-century Italy and the Iberian peninsula, living in some prosperity. The Hebrew Bible manuscripts which they used were mostly of no especial antiquity but had by tradition always been copied with extraordinary care. As a generalization, Hebrew biblical manuscripts were transcribed with far greater fidelity to their exemplars than the equivalent Christian books in Latin. Meticulous copying, with no allowance for error or variation, was

a religious obligation to Jewish scribes. Hebrew printing began around 1470 (the earliest books are undated). The complete Hebrew Bible (which is to say, of course, only the Old Testament in the Christian definition) was printed for the first time in 1488 in the town of Soncino, between Milan and Mantua. It was reprinted in

1491–3 and again in 1492–4. When the Jews were expelled from Spain in 1492 and from Portugal in 1498, many valuable Hebrew manuscripts remained behind and they evidently intrigued Christians into whose hands they fell. Hebrew books in the fifteenth century were made for use by practising Jews, not for any antiquarian interest among Christian biblical scholars; but no one in the late fifteenth century was unaware of the parallel universe of Jewish culture, with its curiously fascinating corpus of texts which looked back to the Old Testament from a period far earlier than the Vulgate. Martin Luther himself owned a copy of the

1494 edition of the Soncino Bible in Hebrew (Pl. 158).

Constantinople fell to the Muslims in 1453, as we saw in the previous chapter. Greek-speaking refugees escaped, some bringing books. For the first time, early Greek manuscripts became available in quantity in the West. The great fourth-century biblical *Codex Vaticanus*, for example, was acquired by the Vatican by 1481 (perhaps by 1475). Humanist scholars could now confront the kind of manuscript and text which Jerome himself could have used as exemplars in translating the Bible.

Medieval pictures of Saint Jerome often emphasize the ascetic and self-mortifying life of a penitent saint praying in the wilderness. In the Renaissance, the iconography of Saint Jerome changes into something infinitely more agreeable and appealing. Jerome begins to be shown as a Christian humanist, his cardinal's hat hung on a peg, sitting among his books and surrounded by all the comforts of the life of a bachelor scholar in his university study. The earliest woodcut securely attributed to Albrecht Dürer, datable to 1492 (and frequently reprinted), shows Jerome in just such a setting, with three Bibles lying open in his library cell, one each in Hebrew, Greek and Latin. Two Renaissance scholars who probably consciously modelled themselves on an image like this were Francisco

Ximénes de Cisneros (1436–1517) and Desiderius Erasmus (c.1469–1536).

Ximénes, like Jerome, lived for a time as an anchorite. He later became confessor to Isabella of Castile (1492), archbishop of Toledo (1495), cardinal, like Jerome also (1507), and, during the minority of Charles V, regent of Castile. He was a politician but also, by passion, a scholar. Around 1498–1500, he decided to found an entire university dedicated to the three ancient biblical languages of Hebrew, Greek and Latin. He endowed it out of his own income. The university was built at Alcalá de Henares (*Complutum* in Latin), about 30 kilometres (20 miles) east of Madrid. Probably in the summer of 1502, Ximénes devised a plan for one of the most extraordinary and revolutionary Bibles of the Renaissance. This is the publication now known as the 'Complutensian Polyglot', a Bible printed in multiple languages. The word 'polyglot' means 'many tongues'. It was conceived on the model of the *Hexapla* of Origen. This was the famous long-lost third-century compilation which Saint Jerome is reputed to have brought back to Bethlehem to use for his own preparation of the Vulgate text. The ancient *Hexapla* manuscript had six parallel columns of text, with the Hebrew text and its various different translations into Greek. Ximénes proposed a latter-day version, specifically as a printed book.

Cardinal Ximénes assembled an impressive editorial team and purchased or borrowed as many early manuscripts as could be found. Pope Leo X lent a Greek manuscript from the Vatican collections; others came from as far away as Venice and the island of Rhodes. The cardinal is reputed to have spent 4,000 ducats on buying seven Hebrew manuscripts. Among the most innovative textual critics employed on the project was the Hebrew scholar, Elio Antonio de Nebrija (1441–1522). There is an agreeable image of Ximénes and his editors in the biographical notes by his contemporary, Alvar Gómez. He describes how the cardinal, on his way to his office in the university each morning, would pass by the printing shop and along the street where Nebrija lived. Ximénes would stop to chat, he in the street, Nebrija leaning on the window sill. Printing of the first instalment of the Complutensian Polyglot was finished in January 1514. This was to become volume V of the set, comprising the New Testament. The Greek text appeared here in print for the first time. The printing of the final volume of the Polyglot was completed in July 1517. Then (and what modern publisher does not sympathize?) the whole publication was suspended. Cardinal Ximénes died that year. The entire stock of printed sheets remained in Alcalá, still unissued. When Pope Leo X sent a commendation in March 1520, this was added on the last page of the first gathering of volume I. The book was probably finally bound up and released for publication between 1520 and 1522, years after it had been set in type.

Let us look at the Complutensian Polyglot. The Bible is in five volumes. The sixth volume comprises dictionaries, grammars and other aids to the reader. The volumes are of large size but not enormous, about the same dimensions as the Gutenberg Bible. Each title-page shows the arms of Ximénes printed in red,

Trãsla.Gre.lxx.cũ interp.latina.

res hec. nõ poterimᵒ tibi ꝗdicere ma
lũ aut bonũ.ecce rebecca corã te: tolles re
uertere. τ sit vxor filio dñi tui: sicut lo
cuτ ẽ dñs:factũ eãt cũ audieret puer abra
am verba coꝝ: adorauit sup terrã
dñs. et pferẽs seruus vasa argētea τ au
rea τ vestem: dedit rebecce. τ bona τ
dit fratri eius. τ comederũt
et biberũtiꝑse τ viri cũ eo erũtes:
et ꝑnoctauerunt. et surges puer: mane dixit. di
mittite me: vt vadã ad dñm meũ.dixerũt
fratres eius τ mater: maneat virgo
nobiscũ dies quasi vece. et post hoc ꝑficisce
tur. ille ãt dixit ad eos: ne detineatis me. τ dñs
ꝑsperauit viã meã:dimittite me: vt per
gã ad dñs meũ.dixerũt: vocemus puel
lam: interrogem̃ os eius. et vocauerũt
rebeccã: et dixerũt. ei. ibis cum hoĩe
isto: illa ãt dixit vadam. et dimiserũt
rebeccã sororem eorũ: et substantiã
eius: et seruũ abraã: et eos ꝗ co.
et bñdixerũt rebecca sororẽ eorũ: et bi
xerũt ei. soror nfa es. fias in milia vecẽ
pτ. et ꝓlem fiant ꝗ aduersáτ eis et ancille
eius: ascederũt sup camelos: τ abierũt
cum hoĩe. et accipiẽs puer rebeccã:

Trãsla.B.Hiero.

sermo. Nõ possumus
extra placitú eius quic
ꝗ aliud loqui tecú. En
rebecca corã te ẽ:ᵐtolle
eam:ⁿ& proficiscere:⁰&
sit ᵖvxor filii dñi tui:
sicut � locutus est domi
nus. ʳQuod cum ꝏꝏꝏꝏꝏ
audisset puer abraam:
procidens ʳadorauit in terrã ˢdñm.
ᵗProlatisꝗ ꝏꝏꝏꝏꝏꝏ
vasis ᵘargenteis ᵛ&au
reis ac vestibus ꝏꝏꝏꝏꝏ
qdedit ea ʷrebecce. τ ˣbona
ᵞmunere. ᶻFratribus ᵐ quoꝗ
eius & matri ᵃdona ob
tulit.ᵇInito cõuiuio ᶜve
sceṫes pariter ᵈ& bibeṫes
manserunt ibi.ꝏꝏꝏꝏꝏꝏ
ᵉSurgens aút ᶠmane lo
cutus est puer. ᵍDimitte
me vt vadã ʰad dñm me
um.ⁱRñderútꝗ ᵐfrater
eius ᵏ& mr.ᵒMãeat ᵖpuel
la saltê ᵠdecê ʳdies ˢapud
nos:ᵗ& postea ᵘproficisce
tur.ᵛnolite ait ʷme ˣretie
re:quia ᵞdñs direxit viã
meã.ᶻDimittite me ᵐ
vt pgã ᵃad dñm meum.
ᵇEt dixerút. ᶜVocemus
ᵈpuella & ꝗramus ᵉipsi
us volútate. ᶠCúꝗ voca
ta venisset:ᵍsciscitati sút.
ʰVis ire ꝏꝏꝏꝏꝏꝏꝏꝏ
cum ⁱhomine ᵏisto? ˡQue
ait.ᵐVadam. ⁿDimise
runt ergo ⁰eam ꝏꝏꝏꝏꝏ
ᵖ& ꝏꝏꝏꝏꝏꝏꝏꝏꝏ
nutricem illius:ᵠseruú
ꝗ ʳabraam ꝏꝏꝏꝏꝏꝏ
ˢcomites eius ᵗippecãtes
ᵘpspa sorori sue atꝗ di
cẽtes.ᵛSoror nostra ʷes.
ˣCrescas ᵞin mille milia:
ᶻ& possideat semen tuú
ᵐportas ᵃinimicorú suo
rú. ᵇIgr rebecca ᶜ& puel
le illius ᵈascensis ꝏꝏꝏ
ᵉcamelisᶠsecute sunt ꝏ
ᵍviru:q festinus reuerte
batur ad dñm suú. Eo ãt

Tex.Heb. Geñ. Ca.xxiiii. Púítiua heb.

Hebrew text	Root
הַדָּבָר לֹא נוּכַל דַּבֵּר אֵלֶיךָ רַע	תֵּל רֹעַ
אוֹ טוֹב הִנֵּה רִבְקָה לְפָנֶיךָ קַח	פָּנָה לֶחֶם
וָלֵךְ וּתְהִי אִשָּׁה לְבֶן אֲדֹנֶיךָ	יָלַךְ הָיָה
כַּאֲשֶׁר דִּבֶּר יְהוָה וַיְהִי כַּאֲשֶׁר	
שָׁמַע עֶבֶד אַבְרָהָם אֶת דִּבְרֵיהֶם	
וַיִּשְׁתַּחוּ אַרְצָה לַיהוָה וַיּוֹצֵא	שָׁתָה יָצָא
הָעֶבֶד כְּלֵי כֶסֶף וּכְלֵי זָהָב וּבְגָדִים	כָּלָה
וַיִּתֵּן לְרִבְקָה וּמִגְדָּנֹת נָתַן לְאָחִיהָ	נָתַן
וּלְאִמָּהּ וַיֹּאכְלוּ וַיִּשְׁתּוּ הוּא	אָכַל שָׁתָה
וְהָאֲנָשִׁים אֲשֶׁר עִמּוֹ וַיָּלִינוּ	לָן
וַיָּקוּמוּ בַבֹּקֶר וַיֹּאמֶר שַׁלְּחֻנִי	קוּם
לַאדֹנִי וַיֹּאמֶר אָחִיהָ וְאִמָּהּ תֵּשֵׁב	יָשַׁב
הַנַּעֲרָ אִתָּנוּ יָמִים אוֹ עָשׂוֹר אַחַר	יוֹם עָשַׁר
תֵּלֵךְ וַיֹּאמֶר אֲלֵהֶם אַל תְּאַחֲרוּ	יָלַךְ אָחַר
אֹתִי וַיהוָה הִצְלִיחַ דַּרְכִּי שַׁלְּחוּנִי	צָלַח
וְאֵלְכָה לַאדֹנִי וַיֹּאמְרוּ נִקְרָא	קָרָא
לַנַּעֲרָ וְנִשְׁאֲלָה אֶת פִּיהָ וַיִּקְרְאוּ	שָׁאַל פֶּה
לְרִבְקָה וַיֹּאמְרוּ אֵלֶיהָ הֲתֵלְכִי	
עִם הָאִישׁ הַזֶּה וַתֹּאמֶר אֵלֵךְ	
וַיְשַׁלְּחוּ אֶת רִבְקָה אֲחֹתָם וְאֶת	שָׁלַח
מֵנִקְתָּהּ וְאֶת עֶבֶד אַבְרָהָם וְאֶת	יָנַק
אֲנָשָׁיו וַיְבָרְכוּ אֶת רִבְקָה וַיֹּאמְרוּ	בָּרַךְ
לָהּ אֲחֹתֵנוּ אַתְּ הֲיִי לְאַלְפֵי רְבָבָה	הָיָה
וְיִירַשׁ זַרְעֵךְ אֵת שַׁעַר שֹׂנְאָיו	יָרַשׁ
וַתָּקָם רִבְקָה וְנַעֲרֹתֶיהָ וַתִּרְכַּבְנָה	קוּם רָכַב
עַל הַגְּמַלִּים וַתֵּלַכְנָה אַחֲרֵי	יָלַךְ
הָאִישׁ וַיִּקַּח הָעֶבֶד אֶת רִבְקָה	לָקַח

Transla.Chal.

בְּתִגְמָא לֵית אֲנַחְנָא יָכְלִין לְמַלְלָא עִמָּךְ בִּישׁ אוֹ טָב: הָא רִבְקָה קֳדָמָךְ דְּבַר וַאֲזִיל
וּתְהֵא אִתְּתָא לְבַר רִבּוֹנָךְ כְּמָא דְּמַלִּיל יְיָ וַהֲוָה כַּד שְׁמַע עַבְדָּא דְּאַבְרָהָם יָת פִּתְגָּמֵיהוֹן
וּסְגֵיד עַל אַרְעָא קֳדָם יְיָ וְאַפֵּיק עַבְדָּא מָאנִין דִּכְסַף וּמָאנִין דִּדְהַב וּלְבוּשִׁין וִיהַב
לְרִבְקָה וּמַגְדָּנִין יְהַב לְאָחוּהָ וּלְאִמַּהּ וַאֲכָלוּ וּשְׁתִיאוּ הוּא וְגֻבְרַיָּא דְּעִמֵּיהּ וּבָתוּ
וְקָמוּ בְּצַפְרָא וַאֲמַר שַׁלְּחוּנִי לְוָת רִבּוֹנִי וַאֲמַר אֲחוּהָא וְאִמַּהּ תֵּתֵיב עוּלֵימְתָא עִמָּנָא
עִדָּן בְּעִדָּנִין אוֹ עַסְרָא יַרְחִין בָּתַר כֵּן תְּהַךְ וַאֲמַר לְהוֹן לָא תְאַחֲרוּן יָתִי וַייָ אַצְלַח
אָרְחִי שַׁלְּחוּנִי וְאֵיזֵיל לְוָת רִבּוֹנִי וַאֲמָרוּ נִקְרֵי לְעוּלֵימְתָא וְנִשְׁמַע מַה דְּהִיא אָמְרָא
וּקְרוֹ לְרִבְקָה וַאֲמָרוּ לַהּ הֲתֵזְלִין עִם גַּבְרָא הָדֵין וַאֲמֶרֶת אֵיזֵיל וּשְׁלַחוּ יָת רִבְקָה
אַחַתְהוֹן וְיָת מֵינִיקְתַּהּ וְיָת עַבְדָּא דְאַבְרָהָם וְיָת גֻּבְרוֹהִי וּבָרִיכוּ יָת רִבְקָה וַאֲמָרוּ לַהּ
אֲחָתַנָא אַתְּ הֲוֵי לְאַלְפִין וּלְרִבְּוָן וְיֵירְתוּן בְּנַיְכִי יָת קִרְוֵי שַׂנְאֵיהוֹן וְקָמַת רִבְקָה
וְעוּלֵימְתָהָא וּרְכִיבָן עַל גַּמְלַיָּא וַאֲזָלוֹ בָּתַר גַּבְרָא וּדְבַר עַבְדָּא יָת רִבְקָה וַאֲזַל

Interp.chal.

sermo:non possumus nos loqui tecú malú aut bonú.
Ecce rebecca corã te est: tolle eam & vade: & sit vxor
filio dñi tui: sicut locutus est dñs. Et facti est cum au
disset seruus abzahe verba eorum: adorauit in terra
corã dño. Et protulit seruus vasa argentea et vasa
aurea & vestes: & dedit rebecce & munera dedit fratri
eius & matri. Et comederút & biberunt ille & viri qui
erant cum eo & dormierunt & surrexerunt mane. Et
dixit.Mittite me ad dñm meum. Et dixit frater eius
& mater. Maneat puella nobiscum aliquo tempore:
aut decem mésibus: & postea ibit.Et dixit eis. Ne re
tineatis me quia direxit viam meam: dimittite
me vt vad adã dñm meum. Dicerútꝗ vocemus puel
lam: & audiamus quid ipsa dicat. Vocaueruntꝗ re
beccam: & dixerunt ei. Anquid ibis cum viro isto?
Et dixit: vadam. Dimiseruntꝗ rebecca sororem suam
et nutricem eius: & seruum abzahe et viros eius. Et
benedixerunt rebecce atꝗ dixerút ei. Soror nostra
tu sis in millia millisi: & possideant filii tui ciuitates
inimicorum suosú.Et surrexit rebecca et puelle eius:
et ascenderunt super camelos: & ibant post virum. et
tulit seruus rebecca & abijt

Púítiua chal.

Root
טוֹב
הֲוָה לֶהֱוֵא
דְּבַק
שְׁתָה
קוּם רַבָּה תֵּב
עֲלַם אֲזַל אַחַר
שְׁמַע אֲזַל קְרָא
אֲזַל
הֲוָה רַבּוֹ יְרַת
סְרַךְ רַבָּה קוּם

f

beneath a many-tasselled cardinal's hat. The page layout of the text is immensely elaborate (Pl. 160). In the centre of each page is a narrow and unvarying vertical column in Latin, 38 mm wide (about an inch and a half). It is printed in a small round roman type. Where necessary, the text is padded out with meaningless rows of circles, like little 'o's, so that it has no blank spaces. This is the sacred text of the Latin Vulgate, in as accurate an edition as the editors could make it. The general preface compares it with Christ on the Cross, flanked by thieves. For most of the Bible, then, the thieves on either side of the Vulgate are the Hebrew text in the outer margin and the Greek in the inner margin, each spiritually flawed (according to the preface) by association with Judaism or Greek Orthodoxy. Beyond this remark, however, the parent texts are presented with care and respect. The Greek text is edited from the Septuagint in the Old Testament and from the original Greek for the New Testament. It is printed in an italic script. Above each Greek word is a precise translation into Latin, so that it could be compared exactly with the Vulgate, even by a reader who knew no Greek. This is not so simple for the broad column of Hebrew text on the outer side of the Vulgate, because (of course) Hebrew is written from right to left. If translations were written above each word, every line of text in Latin would emerge in reverse. This problem must have preoccupied many editorial committee meetings in Alcalá de Henares. The solution was to place a tiny letter of the Latin alphabet, lower-case, in order from 'a' to 'z' and back to 'a' again, just above the start of each word in Hebrew. These are then keyed to the Latin text, with corresponding superscript letters above the nearest equivalent word in the Vulgate. The different word order between Hebrew and Latin means that the key letters are not always in alphabetical sequence when they appear in the Vulgate column, but by following the letters in order one can disinter the ancient Hebrew in its own stilted sentence structure.

This sounds complicated, but in practice it is extremely easy to use. Even without knowing a word of Hebrew, one can compare the Hebrew text with a precision which is strangely satisfying and compulsive. There are indeed slight differences, mostly of the inclusion or omission of words which affect the phrasing but not the overall sense. To help those readers who might try to teach themselves Hebrew from the Polyglot, the outer margins again include the roots of Hebrew compound words which occur in the adjacent text. In the Pentateuch volume there is a further text in the lower margin as well. This is the ancient *Targum of Onkelos*, the Aramaic version of the Hebrew Pentateuch, written in Hebrew characters. It too had survived with the Jewish scriptures. The Complutensian Polyglot calls it the 'Chaldean' translation (not strictly correctly but following Jerome's terminology). It appears here in blocks of Hebrew type beside a literal Latin prose translation.

This is a thoroughly orthodox book. There is not a hint of proto-Protestantism or disrespect for the traditional Latin of the Vulgate. Nonetheless, the Polyglot is

160

The Complutensian Polyglot Bible was printed in 1514–17. The page here shows the text of Genesis 24:50-62, with the Greek Septuagint version in the left-hand column, the Latin Vulgate in the centre column, the Hebrew text in the right-hand column, and the Aramaic version (with Latin translation) below. The column on the far right shows the roots of the compound Hebrew words

a scholarly edition, attempting to restore the original texts by intelligent critical conjecture and collation. Occasionally the Greek text is actually corrected by comparison with the Latin, rather than the other way round. A famous example is the end of the Lord's Prayer (Matthew 6:9–13). Most Greek manuscripts of the Gospels conclude these verses with the formula 'for thine is the kingdom, the power and the glory, for ever and ever'. This is not in the Latin Vulgate. The editors of the Complutensian Polyglot recorded that the Vulgate tradition was probably more ancient and that the concluding clause had probably been carried across unconsciously from its liturgical use in the Greek Mass. Therefore, by editorial decision, it was omitted from the Greek text as printed in the Polyglot. No medieval scholar would have been capable of making such a distinction, and even if they had become aware of a difference in text, no one would ever have selected one reading as preferable to another. The Complutensian Polyglot

161

Desiderius Erasmus (c.1469–1536), painted here by Quentin Matsys
(ROME, PALAZZO BARBERINI)

162 opposite

Erasmus's edition of the Greek and Latin Novum Instrumentum, *his provocative title for the New Testament, was published in Basle in 1516*

shows Renaissance biblical scholarship at its very best, just before even textual criticism descended into desperate polemic between Catholics and Protestants.

While the printing of the Polyglot was proceeding in Spain, the most famous northern humanist, Desiderius Erasmus, was then working on his own edition of the Gospels in the original Greek. Erasmus was one of the very great figures of the Renaissance. He was educated by the Brothers of the Common Life at Deventer and joined the priesthood in 1492. He studied in Paris, Oxford, Louvain and Cambridge. From 1521 he lived mostly in Basle. Erasmus was an international scholar of remarkable breadth and sophistication. Everyone of merit or culture sought to become his friend and correspondent, and Erasmus obliged them all. He gave much attention to his own public image. Like many men who use their cleverness to reassure themselves, he sometimes failed to distinguish wit from sarcasm. Not everyone trusted him, therefore, but no one doubted his piety, scholarship or intellect, certainly not Erasmus himself. Holbein and other artists painted him in the agreeable image of Saint Jerome among his books (Pl. 161).

Erasmus found a manuscript of Lorenzo Valla's *Collatio Novi Testamenti* in the library of Parc Abbey, on the outskirts of Louvain. This text, which we encountered above, had not circulated widely. Only two manuscript copies have survived today. The scholarly curiosity of Erasmus, however, was aroused by the idea of comparing and judging the Latin of Saint Jerome against the Greek original, and he seized upon Valla's text and edited it for its first publication, printed in Paris in 1505. At this time, the Bible in Greek was still not available in print. Around the end of 1511, Erasmus began work on an edition of the Greek New Testament.

As he did so, he constantly checked it against Jerome's translation in the Latin Vulgate, taking upon himself the brave responsibility of furnishing textual improvements to the Latin which he believed Jerome had overlooked or had translated misleadingly from the Greek. In July 1514, he reported confidently to a colleague from his former monastery that by examining the Greek original he had already improved Jerome's version in over a thousand places. Erasmus used the verb *castigare* for what he was doing to the Latin text – to beat it into shape and to teach it a lesson. The high and unquestionable reputation of Erasmus saved him from outright accusations of interference with Holy Writ, but even his friends were distinctly uncomfortable that Erasmus was apparently rewriting the familiar Latin Bible. Martin Dorp drafted a long and reasoned letter to Erasmus in October 1514, begging him to be careful. The Church had used the Vulgate for countless generations, Dorp said, and it would be unreasonable to suppose that all Church fathers and general councils who had relied on the precise wording of the Vulgate were simply in error, especially as their judgements, based on the Vulgate, were indisputable. Erasmus preserved the letter (it is no. 304 in his collected correspondence) but continued work.

The result was an edition of the New Testament edited by Erasmus. It is substantial and heavy book, handsomely printed by Johann Froben in Basle in 1516. It has a very long Latin title beginning *Novum Instrumentum omne, diligenter ab Erasmo Roterodamo recognitum & emendatum ...* (Pl. 162). Even in the title, Erasmus could not resist being clever. The words *Novum Instrumentum* are what everyone else would call the 'New Testament'. He afterwards explained that a 'testament' is strictly a statement of intent: a person leaving a will or covenant, for example, might make an oral testament. The written document which subsequently embodies that statement, however, is called an 'instrument'. Therefore Christ may have left a testament to his disciples but when it was written down it became an instrument, and so the Bible was formed of Old and New Instruments, not Testaments. Erasmus enjoyed being provocative. No one accepted his ingenious improvement, however scholarly and plausible, and in later editions the New Testament version of Erasmus slipped back to its more familiar name.

His *Novum Instrumentum* of 1516 is in two parts. The first comprises parallel columns of the original Greek text, as accurately as Erasmus could edit it, and beside it a precise translation into the Latin which Erasmus thought Jerome should have used (Pl. 163). The second part consists of a commentary on the edition with alternative translations of words. The Latin which Erasmus proposed included many thoughtful but controversial choices of words. For example, the famous opening of Saint John's Gospel in the traditional Latin Vulgate is 'In principio erat verbum ...' Erasmus suggested 'In principio erat sermo ...' Both *verbum* and *sermo* mean 'word' in Latin, *logos* in Greek, but there is a very subtle and disconcerting difference. *Verbum* is a grammatical entity; *sermo* is that entity being spoken. Maybe Erasmus was actually right. Similarly, one of the most famous phrases of the New Testament was the greeting which Gabriel gave to the Virgin Mary at the Annunciation: *Ave gratia plena*, 'Hail, full of grace' (Luke 1:28), three words reproduced in every Book of Hours and almost every altarpiece of the late Middle Ages. Erasmus rephrased it *Ave gratiosa*, 'Hail, graceful one', almost the same but not quite. The Vulgate implies a state of having been filled with grace; the Greek, as translated by Erasmus, suggests that the grace was already there. This may seem like hair-splitting to us, five hundred years later and accustomed to a variety of Bible translations, but half the theology of the late Middle Ages hinges on an exact understanding of God's relationship to the Virgin Mary at the moment of the Incarnation. Erasmus's choice of word gave an unexpected new interpretation, shocking to many of his readers. A final example of Erasmus's rendition of the Greek leads us to what became one of the most disputed biblical phrases of the sixteenth century. John the Baptist, preaching in the wilderness, urged his listeners to repentance. The word he used in Greek is *metanoeite* (Matthew 3:2). The Vulgate translates this as *penitentiam agite*, 'do penance'; Erasmus proposed *Resipiscite*, 'be penitent'. To Luther, the interpretation of Erasmus justified a spiritual turning to God; to the Catholic Church of the Middle Ages, the doing of penance was a physical activity. There is an enormous difference of doctrine between those two meanings. Erasmus was not one of the Protestant Reformers, and he always remained a Catholic. However, his *Novum Instrumentum* in 1516 laid out a technique for interpreting the original Greek which the Lutheran reformers would find very valuable.

There is some evidence of haste in the preparation of the Greek text to be printed in the *Novum Instrumentum* of Erasmus. Many manuscripts were used, but probably mostly these were selected for convenience of access than for textual supremacy. On its publication in March 1516, the *Novum Instrumentum* became the first edition of the New Testament in its original language. The New Testament volume of the Complutensian Polyglot was already printed, but it was still in its loose sheets in storage in Alcalá and it was not yet published or available for study. It is probable that Froben knew of this project and was therefore especially anxious to bring out Erasmus's edition as soon as possible. In a letter to Guillaume Budé in June 1516, Erasmus described the frenetic business

The Novum Instrumentum *of Erasmus prints the Bible text in Greek beside a literal translation of the Greek into Latin. This page shows Matthew 1:1–8*

QVATVOR EVANGELIA, AD VETVSTISSIMORVM
EXEMPLARIVM LATINORVM FIDEM, ET AD
GRAECAM VERITATEM AB ERASMO ROTE
RODAMO SACRAE THEOLOGIAE PROFES
SORE DILIGENTER RECOGNITA.

ΕΥΑΓΓΕΛΙΟΝ ΚΑΤΑ
ΜΑΤΘΑΙΟΝ.

EVANGELIVM SECVNDVM
MATTHAEVM.

ΙΒΛΟΣ γενέ
σεως ΙΗΣΥ ΧΡΙ
ΣΤΟΥ, ἠοῦ Δα
βίδ, ἠοῦ ἀξρα
ἀμ. Αξραἀμ ἐ
γἐννησεν τ̃ ἰσα

ἀκ.ἰσαἀκ δὲ, ἐγἐννησεν τὸμ ἰακώβ. ἰακώβ
δὲ, ἐγἐννησεν τὸμ ἰοὐδαμ, καὶ τὺς ἀδ'ἐλ
φοὺς αὐτου. ἰοὐδας δὲ, ἐγἐννησεν τὸμ φα
ρἐς, Ὁ τὸμ ζαρἀ,ἐκ δοὶ θἀμαρ.φαρἐς δὲ,
ἐγἐννησεν τ̃ ἐσρώμ, ἐσρωμ δὲ, ἐγἐννησεμ
τὸμ ἀρἀμ, ἀρἀμ δὲ ἐγἐννησεν τὸμ ἀμι
ναδ'άβ, ἀμιναδ'αβ δὲ, ἐγἐννησεν τ̃ ναασ
σὀμ.ναασσὀμ δὲ, ἐγἐννησεμ τ̃ σαλμὡμ.
σαλμὡμ δὲ, ἐγἐννησεν τὸμ βοοζ ἐκ δοὶ ρα
χάβ.βοοζ δὲ, ἐγἐννησεν τὸμ ωβἠδ, ἐκ δοὶ
ρὀθ.ωβἠδ δὲ, ἐγἐννησεν τὸμ ἰεσσαί. ἰεσσαί
δὲ, ἐγἐννησεν τὸμ δαβἰδ τὸμ βασιλἐα.
Δαβἰδ δὲ ὁ βασιλευς ἐγἐννησεν τὸμ σο
λομῶνα ἐκ δοὶ τῦ οὐρίου.σολομὡμ δὲ,
ἐγἐννησεμ τ̃ ροβοἀμ.ροβοἀμ δὲ, ἐγἐννησεμ
τὸμ ἀβιἀμ.ἀβιἀμ δὲ, ἐγἐννησεμ τ̃ ἀσἀ. ἀσὰ
δὲ, ἐγἐννησεμ τὸμ ἰωσαφἀτ. ἰωσαφἀτ δὲ,
ἐγἐννησεμ τὸμ ἰωξἀμ. ἰωξἀμ δὲ, ἐγἐν.ἠ
σεμ τὸμ

Iber generatio
nis Iesu Christi
filij Dauid, Filij
Abrahā, Abra
ham genuit Isa
ac.Isaac aūt,ge
nuit Iacob. Ia
cob aūt,genuit Iudā, & fratres eius.
Iudas aūt, genuit Phares, & Zarā,
e Thamar. Phares autē, genuit Es
rom. Esrom aūt, genuit Aram. Arā
autem,genuit Aminadab. Amina
dab aūt,genuit Naasson. Naasson
aūt,genuit Salmon. Salmon autē,
genuit Boos, e Rhachab.Boos aūt,
genuit Obed, e Ruth. Obed autē,
genuit Iesse, Iesse aūt,genuit Dauid
regem. Dauid autē rex,genuit So
lomonem,ex ea q̃ fuerat uxor Vrie.
Solomon autem,genuit Roboam.
Roboam aūt,genuit Abiam. Abia
autem, genuit Asa. Asa autem, ge
nuit Iosaphat. Iosaphat autem, ge
nuit Ioram. Ioram autem , genu
A   it Oziā.

IOANNES
FROBENI
VS SVIS
TYPIS
EXCV
DE
BAT

of simultaneously writing, correcting and proof-reading the text. Between them, he said, he and Froben produced a printed sheet a day. Erasmus sometimes worked faster than he would have preferred. 'Some things I purposely passed over,' Erasmus told Budé, 'and shut my eyes to many points upon which soon after publication I had a different opinion.' Every author, being chased by his publisher, knows that feeling.

There is no doubt that the publication of the *Novum Instrumentum* marked a major step towards the Bible translation by Martin Luther. It presented the New Testament as a text which dated back beyond the Latin Vulgate and claimed therefore to be potentially more authentic. It offered a means of blocking out the traditional interpretation of the medieval Church and of coming face-to-face with apostolic Christianity instead. Already by 1516, Luther was preaching the doctrine of justification by faith, which is that Christ offers salvation to those who

turn to him directly and place their total trust in him, without any mediation of priests or penances imposed by a hierarchical Church. He based this on a close reading of Romans 1:17. It was axiomatic that every person should understand the Bible as directly as possible, without hindrance of language or tradition.

In 1517, a year after the publication of the *Novum Instrumentum* and while the Complutensian Polyglot was still in press, Luther proclaimed his famous 95 theses from the door of the Schlosskirche in Wittenberg. Luther's final break with Rome occurred in 1520, when he denounced the Roman Church and all its doctrines, and he invited all German princes to follow him. In June 1520, the pope declared all writings by Luther to be heretical and ordered their destruction. In reply, Luther burned the papal bull. On 3 January 1521 he was excommunicated, and he withdrew into tactical hiding at the twelfth-century castle of the Wartburg, near Eisenach in Thuringia. His principal occupation at the Wartburg was to translate the New Testament into modern German.

The Bible had existed in German before Luther. There were manuscripts in the German language in the fifteenth century. They passed almost unnoticed, attracting neither favour nor disapproval. As many as 18 editions of the Bible in German translations were published between 1466 and 1522. They were all large books for a popular market, mostly with homely woodcuts of boisterous and familiar stories from the Bible. They follow an anonymous translation prepared for the first edition, published in Strassburg in 1466, revised especially in

1473 and 1483. The text had been adapted directly and uncritically from the Vulgate, and its stilted sentences often emerge into the German language as endearingly quaint and incomprehensible as many of those in the earlier version of the Wycliffite Bible. Luther discarded all this. He must have known the German versions current in his own time but there is not a hint of them in his new translation. Luther was fluent in Latin and Greek and competent in Hebrew. He took with him to the Wartburg a copy of the second edition of the *Novum Instrumentum* (1519), and he began to translate directly from the original Greek in the edition of Erasmus.

Visitors to the Wartburg today are shown the room where Luther is reputed to have translated the New Testament. As furnished now, it is quite as agreeable as any sixteenth-century engraving of the cell of Saint Jerome. Luther himself referred to it as his Patmos, comparing it to the island where the exiled Saint

John is supposed to have written the Apocalypse. The castle is on a high rock surrounded by forests, near the old East German border (Pl. 164). Luther's room and its adjoining bedroom are in the northern bastion of the Wartburg above the warden's quarters. Here, during the winter of 1521–2, Luther produced a first draft of the New Testament from Greek into idiomatic contemporary spoken German. In early March 1522, he returned to Wittenberg with his manuscript translation and he discussed it sentence by sentence with his friend, Philipp Melanchthon (1497–1560), a remarkably young and extremely able professor of Greek. The text was ready for printing by the late spring. The Wittenberg printer, Melchior Lotther, originally devoted two presses to printing it, and had brought a third into operation by the end of July. The book was finally published on 21 September 1522 (Pl. 165). Because of this date, it is often known as the *September Testament*, though the calligraphic title-page itself declares the book to be simply *Das Newe Testament Deutzsch*. The translator's name does not appear.

One of Martin Luther's great strengths was his extreme ability to write clearly and articulately. The fluent literary style of his biblical translations must have had an enormous influence in promoting the Reformation in Germany. The nineteenth-century philosopher Friedrich Nietzsche (perhaps not the most reliable of critics) described it as not only the finest work in the German language but as the greatest work of literature of any age. Many would probably agree. It is the standard translation used by millions of German-speakers today. In the 1520s, German had still been a language of many local dialects. Luther attempted to select vocabulary which was as neutral and mainstream as possible. Occasionally provincial words reveal Luther's rural upbringing in Saxony, such as the then rare term *Krippe*, for 'manger', which thus through the Bible translation entered into modern German.

Luther's Greek text was that of Erasmus. He adopted its decision to place the book of Acts immediately after the Gospels, as in most modern Bibles, instead of between Hebrews and the Catholic Epistles, as had been usual in the Vulgate. Luther certainly studied Erasmus's Latin translation and notes as well as his Greek text. Some of the innovative words used in the *Novum Instrumentum* entered into Luther's German translation and became immortalized, such as the *gratiosa* in Gabriel's greeting to Mary (Luke 1:28), as described above, which emerges in Luther's translation in the single corresponding word *Holdselige*. Where the Greek text seemed to allow it, Luther gladly chose words consistent with a Protestant interpretation of concepts of grace and salvation. Luther's translation, however, is not polemical or deliberately phrased to favour Protestant doctrine. It aims for simple faithfulness to the apostolic original, which was precisely what Protestantism claimed to represent. The last page includes a list of eight corrections to the text noticed while the book was in press. From the moment of publication, the *September Testament* must have given the impression of diligence and authenticity.

The volume includes woodcut illustrations. These mostly take the form of large initials at the opening of each book enclosing pictures of the various authors, the four evangelists, Saint Paul, and so on. This is a formula for identifying books in Latin Bibles which goes back beyond the thirteenth century and which would have been very familiar to Luther's readers, even those who had not previously used the text in German. The portraits are applied in the *September Testament* with a certain haphazard charm. Thus the woodcut initial of Saint John with his eagle used for the opening of John's Gospel is reused for the start of the Epistle of Saint James, probably because no other initial 'I' was available. The Apocalypse opens with a woodcut 'D' which actually shows Saint Matthew with his angel. It was originally printed at the beginning of Matthew's Gospel, but was reused later because the letter 'D' was required in both texts, and the subject seemed similar enough to Saint John's encounter with the angel of God in the Apocalypse. This careless pragmatism vanished in the printing of the Apocalypse itself, which is unexpectedly embellished with 21 full-page pictures illustrating the text. They stand out as incongruous in a publication which was mostly understated and unprovocative. The Apocalypse woodcuts were evidently designed in the workshop of the artist Lucas Cranach the elder, one of the two publishers of the *September Testament* (the other was Christian Döring, a local goldsmith and businessman). It may be that Cranach himself requested their inclusion. The pictures echo those of the majestic Apocalypse of Dürer (1498) and even the crude blockbook Apocalypses of the 1450s, but they are adapted here into a visual assault on the papacy. The evil city of Babylon, doomed to destruction by earthquake, is recognizable in its woodcut as Renaissance Rome, with the Castel San

166

The Apocalypse at the end of the September Testament *includes a series of 21 full-page woodcuts. Here the blasphemous Whore of Babylon is shown wearing the triple tiara of the popes of Rome*

Angelo unambiguously beside the Tiber. The beast from the bottomless pit (Apocalypse 11:7), the dragon which spewed out foul spirits like frogs (Apocalypse 16:13) and the blasphemous Whore of Babylon (Apocalypse 17:3) are all shown wearing the triple tiara of the popes (Pl. 166). The scarcely veiled insult was extraordinary in 1522. Luther's text may have been restrained and intellectual but, in the silent gloss provided by the woodcuts, he used the medium of the Bible to curse the Church of Rome.

It is credibly reported that 3,000 copies of the *September Testament* were printed. They cost between half a *gulden* and one and a half *gulden* each, probably depending on the binding. Compare this with 100 *gulden*, apparently the contemporary price of the Huntington Library copy of the Gutenberg Bible on parchment, or the 133 *gulden* paid by the collegiate church of Namur for a manuscript Bible in 1478. Here was a book aimed at the most popular market the Bible had addressed since the early years of Christianity. Luther himself took no fee or royalty for his work. The pope's ban on writings by Luther had no obvious effect, and the translation evidently sold extremely rapidly. The provocatively anti-papal woodcuts caused political anxiety to Duke Georg of Saxony (1471–1539). On 6 November 1522 he prohibited the sale of the book in his territories and stated that no woman or man was to use the translation (*niemands es were Weib oder Man*, note that women are mentioned first). With an agreeable nod to the mercantile mentality of the north Germans, the duke offered to refund the purchase price of any Luther New Testaments surrendered to the authorities before Christmas. By then, however, the edition had already sold out. A reprint appeared in Basle in December 1522, and a new edition with many textual corrections by Luther was published from Wittenberg in the same month. This is commonly known as the *December Testament*. The woodcuts in the Apocalypse were repeated but were arranged differently, often as pairs facing each other across the open pages. However, the papal tiaras had now been carved away from the woodblocks and the most controversial aspect of the publication was thereby evaded.

Over the next twelve years, Luther worked on his translation of the Old Testament. This was a period of extreme activity in his life, including his marriage to a former nun in 1525, and parts of the biblical work were delayed by the extraordinary pressures of defining and defending the Reformation. Luther found himself the spokesman for a movement which was transforming and dividing all of Europe, and Bible translation, however important, is slow work. As each section was finished, it was published separately. Luther's translation of the Pentateuch appeared in 1523. The following year he added German translations of the texts from Joshua to the Books of Solomon

167

Luther's heavily corrected autograph draft of his translation of Psalms 22-3, probably written in 1524
(FORMERLY BERLIN, DEUTSCHE STAATSBIBLIOTHEK)

168 opposite

Luther's translation of the New Testament was an immense success. It was reprinted more than 50 times in the 1520s. This edition was published in 1523

followed by the Psalter (Pl. 167). Work on the Prophets was greatly delayed. The books began appearing in 1526 but were not complete until 1532. Luther then turned to translating the Apocrypha. At each stage, he was constantly revising and reprinting parts which were already in print. The New Testament and the Psalms, especially, went through many editions, often with extensive corrections by Luther, during the 1520s and early 1530s. There were over fifty editions and reprints of Luther's New Testament between 1522 and 1529 alone (Pl. 168), not including further editions of separate portions of the New Testament. The peak was in 1524, when there were 47 different editions of parts of Luther's translation. Many were printed under Luther's general supervision in Wittenberg by Hans Lufft, but others were reprinted freely in Basle (especially), Augsburg, Strassburg, Zurich, and occasionally elsewhere. There was no copyright in the early sixteenth century. Once a book was in print and was demonstrably selling well, there was little to prevent other publishers from making their own reprints. The entire Bible in Luther's translation was finally published as a single consecutive entity in Wittenberg in the autumn of 1534 (Pl. 156). It was called *Biblia, das ist die gantze Heilige Schrifft Deudsch* ("The Bible, that is the entire Holy

Writing in German') and Martin Luther's name appeared on the title-page.

Most of the Old Testament was translated from the Hebrew. Luther does not seem to have had access to a copy of the Complutensian Polyglot. He certainly used the 1494 Soncino edition of the Hebrew Bible, for his marked-up copy survives in the Deutsche Staatsbibliothek in Berlin (Pl. 158), and he owned the Hebrew edition of the Psalms printed by Froben in 1516. He used the Vulgate and the Greek Septuagint. Luther was competent in Hebrew, though never a great Hebraist. Just as he revised his Greek translations with Melanchthon, so Luther took advice in Hebrew from the scholar Matthäus Aurogallus (c.1490–1543). Many Jews in the 1520s had sympathy with Luther, and the Jewish biblical commentator, Abraham Farissol (c.1451–c.1525), had hopes of Luther's conversion. In later years Luther turned against the contemporary Jews and his hostility led at least in part to their expulsion from Saxony in 1543.

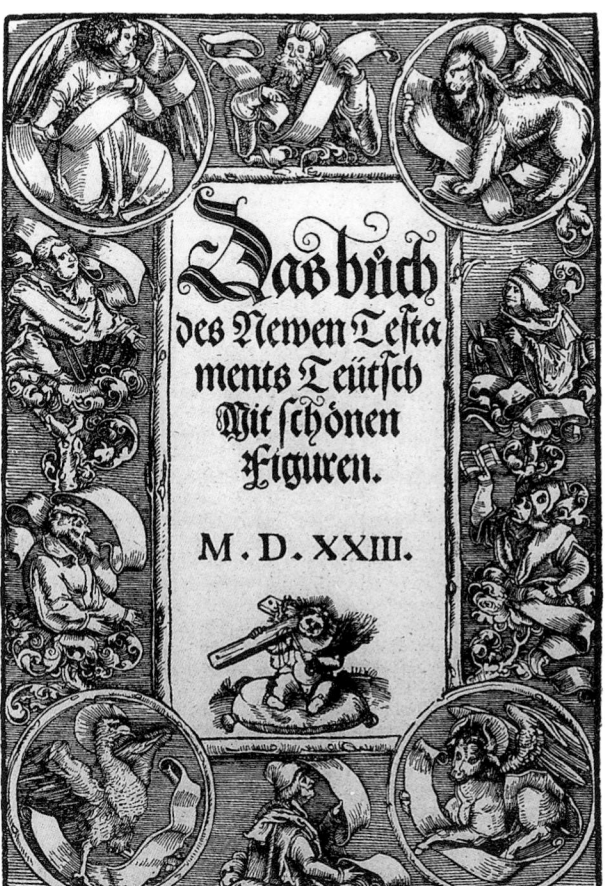

A major part of the success of Luther and of all early Protestant Bibles was the insistence that the texts were taken directly from the original languages. This caught the public imagination. Even people with no scholarly background became fascinated with the apparent authenticity conferred by translating from Greek and Hebrew scriptures. We can illustrate this with an eye-witness description of an encounter with Martin Luther. A Swiss student of theology, Johann Kessler, wrote an account of his travels in the 1520s, called the *Sabbata*. One day in February 1522, he recounts, he and a friend escaped from heavy rain into the Black Bear inn in Jena. Seated at a table was a strange-looking man in breeches, doublet and a red hat. Unknown to them, this was Martin Luther in disguise, travelling from the Wartburg back to Wittenberg. He was reading a Hebrew Psalter. Two merchants joined them at one of the tables and they all fell into conversation together, over drinks and later during dinner. One of them remarked that he would give one finger to be able to read the Scriptures in Hebrew. Luther said that he too wished to master Hebrew and so he practised reading it daily. He added that it was necessary to know Greek and Hebrew to understand the Bible. One of the merchants produced a copy of one of Luther's biblical commentaries, just published, and asked if his new companions had seen it yet. Luther, still unrecognized, said he hoped to acquire one when he reached Wittenberg. The landlord, unable to contain himself, announced that this man was Luther himself, but none of the other diners believed him. Even in a country inn, then, in the first years of the Reformation, travellers of no great distinction did not find it odd or out of place to be discussing the fascination of the Bible in Hebrew and Greek. That is a situation which would have been inconceivable even a hundred years earlier.

Luther honoured and preserved the entire Bible. His more radical colleagues might not have agreed with him. Since the Gospels were the central text of Christianity, some Reformers argued that no other texts were necessary, or that other parts of the Bible had no logical purpose except in so far as they predicted or proclaimed the Gospels and the life of Christ. This line of reasoning opened the possibility of radical reformation of the Bible too. If the pope and bishops could be pruned away as unnecessary accretions, why not parts of the Bible too? There was a moment in the 1520s when the Reformers were casting off so many of the long-established traditions of the Roman Church that they might easily have been carried away into paring away considerable parts of the Bible and the Apocrypha as irrelevant. The canon of the Bible was probably in more danger in the early sixteenth century than at any period since the fourth century. Reformers looked again at the credentials of each biblical text. It is difficult to find explicit allusions to Christ in some books of the Bible, such as the Song of Songs (always a strangely worrying text), or the book of Esther (which never even mentions God), or the Apocalypse. Other Old Testament books were mainly concerned with laws and patterns of behaviour which were self-evidently addressed specifically to Jewish life in ancient Palestine. By the Renaissance, scholars knew enough ancient history to place such texts in context. In the end, however, Luther evaded the issue. He drew a distinction between parts of the Old Testament which had a historical relevance to the ancient Jews to whom they were directed, and those which were still to be regarded as the active precepts of God. He simply accepted all books of the Bible as inspired by the Holy Ghost, but not all as being of equal value. He compared the lesser books of the Bible with the straw in the manger in Bethlehem, which was laid there by the Holy Ghost to support the Christ Child. Elsewhere he compared them with the swaddling bands which wrapped the Child.

Let us look at the Luther Bible as a book. The first complete edition, Wittenberg, 1534, is a large heavy quarto, usually bound in two volumes. The title-page to each volume has a full architectural border (Pl. 169). At the top, leaning over the balustrade of a kind of mezzanine gallery, is a bearded figure, apparently God himself, writing a scroll inscribed *Gottes wort bleibt ewig* ('God's word remains forever', from Isaiah 40:8). There are cherubim on either side of him. Those on the left hold an open manuscript, doubtless a Bible. One of those on the right struggles with a vast book in a Gothic binding while the other holds a document with a hanging seal. This must be God's covenant. On each side of the title are Germanic knights in armour, holding banners. At the foot of the page, a crowd of cherubim has gathered on the steps to read, admire and adore an open book. This

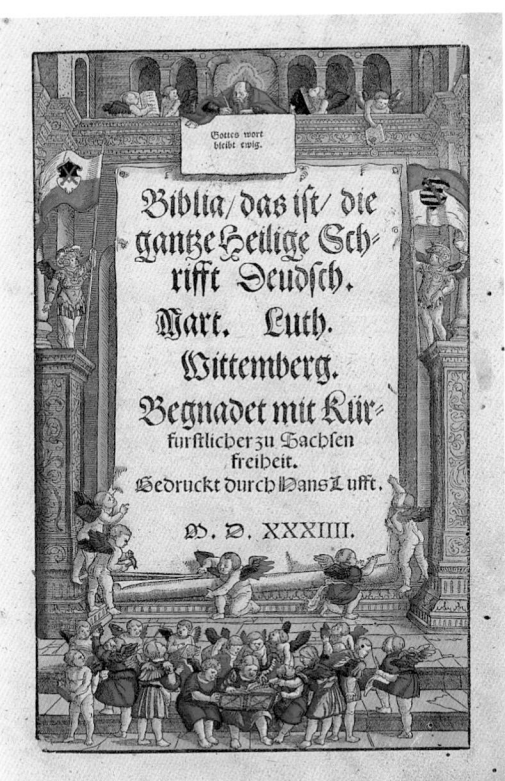

169

*The first edition of the complete
Bible in Luther's translation
was published in Wittenberg in
1534*

is a title-page, therefore, which venerates the Bible as a physical object distributed from the court of Heaven. The German knights give a reassuringly contemporary chivalric endorsement. Turn the page and this is reinforced, for there is a charter of privilege from Duke Johann Friedrich of Saxony (1503–54). It is a book which brings a certain authority to itself. In later editions, the duke's portrait appears.

The Bible itself is divided into seven sections, each with separate sequences of folio numbers. These correspond with the distinct campaigns in which Luther translated the text. They comprise the Pentateuch (133 leaves), Joshua to Esther (212 leaves), Job to the Song of Songs, including the Psalter (85 leaves), the Major and Minor Prophets (94 and 59 leaves respectively), the Apocrypha (106 leaves) and the New Testament (200 leaves). This adds up to 889 leaves, almost 1,800 pages of text. The book has a total of 184 woodcuts, mostly printed for the first time in this edition. The inclusion of pictures in early copies of the Luther Bible must tell us something about the anticipated use of the book by its readers. The great public folio Bibles, like the Gutenberg Bible or the English 1611 Authorized Version, have no illustrations. Even illuminated manuscript Bibles usually had no pictures beyond miniatures enclosed in initials. The Luther Bibles, however, were clearly intended for domestic use, perhaps by people whose level of literacy was often unsophisticated. All owners of Luther Bibles must already have known Bible stories from pictures, for no one in the late Middle Ages or Renaissance could have avoided the multitude of biblical imagery appearing everywhere from church walls to inn signs. The use of woodcuts in Luther Bibles would provide a reassuring anchor. The illustrations occur mainly in the narrative books. Genesis, for example, includes pictures of familiar subjects such as the Garden of Eden, Noah's flood, Noah's family kneeling before the rainbow, Lot being led from Sodom by angels, the sacrifice of Isaac, and so on. From the books of prophets to the New Testament epistles, the woodcuts occur only at the opening of books. The Psalms, for instance, open with a beautiful half-page image of King David in his bedroom in a sixteenth-century castle. There are no pictures from the life of Christ. The Protestants did not outlaw devotional art (Luther himself regarded the commandment about graven images to be one of those directed specifically to the ancient Jews in Sinai) but they were anxious to avoid any possibility of idolatry. Pictures of Christ or (especially) of the Virgin Mary would seem inappropriate. The Gospels in the Luther Bible are therefore illustrated by pictures of the Evangelists, such as Saint Matthew seated at a cluttered table in an elegant garden bower, with his angel opposite him and the Holy Dove above. It is a civilized and uncontroversial scene. The Apocalypse, however, returns with its damning woodcuts, now recut in oblong shape and increased to 26. The beasts and the Whore of Babylon are once again shown unambiguously as the pope in papal tiaras.

Typographically, Luther Bibles are very easy to read, especially the editions produced in Wittenberg. This too must have been a deliberate policy. The text

is in a single column of large print. It is presented in a rounded Gothic type, then traditional for vernacular texts. It is divided up by sense into short and visually distinct paragraphs, and the sentences are punctuated by neat oblique strokes. Marginal notes are in a smaller and distinctive type, and there is no confusion as to what is biblical. Chapters are marked by woodcut initials on square panels, usually in classical or leafy designs. The pages have folio numbers as well as the traditional thirteenth-century running-titles and chapter numbers. The Luther Bible is not only in a language which was easy to understand but was arranged in print in a way that made it extremely accessible.

It is worth emphasizing the extraordinary use which the Reformers made of the printing press. The impact of the Reformation would have been inconceivable without the invention of printing in the fifteenth century. Gutenberg had produced an orthodox Latin Bible and he had taken advantage of a huge market for printed indulgences. Luther launched the Reformation by an attack on indulgences and he dethroned the Latin Bible from the heart of western Christendom, but he used the printing press as no one had ever done before. Over 3,700 separate editions of books and pamphlets by Martin Luther were published in his lifetime, not including Bible translations. This is an immense number for any one author, even by today's standards. It is an average of almost two publications a week for most of his adult life. In his time, Luther was by far the most extensively published author who had ever lived. Many contemporary portraits show him holding a book. The Reformers fully understood and exploited the propaganda value of the printing press, and of engravings and woodcuts (Pl. 170). The Luther Bible was printed and reprinted over and over again. Most editions were of several thousand copies. When the Wittenberg printer, Hans Lufft, retired from business in 1572, it was said that he had by then printed almost 100,000 Bibles in Luther's translation. At 1,800 pages a copy, that would be nearly 180 million pages of the Bible passing through Lufft's press alone. It was a fundamental part of the Protestant belief that the Word of God should be made available to speak directly to all people. The printing press provided a means of achieving this which some saw as divine intervention and which confounded critics of the Reformation because it was completely irreversible. The first public burnings of Protestant books took place as early as 1521, and the first burning of a printer in 1527. To offer martyrdom to any opponent is a risky political manoeuvre, which often achieves an opposite effect.

Destruction of some copies of a book only adds to the value of those that remain. The fact that the Catholic Church reacted so violently to the printed texts of the Reformation is evidence that they realized and feared the power of the press. In no way did the Protestants invent the art of printing, but they found themselves in possession of a tool for propaganda which made the Reformation unstoppable.

We have so far looked principally at the Reformation Bible in Germany, for it was there that Luther established a pattern of Bible translation and publication which was rapidly repeated across northern Europe. Luther's *September Testament* was published in 1522. A New Testament in Dutch, translated from Luther's edition, appeared as early as 1523. In 1524 and 1526 respectively, the text was already in Danish and Swedish, both translated from Luther's version. The whole Bible was in Dutch by 1526, Swedish by 1541 and Danish by 1550 (Pl. 171). There was even a Finnish New Testament published in Stockholm in 1548, translated directly from the Greek. It is a squat little book, like a miniature Luther Bible. Holland and Scandinavia eventually became uncontroversially Protestant. Denmark and Sweden are still soundly Lutheran.

Italy remained Roman Catholic throughout the Reformation, and still is. The Catholics found themselves in a difficult position with regard to the Bible in vernacular translations. On the one hand, they sought to defend the traditional position of the Church as the interpreter of the Bible as transmitted from Saint Jerome. On the other, it was abundantly clear to Catholic scholars and humanists that editions based on the Greek and Hebrew were probably closer to the original texts. The Bible was available in an Italian translation made from the Vulgate by

170 opposite

Luther's supporters used the printing press ceaselessly for propaganda, publishing vast quantities of tracts and leaflets and many pictures of Luther himself
(NUREMBERG, GERMANISCHES NATIONALMUSEUM)

171

Luther's Bible was translated into Danish in 1550. This is the second edition, published in Copenhagen in 1588–9

a Venetian monk, Niccolò Malermi (*c.*1422–81), abbot of the monastery of San Michele di Murano, on the island in the lagoon of Venice. His translation was first printed in 1471 and remained in print until 1567. The final edition proclaims its endorsement by the Holy Inquisition, an assembling of papal credentials in support of a work of patently obsolete scholarship (Pl. 172). In the meantime, another translation had been made by the Florentine humanist, Antonio Brucioli

172

The Italian translation of Niccolò Malermi remained in print until this edition of 1567, which proudly (and by then out-datedly) proclaims that it is based on the Latin Vulgate of Saint Jerome

173 *opposite*

The first truly Protestant Bible in Italian was published by Giovanni Diodati in Geneva in 1607. It was translated from the Hebrew and Greek

(*c.*1495–1566). His edition pretends to be taken from Greek and Hebrew sources but it derives mostly from the Latin of Erasmus. His text of the New Testament was printed in Venice in 1530 and the complete Bible in 1532. Although Brucioli was a Catholic, his sympathies towards Protestantism made his translation open to suspicion. It was placed on the papal Index of banned books in 1559.

The first true Protestant Bible in the Italian language was that of Giovanni Diodati (1576–1649), professor of theology in Geneva. It was addressed primarily to Italian-speaking Protestants in Switzerland. It was trans-lated directly from the Hebrew and Greek and was first published in Geneva in 1607. The woodcut on the title page conveys an agreeably rustic image of Reformation Switzerland, showing a farmer sowing a field on a mountainside, with the motto in French, *Son art en Dieu* (Pl. 173). Facing the opening page of Genesis is a quotation from II Timothy 3:16–17, on the value of the Scriptures to all people of God, for teach-ing, reproof, correction and training in righteousness. These are all acceptable Protestant virtues. Diodati's translation has remained in print ever since and is even now a principal version of the Bible in the Italian language.

If anything, Spain remained even more aggressively Catholic than Italy. This was the country of the Spanish Inquisition, originally set up in 1479 to cor-rect elements of Islam and Judaism. Cardinal Francisco Ximénes de Cisneros, genial and humane editor of the Complutensian Polyglot, was himself the Grand

Inquisitor of Spain. In the sixteenth century, however, the Inquisition turned on Protestantism with great vigour and relentless cruelty. It was extremely effective. A few portions of the Bible translated into Spanish from 1490 onwards survive only as fragments. The first index of banned books issued by the Inquisition in Toledo in 1551 prohibited absolutely any Bible in Castilian or any other vulgar tongue. The first complete Bible in the Spanish language was the translation of Cassiodoro de Reyna (*c.*1520–94), a former monk from Seville. He converted to Protestantism and ministered to a Spanish congregation in London in the late 1550s. Pursued by charges of heresy and homosexuality, Reyna moved across to Antwerp in 1563 and later to Frankfurt-am-Main. His Spanish Bible was published in Basle in 1569. He used sources in Hebrew, Greek and Syriac. Like the Luther Bible, the title-page of Reyna's edition cites Isaiah 40:8 on the eternity of the Word of God, but this time (defiantly) it quotes it in Hebrew.

France suffered terrible anguish at the Reformation. Protestants and Catholics confronted each other intemperately for centuries. In the end, the Protestants, or Huguenots, withdrew from France but not without experiences of fearful persecution. Each camp translated and promoted multiple versions of the Bible in the French language, pretending to exclusive accuracy and no knowledge of each other's editions. Events began innoculously enough. Jacques Le Fèvre d'Étaples (*c.*1455–1536) was librarian of the monastery of St-Germain-des-Prés in Paris and a humanistic scholar in the circle of Erasmus. He was a liberal churchman but a Catholic. He had translated works of Aristotle. He was well connected in the royal court and Church hierarchy. An anonymous French translation of the New Testament, securely attributed now to Jacques Le Fèvre, was published in Paris in 1523, and a complete Bible in 1530. The title declares its loyal Catholic source *selon la pure et entiere traduction de sainct Hierome*, 'in accordance with the pure and complete translation by Saint Jerome'. Revised editions appeared in 1534 and 1541. In a final revision, it became the model for the so-called Louvain Bible (*selon l'edition Latine*), published in Louvain in 1550. This text was then promulgated by the Catholics. Many other supposed translations which followed (including those of Besse, 1608, Deville, 1614, and Frizon, 1621) were little more than the Louvain Bible slightly adapted. Altogether the text probably appeared in upwards of 200 subsequent editions.

In the meantime, a cousin of John Calvin, the Swiss reformer, had produced the first French Protestant edition. The translator was Pierre Robert Olivetan (*c*.1506–38). He was a native of Noyon, in northern France. He joined a group of French-speaking Swiss Reformers in 1532. Olivetan's translation of the Bible was published in Neuchâtel in Switzerland in 1535, with a preface dated *des Alpes* on 12 February 1535. The text, like all Protestant Bibles, declares itself to be taken directly from the Hebrew and Greek. In practice, it was evidently based on the text of Le Fèvre, collated against the Latin of Erasmus and others. The mutual indebtedness across enemy lines becomes even more complicated, for Olivetan's translation was apparently then used for the Louvain revisions of the Catholic Bible in 1550. The French Protestants and Catholics would gladly have massacred each other (as happened on Saint Bartholomew's day in 1572 when between 5,000 and 10,000 Huguenots were killed in Paris and elsewhere) but they silently took phrases from each other's French Bibles. Olivetan's translation was corrected and reprinted often, especially in Geneva (Pl. 174). The edition published by Robert Estienne in Geneva in 1553 was the first printed Bible with its text divided into numbered verses. That device has survived ever since, in almost all Bibles, Protestant and Catholic.

The official Catholic position throughout this period was one of defending the primacy of the medieval Latin Vulgate as the only true Bible, supported by a thousand years of tradition. The status of the Vulgate was confirmed in 1546 at the Council of Trent (1545–63), the conference held by Catholics to define and strengthen their traditional Church against the advances of Protestantism. In order to deflect accusations that the Latin text itself might have become inaccurate over centuries of copying, a new and scholarly edition of the Vulgate Bible was commissioned by Sixtus V (pope 1585–90). A commission of bishops and scholars collated the text against many early manuscripts, including the *Codex Amiatinus* (above, p. 33). They produced what is known as the 'Sixtine' edition, finally published by the Vatican in 1590. Political wrangles and criticisms within the Church required its withdrawal and replacement by a monumental revision in 1592, usually called the 'Clementine' edition, after Clement VIII (pope 1592–1605). This then became the standard Catholic Bible, endorsed as the true Bible for the next 350 years. Any subsequent translations for use by Catholics were taken from the Clementine Vulgate. A version for German Catholics was made by Kaspar Ulenberg (1549–1617), revised and reissued in Mainz in 1662. A French Catholic translation was made by two brothers, Antoine le Maistre (1608–58) and Louis Isaac le Maistre (1613–84, known as 'De Saci'), published in 1667. Italian and Spanish translations from the Clementine Vulgate eventually followed, but only as late as the end of the eighteenth century.

This has already become a long chapter, but let us finally look at England. The situation there was different from elsewhere in Europe, because (as we saw in Chapter 7), the vernacular Bible was already illegal long before the Reformation. It therefore began with an official handicap. Once England became Protestant,

174

The French Bibles printed in Geneva by Robert Estienne were the first with numbered verses. This is the edition of 1588

however, the translated Bible then became a symbol of state. This is unique in Europe. Only England has an 'Authorized Version' of the Bible, issued under the auspices of a king who was head of the Church.

William Tyndale (*c.*1494–1536) is the saintly hero of English Protestants. He was a man of good academic credentials and Christian piety. He lacked the physical presence of Luther and the self-confidence of Erasmus: he was short, 'of no great stature', according to John Foxe. At the time of the publication of Luther's *September Testament* in 1522, Tyndale conceived the idea of producing a contemporary rendering of the Bible in English. The anti-Wycliffite constitutions of Archbishop Arundel were still legally valid in England, prohibiting any translation of the Bible unless it had been approved by the local diocese. Tyndale therefore applied to Cuthbert Tunstall, bishop of London, to endorse his work as translator. The bishop declined. Here we see the refreshing internationalism of Renaissance scholarship, for Tyndale simply moved to Germany, probably in April 1524, and continued work as normal, beyond the close scrutiny of English law. He knew Greek and Hebrew. He used the Greek text in the *Novum Instrumentum* of Erasmus and the German translation by Luther. Within a year he had already completed a New Testament in fluent contemporary English. It was being printed in Catholic Cologne in 1525 when, it is said, the printers boasted in a tavern that they were producing a text that would make England Lutheran. The printing press was raided by local magistrates and Tyndale escaped up the Rhine to Worms, taking with him those sheets of his New Testament which had already been printed. Only a single fragment of that unfinished publication still survives, now in the British Library, one of the absolute rarest of any major printed books (Pl. 175). It is a section of 31 leaves in quarto, comprising Saint Matthew's Gospel as far as chapter 22. It includes a woodcut author-portrait of Saint Matthew and marginal notes, all of which closely resemble the *September Testament* of Luther.

On arrival in Worms, Tyndale initiated a new edition, probably completed in 1526. Its title-page emphasizes its authentic pre-Vulgate credentials, 'as it was written'. Unlike the stately Cologne fragment or the first Luther Bibles, this was a little pocket-sized book, on the scale of many manuscripts of the Wycliffite Bible, easy to conceal. Unbound copies were smuggled into England, apparently through Antwerp, and were sold furtively. Records of trials give some flavour of the trade, such as 'About Christmas last, there came a Duche man, beyng now in the Flete, which wold have sold this Respondent ii or iii Hundreth of the said N. Testaments in English', priced at 9 pence each. This illegal first edition too is now a book of extreme rarity. For many years, only two copies were known, a very imperfect volume (lacking 71 leaves) in the library of St Paul's Cathedral in London, and an enchanting illuminated copy, lacking only its title-page, in the

175

Tyndale's first attempt at publishing an English translation of the New Testament was interrupted by legal action in 1525. Only a single fragment survives, now in the British Library

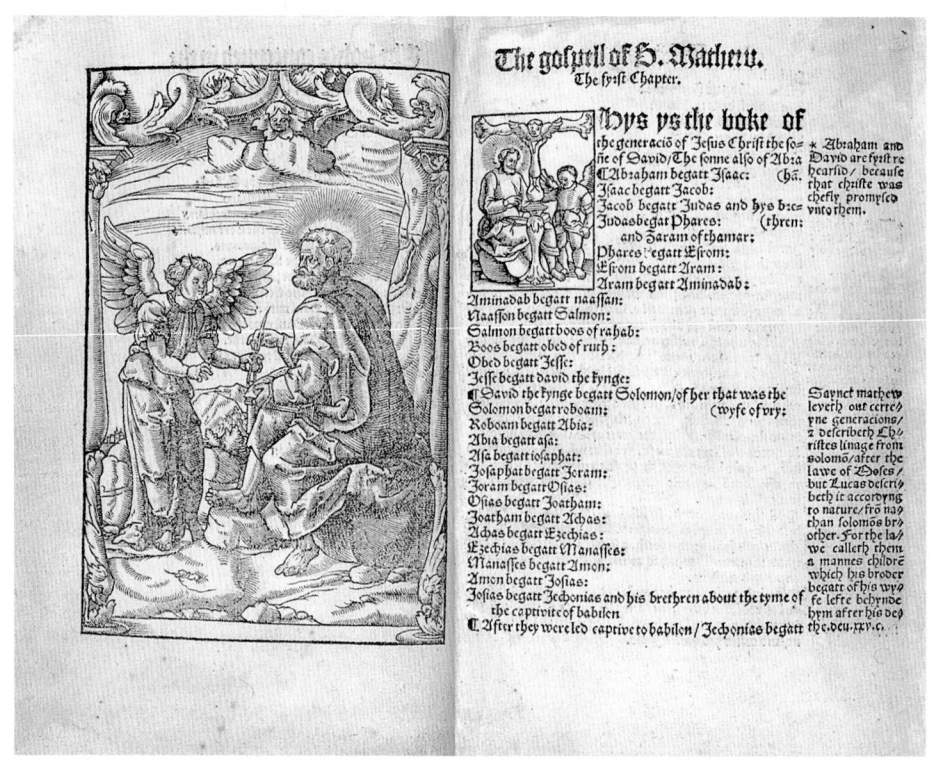

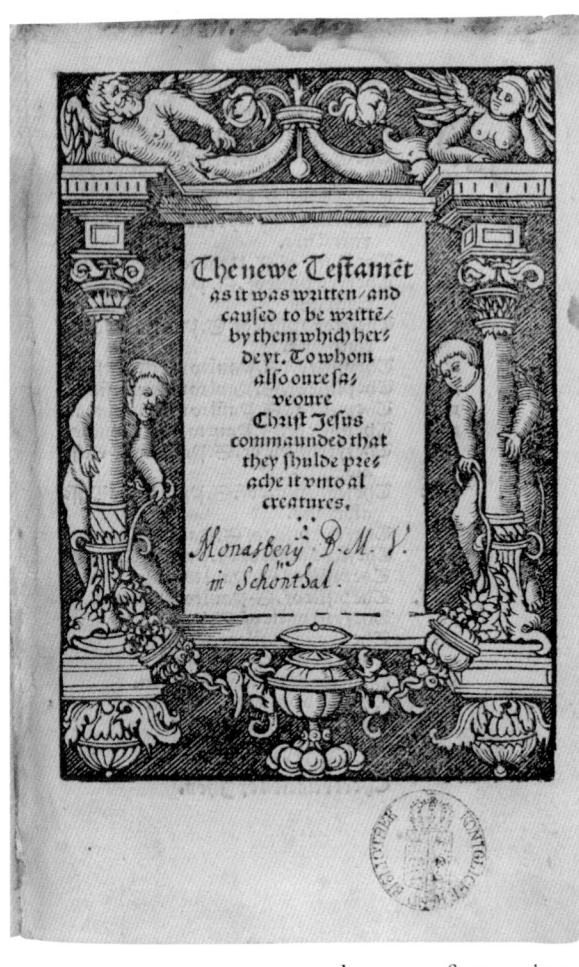

176

The first printed edition of the whole New Testament in English was published illegally in 1526. Until recently, only two copies were known, both incomplete. This third copy, complete with its title-page, was recognized in Germany in 1995
(STUTTGART, WÜRTTEMBERGISCHE LANDESBIBLIOTHEK)

collection of the Bristol Baptist College. In 1994 the Bristol copy was acquired by the British Library. The publicity which ensued flushed out a third surviving copy, entirely complete, which had been unacknowledged for centuries in the Bibelsammlung of the Württembergische Landesbibliothek in Stuttgart (Pl. 176).

Like Luther, Tyndale then moved back to the beginning of the Bible and translated the Pentateuch. He worked directly from the text in Hebrew. The translation was apparently published in Antwerp in January 1530, though it has a colophon pretending that it was 'emprented at Malborow in the lande of Hesse, by me Hans Luft'. Malborow is Marburg and Hans Lufft was the name of Luther's busy printer in Wittenberg; both are spurious names to obfuscate the provenance. Antwerp was a possession of the Holy Roman emperor, still aggressively Catholic and allied to England in league against Lutheranism. Tyndale in the meantime was translating the Old Testament (Jonah was published in 1531) and revising the New Testament. This was printed in Antwerp in 1534, with a true colophon naming the printer and Tyndale as translator. Tyndale was arrested in May 1535 and was imprisoned at Vilvorde, north of Brussels. There is a heart-rending letter which he wrote from prison, begging for warmer clothes to see him through the coming winter in his unheated cell and asking for his Hebrew Bible, grammar and dictionary, all of which had been impounded. He was convicted of heresy in August 1536 and was strangled first and then burnt at the stake in Vilvorde. According to Foxe, his last words were 'Lord, open the king of England's eyes'.

The eyes of Henry VIII were already opened very wide indeed. In 1533 he had married Anne Boleyn, the second of his six successive wives. To do so, he had been obliged to divorce Catherine of Aragon and to declare England's independence from the Church of Rome. Anne herself was openly sympathetic to Protestantism. She patronized Miles Coverdale (1488–1568), a former assistant to Tyndale. Coverdale prepared a second English translation of the Bible, mostly from the Vulgate and from Luther's German text, rather than from the Greek or Hebrew. This was printed probably in Cologne in 1535 and was imported into England, where a fulsome dedication to Henry VIII was quickly inserted into to every copy. Henry was as susceptible to flattery as to women. A combination of religious needs and political expediency brought about a very rapid change of royal policy towards the Bible in the English language. The king embraced Protestantism with passionate enthusiasm. He allowed himself to be made head of the Church of England. The prologue to Coverdale's Bible suggested that Henry VIII's title 'Defender of the Faith', which the pope had conferred on the king in 1521 for his opposition to Luther, could as well be used by Henry in defence of the Protestant Bible in English. In 1537 two printing-shops issued Bibles in London, including two further editions of Coverdale's Bible and a new version again, under the pseudonym of Thomas Matthew, dedicated to 'the moost noble and gracyous Prynce Kyng Henry the eyght'. On 5 September 1538 the king commanded that a copy of the Bible in English should be placed in every church in England.

177

The image of Henry VIII distributing English Bibles in 1539 can be compared with the ninth-century picture of Saint Jerome handing out copies of the Latin Bible illustrated above, Pl. 21

178 opposite

The first edition of the 'Authorized Version' of the English Bible was published in 1611 and has remained in print ever since. This page shows the difference between two printings of 1611. The first has the reading 'he wente into the citie' at Ruth 3:15 in the centre of the left-hand column here; the second printing is otherwise identical but reads 'she went into the citie'

The history of the English Bible since 1538, like that of the Church of England itself, has largely been shaped by committees. The so-called *Great Bible* of 1539 was a composite translation, assembled by 'dyverse excellent learned men', according to its title-page. The woodcut which surrounds the title shows Henry VIII himself distributing copies of the Bible to his grateful subjects to the right and left (Pl. 177). It is pleasantly reminiscent of the ninth-century miniature in the First Bible of Charles the Bold (Bibliothèque Nationale de France, ms. lat. 1), which we encountered at the end of Chapter 1, showing Saint Jerome distributing Bibles to his monks (Pl. 21). The difference is that Jerome was the translator; and Henry VIII was, at best, a late-come convenor of translators. Further English Bibles of the Reformation were all the results of multiple enterprises. The 'Geneva' (or 'Breeches') Bible of 1560 was the work of at least three translators. The Bishops' Bible of 1568 was prepared by a committee of approximately seventeen scholars, mostly bishops, chaired by Matthew Parker, archbishop of Canterbury 1559–75. The most influential English Bible of them all was entirely the product of committees. The meeting of the Hampton Court Conference in January 1604 suggested that a definitive Bible in the English language should be prepared under the patronage of the King James (king of Scotland 1567–1625, king of England from 1603). The king himself announced the appointment of 54 different translators. Forty-seven of them are recorded by name. They were divided into six sub-committees, meeting in Westminster, Oxford and Cambridge. The result was the monumental 'King James' or 'Authorized Version' of the Bible, first printed in 1611 and since then probably the most widely read and best-known book ever published in English (Pl. 178).

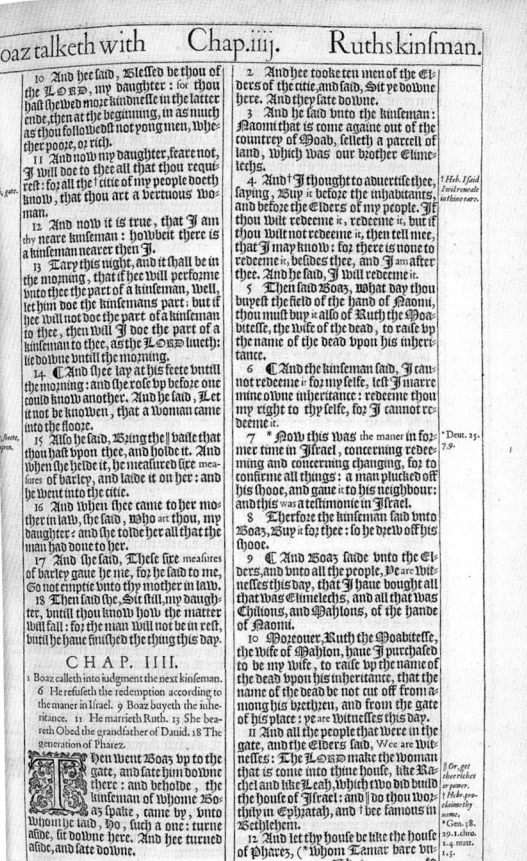

These English Bibles are Protestant translations. It must be emphasized that the fundamental differences of meaning between the traditional Latin Vulgate text and the Lutheran or Anglican translations are usually very slight. Versions vary only in their choice of words to express the same meaning. Even when the Reformers went back to the original Hebrew or Greek, the text of the Scriptures was found to have survived the Middle Ages more or less accurately. Fanatical adherents of the Reformation and the Counter-Reformation in the sixteenth century wrote hysterical pamphlets deploring each other's corruption of the sacred Scriptures. They exaggerate outrageously. In practice, Protestant and Catholic versions of the Bible told exactly the same story. Some individual words are understood slightly differently. A Roman Catholic Bible might opt for vocabulary like 'church', 'priest', 'chalice', and 'charity'. A Protestant Bible might translate those same words from the Greek as 'congregation', 'elder', 'cup' and 'love'. The cumulative effect of such vocabulary might convey a different emphasis to accounts of primitive Christianity in the Acts of the Apostles, for example, or the Epistles of Saint Paul. The Catholics pointed to the proven traditions of the Church for over a thousand years. The Protestants constantly emphasized that they were going back far beyond the time of Jerome. That is the great difference. That is why, until recently, the Protestant translations triumphed. The Great Bible of 1540 proclaimed itself as 'translated after the veryte of the Hebrue and Greke textes'. The Geneva Bible of 1560 described itself as 'translated according to the Ebrue and Greke'. The 1611 Authorized Version is called the Holy Bible 'translated out of the Originall Tongues and with the Former Translations diligently compared and revised'. This is the most famous book title in the English language.

10 | The English and American Bible Industry

THE AUTHORIZED VERSION of the English Bible, first printed in 1611, was so successful and so protected by legal privilege that it remained unaltered for 250 years and it is still in print today. It is the most widely-published text in the English language. During many generations, large portions of it were known by heart by people on both sides of the Atlantic. With Shakespeare, its exact contemporary, the Authorized Version has contributed countless quotations and expressions which have slipped, hardly noticed, into English language and idiom. The text had a vast readership but not simply because it was a captivating text. The words 'The Bible' are not neutral. The title of no other book is so charged with meaning, positive or negative. Whether one regards it as a divinely inspired guide to life or as an obsolete record of credulity, the Bible is universally acknowledged to be a publication with an extremely unusual status. In commercial terms, the Bible is a commodity with international market recognition. It is this phenomenon that makes it such an interesting part of English-speaking culture, both in Britain and in North America.

Let us look first of all at the legal status of the Authorized Version, for (strangely for a text which declares itself to be the essential birthright of all people) it was protected by copyright. Only certain publishing houses were licensed to print Bibles. From the seventeenth century onwards, many attempts were made by other commercial enterprises to capitalize on the Bible and eventually to dislodge it from its position as a protected commodity.

First of all, the term 'Authorized' has no real historical validity. The book was dedicated to King James I, who had initiated the translation, but no legal or royal endorsement was conferred on the text itself. The privilege was associated with the printers, not the text. The royal privilege for printing Bibles goes back to the

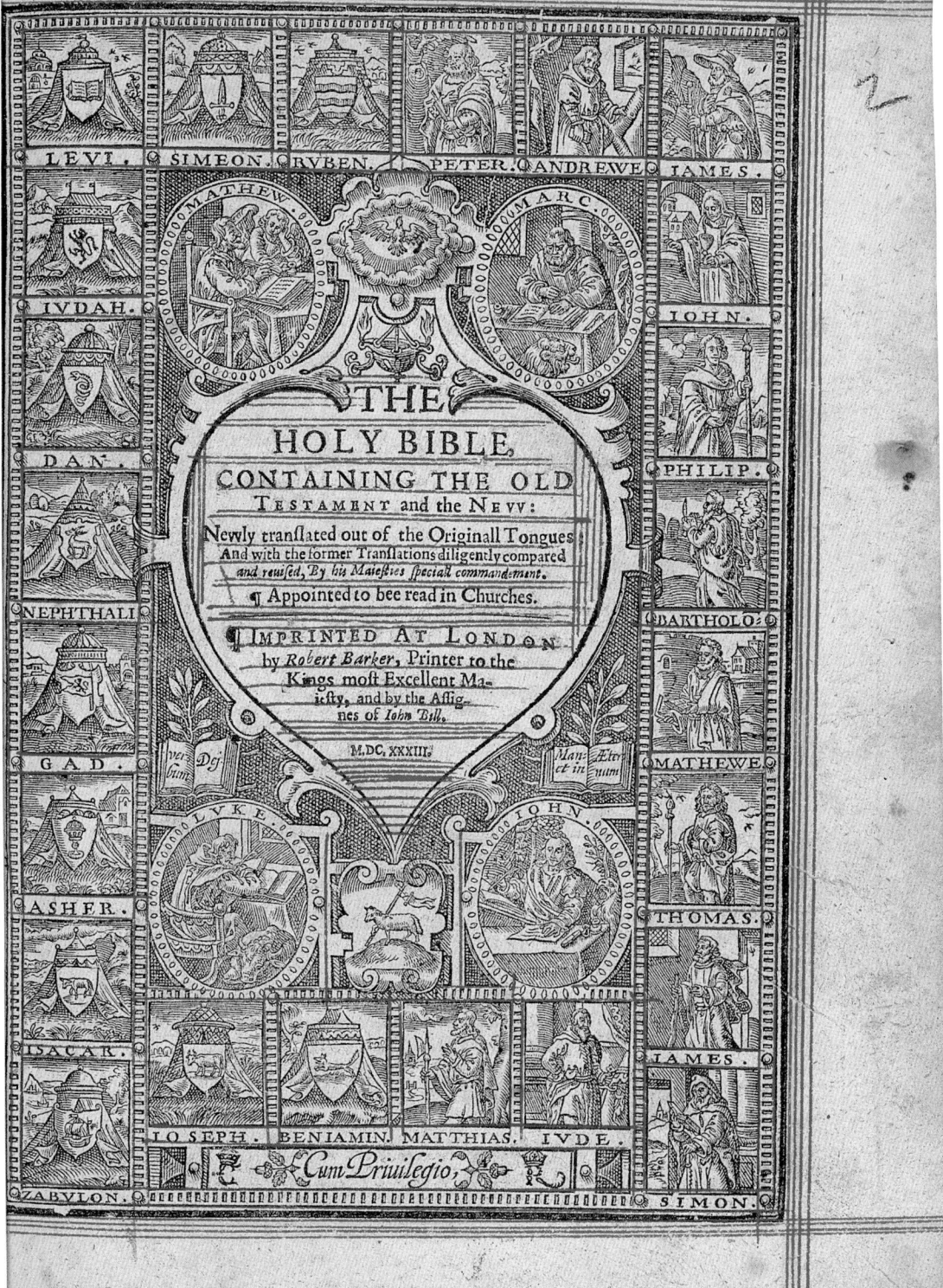

sixteenth century. In 1589, Queen Elizabeth had granted an exclusive patent for
the publishing of Bibles in English to Christopher Barker (c.1529–99). In a Bible
printed in London that year, Barker first calls himself the printer to the Queen.
This right was inherited by his son, Robert Barker (d.1645), who is described on
the title-page of the original Authorized Version in 1611 as 'Printer to the Kings
most Excellent Majestie'. When monopolies were abolished in England in 1623,
an exception was made for royal grants of the sole right to print certain books.
The privilege was interrupted, but not abolished, during the Commonwealth,
1649–60, when the English monarchy was forced into abeyance by Parliament.
The right to print Bibles was restored to private enterprise under Charles II
(king of England 1660–85) and it remained nominally in the possession of the
Barker family until 1709 (Pl. 179). At certain times the Barkers raised money
by selling leases in their monopoly to other London booksellers, including
John Bill (d.1630) and his son, John; Thomas Newcombe (d.1682) and his son,
Thomas; and Henry Hills (d.1689) and his son Henry. These names appear in the
imprints of seventeenth-century English Bibles with epithets such as 'assigns' or
'deputies' of each other, as the balance of the partnership was constantly adjusted
between them. In a series of moves between 1709 and 1712, the patent was
finally bought out from the various Barker heirs by John Baskett (d.1742), the

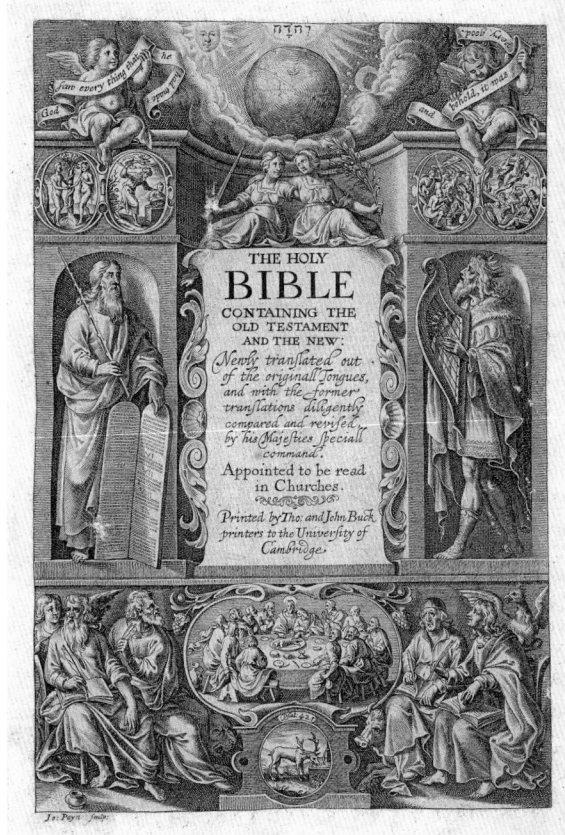

supreme businessman in printing and promoting Bibles
in the early eighteenth century. On his death, the exclusive right passed first to his son, Thomas (d.1761), and
then to his grandson, Mark. It was sold for £10,000 in
1769 to Charles Eyre and his partner William Strahan
(d.1785). After many renewals and commercial trans-
formations, the privilege survived until the late twentieth
century, until recently in the possession of the publishers,
Eyre and Spottiswoode. Now even this company has closed
and (for the moment) this line of the privilege seems
finally to have lapsed.

In the meantime, the right to print Bibles had been
extended in the seventeenth century to the university
printers of Oxford and Cambridge (both by invoking
earlier rights) and to the royal printer in Edinburgh.
Cambridge took rapid advantage of a royal charter of
1628 and published a New Testament that year and a
full edition of the Authorized Version in 1629 (Pl. 180).
It was printed by Thomas and John Buck, 'printers to the
University of Cambridge'. Oxford received a charter in
1636 but initially leased its rights back to the Stationers'
Company. This lease expired in 1673 and the first Oxford
Bible was printed in the Sheldonian Theatre in Oxford in

1675. In 1711–12, John Baskett negotiated deals with both Oxford and Cambridge and he bought a partnership with Edinburgh in order to operate their various printing privileges himself. The two university presses today have resecured their rights and both are still major printers of Bibles in England.

The question of what was or was not covered by the privilege was never completely clear, even in the seventeenth and eighteenth centuries. It came to be accepted that it applied specifically to the Bible of 1611. The book was always printed according to a very precise formula. The lengthy wording of the title-page was unvarying. Every Bible opened with the standard preface to James I, 'To the Most High and Mighty Prince James…', beginning 'Great and manifold were the blessings…' The text of the Bible was arranged in strict convention. It was generally laid out in two columns, with separate numbered verses. Each chapter opened with a short summary of its content. There were no interpretative notes, but there were brief references in the margins to parallel passages or variant readings. Occasional words which the translators had inserted into the text to help the sense in English but which did not appear in the original languages were printed in italics. These are very often forms of the verb 'to be' (such as 'darkness *was* upon the face of the deep' at Genesis 1:2) or slight expansions required by English usage (such as 'God called the dry *land* Earth' at Genesis 1:10). In this distinctive form, then, the Authorized Version hs been printed in many thousands of copies every year since 1611, and still is, by its authorized publishers.

In its established format, the Authorized Bible has no pictures. It was published in 1611 in a large size suitable for use on a public lectern, 'Appointed to be read in Churches', according to its title. A book to be read aloud, whether in church or even by the head of a household to his assembled family and servants, does not need illustrations. Early editions of the Authorized Version were sometimes punctuated by large woodcut initials but they never had integral illustrations like the Luther Bibles.

Some seventeenth-century English booksellers made a business of buying up German and Dutch prints of biblical scenes which they would then bind into English Bibles for resale. By this means they produced attractive Bibles for domestic use, without infringing the copyright on printing the text. A number of continental artists published sets of engravings for this purpose (Pl. 181), including Matthaeus Merian the elder (1593–1650) and Nicolaes Visscher (1587–1652). Several of the earliest surviving examples of English Bibles embellished in this way are editions published in Edinburgh in 1633 by the royal printer there, Robert Young. This was tactless, for the Scots

179 page 247
From 1589 to 1709, the right to print the Authorized Version of the Bible in London lay exclusively with the Barker family and their associates. This Bible was printed by Robert Barker in 1633

180 opposite
The Universities of Oxford and Cambridge also claimed the right to print Bibles. This is the first Bible printed in Cambridge, 1629

181
Some continental publishers printed books of engravings intended for sale in England in order to illustrate Bibles. These were printed in Amsterdam in the 1640s

GENES. III.

were puritanical. They deeply opposed any gestures which might suggest idolatry. The printer himself described several years later how he had received 'most tragicall complaints' when copies of his austere Edinburgh Bible were found to include pictures. From indignant accounts written by Puritans, we are told that a principal culprit was the London print dealer, one Robert Peake. He dealt in sets of continental engravings of Bible scenes, and he also made his own copies of pictures, re-engraved with English captions. According to a pamphlet written in 1652 by the Puritan printer, Michael Sparke, these sets of engravings were sold on by Peake to a Worcester bookbinder, Francis Ash, who bound them into copies of the English Bible at the appropriate places in the text. Ash and Peake thus made a large profit in reselling Robert Young's blameless Scottish edition of the Authorized Version as a Catholic-looking book filled with pious images. Sparke takes immodest pleasure in adding that when the Royalist armies besieged Worcester in 1642, Ash hid his illicit fortune down the privy and, in trying to dig out his money some weeks later, was overcome by the smell and died. Peake, however, lived on, was knighted by Charles I in Oxford in 1645 and died in 1667.

Other more happy attempts at restructuring the Authorized Version to include pictures were undertaken by Nicholas Ferrar (1592–1637). He and his family assembled what they called 'Gospel Harmonies'. These were large hand-made illustrated albums assembled by the religious commune established by Ferrar at Little Gidding, in Huntingdonshire. The Harmonies were made by cutting up printed Bibles into separate verses which were then pasted together to form single consecutive narratives of the Gospel stories, illustrated throughout with cut-out engravings and prints. About a dozen copies survive. They are not strictly Bibles, but were constructed entirely from biblical components and engravings. The books

182

The Ferrar family at Little Gidding created their own picture Bibles by cutting up printed texts and pasting them into albums with engravings. This copy was given to Charles I in 1635
(LONDON, BRITISH LIBRARY)

183 opposite

In 1660 John Ogilby bought up the entire edition of a Bible printed in Cambridge the previous year. He commissioned a new title page, inserted illustrations, and then resold the edition as his own publication

only to *Promote the Reading of the Holy Scriptures in Families and Schools, but also to Remove that great Uneasiness observable in Children upon the Appearance of Hard Words in their Lessons,* 1766, which is little more or less than a complete pirated New Testament. *The Protestant's Family Bible … Illustrated by Explanatory Notes,* 1780, includes engravings by William Blake.

Several Bibles printed around 1800 evaded the copyright restrictions by appearing as picture Bibles. A plan for a magnificent edition was hatched about 1790 by Thomas Macklin (d. 1800), a former gilder of picture frames who had opened a gallery in Pall Mall in London. He issued a prospectus, saying that copies of Bible were 'scarcely to be found in such a state, with respect to ornaments, as to merit a place in an elegant library'. He reported in 1792 that his subscription list was filling briskly and was already 'decorated with the most august and respected names'. Macklin's Bible book was finally published in 1800, in six gigantic and heavy volumes, usually about 465 by 368 mm (18¼ by 14½ inches). It includes 71 plates, engraved from biblical pictures by contemporary English artists such as Joshua Reynolds, James Northcote, John Opie, Angelica Kauffmann, and others, especially Philip de Loutherbourg, who painted 22 illustrations specially for the book.

The text was the Authorized Version again, unacknowledged. Macklin had actually applied to Oxford University Press for official permission to print the text of the Bible. The Delegates of the Press had considered his request in January 1790, but the minutes of the meeting reported that it was 'resolved, that the Board do not think it proper to grant his Request, having no Precedent on their Books'. Therefore, Macklin was obliged to follow what had become the standard technique for circumventing the royal licence. He supplied a minimum number of insignificant footnotes, which were printed in microscopic type in the extreme lower borders, right on the deckle edge of the paper. Therefore, his book was now a commentary, not a Bible. In most copies the notes were automatically trimmed away as soon as the book was first bound. The typography of the text itself is exceptionally large and handsome, in clear round type. It was one of the last books printed in England with the old-fashioned long 's', resembling 'f'. Even in the typography there is an oddity which was used to distinguish the text from the normal convention of the copyright editions. In order not to employ italics for those words which the translators had inserted for reasons of sense, the printers of the Macklin Bible instead placed a tiny dot under the first vowel of any word which would have been in italics in an official printing of the Authorized Version. This is almost invisible. Probably hardly a single user of the Macklin Bible has ever noticed this.

Even during the preparation of the book, Macklin's enterprise attracted imitations. In 1795, his neighbour and competitor in Pall Mall, Robert Bowyer, rushed out a small-scale edition of the Bible with pictures engraved from paintings ascribed to Dürer, Rembrandt, Rubens and others, then in English noble collections. A three-volume Bible, with some of the same pictures differently engraved, was published in 1811–12 under the guise of notes by the Reverend John Hewitt but really to include 120 engravings 'from the best pictures of the great masters in the various schools of painting', as it asserts on the title. Artists especially represented were Raphael, Poussin and Salvator Rosa.

This use of works by Old Master painters to ornament Bibles was then a recent phenomenon. The cycles of biblical pictures published by Richard Ware and others might have claimed to be based on 'the designs of the greatest masters', but no prototypes are recognizable. The Fawkes Family Bible of 1762 included a few engravings which had derived from the Raphael cartoons, then at Windsor Castle. The Bowyer Bible of 1795 tended to trumpet the names of the aristocratic and other distinguished owners of the originals of the pictures reproduced; by the time of the Macklin and Hewitt editions, captions drew attention to the names of artists.

The passion for Old Masters is represented by an intriguing use to which the Macklin Bible was often put. Owners of the book would disassemble their copies and insert original prints and drawings to illustrate the text. The books would then be rebound in expanded form. This practice is known as 'Grangerizing' after James Granger (1723–76), who had initiated the pastime for embellishing historical and biographical texts. With sufficient patience, a collector could acquire an appropriate Old Master print or woodcut for almost every passage of the Bible. Copies of the Macklin Bible were swelled up by inserted pictures and would need to be rebound in many more than their original six volumes. One set, sold at Sotheby's in 1973, was enriched by Elizabeth Bull (d.1809), daughter of the print collector Richard Bull (1721–1805), and was expanded to 25 volumes by the insertion of several thousand woodcuts and engravings, including originals of Lucas van Leyden, Urs Graf, Dürer, Rembrandt and others. Another is now in the Parsons Collection at the University of Texas in Austin. It was extended to 31 volumes by the inclusion of approximately 5,000 prints and 786 original drawings, mostly of the sixteenth century. A third copy of Macklin's Bible must be the largest of all. It was put together by Robert Bowyer (1758–1834), Macklin's competitor and publisher of the illustrated Bible of 1795. Bowyer's name appears on the published subscription list for the Macklin Bible. He became completely obsessed with grangerizing his copy. He later claimed to have spent some £4,000 in buying old prints and that the cost had rendered him bankrupt. He acquired 6,293 different prints of biblical events. His Macklin Bible needed to be rebound in 45 volumes to accommodate them and it was housed in a specially built bookcase (Pl. 187). The first volume takes the text only as far as the opening words of Genesis 4, but already it is enhanced with 126 inserted prints, illustrating a mere 81 verses. Boywer's vast set was acquired in 1948 by the municipal corporation of Bolton, Lancashire.

From the elephantine, let us turn to the miniature. An engaging class of books was published throughout this period. They often purport to be Bibles but comprise only summaries or strings of extracts. These are the books generally known as 'Thumb Bibles'. Like 'jumbo', the word 'thumb' in this context derives originally from advertising by Barnum's Circus. In 1844, the Circus achieved a sensation by exhibiting in England a human midget, who used the stage name of General Tom Thumb. By the late 1840s, tiny books were being sold as Thumb Bibles. In fact, miniature Bibles go back very much earlier. Diminutive books of devotion are found far back in the Middle Ages. Paris, BNF, ms. lat. 10439 is a little Gospel of Saint John, for example, written around 500 AD, about 71 by 51 mm (a little under 3 by about 2 inches). Truly miniature books, about half that size, existed by the late fifteenth century. Thumb Bibles are usually said to begin with verse summaries of the biblical narratives by

187
Thomas Macklin published a luxury Bible in six volumes in 1800. Buyers of the book often had further pictures bound in, greatly expanding the size of the publication. A copy owned by Robert Bowyer was thus increased to 45 volumes, shown here in their special bookcase in a nineteenth-century engraving
(BOLTON PUBLIC LIBRARY)

THE BOWYER BIBLE AND CABINET.
VALUE THREE THOUSAND ONE HUNDRED GUINEAS;
THE HIGHEST PORTION IN MRS MARY PARKES'S LAST GRAND CLUB SUBSCRIPTION.
SHARES, ONE GUINEA EACH.

John Weever (1576–1632) and John Taylor (1580–1653), which first appear in miniature format around 1600. At about the time that publishers were testing the monopoly of the Authorized Version with dissimulated variants, so miniature books in prose began to appear with the aim of appealing to the limitless market for Bibles (Pl. 188). An early example was *Biblia, or a Practical Summary of ye Old & New Testaments*, printed in London for R. Wilkin, 1727. It consists of 284 leaves, but is 36 by 24 mm (about 1½ inches by less than an inch). Another pretended to be published on the island of Lilliput, the miniature kingdom described in *Gulliver's Travels* (1726). It is called *A History of the Bible, Compiled for the Use of the Emperor of Lilliputia, Lilliput, Printed in 1775*. That edition is 38 by 29 mm (1½ inches by a little more than an inch). The most common is a tiny book published in London in 1780 by Elizabeth Newbery (d.1821), widow of Francis Newbery (d.1780), printer of children's books. It appeared as *The BIBLE in Miniature, or a Concise History of the Old and New Testaments*. It has 256 leaves and measures 38 by 28 mm (about 1½ inches by just over an inch). Copies were still for sale 20 years later in 1800, at the original price of one shilling bound in calf, two shillings in morocco. It is a proper book, in very small print, 8 lines to the page. It has 14 full-page engravings. The preface explains that although Bibles are now in the hands of everyone in the country, too few people know its text. The summary here is in six books. The first is on God. The second gives the accounts of the Creation and Garden of Eden from Genesis. Book III summarizes

the rest of Genesis and Exodus into seven chapters. Book IV completes the Old Testament from Joshua until the birth of John the Baptist. Book V abridges the Gospels and Acts in ten chapters. The final book is on the Last Judgement. All this is contained in a book so small that it can be concealed entirely within one's closed fist.

Similar Thumb Bibles were produced abroad. There were many tiny editions published in Germany of *Biblia oder Inhalt und Kern gantzer h. Schrift*, from at least 1705 to 1735. Miniature editions of Taylor's verse summary of the Bible were printed in North America from the mid-eighteenth century. One, published in Boston in 1765, describes itself as a third edition. It is 45 mm (about 1¾ inches) square. Another, printed in Boston in 1786, has a little verse opposite the title:

Reader, come buy this Book,
for tho' it's small,
'Tis worthy the perusal
of us all.

Who, then, were these doll's house Bibles intended for? The traditional answer is that they were made for children. If true, this is early evidence of a whole new use for the Bible. Before the seventeenth century it would probably have been inconceivable to place the holy scriptures in the hands of children. The popularity of Thumb Bibles coincides with the dates of the first Family Bibles, with their emphasis on educating children in biblical virtue. Miniature Bibles were probably too fragile for daily use as lesson books in the nursery and their print is far too small for anyone learning to read. They were perhaps given as rewards for good behaviour, to be kept safe for careful admiration on Sundays. One Thumb Bible of *c.*1815 is described on its title-page as 'Intended as a PRESENT for *Youth*'. An American edition, called *Miniature Bible … For the use of Children*, Brattleborough (Vermont), 1816, has a frontispiece showing two children kneeling together holding a book between them, captioned 'John and Sarah reading the little Bible'. Another, from Hartford (Connecticut), 1817, shows three well-dressed children seated on chairs, 'Eliza, William, and Julia, Reading the Little Bible'. A Philadelphia edition of 1839, *Miniature Bible, with Engravings*, includes an illustration of the rarely depicted scene of II Kings 2:24, with the alarming caption (perhaps more credible in America than London), 'Children destroyed by bears'.

After declaring independence from Britain in 1776, the Americans considered themselves absolved from the royal privileges which restricted publication of the Authorized Version. It had not been legal to publish any English Bible in North America while it was a British colony. The first book of the Bible printed in English in the newly founded United States was probably the New Testament issued in Philadelphia towards the end of 1777 by Robert Aitken (1734–1802). There was an evident market for Bibles, even (or especially) during the Revolutionary War. A petition had been sent to the Continental Congress in the summer

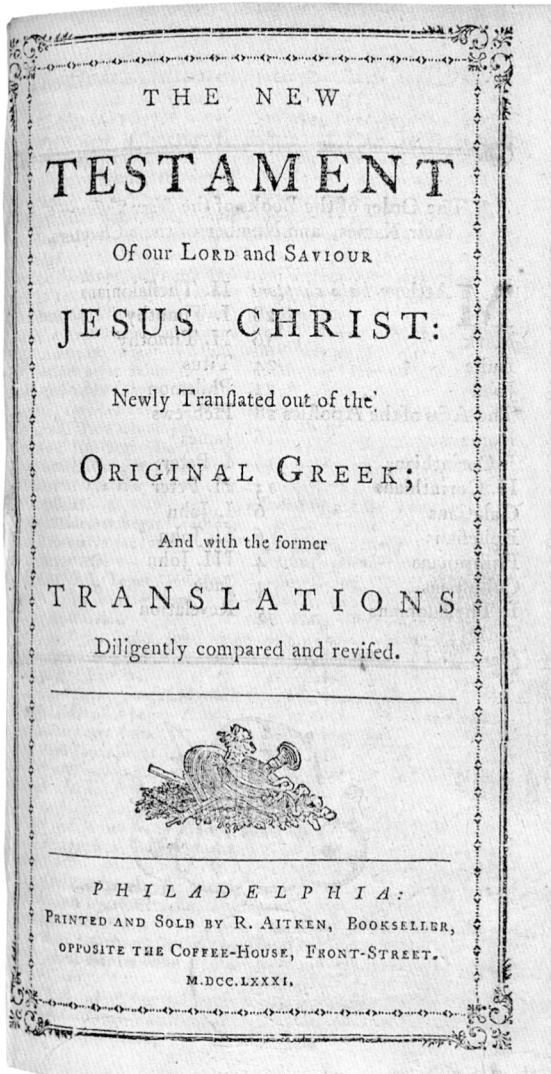

of 1777 complaining of the current difficulties in obtaining Bibles from England. Congress invited estimates from local printers for an American edition. In the event, the plan for this government-sponsored Bible was abandoned, as was a second idea to import 20,000 ready-made English Bibles from Holland. Aitken, who was one of the five local printers who had submitted a tender, undertook the task on his own initiative. His New Testament was a considerable success, and it was reprinted annually until 1781 (Pl. 189). In 1782, he printed the whole Bible, in the Authorized Version, in an edition of 10,000 copies. This was over-ambitious, for he lost money on the invest-ment. It is book of quite small dimensions, 143 by 80 mm, a little more than 5½ by 3 inches, sometimes bound in two volumes. Opposite the opening page of Genesis, Aitken added an endorsement from Congress, expressing their approval of 'the plans and laudable undertaking of Mr. Aitken, as subservient to the interests of religion, as well as an instance of the progress of arts in this country'. In flouting the British laws which copyrighted the Authorized Version, Aitken was glad to be the recipient of government privilege himself.

The history of the Bible in the United States is similar to that of England in the late eighteenth and first half of the nineteenth centuries. The American business ethic has always welcomed private enterprise. There were no inhibitions about printing the Authorized Version, although occasionally they felt obliged to explain on a title-page 'translated ... by the Special Command of King James I., of England' (Worcester, Mass., 1793). Today Americans usually refer to the translation as the 'King James Bible' rather than by the more British term

'Authorized Version'. Competition was provided not by royal printers, protected by licence, but by huge businesses which maintained their own monopolies through technology. Cheap Bibles were produced in enormous numbers from 1801 onwards by the energetic Philadelphia printer, Matthew Carey (1760–1839). His prices were as low as $3.50 a copy. Even Carey's pre-eminent position was dislodged by the introduction of stereotyping. This is a process of book production by which a printer keeps an impression in plaster of Paris of each page of printing type. If ever the text needs reprinting, a new single block of metal type can be made from the plaster mould rather than by laboriously re-setting each page by hand. The technique of stereotyping was first used for printing Bibles in Cambridge in England in 1805. In 1812, a set of plaster moulds for stereotyping Bibles was sent from England to the Bible Society of Philadelphia, with the aid of a £500 grant from the British and Foreign Bible Society. The United States government contributed by admitting the moulds without import duty.

Stereotyping was a technique enthusiastically adopted by the American Bible Society, founded in 1816. They began publishing Bibles immediately, at prices which could undercut those of almost all other competitors (Pl. 190). The Society was soon mass-producing Bibles by the use of the new techniques of stereotyping, machine-made paper and (from 1829) steam-powered printing presses.

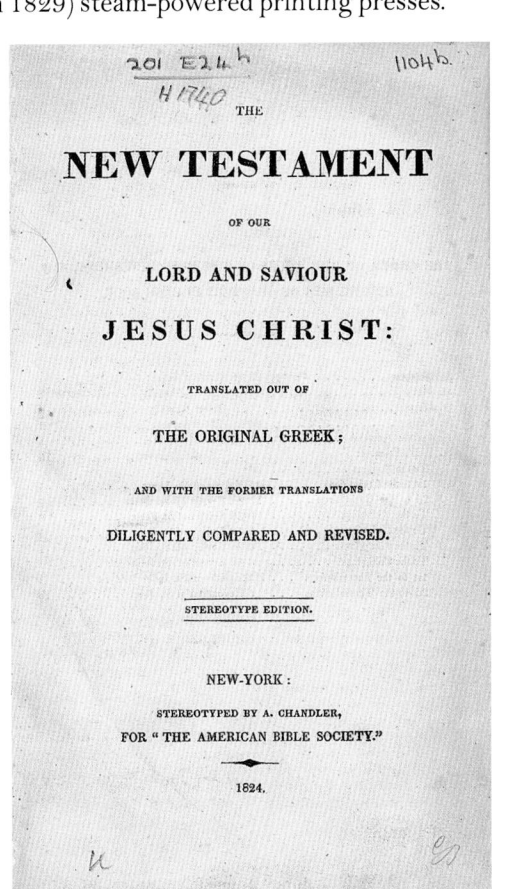

Within a generation, they had a complete command of the market. By the 1840s, the American Bible Society could offer New Testaments for only 6 cents each, and whole Bibles for 45 cents. From their own records, we know that the Society printed over 6,000,000 Bibles in their first thirty years of publishing, and by 1862 were selling a million copies a year. By 1880, they had printed more than 32,000,000 copies. All these were the unchanged King James Bible of 1611, freed of legal restriction by being printed outside Britain.

When other American publishers found themselves unable to compete on price, they turned to imaginative and unusual ways of presenting the Bible. Such books were significantly more expensive, but more profitable. The first

189 opposite

After declaring independence from Great Britain in 1776, American printers considered themselves freed from copyright restrictions. This New Testament was published in Philadelphia in 1781

190

Technical advances allowed mass production of Bibles in America in the first half of the nineteenth century. This edition was printed by stereotyping in 1824

American illustrated Bible was a luxurious folio printed in Worcester, Mass., by Isaiah Thomas in 1791. It has 50 copperplate illustrations by American artists. It was heralded as a great patriotic masterpiece. American Bibles were often marketed with names that would distinguish them from ordinary plain copies. They were published with titles such as *The Christian's New and Complete Family Bible* (Philadelphia, 1788), *The Self-Interpreting Bible* (New York, 1792), *The Family Expositor, or a Paraphrase and Version of the New Testament, with Critical Notes* (Charlestown, Mass., 1808), *The New Testament, in an Improved Version* (Boston, 1809), *The Pronouncing Testament* (Boston, 1822), *The Collateral Bible* (Philadelphia and New York, 1826–8), *The Comprehensive Bible* (Hartford, 1832), or *The Cottage Bible* (New York, 1833–4).

The most innovative of all American Bibles was *Harper's Illuminated and New Pictorial Bible* of 1843–6 (Pl. 191). This was a project devised by the engraver Joseph Adams (1803–80). He persuaded the New York publishers, Harper and Brothers, to undertake what was announced as 'the most splendidly elegant edition of the Sacred Record ever issued'. It would have over 1,600 illustrations. The pictures were generally integrated into the pages of biblical text, instead of being bound in as separate plates. The title of 'illuminated' was an over-statement, for the pictures were mostly in black and white, but the book does indeed resemble a lavish manuscript of the Middle Ages, with large ornamental initials and decoration and illustrations on almost every page. The enterprise was vigorously promoted by all the new wiles of advertisers and travelling salesmen. It

191

Harper's Illuminated and New Pictorial Bible *was published in 54 instalments from 1843 onwards and was then reissued as a book in 1846. It sold over 75,000 copies*

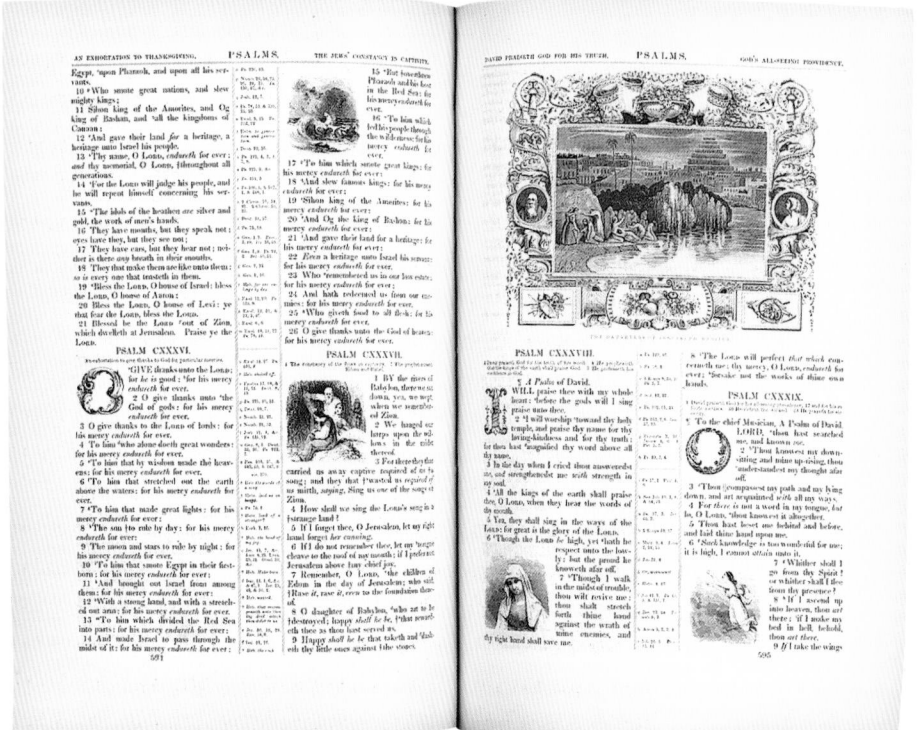

was the first book printed in America by electrotyping, a technique of hardening

the printing plates by electrochemically coating them in copper. This permitted
mechanical printing at extremely high speed. The book was initially published
like a magazine in 54 separate numbers from 1843, each section with 25 to 60
pages, priced at 25 cents each. There were 50,000 subscribers. Those who bought
the whole set, which would have cost $13.50 altogether, could then receive a bind-
ing for the whole Bible. For an extra sum, the owner could have his or her named
blocked in gold on the cover, with a picture of the customer's local church. This
was a touch of advertising genius, for it was irresistible. On completion of the
issue in 1846, Harper's then republished a further 25,000 copies of the complete
book. The engraver Adams, who had negotiated for himself a 50 per cent share of
the profit, retired at once, a very wealthy man. The *Illuminated and New Pictorial
Bible* was reprinted again in 1859 and 1866.

An important aspect of the promotion of the *Illuminated Bible* was that the
illustrations claimed to be authentic representations of life in biblical lands. The
covers of the separate issues of the edition in 1843 carried a statement emphasizing the 'accuracy of its pictorial designs, as to architecture, costumes, localities,
and characters … in strict accordance with the recent important discoveries of
ancient relics in the East'. Topographical authenticity was of ever greater interest
in nineteenth-century biblical illustrations. Even as late as the pictures commissioned for Macklin's Bible in the 1790s, there had been little concession to
locations in Egypt or Palestine, apart from the occasional palm tree or pantomime
turban. Improved shipping and a passion for Orientalism opened up the Near
East for travellers in the second quarter of the nineteenth century. In his prospectus for a book, *Illustrations of the Bible* to be published in London in 1834,
John Murray offered his customers authentic scenes from the Holy Land, made
from drawings taken on the spot by artists such as Charles Barry, C.R. Cockerell
and Robert Ker Porter. These, he said, 'will be esteemed a more appropriate illustration for such a work, and more suitable to its character, than any *fictitious or
imaginary* representations' of the events in the Bible. Pursuit of authenticity, often
romantic, is a feature of biblical illustrations in the mid-nineteenth century. The
Pre-Raphaelite painter, William Holman Hunt (1827–1910), travelled extensively
in Palestine in 1854–6 to achieve credible settings for his biblical pictures.

Photographs of the Holy Land were understandably of great interest in Western Europe and America. The travel photography of Francis Frith (1822–98)
was in constant demand. He issued *Egypt and Palestine Photographed and Described*,
London, 1858, published in 25 monthly parts, each with three albumen prints by
Frith, reissued in two volumes in 1859, with 76 original photographs. Twenty
more albumen prints by Frith appeared in a massive album of 1860, *Egypt, Sinai
and Jerusalem*. Each print is 385 by 490 mm (a little over 15 by 19¼ inches) – these
are contact prints, not enlargements – within a book 760 by 560 mm (30 by 22
inches). The public was mesmerized by actual images of places mentioned in the

Bible. It was only a matter of time before photographs started to illustrate Bibles themselves. They appeared in *The Queen's Bible containing the Old and New Testaments*, published by William Mackenzie, London and Glasgow, 1862, with 20 photographs by Francis Frith (Pl. 192). It was published in 170 copies and cost 50 guineas. The book was reprinted about a year later in a larger edition with 56 photographs, now priced at 20 guineas, still expensive. The publishers Eyre and Spottiswoode, holders of the royal licence for the Authorized Version, joined the trend with a quarto Bible in 1862 illustrated with 20 original photographs of biblical scenery by Frith, mounted onto pages of thin card. The frontispiece shows the wells at Beer-Sheba (Genesis 26:32–3); Rachel's tomb illustrates Genesis 35:19; a view of Elim at Sinai faces Exodus 15; and so on. The book was priced at 7 guineas.

The twentieth-century equivalent was the epic film. These were a logical evolution from *Harper's Illuminated and New Pictorial Bible* and Frith's *Palestine Photographed and Described*. They proved to be enormously successful, even in an age when cynics – and there are many in Hollywood – would have said the popular appeal of Bible illustration had run its course. Films with biblical themes and meticulous period settings were box office triumphs time after time. The most famous are those of the producer, Cecil B. DeMille (1881–1959), who made *The Ten Commandments* (1923, remade 1956), a phenomenal success both times (Pl. 193),

The King of Kings
(1927) and *Samson
and Delilah* (1949).
Other early films
included *Judith of
Bethulia* (1913),
produced by D.W.
Griffith, the first *Quo
Vadis?* (also 1913)
and *Noah's Ark*
(1929). In the 1950s,
spectacles set in or
around the Bible
were the highest
income earners for

the film industry, year after year. They included the remakes of *The Ten Commandments* and *Quo Vadis?* (1951), and *David and Bathsheba* (1951), *The Robe* (1953)
and *Ben Hur* (1959).

In England in the nineteenth century, the Authorized Version of the Bible was
still being sold in enormous quantities. The figures compare well with those of
America. In a single year, 1860, for example, Oxford University Press sold over
a million Bibles. These were copies of the Authorized Version, still protected by
copyright. This was the century of patriotism, colonialism and an unshakable
conviction that the British way of life represented the highest point of civilization.
The Authorized Bible, in its now quaint Shakespearean English, was a symbol of
that secure and confident way of life. Victorian Bibles, with heavy leather covers
and brass fittings, were in almost every household.

The fact that the Bible was an instantly recognizable commodity made it the
obvious candidate for demonstrations of the advances of printing technology, in
which the nineteenth century gloried. For instance, a special edition of the Bible
was printed to commemorate the Caxton anniversary of 1877. (William Caxton
actually began printing in Westminster in 1476, not 1477, but this was not
discovered until recently.) The edition printed for the celebrations is called the
Caxton Memorial Bible (Pl. 194). A note in Gothic type opposite the title-page
records: 'Wholly printed and bound in twelve hours, On this 30th day of June,
1877, For the Caxton Celebration – Only 100 copies were printed …' The book
has 1,052 pages. Printing began in Oxford at 2 am that morning from standing
type. The sheets were rushed by the morning train to London, where they were
bound and lettered in gilt, and the entire edition of finished Bibles was delivered to
the exhibition by 2 o'clock in the afternoon. It symbolized patriotism, machinery,
and the Bible. A similar triumph of technology was exemplified in the smallest
complete Bible ever printed (at least until that time). It was published in 1896 in

192 opposite
The Queen's Bible, *published
in London and Glasgow in
1862, includes real
photographs of views in the
Holy Land*

193
*Epic films based on the Bible
were among the great box office
triumphs of the twentieth
century. This is Charlton
Heston as Moses in* The Ten
Commandments, *1956*

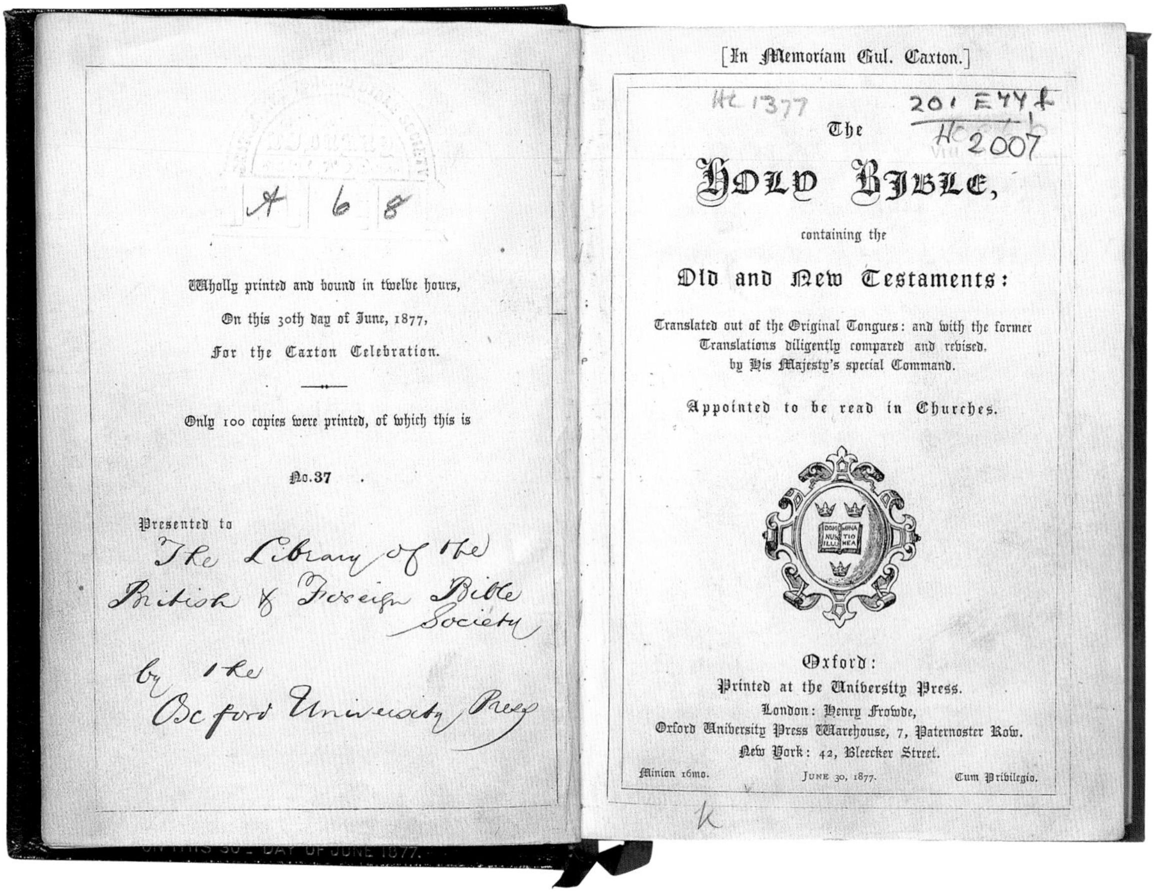

25,000 copies by David Bryce and Son, Glasgow, under specific licence from the royal printer in Scotland. It is a photographic reduction of the whole Authorized Version into microscopic size. The printers achieved 23 lines to the centimetre (49 lines to the inch). The text is entirely legible under a magnifying glass, and a tiny one was provided inside the upper cover of each copy. The whole Bible is 43 by 30 mm (less than 1¾ by 1¼ inches). It was patriotically reprinted for the coronations of Edward VII (Pl. 195) and George V in 1902 and 1911 respectively.

Although the archaic language of the Authorized Version was a very great part of its charm and quintessential Englishness, the text of the Bible was already reaching an age when it was becoming increasingly difficult to understand. Campaigns of textual updating resulted in the publication in England of the Revised Version in 1881–5, and the American Standard Version in New York in 1901, both based on the text of 1611.

The public arguments for and against changing the words of the Bible were as vigorous and as one-sided as they had been when Saint Jerome had dared to revise the Old Latin text of the Bible fifteen hundred years earlier.

New English translations of the Bible proliferated in the twentieth century, especially (but not exclusively) in America. Some were the result of private enterprise, like that of James Moffatt (1870–1944), 1913–24, revised in 1935. Others were promoted by churches, missionary groups and Christian publishers, Catholic and well as Protestant. In 1943 Pope Pius XII issued an encyclical freeing Catholic scholars from their obligation to translate exclusively from the Latin Vulgate and encouraging new translations from the original sources. It would become unwieldy and inappropriate to try to list here every modern translation or edition of the English Bible. The huge number of such books, and the apparently insatiable market for them, is evidence of the very special status that the Bible still has in our own times. This can be seen in any modern religious bookshop. Bibles are still very saleable merchandise. We have already glanced at the businesses which sold Bibles in the seventeenth and eighteenth centuries, enterprises run by Francis Ash, John Ogilby, Richard Ware, and others. Let us now simply look round two bookshops today. These examples must suffice to represent what one might find similarly in hundreds of specialized bookshops in Britain and America where Bibles are sold.

The first is Pauline Books and Media in North Michigan Avenue in Chicago. It is a Catholic bookshop, run by the Daughters of Saint Paul. There are several priests and nuns in the shop. The Bible is represented by videos and interactive computers (for this is America), and by several bays of printed Bibles along the far right-hand side of the shop. The King James Bible is here, freely printed in America by any publisher who cares to produce it, and its most traditional descendants, the *American Standard Version* and the *New Revised Standard Version* (1991). Even these Bibles vary immensely in appearance. Some, like the candles and religious statues in the window, seem hardly to have changed in appearance since the thirteenth century, for there are Bibles in two columns, with initials and running-titles, and bindings of brown and red leather, almost exactly like medieval manuscripts. Some are in modern versions of 'chemise' bindings, the kind of soft leather which wraps around the fore-edge of the book to close up into a self-contained package. That is a style of book covering at least as old as the time of Charlemagne. There are Bibles in padded white satin bindings, for confirmations and weddings. There are large-print Bibles. Others are innovative and multi-coloured, aiming for new and youthful audiences. There are many editions of the *Good News Bible* (1976), or *The Bible in Today's English Version*, translated for the United Bibles Societies in 1966–76. It is evidently the basis of the *New Catholic Study Bible*, Saint Jerome Edition (1985), and one called *Precious Moments Bible, for Catholics*. The word 'New' often appears in titles, such as the *New International Version*, described as translated by over a hundred scholars from the Greek for

194 opposite above
The Bible was such a familiar artefact in the late nineteenth century that it was often used to demonstrate the technical advances of printing. The whole edition of this Bible was printed and bound in 12 hours in 1877

195 opposite inset
This Bible is shown here actual size. It was printed in miniature, complete with a magnifying glass, to commemorate the coronation of Edward VII in 1902

196

This is a modern polyglot.
It shows the opening of Ecclesi-
astes in The Complete
Parallel Bible, *published by*
Oxford University Press in
1993. The four texts in parallel
columns are from the New
Revised Standard Version,
the Revised English Bible, the
New American Bible and the
New Jerusalem Bible

the Christian Reformed Church and National Association of Evangelicals (1978). An edition of it appears as the *Women's Devotional Bible.* There is the *Contemporary English Version* (begun in 1985), in easy, conversational style. There are copies of the classic *Jerusalem Bible* (1966), the English version of a French Catholic translation of 1948–54, still derived in part from the Latin Vulgate, and its retranslation, the *New Jerusalem Bible* (1985). There are Bibles which look as eye-catching as paperback fiction, such as *The Amplified Bible,* with a cover blocked in gold ('Unlocks Subtle Shades of Meaning'). It piles up variant readings almost as thickly and as indecisively as the old Dominican *Correctiones Bibliae,* promulgated in 1236 (above, p. 122). There are a number of Catholic translations directly from the Greek and Hebrew. These include the *New American Bible,* dedicated to Saint Joseph, Patron of the Universal Church, first published in 1970. Revisions began in 1987 to find suitably neutral expressions for biblical terms which to modern ears might seem to discriminate against Jews or women, for example. *The New American Bible* is the basis for the *Catholic Study Bible,* edited by Donald Senior (1990). Other Catholic Bibles are specifically evangelical. Here is *The Alba House*

NEW REVISED STANDARD VERSION

Ecclesiastes

1 The words of the Teacher,ᵃ the son of David, king in Jerusalem.
2 Vanity of vanities, says the Teacher,ᵃ
  vanity of vanities! All is vanity.
3 What do people gain from all the toil
  at which they toil under the sun?
4 A generation goes, and a generation comes,
  but the earth remains forever.
5 The sun rises and the sun goes down,
  and hurries to the place where it rises.
6 The wind blows to the south,
  and goes around to the north;
  round and round goes the wind,
  and on its circuits the wind returns.
7 All streams run to the sea,
  but the sea is not full;
  to the place where the streams flow,
  there they continue to flow.
8 All thingsᵇ are wearisome;
  more than one can express;
  the eye is not satisfied with seeing,
  or the ear filled with hearing.
9 What has been is what will be,
  and what has been done is what will be done;
  there is nothing new under the sun.
10 Is there a thing of which it is said,
  "See, this is new"?
  It has already been,
  in the ages before us.
11 The people of long ago are not remembered,
  nor will there be any remembrance
  of people yet to come
  by those who come after them.

12 I, the Teacher,ᵃ when king over Israel in Jerusalem, 13 applied my mind to seek and to search out by wisdom all that is done under heaven; it is an unhappy business that God has given to human beings to be busy with. 14 I saw all the deeds that are done under the sun; and see, all is vanity and a chasing after wind.ᶜ
15 What is crooked cannot be made straight,
  and what is lacking cannot be counted.
16 I said to myself, "I have acquired great wisdom, surpassing all who were over Jerusalem before me; and my mind has had great experience of wisdom and knowledge." 17 And I applied my mind to know wisdom and to know madness and folly. I perceived that this also is but a chasing after wind.ᶜ
18 For in much wisdom is much vexation,
  and those who increase knowledge increase sorrow.

2 I said to myself, "Come now, I will make a test of pleasure; enjoy yourself." But again, this also was vanity. 2 I said of laughter, "It is mad," and of pleasure, "What use is it?" 3 I searched with my mind how to cheer my body with wine—my mind still guiding me with wisdom—and how to lay hold on folly, until I might see what was good for mortals to do under heaven during the few days of their life. 4 I made great works; I built houses and planted vineyards for myself; 5 I made myself gardens and parks, and planted in them all kinds of fruit trees. 6 I made myself pools

ᵃ *Heb* Qoheleth, *traditionally rendered* Preacher   ᵇ *Or words*
ᶜ *Or a feeding on wind. See Hos 12.1*
1432

REVISED ENGLISH BIBLE

Ecclesiastes

1 THE words of the Speaker, the son of David, king in Jerusalem.
2 Futility, utter futility, says the Speaker, everything is futile. 3 What does anyone profit from all his labour and toil here under the sun? 4 Generations come and generations go, while the earth endures for ever. 5 The sun rises and the sun goes down; then it speeds to its place and rises there again. 6 The wind blows to the south, it veers to the north; round and round it goes and returns full circle. 7 All streams run to the sea, yet the sea never overflows; back to the place from which the streams ran they return to run again. 8 All things are wearisome. No one can describe them all, no eye can see them all, no ear can hear them all. 9 What has happened will happen again, and what has been done will be done again; there is nothing new under the sun. 10 Is there anything of which it can be said, 'Look, this is new'? No, it was already in existence, long before our time. 11 Those who lived in the past are not remembered, and those who follow will not be remembered by those who follow them.
12 I, the Speaker, ruled as king over Israel in Jerusalem; 13 and I applied my mind to study and explore by means of wisdom all that is done under heaven. It is a worthless task that God has given to mortals to keep them occupied. 14 I have seen everything that has been done here under the sun; it is all futility and a chasing of the wind. 15 What is crooked cannot become straight; what is not there cannot be counted. 16 I thought to myself, 'I have amassed great wisdom, surpassing all my predecessors on the throne at Jerusalem; I have become familiar with wisdom and knowledge.' 17 So I applied my mind to understanding wisdom and knowledge, madness and folly, and I came to see that this too is a chasing of the wind. 18 For in much wisdom is much vexation; the more knowledge, the more suffering.

2 I said to myself, 'Come, I will test myself with pleasure and get enjoyment'; but that too was futile. 2 Of laughter I said, 'It is madness!' And of pleasure, 'What is the good of that?' 3 I sought how to cheer my body with wine, and, though my mind was still guiding me with wisdom, how to pursue folly; I hoped to find out what was good for mortals to do under heaven during the brief span of life. 4 I undertook great works; I built myself palaces and planted vineyards; 5 I made myself gardens and orchards, planted with every kind of fruit tree. 6 I constructed ponds

1:1 the Speaker: *Heb.* Koheleth, *Gk* Ecclesiastes.   1:5 then ...
place: *prob. rdg: Heb.* panting to its place.

NEW AMERICAN BIBLE

Ecclesiastes

1 The words of David's son, Qoheleth, king in Jerusalem:
2 Vanity of vanities, says Qoheleth,
  vanity of vanities! All things are vanity!
3 What profit has man from all the labor
  which he toils at under the sun?
4 One generation passes and another comes,
  but the world forever stays.
5 The sun rises and the sun goes down;
  then it presses on to the place where it rises.
6 Blowing now toward the south, then toward
  the north,
  the wind turns again and again, resuming
  its rounds.
7 All rivers go to the sea,
  yet never does the sea become full.
  To the place where they go,
  the rivers keep on going.
8 All speech is labored;
  there is nothing man can say.
  The eye is not satisfied with seeing
  nor is the ear filled with hearing.
9 What has been, that will be; what has been done, that will be done. Nothing is new under the sun. 10 Even the thing of which we say, "See, this is new!" has already existed in the ages that preceded us. 11 There is no remembrance of the men of old; nor of those to come will there be any remembrance among those who come after them.

12 I, Qoheleth, was king over Israel in Jerusalem, 13 and I applied my mind to search and investigate in wisdom all things that are done under the sun.

A thankless task God has appointed
for men to be busied about.

14 I have seen all things that are done under the sun, and behold, all is vanity and a chase after wind.
15 What is crooked cannot be made straight,
  and what is missing cannot be supplied.
16 Though I said to myself, "Behold, I have become great and stored up wisdom beyond all who were before me in Jerusalem, and my mind has broad experience of wisdom and knowledge"; 17 yet when I applied my mind to know wisdom and knowledge, madness and folly, I learned that this also is a chase after wind.
18 For in much wisdom there is much sorrow,
  and he who stores up knowledge stores up grief.

2 I said to myself, "Come, now, let me try you with pleasure and the enjoyment of good things." But behold, this too was vanity. 2 Of laughter I said: "Mad!" and of mirth: "What good does this do?" 3 I thought of beguiling my senses with wine, though my mind was concerned with wisdom, and of taking up folly, until I should understand what is best for men to do under the heavens during the limited days of their life. 4 I undertook great works; I built myself houses and planted vineyards; 5 I made gardens and parks, and set out in them fruit trees of all sorts. 6 And I constructed for myself

1433

NEW JERUSALEM BIBLE

Ecclesiastes

1 Composition of Qoheleth son of David, king in Jerusalem.
2 Sheer futility, Qoheleth says. Sheer futility: everything is futile! 3 What profit can we show for all our toil, toiling under the sun? 4 A generation goes, a generation comes, yet the earth stands firm for ever. 5 The sun rises, the sun sets; then to its place it speeds and there it rises. 6 Southward goes the wind, then turns to the north; it turns and turns again; then back to its circling goes the wind. 7 Into the sea go all the rivers, and yet the sea is never filled, and still to their goal the rivers go. 8 All things are wearisome. No one can say that eyes have not had enough of seeing, ears their fill of hearing.
9 What was, will be again,
  what has been done, will be done again,
  and there is nothing new under the sun!
10 Take anything which people acclaim as being new: it existed in the centuries preceding us. 11 No memory remains of the past, and so it will be for the centuries to come—they will not be remembered by their successors.
12 I, Qoheleth, have reigned over Israel in Jerusalem. 13 Wisely I have applied myself to investigation and exploration of everything that happens under heaven. What a wearisome task God has given humanity to keep us busy! 14 I have seen everything that is done under the sun: how futile it all is, mere chasing after the wind!
15 What is twisted cannot be straightened,
  what is not there cannot be counted.
16 I thought to myself: I have acquired a greater stock of wisdom than anyone before me in Jerusalem. I myself have mastered every kind of wisdom and science. 17 I have applied myself to understanding philosophy and science, stupidity and folly, and I now realise that all this too is chasing after the wind.
18 Much wisdom, much grief;
  the more knowledge, the more sorrow.

2 I thought to myself, 'Very well, I will try pleasure and see what enjoyment has to offer.' And this was futile too. 2 This laughter, I reflected, is a madness, this pleasure no use at all. 3 I decided to hand my body over to drinking wine, my mind still guiding me in wisdom; I resolved to embrace folly, to discover the best way for people to spend their days under the sun. 4 I worked on a grand scale: built myself palaces, planted vineyards; 5 made myself gardens and orchards, planting every kind of fruit tree in them; 6 had

Gospels, in dark blue paper covers, subtitled *So you may believe*, translated by Mark A. Wauck, and a stout polychrome paperback, *The African Bible, Family Edition*, with an introduction by the archbishop of Nairobi, Cardinal Otunga (1995).

Our second visit is to the SPCK bookshop in King's Parade, across the road from King's College chapel in Cambridge, England. The assistant here is Scottish and the books are Protestant. Reassuring English hymn tunes are played quietly over the bookshop's sound system. The shop is full of customers of all ages. Many shelves of Bibles line the left-hand wall, nearly as extensively as in Chicago. The Authorized Version is very prominent in Cambridge, in various forms. Copies published by Cambridge University Press, which still holds the royal privilege confirmed in 1628, are described proudly on their slipcases as being 'from the oldest Bible publisher in the world'. There are also the British *Revised Standard Version*, still printed by both Oxford and Cambridge, and the *New Revised Standard Version* with a series of Study Bibles, as they are called, based on this translation, such as the *Cambridge Annotated Study Bible* (1993). There are Bibles for special presentations and weddings, and there are Bibles for children. Many translations are the same as in Chicago. There is the *Good News Bible* again. The *New International Version* appears here as a maroon paperback showing the world turning in space, sub-titled *The Greatest Book on Earth*. The preface begins, 'Welcome. Start here for a journey of discovery.' Beside it are the *New Century Version* (1987) and its derivative *The Youth Bible*. The word 'Bible' is so loaded with meaning that some contemporary translations hardly admit to being Bibles at all. An example is the *New Living Translation, For Those who Thirst* (1996), published in America by the Tyndale Charitable Trust, and its later editions, *The Word, Live it Now* (2000) and *Living Water* (2000). The prefatory matter of the latter refers readers to an 'exciting Web site'. Despite that, let us move on instead to the next bookcase to the right. Beside all these modern Bibles are the oldest texts of all. There, still in print, are editions of the Hebrew Bible and the Greek New Testament, available for purchase in their original languages. There is a market for them too. Their unchanging presence seems to give credibility to the mass of popular English translations.

Kap. I.

Chriſtuſim Ekkartle tamane raviei. Joſeſiblo Maria Kemeis-
ſtegalloæringo: Engelible okaumane Gud Niæmanik erniſerô-
mik, nejorpa Kemengnauerdugo,

Jeſuſe Kriſtuſib Ekkarlénik okauſek, Da-
vib Niarnæt, Abraham-ib Niarnæt.
2. Abraham-ib ernera Iſaak. Iſaak-ib
ernera Iakob. Iakob ernera Iuda nukeilo.
3. Iudab ernera Fares, Zaralo Tamarmir.
Fares-ib ernera Eſrom. Eſrom-ib ernera

11 | Missionary Bibles

THE *MAMUSSE WUNNEETUPANATAMWE*

Up-Biblum God must be the most important unreadable book in the world. It is commonly known as the Eliot Indian Bible (Pl. 198). It was printed in Cambridge, Massachusetts, by Samuel Green and Marmaduke Johnson between 1660 and 1663. It comprises the entire Bible translated by John Eliot (1604–90) into the Natick dialect of the language of the Algonquin American natives then living in Massachusetts and along parts of the east coast of New England. It is the first complete Bible printed in the western hemisphere and it is the first translation of the Bible into any new language for use by missionaries. It was printed on what is now the site of Harvard University, near Boston, only 40 years after the Pilgrim Fathers had crossed the Atlantic in the *Mayflower* in 1620.

John Eliot was an English Puritan clergyman, a graduate of Jesus College, Cambridge, who emigrated to America in 1631 (Pl. 197). In 1632 he became pastor of Roxbury in Massachusetts. Almost from the beginning, he was fascinated by the American Indians and began to learn their languages and dialects and to translate for them the basic textbooks of the Christian life. His translation of Saint Matthew's Gospel was printed in 1655; in the meantime he was working on an entire Bible translated into the dialect of the natives of Natick. This marks a notable step in the history of the Bible. Until now, we have seen scholars over many centuries translating the Bible from ancient or unfamiliar languages into their own. In the *Indian Bible* the process begins to go the other way. Eliot translated the Bible from everyday English into one of the most obscure languages on earth. The colonists' relationship with the American Indians was always a delicate one. On the one hand, they regarded them as fellow exiles from the Garden of Eden, cut off from the benefits of civilization and prosperity for thousands of

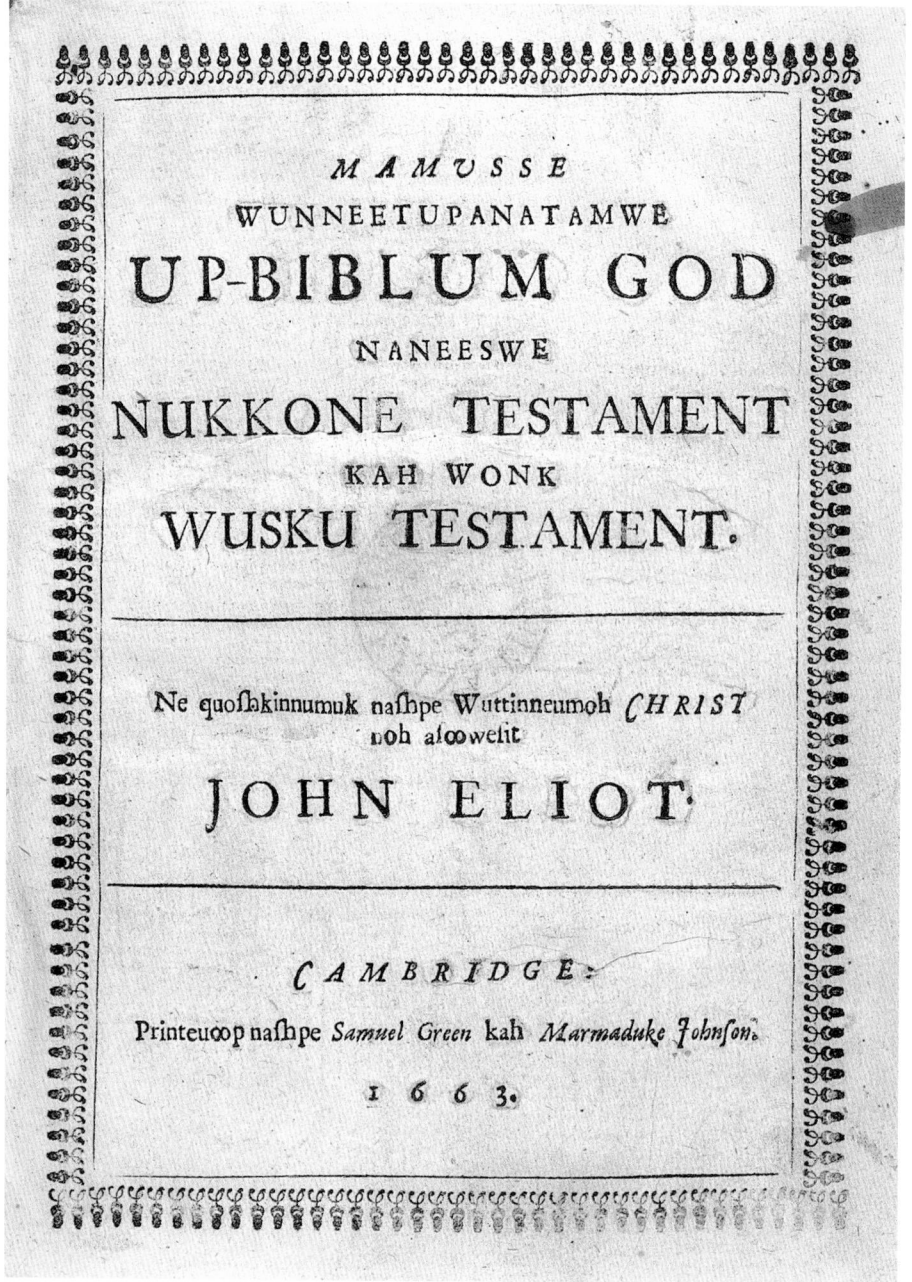

MAMUSSE
WUNNEETUPANATAMWE
UP-BIBLUM GOD
NANEESWE
NUKKONE TESTAMENT
KAH WONK
WUSKU TESTAMENT.

Ne quoſhkinnumuk naſhpe Wuttinneumoh *CHRIST*
noh aſoowefit

JOHN ELIOT.

CAMBRIDGE:
Printeuꝏp naſhpe *Samuel Green* kah *Marmaduke Johnſon.*
1663.

197 previous page
John Eliot is here depicted
in his role as 'apostle to the
Indians', in a nineteenth-
century engraving

198
The Eliot Indian Bible
was completed by the printers
Samuel Green and Marmaduke
Johnson in Cambridge,
Massachusetts, in 1663

years. The Great Seal of the colony of Massachusetts Bay had a figure of a native saying 'Come over and help us' (Acts 16:9). On the other hand, many European settlers feared the indigenous peoples as dangerous and unpredictable barbarians, often (they felt) with good reason. As late as 1776, one of the clauses of the Declaration of Independence accuses the distant British of ill-informed co-operation with what they still regarded as 'merciless Indian Savages'.

The seventeenth-century Puritans in particular took a relatively enlightened view of a people whose apparent lack of civilization seemed to be caused by their having no recognizable religion. If the Lutherans and other Protestants believed, as they did, that all Europeans could see the evident truth of Christianity if only they could read the Bible accurately in their own languages, it was logical that if the native Americans could do the same they would become as instantly civilized and humane as Europeans. A society was set up in England under Oliver Cromwell in 1649, the Corporation for the Promoting and Propagating the Gospel of Jesus Christ in New England. Already by 1658 the Corporation was in correspondence with the New England Commissioners in Plymouth, Massachusetts, about printing Eliot's translation of the Bible. We can follow the progress of the publication very closely from copies of the letters preserved on both sides of the Atlantic.

Since 1638, Samuel Green had been a printer in Cambridge, Massachusetts, operating a relatively small press for Harvard College. He normally depended on local merchants for supplies of paper and other printing equipment. He was evidently greatly alarmed by the plan to print an entire Bible in a language so alien that it would be immensely time-consuming to set in type. In December 1658 he petitioned for a special supply of paper from England and the services of an assistant compositor. In April 1660, the Corporation for the Promoting and Propagating the Gospel announced that they were sending him a stock of paper and a young printer, one Marmaduke Johnson, on a three-year contract from 14 May 1660, the day that Johnson set sail from Gravesend to Boston. They asked that Marmaduke Johnson's name should appear on the title-page as co-printer. Johnson had arrived by late July and took lodgings with Green's family. His rent was £15 a year.

By September 1660, Green and Johnson were working conscientiously together on setting Eliot's manuscript text into print. They were able to keep up a rate of a sheet a week. This was eight pages (four on each side), and for each sheet the printers received £4, forwarded to them by Hezekiah Usher, the Boston merchant charged with covering the expenses of the Bible from a payment of £800 a year which was being lodged with him from London. The print was in two columns of extremely small roman type, usually set in 62 lines to a column. They began with 1,500 copies of the New Testament and they had apparently finished this part of the Bible by March 1661. They started at once on the Old Testament, and had already completed the Pentateuch (26 sheets) by September that year. At that time they printed a special title-page in English and a dedication to Charles II, who had been restored as king of England in 1660. The preface reports thoroughly satisfactory progress in evangelizing the natives, even making the remarkable claim that some of 'the wilde *Indians* … have proceeded further, to attain the knowledge of the Latine and Greek Tongues.' This title-page, dated 1661, and the preface to the king were added to 40 copies of the New Testament which were then sent in two shipments back to London for presentation to Charles II, the Lord Chancellor, and others. Once these had been dispatched, 200 further copies were sent to be bound in Boston, at a cost of six pence a copy, to be distributed at once to the Indians. One of these is now in the Bodleian Library in Oxford, acquired in 1706. It is inscribed several times 'Samuel ponompam his booke 1662'. Ponompam was one of four Indian schoolmasters employed by Eliot on a salary of £10 a year, and he seems to have taught in the Indian settlement of Wamesit, on the Merimack River about 20 miles (32 kilometres) from Boston. Thus we know that the text of the New Testament had demonstrably reached the American Indians even while the Old Testament was still in press.

So far, the progress seems thoroughly satisfactory but two things went badly wrong, one on each side of the Atlantic. In London, the Corporation for the Promoting and Propagating the Gospel unexpectedly found itself in abeyance. It had been founded under Oliver Cromwell, during the abolition of the English monarchy. Its wealth derived from lands sequestered from the defeated royalists. With the restoration of Charles II in 1660, institutions of the previous regime were generally abolished and properties were returned to the families from which they had been seized. For almost a year from April 1661 until its refoundation by Royal Charter in February 1662, no one knew if the Corporation would be able to continue its sponsorship of the Indian Bible.

In America, the problem was much more domestic. In October 1661, the assistant printer, Marmaduke Johnson, was indicted by the Grand Jury of Middlesex County, Massachusetts, on a charge of 'obtaining the affections' of Samuel Green's daughter, Elizabeth, without her father's consent. With the fascinated outrage which the Americans show even today in romantic scandal, the records of the court supply us with intimate details of Johnson's trysts with his master's daughter. She confessed that Marmaduke had proposed marriage to her. This, one might think, would be as satisfactory as Peter Schoeffer marrying the daughter of Johann Fust in Mainz in the 1450s, except that it emerged during the trial that Johnson already had a wife in England. She, in turn, had run off with a married silk stocking weaver, called Jeoffries. Subsequently, Jeoffries's own wife intervened and the hapless Mrs Marmaduke Johnson was sent off to Barbados and (to everyone's convenience) died on the voyage. Johnson himself was at first held in prison in Massachusetts and in April 1662 he was fined £5 and required to give a £20 surety against future good behaviour, both of which he was unable to pay. Eventually he was released through the intervention of John Eliot himself, and he apparently returned to work with Samuel Green in the summer of 1662. Relations must have been frosty in the printing shop.

Although now badly behind schedule, the printers still managed to complete the Indian Bible exactly within contract, in May 1663, three years after Johnson's appointment. The names of both Green and Johnson duly appear on the title-page. The Old Testament was printed in 1,000 copies and was added to the remaining copies of the New Testament, finished two years earlier. The combined book is a stout quarto. It is easily recognizable as a Bible, in that its page layout and chapter

199 opposite

Twenty copies of the newly printed Indian Bible were sent back to England for special presentations to appropriate institutions and noblemen. They are recorded as being bound on arrival in February 1664 by Samuel Gellibrand. It has been suggested that this copy, afterwards in the Doheny Collection, might have been presented to Charles II

numbers are all familiar. As a piece of printing, it is not of great beauty. The type
is extremely small and deeply impressed into the paper. The inking is inconsistent
and uneven. Margins are narrow and the columns of text sometimes lean tipsily
to the left or right from one page to another. By September 1663, the printers
added another English title-page and dedication to 20 special copies and sent
these off to England. The records are so precise that we even know that packing
the books in two chests for the journey cost five shillings. On arrival, the Bibles
were bound in black morocco by Samuel Gellibrand in February 1664 (Pl. 199).
Copies were to be distributed at the discretion of the Governor of the Corporation

for the Promoting and Propagating the Gospel, and John Eliot himself suggested a number of appropriate institutions, including his old college, Jesus College in Cambridge, which still owns the book. On 21 April 1664, the Governor of the Corporation reported back to Eliot in America: 'I waited this day upon the King with your translation of the Bible which, I hope I need not tell you, he received according to his custom very graciously ... He looked a pretty while on it, & showed some things in it to those who had the honor to be about him in his bed-chamber, into which he carryed it.' The scene reminds one of those in which Bibles were presented to Mangu Khan in 1254 or to Shah Abbas in 1608. On this occasion, however, it was the strangeness of the language rather than unfamiliarity with the Bible which must have engaged the king.

Back in Massachusetts, the printers now had 980 Indian Bibles and no immediate market for them. John Eliot must have taken some copies for his Indian mission. In the first year, ending in August 1664, the annual audit in Boston showed an order of 42 copies sent for binding at a cost of 2s. 6d. a volume (the binder, John Ratliffe, complained that the materials alone cost him a shilling a volume). Eliot had set up fourteen Christian communities, which he called 'Praying Towns', for his converts among the native Americans. The odd figure of 42 copies could perhaps be explained neatly by supposing that Eliot ordered three Indian Bibles for each of his fourteen Praying Towns. Beyond that, no other copies seem to have been required for upwards of three years. In September 1667, 200 further copies were sent for binding. Not all of these circulated among the Indians. A copy was given in that year by the Overseers of Harvard College to one of their benefactors, Raufe Freke (d.1684), who gave it in 1668 to the Bodleian Library (Pl. 200). It is one of those originally intended for use among the Americans, for it has no English title-page. Its binding is original (the presentation inscription from Harvard in 1667 is on its flyleaf) and so it was doubtless one of the 200 copies 'bound and clasped' in that year, still at 2s. 6d. each. The clasps are interesting, crudely cut out of metal and decorated with zig-zags of double dotted lines, like the ornament of native American headdresses.

It is difficult to guess how many Indian Bibles were actually used by native Americans. One copy, sold at Sotheby's in New York in 1994, has almost 200 contemporary corrections or notes in the Indian language, which show that it was at least owned by someone who could read it, whether missionary or native. Several other copies seem to have belonged to Indians in the eighteenth century. One was bought by the Gardiner family of New York from an Indian tribe in 1813. Most of the surviving copies, however, were evidently preserved by Europeans, who cannot have understood a word of them but simply regarded the books as extreme curiosities. It is commonly asserted that much of the edition was destroyed during the Indian wars of 1675–6. John Eliot remained passionately convinced of the potential value of his Bible among the Indians. In 1681 he wrote to the Governor of the Corporation for the Promoting and Propagating the Gospel, 'Untill we have Bibles, we are not furnished to cary the Gospel unto ym for we have no means to cary religion thither, saving the Scriptures.' He persuaded them to issue a new edition of the Indian Bible, printed again by Samuel Green (but without Marmaduke Johnson) in 1680–5. Each chapter now opens with a little summary of contents in English, which makes the book slightly less incomprehensible to Europeans. Nonetheless, it must always have been a publication of extraordinary unintelligibility. After Eliot's death in 1690, it was never printed again. The language itself is now entirely extinct.

Throughout this period, the Governor of the Corporation for the Promoting and Propagating the Gospel in New England, whose involvement we have quoted several times, was none other than Robert Boyle (1627–91), the physicist

(Pl. 201). Boyle is especially famous now for his scientific work and as the proponent of 'Boyle's Law' in physics. He was also a remarkable student of the Bible. He knew Hebrew, Greek, Chaldee and Syriac. He took a great interest in translating the Bible for missionary work. This was still a new concept. Although the Catholic (especially Jesuit) missionaries were active in the Far East in the seventeenth century, they apparently never considered translating the Bible into the languages of those they hoped to convert. This is one of the differences between Catholic and Protestant missions. Catholics sent priests. They would hope to convince by preaching and by bringing the catechism and liturgy into alien communities. Converts could eventually be educated to a level where they might wish to read the European Bible. Protestant missionaries, by contrast, were often laymen. They wanted to make the Bible available first of all, believing that anyone who read it would then be led to Christianity. The first translation of the Scriptures into any Asian language was the work of Dutch traders, mercantile Protestants, who began adapting sections of the Gospels into Malay in 1629. The English were not far behind.

Robert Boyle was also a director of the East India Company. In addition to his interest in the conversion of the native Americans, he looked to the Far East too. In 1677 he personally gave £200 to John Fell, newly appointed bishop of

Oxford, either for sponsoring four missionaries in the East Indies or, if that was impracticable, 'to goe for translating such parts of scripture into their languages as should be advisable'. The result was *Jang ampat Evangelia derri Tuan kita Jesu Christi*, printed in Oxford in 1677. This was the Gospels and Acts in Malay. It is actually a reprint of an Amsterdam edition of 1651 rather than a new translation. It was published at Boyle's expense and the preface thanks him effusively, recollecting the Indian Bible: 'your Charity is not limited only to the East Indians; for the poor Souls of the West-Indians are also bound to blesse you.' Further than this, Boyle had already contributed £70 towards printing the Bible in Turkish (Oxford, 1666) and he spent £700 on the publication of the Bible in an Irish translation, the New Testament in 1681 and the Old Testament in 1685. An Irish typeface was cut especially for this edition. Boyle arranged for the book to

be circulated among the Gaelic speakers of the Scottish highlands as well, where it enjoyed a notable success among those who hardly knew English, if at all. The English title-page of the Irish Old Testament proclaims its publication 'For the publicke good of that Nation'.

This sense of public good was manifested in the foundation in England of two rather similar philanthropic associations soon after Boyle's death. These were the Society for Propagating – later changed to Promoting – Christian Knowledge (1698) and the Society for the Propagation of the Gospel in Foreign Parts (1701). The SPCK and the SPG, as they are universally abbreviated, still exist, and both have been enormously influential in fostering missionary work throughout the world. Both were established by Thomas Bray (1656–1730), whose *Proposals for Encouraging Learning and Religion in Foreign Plantations* was published in 1695. The SPCK was founded primarily for religious work in England, such as establishing charity schools for children of the poor and reconverting the misguided Quakers back into membership of the Church of England. It had a secondary purpose to distribute Bibles and religious publications 'both at home and abroad'. The concern of the SPG was originally to minister to the spiritual welfare of British colonies and trading posts around the world (Pl. 202).

The first active involvement of the SPCK in printing the Bible in translation was actually part of a missionary campaign initiated from Denmark and Germany. Frederick IV became king of Denmark in 1699 and almost at once determined to send missionaries to the Danish trading port at Tranquebar on the east coast of the southern tip of India, in the Tanjore district of Madras. Unable to find suitable Danish missionaries, the king recruited two German Lutherans from Halle, Bartholomäus Ziegenbalg (1682–1719) and Heinrich Plütschau (1677–1752). They were ordained in Copenhagen and arrived in Tranquebar, after an eight-month voyage, in July 1706. The Danish merchants in India did not make them welcome, and initially the missionaries found it difficult to make contact with the native Tamil population. In 1707 they opened a church there, called New Jerusalem. Ziegenbalg began to study the local languages and literature and to collect Tamil manuscripts. He began also to translate the New Testament into Tamil in October 1708. Frederick IV's brother, Prince George of Denmark, was the husband of Anne, Queen of England. He too expressed interest in this Danish initiative and, through his chaplain, inquired whether the SPG would help sponsor the Tamil Bible. When it was decided that their mandate was restricted to British possessions abroad, the matter was referred to the SPCK, who welcomed the idea and opened a public subscription in 1710. They dispatched to India a printing press, a quantity of paper and a trained English printer. The ship was hijacked by French pirates and was taken to Rio de Janeiro where it was held for ransom, £150 of which was paid by the SPCK. When it was eventually released, the ship continued on its long voyage towards Tranquebar. Unfortunately, the printer died on the journey. The press was eventually delivered to Ziegenbalg and Plütschau in 1713. The problems were not yet over. By an agreeable piece of international collaboration, special Tamil type for the projected book was cast in Germany and was sent out to Tranquebar from Halle. The missionaries began printing in this huge type. When they had finished the Gospels in the summer of 1714, they realized they had already filled nearly 500 pages and were running seriously short of paper. Therefore they were obliged to cast their own much smaller type to complete the New Testament, which was finally published in 1715 (Pl. 203).

The book is dedicated to Frederick IV, with a preface to the king printed in parallel columns of Tamil and German. The entire biblical text is set in the very

202 opposite

The Society for the Propagation of the Gospel in Foreign Parts was established in 1701. The design for its seal shows native peoples welcoming a ship, with the text of Acts 16:9 in Latin, 'help us [by] coming across'

203

The first Bible in any language of the Indian subcontinent was the version in Tamil, printed in Tranquebar in 1715 by German Lutheran missionaries sent to India by the king of Denmark

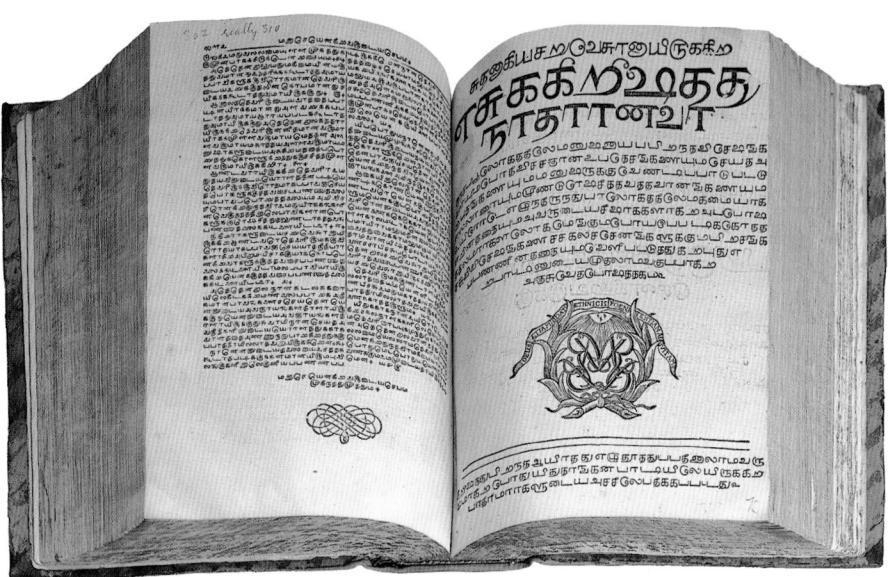

exotic Tamil script (partly made in Halle, partly in Tranquebar) and in that feature the book would have seemed more strange to Europeans than even Eliot's Indian Bible, which was at least in roman type. Nevertheless, the Tamil version looks unmistakably like a Bible. The text is in two columns, clearly divided into verses and chapters, and there are running-titles for each book along the tops of the pages. This is the first New Testament published in any language of the Indian sub-continent. There is an important difference between the so-called Indians of North America and the actual Indians of Tranquebar. The latter were far from illiterate or uncivilized. They were Hindus with very many books and holy writings of their own. While John Eliot might teach the principles of reading and writing in Massachusetts and could thus introduce the Bible as a first reading-book, Ziegenbalg and Plütschau would need to infiltrate the Bible into a corpus of sophisticated literature available locally. For that, the missionaries required a

Bible in a script which their potential converts could read. Apart from the dedication to the king of Denmark, the only words in the Tamil Bible in a European script are in the motto in the woodcut on the title-page, *Deus etiam dat ethnicis poenitentiam ad vitam*, adapted from Acts 11:18, 'God even gives to ethnic peoples the repentance that leads to life.'

The Scandinavians also took the Bible westwards in the eighteenth century. Hans Egede (1686–1758) was chaplain of Vaagan in Norway, 1707–18. He learned that there had been Norwegian settlers in Greenland in the Middle Ages and he wondered if their descendants were still living. He read the injunctions at the end of Saint Matthew's Gospel about going out to make disciples of all nations (Matthew 28:19). He set forth from Copenhagen with his wife and family in 1722 and worked as a missionary in Greenland until 1736. His son, Poul, who had returned to Denmark, then rejoined his father at Disko Bay in Greenland in 1734. Poul spoke Inuit fluently, having learned it among the natives as a child. Poul Egede's translation of the Gospels into Inuit was printed in Copenhagen in 1744. A second edition, including Acts, appeared in 1758. Finally, the entire New Testament in Poul Egede's translation was published in Copenhagen in 1766 (Pl. 204), dedicated to Christian VII, king of Denmark and Norway, and to the faithful congregation of Greenland. All three are stout books in small format, though the New Testament is a thousand pages thick. They are printed in large type in single columns. The New Testament has numbered verses, marginal notes and cross-references to parallel passages, and a table of readings for the liturgical year. It looks, in fact (and as one might expect), like the Lutheran New Testaments of the Reformation. The Greenlanders had no literacy of their own and it was imported in the form of the Bible by the Egede family. A second edition was published in 1799.

The Danish and Norwegian missions were associated with their national trading routes, and so were principally restricted to Scandinavian settlements in the Far East and the north Atlantic. A small exception is the publication of parts of the Gospels and Luther's catechism in the Accra language for use in the Danish schools on the Gold Coast in Africa in 1826. England, on the other hand, had commercial and colonial interests which extended infinitely wider. There were, in effect, two contradictory trends in late eighteenth-century English culture. One was a curiosity about the world and nature, and a delight in science, discovery and rational good order. The voyages of Captain Cook and others brought back to Europe accounts of the southern oceans and of races of people even more distant than the American Indians of Massachusetts or the Tamils of Tranquebar. Improvements in navigation enhanced the possibilities of travel, commerce and empire. The universe was at last being understood as something to be encompassed within a single vision. Conflicting with this trend – or maybe even because of it – was a revival of religious piety at a very popular level. This was the age of Baptists, Methodists, Quakers and Congregationalists. Especially in the second half of the eighteenth century, there was a huge reaction towards prayer, preaching and personal spirituality. These two trends converged in international evangelism. The idea of converting all people to conformity with European Christianity was attractive both to those with a grand view of the world as an exploitable commodity and to those with religious convictions in the spiritual capabilities of all mankind.

One expression of this quite sudden enthusiasm for evangelizing the world occurs in the rapid foundation of whole series of Bible societies, each dedicated to the international dissemination of the Word of God. This is an especially Protestant phenomenon. The English Baptist Society was set up in 1792. The London Missionary Society was founded in 1795, independent of any sectarian affiliations. The Church Missionary Society followed in 1799, established by evangelical members of the Church of England. In the same year the Religious Tract Society was founded. At a meeting of its committee in 1804, it was suggested that the Society might help supply Bibles in the Welsh language for distribution in Wales. One delegate, Joseph Hughes, rose to support the motion, proposing that 'a society might be formed for the purpose; and if for Wales, why not for the Kingdom? – why not for the whole world?' The result was the foundation of the British and Foreign Bible Society, the most important and wide-reaching of all such associations (Pl. 205). It was not a missionary organization as such but actively supported missions by supplying Bibles. The name of the British and Foreign Bible Society will recur many times in the residue of this

204 opposite

The New Testament translated by Poul Egede into the Inuit language of Greenland was published in Copenhagen in 1766

chapter. Other foundations included the Methodist Missionary Society (1813) and local societies and even village groups across the country. By 1815, there were over 400 auxiliary branches of Bible societies in England and its various dominions. The trend was not limited to Britain. The Deutsche Bibelanstalt and the Société biblique de Bâle were both founded in 1804 (they merged in Switzerland in 1806). There were Bible societies in Sweden (1809), Russia, Finland and Hungary (all 1812), the Netherlands (1813), and so on. Societies were established in Philadelphia, Connecticut, Massachusetts, New Jersey, New York, and many other regions of the United States. The American Bible Society was founded in 1816. The camaraderie (and rivalry) of such associations had a huge effect on the promotion and distribution of the Bible, both locally and abroad.

A stirring battle-call to Bible translation was published in 1815 by the two secretaries of the Perthshire Bible Society, W.A. Thomson and W. Orme. It is called *A Historical Sketch of the Translation and Circulation of the Scriptures from the Earliest Period to the Present Time*. It tells of the wickedness of medieval monks who had kept the Bible from the common people and it praises all Reformers and translators. The authors write: 'We cordially agree … that the man who produces a translation of the Bible into a new language (like Wickliffe and Luther, and Zeigenbalg and Carey) is a greater benefactor to mankind than the prince who founds an empire.' That is a strong statement written at the moment when the founding of empires was a European passion. Wycliffe and Luther have been the subjects of entire chapters above. We have looked at Ziegenbalg and his edition of the New Testament in Tamil in 1715. We should now turn to Carey.

William Carey (1761–1834) was an English Baptist pastor and former shoemaker (Pl. 206). In 1792, at the age of 31, he published in Leicester a little book, *An Enquiry into the Obligations of Christians to Use Means for the Conversion of the Heathens*. It invokes the initiatives of Eliot in Massachusetts and of Zeigenbalg in Tranquebar. It gives tables listing the populations of all the countries of the world and their religions. (Under 'California', for example, it records the population as 9,000,000 and their

affiliation as 'Pagans'.) According to Carey's calculations, there were at that time 731 million people in the world of whom 421 million were still in heathen darkness. Carey convinced himself that mission work was the most urgent duty of Christians. With no preparation or support, he sailed to Calcutta in northeastern India in 1793. There he began to learn local languages and financed himself by working part-time in a local indigo factory. In the first seven years he made not a single convert. Two further missionaries joined him in 1799, Joshua Marshman (1768–1837) and William Ward (1769–1823). They moved upriver to the Danish colony, Serampore, on the Hooghly River, about 20 kilometres (12 miles) from Calcutta. They set up a printing press and began to translate and to publish Bibles in local languages.

The first Bible in any language of north India was translated by Carey himself into Bengali. In 1801, the missionaries' new press at Serampore printed 500 copies of the Bengali text of Saint Matthew's Gospel and some biblical prophecies about Christ. The whole New Testament appeared in 2,000 copies in 1801. The Old Testament followed in instalments, from the Pentateuch (1802) to the books from Joshua to Esther (1809). All these were printed in Bengali type. Almost simultaneously, Carey and his colleagues began on the Bible in Hindustani (or High Hindi) in 1802. Their project was postponed when news reached them of a competing translation of the Gospels by Henry Colebrooke (1765–1837), published in Calcutta in 1806. Nonetheless, the Serampore Press eventually issued the Hindustani New Testament in 1811, and the Old Testament in instalments from 1812 to 1818 (Pl. 207). They were printed in exotic Devanagari type.

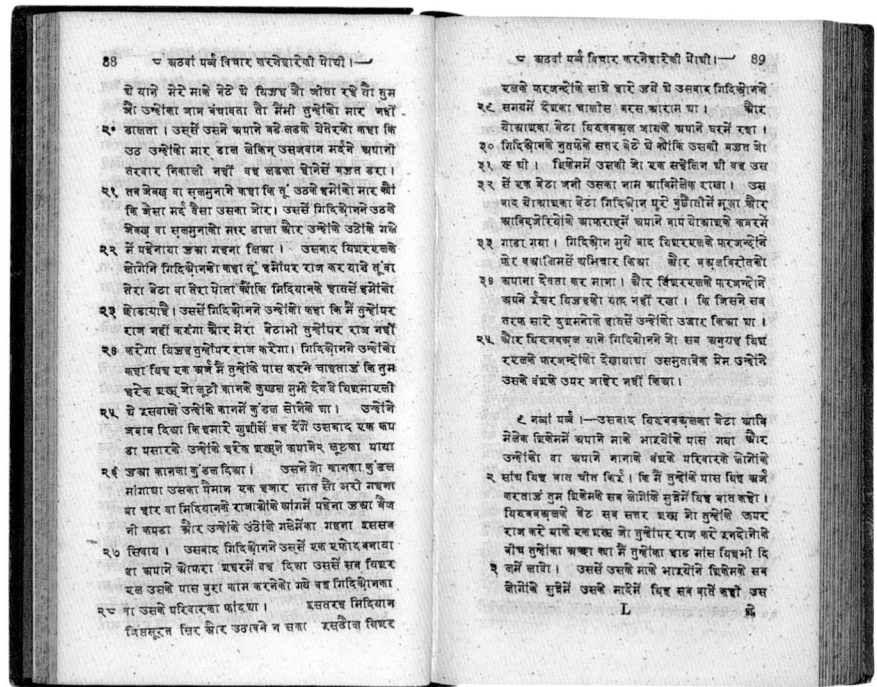

207

*The Hindustani Bible, trans-
lated by William Carey and
his colleagues, was finally
completed in 1818*

208 opposite

*The 5-volume Chinese Bible,
printed in Serampore in
1815–22, is entirely oriental
in appearance and format*

Any European, confronting one of the strangest-looking New Testaments ever printed, cannot but marvel at the English understatement on the title, 'translated … from the Original Greek'.

Even Carey was unable to tackle the Marathi language. His mission station hired a local interpreter to prepare for them Saint Matthew's Gospel (1805, 465 copies) and then the whole New Testament (1811). The Serampore printers used an archaic 'Modi' (or 'broken') type, rather similar to Devanagari. It transpired that the interpreter was not as sophisticated as his credentials and that his own dialect was so local to his home district of Nagpur that no other speakers of the language could understand his translation. Carey was better served by his translator into Chinese. In 1810, the press published Matthew and Mark for the first time in High Wen-li, or classical Chinese. They employed John Lassar, an Armenian born in Macao, who translated from the English with the help from Joshua Marshman correcting the text against the Greek. The practical problems of printing in Chinese characters were enormous. The first editions were printed from woodblocks cut for the missionaries by Bengalis from a nearby chintz-printing factory. They continued with Saint John's Gospel (1813) and, finally, the first complete Chinese Bible, in five parts, 1815–22 (Pl. 208). Nothing obviously suggests that this publication is a Bible. It defers to the oriental style (the Chinese had been printing books for centuries before Gutenberg). Printing is on one side of the paper only, folded into a tall narrow concertina format, bound by stabbing through the inner margins. The volumes are bound in thin brown paper wrappers with crudely printed title-labels in English on the lower cover. One reads, for example, 'THE NEW TESTAMENT IN CHINESE; *PRINTED AT SERAM-PORE*, WITH METALLIC, MOVEABLE CHARACTERS, 1815–22', except that the proud word 'characters' is misspelled 'characrers'.

Typefaces of an extraordinary variety were used in the mission press at Serampore. The printers evidently delighted in the challenge of producing each translation in its distinctive alphabet and format. Publications of the press include: a New Testament in Oriya (1807–9), followed by the books of the Old Testament from 1809 to 1815, printed in Oriya type; Saint Matthew's Gospel in Gujarati (1809) followed by a New Testament (1820), printed in Devanagari type; a New Testament in Asami (1813–20), and Saint Matthew's Gospel (1816) and then the New Testament, both in Khasi (probably 1831), all printed in Bengali type; a New Testament in Urdu (1814), translated from Greek by the late Henry Martyn (1781–1812), printed in Arabic type; the Gospel of Saint Matthew in Burmese (1815), translated by William Carey's eldest son Felix (1786–1822), printed in Burmese type; a New Testament in Panjabi (1815), printed in Gurmukhi type (the printing of this book had begun in 1811 but the special type had been destroyed in a fire at the press in 1812); and a New Testament in Kashmiri (1821), followed by several books of the Old Testament in Kashmiri, 1827–32, all printed in Sarada type, the ancient script of Kashmir.

Many of the Serampore editions were subsidized or entirely paid for by the British and Foreign Bible Society. The Society was effectively the publisher of many books printed by the mission station. By the time of Carey's death in 1834, the Bible Society had contributed a total of £27,230 to the publication programme and the missionaries in Serampore had already produced translations of all or parts of the Bible into a remarkable total of 34 new languages.

The Bible Society also financed the publication of Bibles in many other parts of the world, often in languages of considerable obscurity. Three examples will have to suffice to show the diversity of the books. They are translations into Mohawk, Bullom and Manchu. The first was the Gospel of Saint John in the language of the American Mohawk Indians, printed in 1804. It was translated by a native, Teyoninhokarawen, anglicized (after his conversion) as John Norton. It is a diglot, that is, it comprises two languages, English and Mohawk on facing pages (Pl. 209). Both are in roman script, for the Mohawks had no alphabet. Each verse is numbered and can easily be matched with its corresponding sentence in the other tongue. This would make it extremely simple for a missionary to use, both for preaching and for learning the language. Therefore, if a European wanted to say (for example) 'Peace be unto you' to a group of Mohawks, he could quickly look up John 20:26 and run his eye across the page and pronounce, *skènnen kenhak tsi isewese*. Here and there are words for which no possible Mohawk equivalent could be found, a constant problem for missionaries translating across cultures (even a simple Christian term like the 'good shepherd' would be difficult to render in the language of a Pacific islander who had never seen animals, let alone sheep). The Mohawk edition simply avoids difficult concepts by leaving them in Greek or Hebrew. In the very first verse, the translator could find no native equivalent for *Logos* and *Yehovah*. The Mohawk Saint John was the first book published by the British and Foreign Bible Society, and 2,000 copies were printed in London at a cost of £204 9s. 6d., quite expensive at about two shillings a copy.

Southern Bullom, also known as *Sherbro* or *Mampwa*, is a West African language, spoken in parts of Sierra Leone. The Gospel of Saint Matthew was translated into Bullom by Gustavus Reinhold Nyländer (1776–1824), a German Lutheran chaplain in Freetown, Sierra Leone, sponsored by the Church Missionary Society. First of all, he prepared the ground with *A Spelling-book of the Bullom language, with a dialogue and Scripture exercises*, printed by the Church Missionary Society in 1814. This was followed up by the Gospel, 226 pages, published by the British and Foreign Bible Society as *Biok Hoa Matthew* in 1816. It was the first translation of any part of the Bible into any African language in modern times.

A third example of a book published by the British and Foreign Bible Society is the New Testament in Manchu, printed in St Petersburg in 1835. The translator was Stephan Vasilevitch Lipovtsov, of the Asiatic section of the Russian foreign office. He had learned Manchu in Peking. He compiled a translation of the New Testament in 1821–5 but the Russian authorities refused to give him permission to publish it. The Bible Society appointed a delegate to Russia, the writer George Borrow (1803–81), author of *Lavengro* and *Romany Rye*. His mission was to help transcribe a manuscript of the text so that a copy could be brought to England. He taught himself Manchu in London in January 1833 and set off for St Petersburg. The transcript still survives in the library of the Bible Society (their MS. 349), now in Cambridge, and good parts of it are in Borrow's hand (Pl. 210). Five months into the project, however, the Minister of the Interior relented, after representations from the British ambassador, and consent was given for publication. The Society paid for the printing of the book in Russia, in Chinese script. Borrow saw it through the press, reporting on the frustrations of collaborating on the text with Lipovtsov, since almost the only languages they had in common were Manchu and Latin.

Nineteenth- and even twentieth-century histories trumpet statistics of the numbers of Bible translations which are extremely impressive. The theme of such accounts is commonly one which equates the great march of civilization with the progress of the Bible as it spread across the world. Around 1800, the Bible had been translated into only about seventy languages throughout its long

209 opposite
The first book published by the British and Foreign Bible Society was the Gospel of Saint John in alternate pages in Mohawk and English. 2,000 copies were printed in 1804

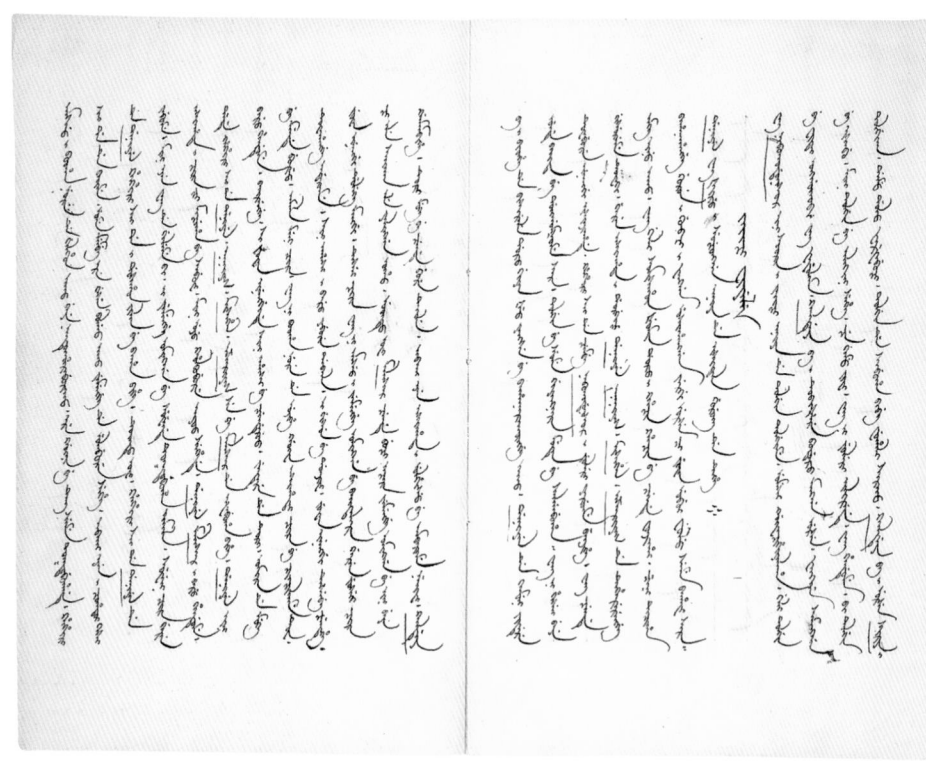

history. A hundred years later, at least parts of the Scriptures had been printed in
well over 500 different languages. By 1925, the figure had reached 835. No one
can deny the immense scholarship and sustained effort involved, or the generosity of time and money freely given by a very large number of people at all levels
of society. It is no longer so easy to judge whether European missionaries imported more culture than they destroyed, or whether motives of colonialism and
commercial advantage were scarcely concealed beneath the cover of pious phil-
anthropy. Critics can point (for example) to David Livingstone's famous speech
in the Senate House in Cambridge in 1857: 'I go back to Africa to try to make an
open path for commerce and Christianity.' It is also fair to say that there was not
always a united policy even within the organizations which promoted the Bible
across the world. On the mission stations, different denominations of the Christian churches sometimes quarrelled with each other and presented very divergent
forms of the Scriptures and the practice of religion.

The British and Foreign Bible Society attempted to remain unsectarian. Bibles
were required to be straightforward texts, without notes or interpretations. Even
that was not always uncontroversial. Members were fiercely divided on whether
or not Bibles promoted by the Society should or should not include the Apocrypha. Martin Luther, as we have seen, gathered it into his German translation,
but more from indecision than endorsement. The Latin Vulgate and all Catholic
translations of the Bible defiantly included the Apocrypha. It became one of the

distinguishing tenets of Catholicism. The English Authorized Version of the Bible consigns it to an appendix or (more usually) excludes it altogether. The doctrinal value of the Apocrypha is rejected in the sixth of the Thirty-Nine Articles, the defining document of the Church of England, written in 1562 and still technically valid. The Westminster Confession, the constitutional charter of the Presbyterian Church (1646–8), banished it utterly. However, the British and Foreign Bible Society also sponsored Bible translations for use in parts of Europe which were Roman Catholic or Lutheran. Some members of the Society accepted that if their work was to be entirely international and without denominational prejudice, then Bibles circulated in Catholic countries, for example, should include the texts which were normally part of Catholic Bibles. Others, especially the Scottish, objected vociferously. The controversy nearly tore the Society apart in the early to mid-1820s, and eventually in 1826 the Society agreed not to publish or endorse any Bibles which included the Apocrypha or to collaborate with other associations unless they too rejected the Apocryphal books.

A second problem within the British and Foreign Bible Society was the fear

that, once the text of the Bible had been put into a strange or exotic language, there was little control as to whether or not it might have become corrupted in translation. Every effort was made to find responsible translators, especially those who could work directly from the original languages, but in practice this was not always possible. The anxiety was brought to a crisis over the Society's publication in Paris in 1819 of a translation in Arabic script of the New Testament in Turkish. The edition was printed from a seventeenth-century manuscript borrowed from Leiden University Library. The 200-year-old translation had been made from a French version by Adalbert Bobowsky, a Pole who as a boy had been sold into slavery in Constantinople and had converted to Islam, taking the name of Ali Bey and joining the court of the Turkish sultan. His Turkish version, it was asserted, had been adapted subtly to suit the taste of his Muslim masters, and the text's nineteenth-century editor, Jean Daniel Kieffer, had failed to notice this. The controversy within the Bible Society lasted for years. Intemperate pamphlets argued for and against withdrawing the edition from print. Both sides had cogent arguments. The Society's eventual view, as expressed by its honorary librarian in 1827, was that it was always desirable to employ translators who could work from the Hebrew and Greek, 'but that, when such men cannot be

212

Slim translations of parts of the Bible into Maori were the first books printed in New Zealand, published at the mission press at Paihia in the far north of the country in the 1840s. The book on the right comprises Daniel and Jonah

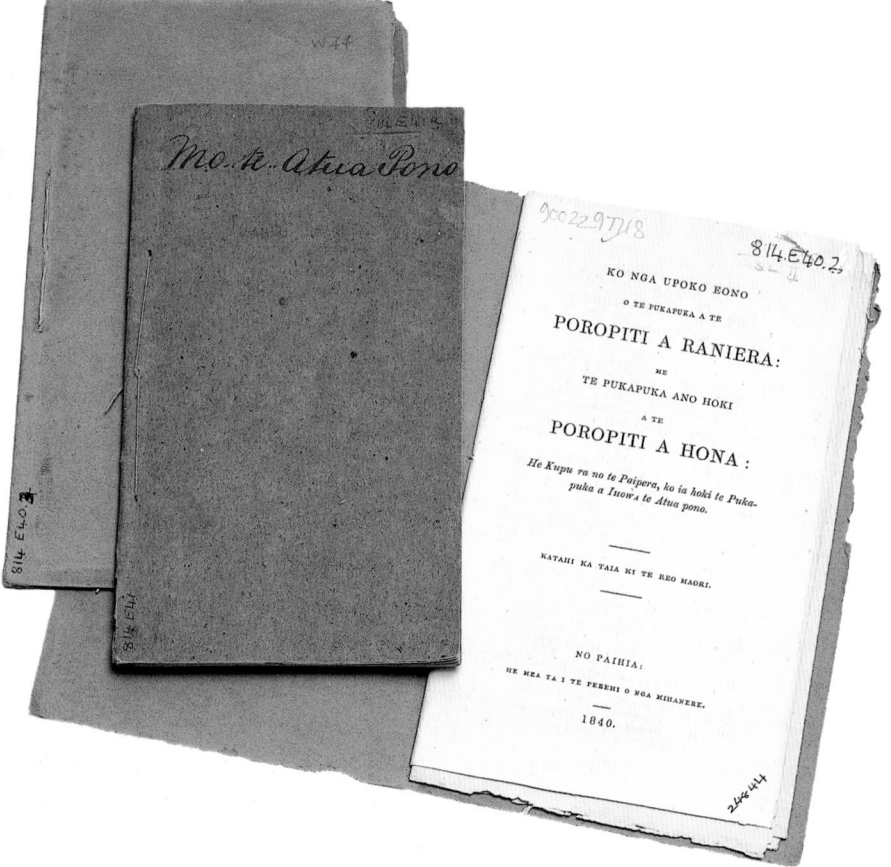

KO NGA UPOKO EONO
O TE PUKAPUKA A TE
POROPITI A RANIERA:
ME
TE PUKAPUKA ANO HOKI
A TE
POROPITI A HONA:
*He Kupu ra no te Paipera, ko ia hoki te Puka-
puka a Ihowa te Atua pono.*

KATAHI KA TAIA KI TE REO MAORI.

NO PAIHIA:
HE MEA TA I TE PEREHI O NGA MIHANERE.
1840.

found, it is better, FAR BETTER, to publish among a people merely the Version

of a Version, than to leave them in utter ignorance of the Word of God'. This
became the common attitude in the years which followed.

The second quarter of the nineteenth century was the great period of the opening up of the Pacific. In many islands the missionaries were the first Europeans
to arrive. The islanders' first experiences of literacy were usually in the form
of translations of parts of the Bible into the local languages. The pattern was repeated over and over again. Missionaries arrived, struggled to master the native
languages and then promptly translated books of Scripture, which (if possible)
they printed themselves by hand in their mission stations. The first books
printed in many Pacific countries, including New Zealand, were Bibles or parts
of Bibles in local translations (Pl. 212). The flimsy publications resemble children's
schoolbooks of the period, little crudely printed and hand-stitched booklets in
large print. Sometimes these pioneer missionaries were university-educated
theologians, competent to translate each time from Greek and Hebrew. Others
simply did the best they could. The enormous distances of the Pacific Ocean
and the utter isolation of the missions made close supervision from Europe very
difficult. It was impossible to judge the exact accuracy of any translation into
a language so obscure that the lonely missionary himself was perhaps the only
European who could speak it.

The first missionaries to Hawaii were sent out by the American Board of
Commissioners for Foreign Missions in 1820. They included Hiram Bingham
(1789–1869) and Asa Thurston (1787–1868), with their wives and families. The
voyage from the United States took 164 days. Between them, they translated the
Gospels from the original Greek into Hawaiian. In 1827 they printed a trial 12
pages of Saint Luke's Gospel, translated by Bingham, followed in 1828 by the
Sermon on the Mount. In 1835, a translation of the whole New Testament was
printed in Honolulu by the missionaries themselves in an edition reputedly of
10,000 copies. The mission was immensely effective. In 1839–41, for example,
more than 20,000 Hawaiians were received into the Christian Church, out of a
native population of about 100,000. The missionaries skilfully linked Christianity
with education. In addition to the Scriptures, Bingham also translated little teaching texts, with names like *Elementary Lessons*, *Scripture Catechism* and *First Teacher*;
Thurston translated *Sacred Geography* and *First Lesson of Arithmetic*.

Bingham's son, also Hiram (1831–1908), was born in Honolulu. In 1857 he set
up his own missionary station on Abiaiang, in the Gilbert Islands in Micronesia,
about 2,250 miles (3,600 kilometres) south-west of Hawaii. He immediately began
learning the native language. With his wife, Minerva, he had completed the first
half of a translation of Saint Matthew's Gospel by the end of 1859 and they sent
it home to Honolulu, where it was printed in 1860, the first book in the Gilbert
Island language. When they had completed the second part of their translation
in 1862, they sent this off too. Thirteen months later, the messengers returned,

having apparently misunderstood or forgotten their instructions. They brought a printing press instead of printed books. By good fortune (for the Binghams, at least), a ship was wrecked on the Gilbert Islands soon afterwards, and one of the survivors, Hotchkiss, had formerly been a printer. He set up their press for them, and completed the Matthew and afterwards printed John and Ephesians. There was very little paper on the island. Hotchkiss used the Binghams' notepaper, for nothing else was available, and was able to print only 64 copies of Saint John's Gospel and 54 of Ephesians before these domestic supplies were exhausted.

The great missionary of the southern Pacific was John Williams (1796–1839), known in the islands by the local version of his surname as 'Viriamu'. He was sent from the London Missionary Society and arrived in Tahiti in 1818. The local chief helped him buy a schooner, the *Endeavor*, and Williams set off to explore islands towards the south-west. He found Rarotonga in the Cook Islands in 1823. He learned the language and translated Galatians into Rarotongan, printed by the London Missionary Society Press at Huahine in the Society Islands, nearly a thousand miles (1,600 kilometres) away, in 1828. It was followed by the Gospels of Saint John (1829) and Saint Mark (1832). In late 1832, a modern metal printing press arrived in Huahine and so the old wooden hand press was dispatched to

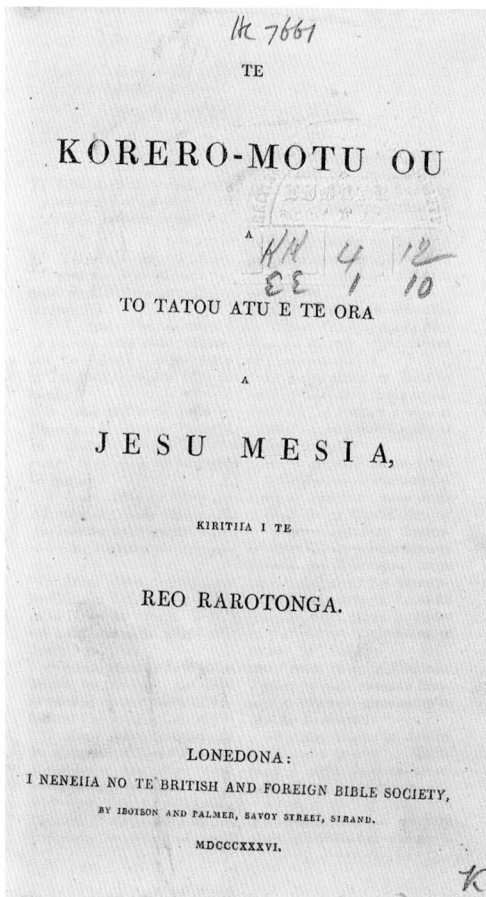

213
This Rarotongan New Testament was printed in London in 1836

214 opposite
As Williams stepped ashore in the New Hebrides in 1839, he was attacked by natives who killed and ate him. The scene is shown in a colour print by George Baxter, published in 1841

Rarotonga, where Williams's missionaries printed almost the whole New Testament in separate pamphlets in Rarotongan. A full text was printed in England (1836), and 5,000 copies were sent out to the islands (Pl. 213). Williams went on to Samoa and eventually to the New Hebrides, where he was killed and eaten by cannibals on the beach in Eromanga (Pl. 214).

Similar tales can be told of many island missions printing Bibles. Two British Methodists, for example, David Cargill (1809–43) and William Cross (1797–1842), met in Tonga and set off together to Fiji in 1835. They opened a mission in Lakemba and immediately translated part of Saint Matthew's Gospel into Fijian, printed in Tonga in 1836. Two years later, they had their own press, even in Lakemba, and printed the Gospel of Saint

Mark in Fijian. Cross died from dysentery in Fiji; Cargill died in Tonga of an overdose of laudanum, taken to combat fever and depression. Both were still young. The dangers of bringing Christianity across the Pacific often outweighed the undoubted adventure and excitement of the enterprise.

Sometimes the Bibles in remote languages were actually printed in London or New York, rather than in the mission field. There is a clear difference in the function and appearance of such books. A single book of the Bible printed locally is likely to resemble a contemporary chapbook, the kind of inexpensive booklet from which the missionaries themselves, as children in Britain or America, would have learned to read. The books are usually little octavos, printed in single columns of text, divided into well-spaced verses. They are teaching books. An example of a Bible printed in London, however, is the first edition of the Bible in Tahitian (1838). The translator was Henry Nott (1774–1844), of the London Missionary

*The first complete Bible in
Tahitian was published in
London in 1847, following the
translation of Henry Nott of
the London Missionary Society*

216 opposite

*Japan did not encourage
foreign overtures for most of
the nineteenth century. The
pencil note on the right makes
the plate appear to be upside
down: the annotator was
wrong, for the book begins at
the back, in Japanese style.
This is Saint John's Gospel,
published in 1837*

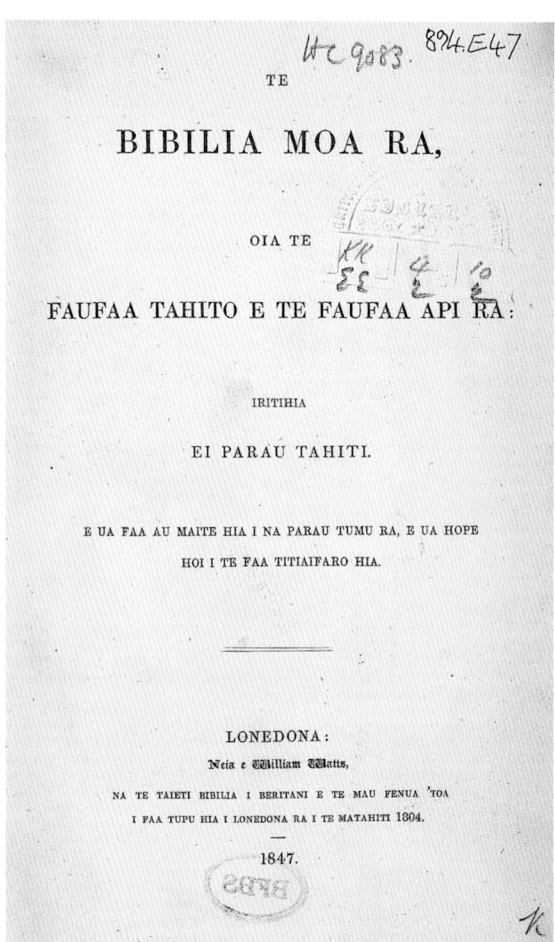

TE

BIBILIA MOA RA,

OIA TE

FAUFAA TAHITO E TE FAUFAA API RA:

IRITIHIA

EI PARAU TAHITI.

E UA FAA AU MAITE HIA I NA PARAU TUMU RA, E UA HOPE
HOI I TE FAA TITIAIFARO HIA.

LONEDONA:
Neia e William Watts,
NA TE TAIETI BIBILIA I BERITANI E TE MAU FENUA 'TOA
I FAA TUPU HIA I LONEDONA RA I TE MATAHITI 1804.
—
1847.

Society, who had arrived in
Tahiti in 1797. He had en-
listed the help of the king
of Tahiti, Pomare II (1779–
1821), in learning the
language and translating
the Bible. A printing press
had been set up at Afareaitu
on Eimeo, the island facing
Tahiti across the lagoon, in
1817. Single books of the
Bible were printed by the
missionaries there from 1818
onwards. From 1836 to 1840,
however, Nott was back in
London to supervise the publication of the entire Bible in
Tahitian, the first in any Poly-
nesian language (Pl. 209). The
result was as different from
the product of an island press
as is possible to imagine. It is
titled *Te Bibilia moa ra, oia te
Faufaa Tahito e te Faufaa Api
ra*. It was published in London
by the British and Foreign Bible Society in an edition of 3,000 copies. It resembles a thoroughly normal Victorian Bible, bound in ecclesiastical blind-stamped
black leather (by Burn and Sons, 37 Kirby Street). The text is in two columns of
small roman type, arranged like a standard European Bible, and the text is in
continuous prose with verse numbers in the outer margins. It could be any Bible
in English, except that the text is in Tahitian. It had become a symbol rather
than a teaching text. It was a Bible as a physical entity, the Holy Bible, an embodiment of Christianity. Copies were sent on publication to the queen of Tahiti and
to Queen Victoria. In Tahiti it would have been a book to own and to carry to
church as a public statement of conversion and culture. It is reported that copies
were keenly sought in Tahiti, and changed hands for the equivalent of eight
shillings each. In Britain, it was presented to public figures and to patrons of the
missionary movement, as a trophy of yet another language from the furthest end
of the earth, which had been captured, tamed and dressed up in the clothing of
English religion.

For much of the nineteenth century, encroaching westernization was resisted
in Japan. While the peoples of the southern Pacific were being proselytized under

the flag of Christianity, the Japanese maintained isolation by imperial edicts against foreigners. A tiny text of Saint John's Gospel was printed in Japanese in Singapore in 1837. It was translated for the American Board of Commissioners for Foreign Missions by three survivors of the shipwreck of a Japanese junk blown in a storm right across the Pacific to the coast of North America. No Bibles were printed in Japan itself until the 1870s. These were small, fragile books in brightly coloured paper wrappers. They look (at least to Western eyes) entirely Japanese in structure, which was perhaps exactly the intention (Pl. 216).

David Livingstone's *Missionary Travels and Researches in South Africa* was published in 1857 and caught the imagination of Europe to a remarkable degree. Africa suddenly seemed to be the continent of adventure and opportunity (Pl. 217). In the second half of the nineteenth century, the Bible was translated into one African language after another. Many were actually printed in Europe, often at

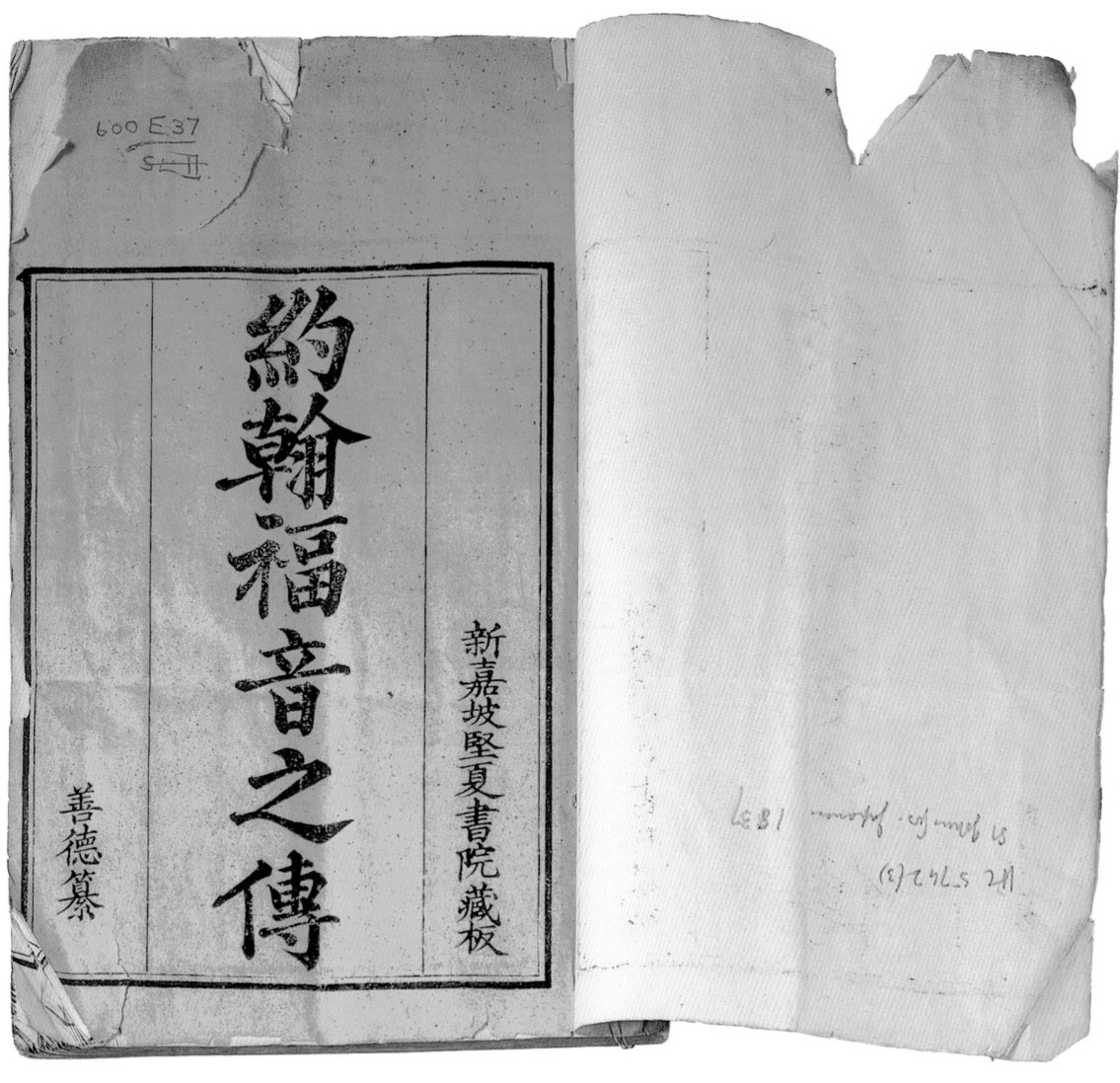

*The adventures of David
Livingstone in Africa caught
the popular imagination and
inspired renewed efforts to
promote African missions and
colonies*

218 opposite
*Saint Matthew's Gospel was
printed in the Isubu language
on the mission station in
Bimbia in west Africa in 1846*

the expense of the British
and Foreign Bible Society.
Examples, among very
many, include: Saint
Matthew in Hausa (spoken
in central Sudan), trans-
lated by James Frederick
Schön (1803–89), London,
1857; the Gospels in
Ashanti (spoken on the
Gold Coast), translated by
Johannes Gottlieb Chris-
taller (1827–95), London,
1859; Saint Matthew in
Ibo (spoken in southern
Nigeria), translated by
John Christopher Taylor
(c.1815–80, the son of an
Isuama slave), London,
1860, revised by Schön;
Saint Matthew 1–7 in
Nupé (spoken in northern
Nigeria), translated by
Samuel Crowther (c.1807–91, himself a former slave), London, 1860, again re-
vised by Schön; Saint Matthew in Benga (spoken on the island of Corisco, West
Africa), translated by G. McQueen of the American Presbyterian Mission, New
York, 1861; the Gospels in Ewe (spoken in Togoland and Dahomey, west Africa),
translated by B. Schlegel of the Bremen Bible Society, Stuttgart, 1861; the New
Testament in Efik (spoken in Calabar, west Africa), translated from the Greek by
Hugh Goldie (1815–95), Edinburgh, 1862; Saint Luke in Dinka (spoken on the
White Nile), translated by the Roman Catholic Central African Mission, Brixen,
1866, a rare instance of a Catholic translation in a profession dominated by Prot-
estants; Ruth and Jonah in southern Swahili (spoken in the region of Zanzibar),
translated by Edward Steere (1828–82), Zanzibar, 1868, and Saint Matthew by
the same translator, London, 1869; Saint Matthew in Susu (spoken in French
Guinea, west Africa), probably translated by J.H.A. Dupont (a West Indian of
African descent, from Codrington College, Barbados), Oxford, 1869; Saint
Matthew in Mende (spoken in the highlands of Sierra Leone), translated by
James Frederick Schön again, London, 1871; Saint John in Kele (spoken in Gabun,
west Africa), New York, 1879; Saint Matthew in Yao (spoken on the eastern and
southern shores of Lake Nyasa), London, 1880; Saint Matthew in Jolof (spoken
in the Gambia, west Africa), London, 1882; Saint Mark in Kongo (spoken along

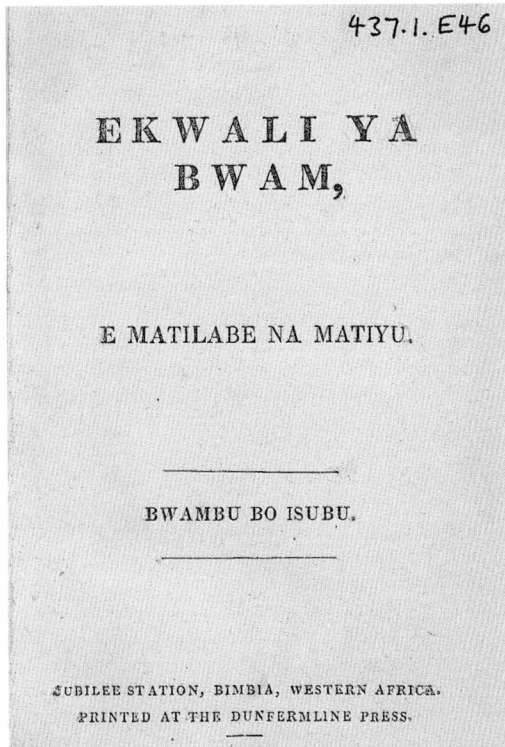

the Congo river in west central Africa), London, 1886; Saint John in Mbundu (spoken in northern Angola), London, 1888; and, finally, Saint Mark in Ngoni (spoken in west central Africa), translated by Walter Angus Elmslie (1856–1935), printed in 500 copies by the missionaries on an Albion hand press at the Livingstonia Mission in Malawi, 1891.

We can choose a single example out of many hundreds. This is *Ekwali ya Bwam, e Matilabe na Matiyu*, the Gospel of Saint Matthew translated into the Isubu language by Joseph Merrick (d. 1849), a native-born African, educated in Jamaica. The book was printed in 1846 at the Dunfermline Press on the Jubilee Station, Bimbia, a missionary outpost which had been opened three years earlier at the foot of the Cameroon mountains in western Africa (Pl. 218). It is small, the size of one's hand, like a children's reading book, printed on thick paper in pale watery black ink, with its single column of text swaying erratically from one page to the next. The Gospel opens, at Matthew 1:1, 'Kalati ya itumba la Jizos Kris, mwana a Devid, mwana a Ebraham', 'The genealogy of Jesus Christ, son of David, son of Abraham'. The book tells of Jizos Kris, his mother Meri, his disciples Pitar, Jon, Andiru, Jemis and others, and his trial before Keefas and Ponshios Pilat, and his crucifixion, death and resurrection. The translation faithfully follows a text which had descended in an unbroken line of transmission since the first centuries AD. It has travelled along an extraordinary journey.

ϮⲘⲘⲀⲟⲨ ⲚⲈⲘⲘⲀ
ⲬⲈⲀⲬⲒⲈⲬⲈⲀ ⲚⲈ
ⲦⲈⲚ Ⲛ ⲚⲔⲀⲦ ⲨⲀϤϤ
ⲈⲘⲀⲚ ⲖⲀϤⲤⲱⲦ
ⲘⲀϤ ⲀⲟⲨⲱⲚⲦⲱ
ⲖⲈⲢⲒⲘⲚⲞⲤ Ⲛ̄ⲦⲀ

THIS FINAL CHAPTER opens in 1859. In that year, Charles Darwin published the *Origin of Species.* In the same year, Constantin Tischendorf finally persuaded the monks of St Catherine's monastery on Mount Sinai to part with their great fourth-century Greek Bible manuscript, now known as the *Codex Sinaiticus.* It was Tischendorf's third visit to the monastery since 1844, when he had first encountered a number of loose leaves of this noble uncial manuscript, apparently then treated by the monks with utter neglect. Tischendorf (1815-74), professor of theology at Leipzig, was the first modern biblical scholar to search scientifically, almost archaeologically, for the earliest evidence of the Bible in Greek. In 1859, after many thwarted attempts during his visit to St Catherine's, he finally gained sight of the manuscript itself, then comprising a vast stack of unbound parchment sheets wrapped in red cloth. Having failed to buy the manuscript outright, which he would have preferred, Tischendorf convinced the monks instead that they would benefit immensely, both materially and spiritually, by presenting their codex to the Tsar of Russia, protector of the Orthodox Church. By this elegant solution, Tischendorf was able to remove the manuscript from the hazardous ownership of an ancient library and to bring it safely to St Petersburg for publication.

Darwin's *Origin of Species* first demonstrated the theory of evolution, the argument that all living creatures have become as they are by an extremely slow process of chance mutation and natural selection over countless millions of years. The process applied to humans as well as to animals. Scientifically, the theory seemed extremely elegant and persuasive. The public reaction to Darwin was extreme, both for and against, for the theory required one to discard completely the account of Creation in the book of Genesis. The biblical narrative records

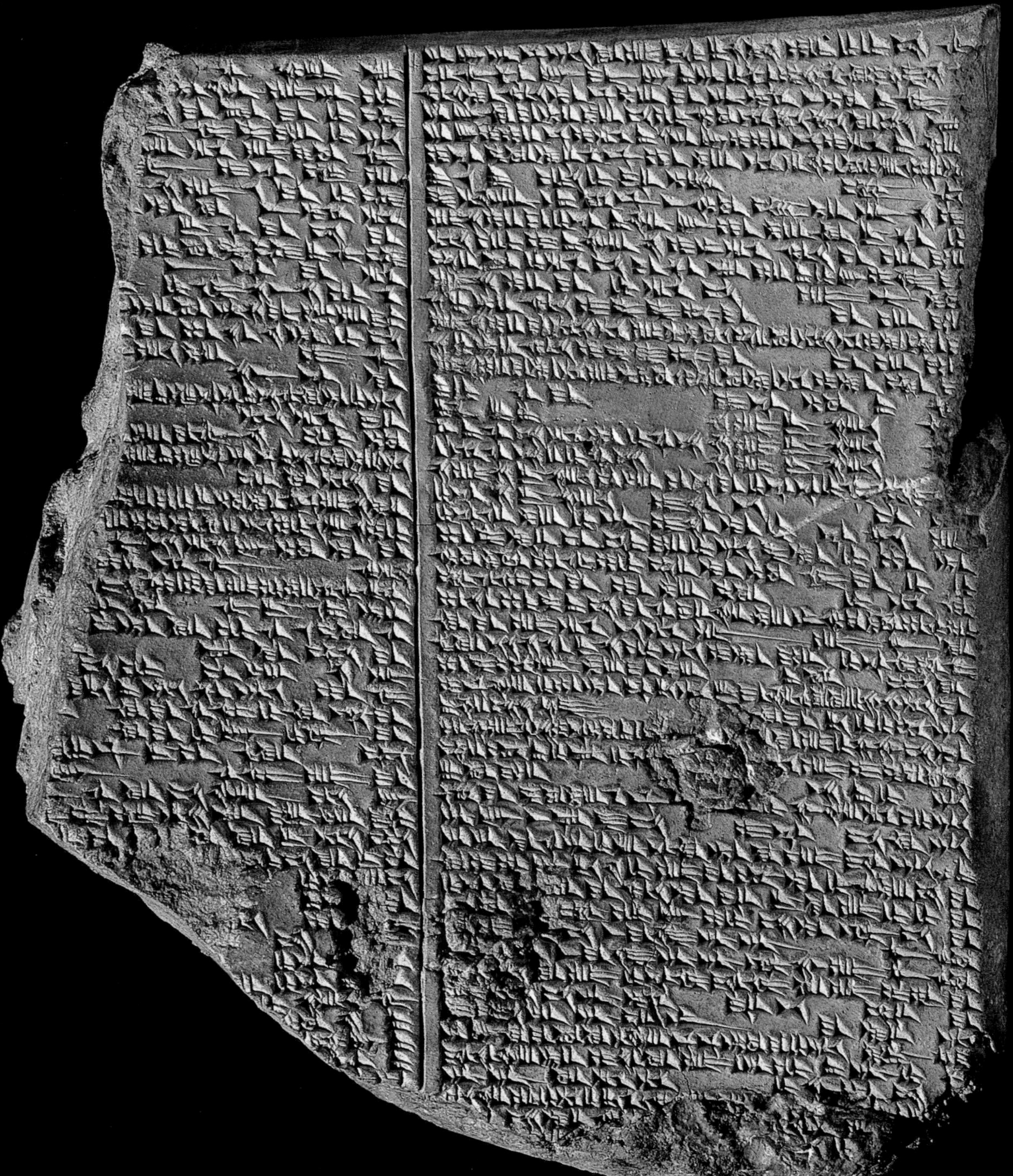

that the formation of the world and all its creatures took place within a single week, and that each step was pronounced by God to be good and perfectly created from its beginning; and it suggests that this all happened within a relatively accessible historical framework. A common calculation, based on the Bible, was that the Creation took place in 4004 BC. With the publication of Darwin's *Origin of Species*, a subtle change took place in popular consciousness. It made scepticism about the Bible fashionable. Before that time, an atheist would generally need to argue for his or her lack of belief. After 1859, the burden of proof began to fall the other way. A believer would now be obliged to defend a faith which revolved around a Bible which unexpectedly seemed to have emerged as contrary to science.

The argument (a false one) was that once it is admitted that even some of the

Bible might not be literally true, then all other parts of it too must be regarded as open to doubt. Equally false reasoning suggests that if one could actually prove the historical truth of some passages of the Bible independently and scientifically, then all the rest of Scripture would stand potentially vindicated. Earlier nineteenth-century rambles in the Near East had focused particularly (and often romantically) on identifying sites and monuments associated with the experiences of Jesus and Saint Paul. Darwin's theory of evolution, however, had primarily challenged the events recounted in the early parts of the Old Testament. It is striking to see how in the 1860s

219 previous page
This cuneiform tablet from excavations at Nineveh was revealed by George Smith in 1872 to contain an apparently independent account of Noah's flood
(LONDON, BRITISH MUSEUM)

220
The ancient monastery of St Catherine on Mount Sinai, seen here in a plate from David Roberts, The Holy Land *(1849), was almost inaccessible to western travellers until the nineteenth century. In 1859, Constantin Tischendorf persuaded the monks there to allow him to take away the* Codex Sinaiticus

and 1870s the public interest turned back towards Old Testament history. While palaeontologists were excavating prehistoric fossils which seemed to be demolishing the credibility of Genesis, there was simultaneously an insatiable interest in archaeological finds which offered tangible confirmation of statements in the early parts of Scripture. Consciously or unconsciously (probably often the latter), many people rejoiced at discoveries which seemed to prove the credibility of those parts of the Bible which were most under threat from science.

There was enormous public interest in 1868 when a German missionary discovered the so-called Moabite Stone, a broken round-topped stele of black basalt, found at Dîbân, in Jordan, east of the Dead Sea. The Stone is now in the Louvre in Paris. It is carved in very primitive Hebrew script, then the oldest ever found, and it commemorates in some detail the defeat of Israel after the death of Achab, around 850 BC, by Mesha, king of Moab. These events are described in II Kings 3:4-27. It was profoundly satisfying to confirm independently the historical veracity of one Bible story, known until then only from having been told and retold through the textual transmission of the Bible during more than two and a half thousand years, far away from the Moabite kingdom.

Even greater excitement was caused by the reading of cuneiform tablets. Many thousands of such tablets were first discovered by French and English archaeologists at Kuyunjik, on the presumed site of Nineveh, in modern Iraq, and these had been sent back to Europe in large numbers in the 1850s. They are mostly little rectangular blocks of hard terracotta, shaped like miniature cushions, inscribed with columns of writing formed from combinations of wedge-shaped patterns impressed into the clay while it was still wet. When baked, cuneiform tablets are almost indestructible. They are quite heavy to hold, and as dense as stones. Those dug from the excavations at Nineveh mostly date from the seventh century BC. Back in the museums of London, Paris and Berlin, scholars began the vast task of reading and transcribing the texts.

The first major revelation of the cuneiform tablets was announced in England in 1872. The public occasion was a meeting of the Society of Biblical Archaeology on 3 December. Rumours of what was about to be revealed ensured that the hall was packed. The Prime Minister, William Gladstone, adjourned Parliament so that he and others could attend. The speaker was George Smith (1840-76), a young deputy keeper at the British Museum. He described a half-tablet, with some of its lines of script nearly perfect, giving part of an independent account of Noah's Flood. The hero of the story had built himself a vast boat. The world was covered with water, as flat as the roof of a house. The boat eventually came to rest on the mountains of Nizir. The hero released a dove, but it returned to the boat, for there was no resting place. He sent a swallow and it too came back. Finally, he released a raven, which never returned. Then they knew that the waters were surely receding (Pl. 219).

This story has an almost exact parallel in Genesis 7:17−8:12. The account in the fragmentary tablet showed that the ancient legend was known in Mesopotamia, quite independently from the Hebrew account in the Old Testament, assumed to have been written in Palestine. The discovery was treated with exultation, as if archaeology had now supplied 'proof' of the Bible. The *Daily Telegraph* newspaper immediately offered Smith 1,000 guineas (£1,050) in order to return to Nineveh in search for the missing piece of his tablet. He took six months' leave of absence from the Museum and set out. Within only a few days of his arrival at the site at Kuyunjik, Smith was able to telegraph home that he had not only fortunately chanced upon the actual lost column of text itself (it describes the building of the boat and filling it with domestic and wild animals), but had also unearthed a cuneiform account of the Creation of the world. This, as he reported later (it was

published in the *Daily Telegraph* on 4 March 1875), described a period of chaos
before the creation of the world, the fall of a celestial creature who initiates a war
in heaven, and the eventual creation of a universe in separate stages, culminating
in man, who is made free from evil but yields to temptation and falls. He wrote a
hugely popular book about his finds. Its long title gives a good idea of its subject.
It is called *The Chaldean Account of Genesis, Containing the Description of the Creation, the Fall of Man, the Deluge, the Tower of Babel, the Times of the Patriarchs, and
Nimrod; Babylonian Fables and Legends of the Gods; from the Cuneiform Inscriptions*,
London, 1876. The public was given a taste of the origins of Genesis. Smith did
not mention Darwin but his conclusions seemed at last to offer a Creation story
more consistent with science than the version in the Bible. The cuneiform
account, he wrote, allows for 'the creation of legions of monster forms which disappeared before the human epoch' (implicit dinosaurs) and an enormous period
of prehistoric time – 432,000 years, if all added up – between the Creation and the
Flood, and a further 34,080 years between the Flood and the Median conquest
of Persia. In effect, the theory of evolution was being applied by archaeology to
the Bible. The Babylonian tablets were parallel to fossils from which all living
creatures descended. The finding of remote ancestors of the book of Genesis
placed even the Bible in a reassuring and fashionable evolutionary context. It
was a first major step into modern biblical scholarship, which seeks to make
the Bible correspond to scientific research rather than the other way round.

The search for documentary confirmation of the Old Testament was vigor-
ously pursued in Germany. The classic textbook was by Professor Eberhard
Schrader, of Berlin, called *Keilinschriften und das Alte Testament* ('Cuneiform
Inscriptions and the Old Testament'), Giessen, 1872, greatly enlarged in 1883,
and translated into English in 1885. It was superseded by Alfred Jeremias, *Das
Alte Testament im Lichte des Alten Orients* ('The Old Testament in the Light of the
Ancient Orient'), Leipzig, 1903, still in print in 1930. American scholars too
joined the search. Thousands more cuneiform tablets were found by American
archaeologists at Nippur in Mesopotamia in 1888-1900, including further
narratives of the Flood. In 1885, the German Assyriologist Paul Haupt (1858–
1926) was recruited from Göttingen to the new Oriental Seminary at Johns
Hopkins University in Baltimore, and founded a tradition of American research
into biblical documents which still flourishes. The supply of cuneiform tablets
from excavations shows no apparent sign of ever abating. In the 1990s, for
example, tens of thousands more were thrown up by the digging of a govern-
mental canal in Iraq.

Modern scholarship requires some of George Smith's pioneering identifica-
tions to be greatly refined. His reading of the tablet with the Fall of Man, for
example, was apparently little more than wishful thinking. The extract on the
great Flood, which caused such a sensation in 1872, is a small part of the tale
now known as the *Epic of Gilgamesh*. The whole text has now been completely

recovered and is widely known. The Flood story of Smith's discovery occurs in
what is called Tablet XI in modern editions. It derives from even older legends,
for similar stories of the Flood have subsequently been found also in tablets from
the Old Babylonian period, datable to around the eighteenth century BC, more
than a thousand years earlier. The supposed missing column, which Smith so
miraculously located in the 1870s, was actually part of a similar-sized tablet
of yet another but different cuneiform text, now called the *Epic of Atra-Hasīs*,
contemporary with Gilgamesh and likewise deriving from the same archaic
Babylonian source. This does not belittle Smith's achievement (there was no way
he could have known otherwise); and, in fact, the knowledge that the stories of
the Flood, for example, were part of the pool of folk legend in early Babylon is
crucial for our modern understanding of the evolution of Genesis. The reasoning
is as follows. Jerusalem was conquered by Nebuchadnezzar (604–562 BC) and the
Jews were deported in 597 and 586 BC, as recounted in II Kings 24:14–16 and
25:11. For several generations the Jews were exiled in Babylon until after that
city was itself conquered by Cyrus the Great of Persia in 538 BC. Before they
were taken captive, the Jews doubtless already had many holy texts, including
the ancient laws of Moses and the graphic accounts of the Israelites' exodus out
of Egypt. The Bible itself offers little information about the existence of sacred
scrolls, for example, in the accounts of religious life in early Israel. We are told
about the Ark of the Covenant and about Temple vessels but not about manuscripts. There is some suggestion that the sacred texts were rendered inaccessible
or at risk while the Jews were in Babylon, or that perhaps they were preserved
only by faithful priestly memory. Some time after King Cyrus had allowed the
Jews to return home and to rebuild and to re-equip the Temple of Jerusalem, so,
the Bible tells us, Ezra the Scribe proclaimed the Law of Moses, dictating the
approved text to five scribes (Nehemiah 8:1–12; and II Esdras 14:23–48). This
event is difficult to date but evidently took place in Jerusalem between about 530
and about 400 BC. It is universally accepted that, from that moment onwards, the
text of the Pentateuch at least was in its more or less definitive written form. It
is the first real evidence in the Bible itself of the existence of a holy and authentic
written scriptural text. It was proposed by German scholars of the late nineteenth
century that the strands of Genesis which have specific parallels in Mesopotamian
folk legend – such as the accounts of the Creation and the Flood – had simply
been absorbed and reconciled into the Israelite sacred traditions during the
time that the exiled Jews were in Babylon in the sixth century BC. Through the
decipherment of cuneiform tablets, therefore, we can see the text of the Bible in
a much wider cultural setting and as subject to general principles of evolution.

The gradual realization that the text of the Bible might have evolved from
various sources became a matter of great public interest from the late nineteenth
century. There were those who challenged the traditional authorship of the texts;
and those who suggested radically redating the writing of the Gospels, for

example, to many centuries later than the lifetimes of the four named evangelists. There was a popular suspicion that the texts might have been greatly contaminated by additions and deliberate alterations during their formative periods in the ancient world. Interest began to focus on the earliest extant copies of the Bible. The *Codex Sinaiticus*, safe but not greatly admired in St Petersburg, was fully edited by Tischendorf in 1862. A vast photographic facsimile of the fourth-century *Codex Alexandrinus* was published by the British Museum in four volumes in 1879-83, in loose sheets enclosed in dark red cloth portfolios. E. Maunde Thompson's preface to the first volume begins: 'The publication of an autotype facsimile of the *Codex Alexandrinus* has been authorized by the Trustees of the British Museum from a desire to place the text within the reach of scholars in a form free from the errors of the printing press and untouched by the hand.' It is worth noting this reassurance that the text was demonstrably uncorrupted by editors. There is no transcription. Interested readers were expected to be able to read the uncial Greek script directly from the dark brown printed photographs. Similar facsimiles were published of the *Codex Vaticanus* in 1889-90, the *Codex Bezae* in 1899, and the *Codex Sinaiticus* in 1911-22 (Pl. 221).

Another line of inquiry into the evolutionary descent of the Bible was to examine the early Christian translations of the Bible into exotic vernacular languages. It was well known (or at least widely accepted) that the original language of the Old Testament was Hebrew and that that of the New Testament

221

There was demand for photographic facsimiles by people interested in checking the sources of the Bible text for themselves. This is the facsimile of the Codex Sinaiticus, *1911–22*

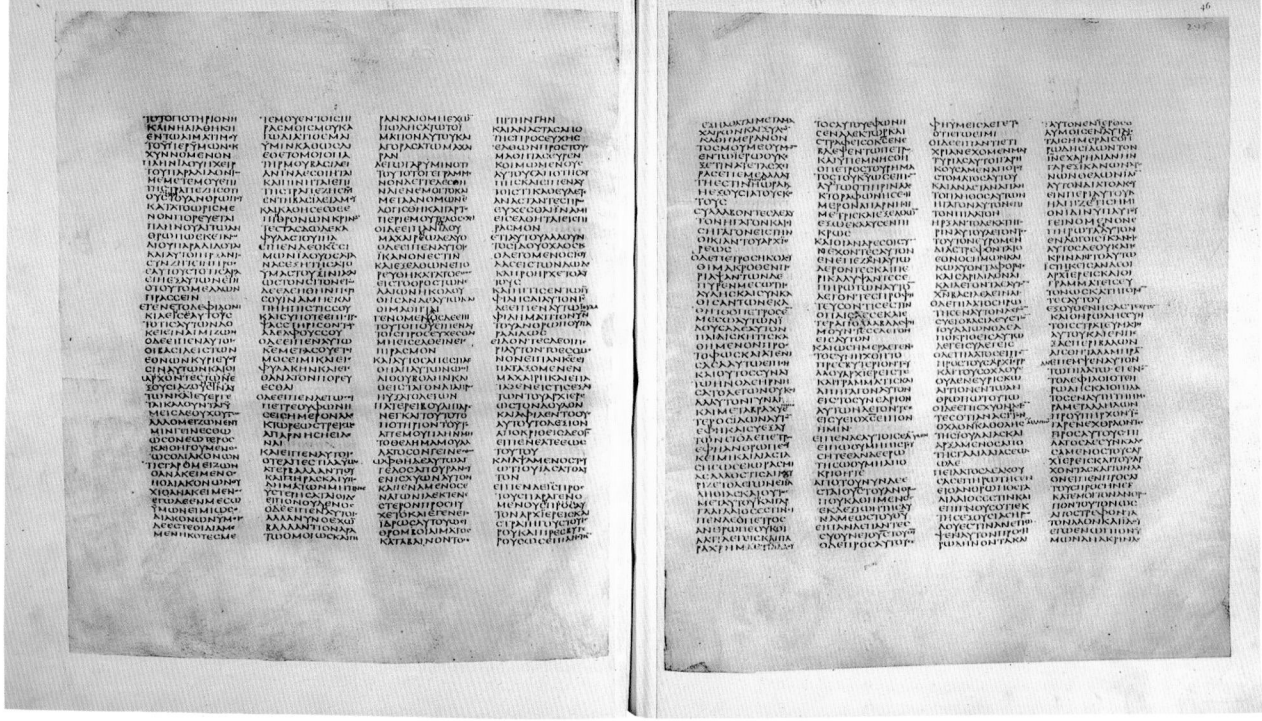

was Greek, but that the oldest extant manuscripts of these were ninth- and fourth-century respectively. A number of primitive translations of the Bible were made for the use of early Christians who did not necessarily understand Greek, and these versions survived in later copies of copies of manuscripts in Syriac, Coptic, Ethiopic, Old Latin, and so on. These are potentially of great interest. If one could show that the translations had actually been made from the Greek text at a period earlier than that of any surviving Greek manuscript, then one might, in theory, have an independent reflection of the Bible in an older stage of its evolution. Even a late manuscript of a very early translation might help reconstruct a retrospective textual tradition of very great value.

One early search was for the lost *Diatessaron* of Tatian. This is a complicated example but is worth examining for what it tells about late nineteenth-century biblical inquiry. The fourth-century historian Eusebius mentions a single-volume Gospel harmony which had been assembled by Tatian, of Syria, who put together a sequence of direct quotations from all four Gospels to form a single consecutive narrative. It was rather like the seventeenth-century Gospel Harmonies of Nicholas Ferrar which we encountered above (pp. 250–1), assembled with scissors and paste. The title '*Diatessaron*' means 'through four' in Greek. Eusebius says that it was widely used in Syriac-speaking churches, in place of the Gospels. It was systematically suppressed in the early fifth century because of concern that Tatian had been a heretic. The importance lies in the fact that Tatian had lived in the second century, and had became a Christian in Rome in *c.*150–65 AD. His *Diatessaron* was evidently already in circulation by about 172 AD when Tatian returned to the east. This is very early indeed in the history of the New Testament, hardly a hundred years after the lifetimes of the reputed evangelists. If, therefore, the text of the *Diatessaron* could be found and authenticated, it would prove that all four Gospels were known and in circulation, presumably in Rome, by the third quarter of the second century, far earlier than any surviving Gospel manuscript known in the late nineteenth century. Many sceptics doubted that the Gospels were as old, or that the *Diatessaron* had ever been a real text.

It was found by the American Unitarian scholar, Ezra Abbot (1819-84), of Harvard. In 1880 he realized that a Latin translation (published in 1876) of a very early Armenian version of the works of Saint Ephraem the Syrian (*c.*306–373) included a Syriac commentary on the *Diatessaron* with quotations from the actual text, translated into Armenian perhaps in the fifth century. Those citations then allowed a medieval oriental manuscript in the Vatican Library (cod. arab. 14) to be recognized as an Arabic translation of the virtually entire *Diatessaron* of Tatian (Pl. 222), which was then published by 1888. The vindication of the *Diatessaron* as a real text gave a date by which the Gospels were already in circulation, a fact now accepted even by those who had initially been sceptical. Although the quotations from the Gospel texts were recovered from an Arabic translation of the Syriac translation of the Greek (presumably), in a

البستان مع حبيب بدأ ثمعون حرم وحلف أني لا اعرف
هذا الرجل الذي كمن كذب لو وفي الوقت وهو في حال كلامه
صقع الديك دفعتين وفي تلك الساعة التفت يسوع
وهو حاح وتامل الصفا وذكر ثمعون كلامه سيدنا التي كان قال
له مراانه من قبل ان يصقع الديك مرتين تكرني ثلث دفعات
لو وخرج ثمعون الى الخارج وبكا كا اءمرا ولماذا الصلح
اجتمع سرقة جمع عظما الكهنه والكتاب ومشيخه الشعب
والجمع كله واعملوا حيله مت ونشاورا واعلى يسوع لكي يميتوه
والتمسوا شهودا زورا يشهدون عليه ليميتوه ولم يجدوا ٥
ووافى كثيرون من شهوه الزور ولم تستوى شهاداتهم واخيرا
نقدم اثنان من شهود الافك وقالا لحن سمعناه قال باني
انقض هذا هيكل الله المعمول بالايدي وابني اخر لم يصنع
بالايدي بعد ثلثة ايام وهكذا ايضا تعقب شهادتهم
وكان يسوع ساكتا وقام عظيم الكهنه في الوسط
وسال يسوع وقال مت الانجيل يحرف عن شئ اذا يشهد
عليك هولاء مت ويسوع كان ساكتا ولم يجبه لشئ لو

manuscript more than a thousand years later than Tatian, it now became possible

third or even in late second century AD (Pl. 237) – and the Boharic, the dialect of northern (or Lower) Egypt. This was apparently somewhat later in date than the Sahidic, perhaps because Egyptians living nearer the Mediterranean were more familiar with Greek. The Sahidic text has a number of textual oddities, including a form of the book of Job which is about one sixth shorter than the standard text of the Hebrew or Greek.

Ethiopia too was converted very early, certainly by the fourth century. An Ethiopian Christian is mentioned in the Bible (Acts 8:27). Very many Ethiopian manuscripts and other works of art found their way back to England as spoils of the Abyssinian War of 1867. The written language of Ethiopia is Ge'ez. The Ethiopian biblical canon preserves several ancient texts long-since eliminated from the Western Bible. One of these is the book of Enoch (Pl. 224), an apocryphal text of the Old Testament which is quoted in the Epistle of Jude, verses 14-15. It remained entirely unknown in Greek or Latin until a good part of the text was unexpectedly excavated in Egypt in 1886, and it was not known in Hebrew until the discovery of the Dead Sea Scrolls. Ethiopian manuscripts raised high hopes when they were first brought to Europe. Many give the appearance of great

antiquity, massive primitive-looking square codices on thick parchment, laced into wooden boards. Generally, however, they have proved to be disappointing, for most copies are very much more recent than their appearance suggests: virtually no Ethiopian book is older than the fourteenth century and most, indeed, are only eighteenth- or even nineteenth-century. If the text is early, which it may be, it was evidently so revised and contaminated in the late Middle Ages that its evidential value for the Bible text is slight.

Throughout the nineteenth and early twentieth century, biblical manuscripts of widely varying textual significance were gathered relentlessly by north European and American collections from ancient neglected monasteries of North

Africa and the Levant. We have seen Tischendorf righteously extracting the *Codex Sinaiticus* from its old home in St Catherine's on Mount Sinai in 1859. Another confident predator of monasteries was the Rev Henry Tattam (1789–1868), archdeacon of Bedford. He acquired several hundred manuscripts from the almost abandoned monastery of St Maria Deipara, in the Nitrian desert in Lower Egypt, most of which were sent back to the British Museum. They include a Peshitta manuscript of Genesis, Exodus, Numbers and Deuteronomy, written in 464 AD, one of the oldest dated biblical manuscripts known (now London, BL, Add. MS. 14425, Pl. 224). Tattam also visited the decaying monastery of Bishoi, in the Wadi Natrun, the desert north-east of Cairo. His stepdaughter wrote an account of searching by lighted taper in a dark vaulted room there, knee-deep in loose leaves of ancient manuscripts. Tattam came away with pieces of the Pentateuch and the Gospels. That same monastic store room furnished further biblical fragments in 1870 (now in the Universitätsbibliothek in Göttingen), in 1873 (now mostly in the British Library), in 1923 (now untraced) and some leaves were even still available from Bishoi as late as 1959 (now in the Staats- und Universitätsbibliothek in Hamburg). Henry Tattam's personal collection of biblical papyri in Coptic was sold at Sotheby's in London in 1868. It was bought then by Lord Crawford and eventually it passed intact to the John Rylands Library in Manchester, where it came to form the nucleus of a major research collection of early biblical fragments.

Other ancient deposits of manuscripts in their final stages of decline included the White Monastery, near Sohag, in Upper Egypt. From the late eighteenth century, this monastery had furnished manuscripts for local antiquities dealers, who kept their source secret for over a hundred years. In 1883 more than 9,000 fragments in Coptic were finally removed from the remains of the White Monastery, mostly now in the

Bibliothèque Nationale de France. Even vaster numbers of manuscript fragments were taken from the Geniza of the Jewish synagogue at Fustat, in the southern suburbs of Cairo. The word *geniza* means 'hiding' in Hebrew. Traditionally even defective Hebrew manuscripts could never be destroyed if they included mention of the divine name. Obsolete and imperfect manuscripts, especially Bibles, would often be collected into a geniza for safe-keeping until they could eventually be taken out and buried. For some reason, the Cairo Geniza seems to have remained unemptied from its foundation in 882 until the nineteenth century, by which time it was said locally to have become the abode of snakes and demons. Dealers had found their way in by 1891. In 1896-8, two Cambridge academics, Solomon Shechter and Charles Taylor, Master of St John's College, travelled to Cairo and they secured tens of thousands of fragments from the Geniza for Cambridge University Library (Pl. 225). Some pieces were as old as any Hebrew biblical manuscripts then known. Among the texts which emerged were leaves of the book of Ecclesiasticus in Hebrew. This apocryphal text had been rejected from the canon of the Hebrew Bible and it was known only from the translations into Greek and Syriac. The Cairo Geniza furnished for the first time many fragments of Ecclesiasticus in the long-lost original language. These were published in 1898–1901.

225

Large numbers of early Hebrew manuscript fragments were recovered from the Geniza of the Jewish synagogue at Fustat, near Cairo, in 1896–8. These are parchment leaves of Hebrew Bibles (CAMBRIDGE UNIVERSITY LIBRARY, TAYLOR-SCHECHTER COLLECTION, T-S A2.7)

From searching half-abandoned buildings to digging in the ground is only a small step. A very large number of relics of early biblical manuscripts were excavated in Egypt in the late nineteenth and twentieth centuries. Many were written on papyrus, the standard writing material throughout the ancient Mediterranean, described above in Chapter 2. Doubtless most or all of the New Testament had originally been written down on papyrus. Until the nineteenth century almost no pieces of original ancient papyrus were known to have survived. Little by little, however, small finds of papyri began to emerge from the dry sands of Egypt. Very early fragments both of classical and biblical texts were brought back in increasing numbers to Europe, to the delight and bewilderment of textual scholars. A tiny piece of third-century papyrus found in the Fayûm in Egypt in 1882, for example, proved to be from a narrative Greek text similar but not identical to Mark 14:27–30, in which Christ predicted that Saint Peter would deny him three times. It appeared to be from an otherwise unknown Gospel. It is now in the Österreich-ische Nationalbibliothek in Vienna. Excavations at Achmîm (ancient Panopolis) on the edge of the Fayûm in 1886-7 furnished portions of several major apocry-phal texts on the fringes of the Bible. These included the first 36 chapters of the Greek text of the book of Enoch, cited above, and two worrying Christian apocryphal texts similar but not identical to anything in the New Testament. Both were published by M.R. James in 1892. One was a codex of the so-called Gospel of Peter, a text recorded in the late second century but of which no other copy has ever been found. The other comprised a number of fragments from the Apocalypse of Peter, a strange text in which Christ grants the Apostles a vision of the life to come. It probably dates from the second century and it was hitherto known from brief quotations by other writers, including Clement of Alexandria (*c*.150-*c*.215).

By the late 1880s, expeditions were being organized to Egypt to excavate for papyri and other early manuscript fragments. The museums of Berlin and London and the Bibliothèque Nationale in Paris all conducted major forays into the deserts of the Fayûm in 1887–8. It would be an exaggeration to compare such searches with gold rushes, but there was certainly an urgent frenzy of digging. One of the most productive of these archaeological safaris was undertaken for Oxford University in 1896–7 at Oxyrhynchus, to the west of the Nile near the modern town of Behnesa, about 120 miles (180 kilometres) from Cairo. Ancient Oxyrhynchus had been well-known in the fourth and fifth centuries for its churches and monasteries. The excavations there produced an immense number of papyrus fragments. At the height of the expedition in 1897 over a hundred men were being employed to dig, and up to 36 basketfuls of manuscript fragments were being brought up out of the excavation every day. All these were diligently sent back to the Ashmolean Museum in Oxford and to the British Museum. The finds are almost all assigned to between about 200 and 400 AD. They include many biblical fragments. The oldest is a piece with the text of Matthew 23:30–9, datable to about 200 AD (Oxford, Ashmolean Museum, P. Oxy. 2683, Pl. 226). One rarity is a papyrus palimpsest. It was originally used in the third century for an epitome of Livy but soon afterwards its script was erased and the manuscript was rewritten on top with the Epistle to the Hebrews. Probably the most famous find from Oxyrhynchus, excavated in January 1897, is what was widely published as the *Sayings of Jesus*. It appeared to be part of an entirely unknown and disconcertingly credible Gospel, with short moral statements, similar to the Beatitudes, spoken by Jesus to his disciples. In 1860 sceptics had wondered if the Gospels might not prove to be largely spurious: by 1900, the Gospels had been not only been securely traced back to the second century, at least, but they seemed to be emerging as only a small part of the early documentary

226

*Excavations at Oxyrhynchus
in Egypt in 1887–8 furnished
many fragments of early
Christian books, including
a piece of Saint Matthew's
Gospel of c.200 AD*
(OXFORD, ASHMOLEAN
MUSEUM, P. OXY. 2683)

227 opposite

*Part of an early Coptic library
was unearthed in 1910 on the
site of an abandoned monastery
near Hamuli in the southern
Fayûm in Egypt. Several manuscripts were still in the remains
of their original bindings; this
covered a Gospel Book in the
Sahidic dialect of the seventh
or eighth century*
(NEW YORK, PIERPONT
MORGAN LIBRARY, M. 569)

evidence for the life and teachings of Christ. These
were heady days for Bible historians.

While European archaeologists were sifting
the sands for fragments, local opportunists
continued to make chance discoveries. Once it
became apparent that manuscripts were potentially valuable, processions of hopeful Egyptians
seem to have brought finds to antiquities dealers
in Cairo. Some of the most important of all early
biblical manuscripts have no known provenance
beyond having been purchased in curio shops in
Egypt. Private collectors entered the market too,
prepared to pay serious prices. The archaeologist
Arthur Hunt bought fragments for Mrs Rylands
(1843-1908), then assembling a library in memory
of her late husband, John Rylands. Her acquisitions included a remarkably early
piece of the first and second chapters of the Epistle of Titus in Greek, written
around 200 AD (now Manchester, John Rylands University Library, Gr. Pap. 5).
A collector whose interests covered a wide range of early biblical languages was
Lord Amherst of Hackney (1835-1908). One of his fragments bought in Egypt,
published in 1900, was a letter on papyrus sent from Rome to a Christian community in Egypt, probably in the Fayûm, datable to c.264-82 AD. The especial
interest is that the letter is written on the back of a sheet which comprises the
first five verses of Genesis, in Greek, the earliest record of the opening of the
Bible in the Septuagint (now New York, Pierpont Morgan Library, Amherst
Papyri G.3). Towards the end of 1906 a dealer in Gizah, near Cairo, came up with
two substantially complete Greek manuscripts of the fifth century, no less, doubt-
less recently excavated. They were sold to a Detroit industrialist, Charles L. Freer.
One was a codex of Deuteronomy and Joshua. The second was a volume with
all four Gospels. Both are now in the Freer Gallery of Art in the Smithsonian
Institution, Washington. The Gospel text joins *Sinaiticus*, *Alexandrinus* and
Vaticanus as one of the fundamental witnesses to the Greek text. The text of
Saint Mark includes one verse not apparently recorded elsewhere. Between
Mark 16:14 and 16:15, Christ adds a statement that the reign of the Devil is over
and that fearful things are about to happen to those sinners whom Christ came
to save, and for whom he has prepared spiritual and incorruptible glory in
heaven. The style and context of the verse suggests the real possibility that
this may indeed be an authentic lost sentence from the Gospel.

Many other chance finds have been made in Egypt. Pieces of ancient mummy
wrappings were bought for the Rylands Library in 1917 because they were made
up from layers of compacted papyrus sheets. When these were carefully peeled
away, they proved to include small fragments of Deuteronomy 23-8 in Greek,

confidently dated to the mid-second century BC (Manchester, John Rylands University Library, Gr. Pap. 458). Even now, this is one of the oldest biblical manuscripts ever found. At such a date, of course, the manuscript must have been made for Greek-speaking Jews. The burial which reused the papyrus Deuteronomy roll was probably in the Fayûm, where there were two Jewish synagogues. In 1920, the Rylands Library was fortunate to obtain an even more spectacular acquisition. It that year the Library bought from Cairo a group of several hundred small papyrus fragments, perhaps originally either from Oxyrhynchus or from the Fayûm. One tiny broken piece, in the shape of a stepped triangle, is clearly from a codex, for it is written on both sides (Gr. Pap. 457). It has part of seven

lines in Greek (Pl. 228). The recto is from John 18:31-3 and the verso from John 18:37-8. This includes the famous verse when Pontius Pilate asks 'What is truth?' Palaeography can never furnish an exact date for any sample of script, but the piece was published in 1935 with the suggested dating of *c.*125 AD. This extraordinarily assured attribution appears to be universally accepted. Assuming the estimated date is really secure, this is by a comfortable margin the oldest acknowledged piece of the New Testament and is the earliest tangible evidence for the existence of Saint John's Gospel.

A major hoard of Greek early Christian manuscripts was unearthed in Egypt in or soon before 1931. The discoveries are known generally as the 'Chester Beatty Papyri', from the fact that most of them were bought *en bloc* by the American mining engineer, Alfred Chester Beatty (1875-1968), who was then living in London and who bequeathed his library to the people of Dublin. 'Their place of origin is unknown', wrote F.G. Kenyon in publishing the papyri in 1933, 'since they reached him through the hands of natives and dealers, whose statements as to *provenance* are not always reliable.' It is generally assumed that the Chester Beatty Papyri are from a single find. To judge from the dialect of Coptic glosses added to one of the manuscripts, it seems likely that the books were used in the region of the Fayûm. The hoard comprised parts or all of at least twelve early Christian codices, mostly biblical. Most are written on tall narrow pages. The latest dates from around the end of the fourth century and most were probably written in the third century. The earliest is a damaged codex with 50 leaves of Numbers and Deuteronomy, apparently of the second century (MS. VI). Another dates from around 200 AD, a nearly complete volume of the Epistles of Saint Paul, the oldest known (MS. II, Pl. 229). Substantial manuscripts of Isaiah (MS. VII) and the Gospels and Acts together (MS. I) are both ascribed to the early third century. Other texts include Genesis (two copies), Ezekiel, Daniel and the Apocalypse. One of the latest is part of a fourth-century copy of the final eleven chapters of the book of Enoch, completing the Greek text of which an earlier part had first been found in 1886, as described above. Between them, the Chester Beatty Papyri provide an impressive run of texts from the Greek Bible, most of them significantly earlier than even the *Codex Sinaiticus.*

The discovery of the Chester Beatty manuscripts was first announced in *The Times* on 17 November 1931 and created great public excitement. It quickly became apparent that the dealers who furnished the papyri must have disposed of portions of their hoard elsewhere. Other parts of the Pauline Epistles manuscript had been sold to the University of Michigan at Ann Arbor (Inv. no. 6238), and fragments of the Gospel Book had been bought by the Nationalbibliothek in Vienna (P. Vindob. G. 31974). A substantial part of the Ezekiel manuscript then emerged in the Scheide Collection, now at Princeton University. It may be that Schøyen MS. 2650, Oslo and London, is from the same source (Pl. 230). This manuscript has resurfaced only recently. It comprises a large part of a fourth-century papyrus codex of Saint Matthew's Gospel in Coptic, not similar to any other copy known in either Greek or Coptic. Its textual status is still unsure but it seems to have been translated from something other than the straightforward Greek text.

It is very noticeable how often the precise origins of manuscript finds are obfuscated. This was prudent of the sellers, for throughout a good part of the last hundred years the export of archaeological artefacts from Egypt has been illegal. Equally striking, as one looks back from a modern cultural perspective, is how European buyers seem almost to have relished the surreptitious trading practices of Levantine vendors. Furtive complicity added to the excitement of collecting. The catalogue of the Coptic manuscripts in the Freer Collection, for example, published in 1923, reports that their dealer supplied misleading provenances: 'Later he owned that the statement was false, and produced the actual finders, who maintained that the manuscripts had been discovered at a spot which … cannot at present be named.' 'When no locality is named', according to the preface to the Rylands catalogue of papyri in 1911, 'it is to be inferred that satisfactory testimony was not forthcoming.' No further questions were asked; vagueness of legal title or export documentation was no hindrance to purchasers. It must have been felt that the end justified the means. Even the most dispassionate of papyrologists evidently experienced a certain excitement and awe at the gathering in of the Bible, which, whether for religious reasons or not, was still the foundation text of European life. That tells us as much about Europe in the first half of the twentieth

228 opposite

This fragment, discovered in 1920, contains part of Saint John's Gospel in Greek and is believed to date from c.125 AD. If the dating is correct, it is the earliest witness to any of the Gospels (MANCHESTER, JOHN RYLANDS UNIVERSITY LIBRARY, GR. PAP. 457)

229

The Chester Beatty Papyri were found in Egypt in or soon before 1931. They include an almost complete manuscript of the Epistles of Saint Paul in Greek, datable to c.200 AD (DUBLIN, CHESTER BEATTY LIBRARY, PAP. MS. II)

century as it does about the papyri themselves. There was undoubtedly a feeling of righteousness and patriotism about bringing the Bible back to Europe and to America, safely into the appropriate possession of Western Christendom.

The same emotion touched the purchase by the British Museum of the *Codex Sinaiticus* in 1933. In the early 1930s it became known that the Soviet government, having more need for hard currency than for religion, would be prepared to part with the great Greek Bible which Constantin Tischendorf had dispatched to the Tsar in 1859. There was no question of offering it back to St Catherine's on Mount Sinai. The *Codex* was initially proposed to buyers in America and Switzerland at dazzling prices. It was finally bought for £100,000 by the British government, aided by public subscriptions. It was carried up the steps of the British Museum, to the sound of cheering and a brass band, on 27 December 1933 (Pl. 231).

Two further very important caches of early Christian manuscripts have been found in Egypt since the Second Word War. On both cases, a great deal of elaborate information has been elicited from the finders about the discoveries. If the stories are to be believed, both hoards were dug up quite near each other, seven years apart. The first group of manuscripts was found in about December 1945 in Upper Egypt, on the right bank of the Nile near Jebel el-Tarif, about 6 miles (9.5 kilometres) east of the town of Nag Hammadi. Because of this place, they are now commonly known as the 'Nag Hammadi Papyri'. They were found by two brothers who were digging for fertilizer. The manuscripts were buried in a red clay jar, sealed with bitumen, hidden at the foot of a cliff at the edge of the desert. The fragile-looking books were deposited for safe-keeping with a local Coptic priest, whose brother-in-law arranged to get them up to Cairo for possible sale. After many delays and rapid changes of ownership, only one manuscript was successfully sold abroad, acquired in 1952 by the Jung Institute in Zurich. The others were eventually acquired by the Egyptian state in 1956 and were assigned in 1959 to the custody of the Coptic Museum in Cairo. The book which had reached Zurich, now disbound, was returned to Egypt a few portions at a time between 1960 and 1975. The lid of the jar in which the manuscripts were found and the detached binding of the former Jung volume are both now in the Schøyen Collection. A half leaf is preserved in the Beinecke Library at Yale. Apart from these salvaged relics, however, the entire Nag Hammadi hoard is now together again, in its country of origin.

The second deposit of manuscripts was found towards the end of 1952, about 7½ miles (12 kilometres) to the east of the Nag Hammadi site, near the village of

Dishnā. The manuscripts are known either as the 'Dishna Papers' or the 'Bodmer Papyri'. Neither term is strictly accurate. Like the Nag Hammadi books, the manuscripts eventually reached the dealers in Cairo through various horrendously devious routes (including a kidnap of a girl and the midnight bribing of police guards). This time foreign buyers were found discreetly and the manuscripts were spirited abroad. Most were acquired between 1953 and 1958 by the

late Dr Martin Bodmer (1899–1971); these are now in the Fondation Martin Bodmer, at Cologny, on Lake Geneva. Other buyers included the Chester Beatty Library again, the Palau-Ribes Collection in Barcelona, Duke University and the University of Mississippi. The two books which went to Mississippi were afterwards resold;

one is now privately owned in Florida and the other is MS. 193 of the Schøyen Collection. Dr Bodmer gave part of one of his manuscripts to the pope, and it is now in the Vatican Library.

Both the Nag Hammadi and Dishnā sites are within easy walking distance of the ruins of two of the earliest monasteries in Egypt, founded by Saint Pachomius (*c.*290–346). One was Chenoboskia, where Pachomius himself had set up his first hermitage. The other was the headquarters of the Pachomian Order at Pabua, a larger monastic complex nearby. We know from contemporary texts that the early Pachomian monasteries encouraged the use of books and lent them out to the monks. On the face of it, it seems likely that the two very substantial burials of Christian manuscripts might have come from the library of the local Pachomian monks. The problem is that the two deposits are extremely different in their nature. The Nag Hammadi books are mostly heretical and mystical texts, seemingly unsuitable for a conventional monastery. The Bodmer Papyri, by contrast, are extremely orthodox and they include a good run of classical texts, as well as books of the Bible. Both are important. Let us consider them briefly in turn.

The Nag Hammadi manuscripts comprise 12 codices and part of a thirteenth, with a total of 52 texts (including six duplicates). They are all written in the Sahidic dialect of Coptic. They date from the third to the sixth century. Many are expressly Gnostic treatises, that is, texts from the mystical Christian sect concerned with religious knowledge (*gnosis* in Greek), based on spiritual revelation. The mainstream Christian Church was deeply suspicious of Gnosticism and condemned its followers as heretics. What is so fascinating from the point of view of

230
This fourth-century papyrus of Saint Matthew's Gospel in Coptic has only recently come to light. It appears to represent an otherwise unknown recension of the text
(OSLO AND LONDON, THE SCHØYEN COLLECTION, MS. 2650)

231
This is Mr Martin Schøyen, the Norwegian collector of biblical manuscripts, with the Codex Sinaiticus *in the old British Museum building in 1995*

biblical history is that the Nag Hammadi hoard includes very many early texts just outside the fringes of the Bible as we know it. Here is the unique copy of the Gospel of Philip, on the quest for salvation, with sayings attributed to Christ. Here too are the Acts of Peter, which includes the earliest reference to the *Quo Vadis?* story, not told in the Bible. There are multiple volumes with the Apocalypses of Paul, James and Adam, and the substantial Apocalypse of Peter, of which the first recorded fragments had been found at Achmîm in the late 1880s. The most famous text of all is the only known complete copy of the Gospel of Thomas (Pl. 232). This is so like part of the actual Bible that it is distinctly unnerving. It is a collection of 114 statements or parables said to have been spoken by Jesus in his lifetime. On its discovery it became apparent that the tantalizing fragment of the so-called *Sayings of Jesus*, excavated at Oxyrhynchus in 1897, was simply a small piece from the newly found Gospel of Thomas. The text includes slightly different perspectives on many tales already known from the four conventional Gospels, such as the parable of the sower (verse 9, cf. Matthew 13:1–9, Mark 4:3–9, Luke 8:4–8), the parable of the vine-yard and the tenants (verse 65, cf. Matthew 21:33–9, Mark 12:1–8, Luke 20:9–15) and the story of the tribute coin which Christ tells his hearers to pay to Caesar, whose portrait it shows (verse 100, cf. Matthew 22:17–21, Mark 12:14–17, Luke 20:22–6). Many are quite new. Verse 37, for example, refers to a habit of small children in all ages. It reads: 'His disciples said, When will you become revealed to us and when shall we see you? Jesus said, When you disrobe without being ashamed and take up your garments and place them under your feet like little children and tread on them, then [will you see] the son of the living one, and you will not be afraid.'

The Bodmer group of papyri is much larger and a great deal more orthodox. It consists of nine rolls and 29 codices. Their dates range from the late second century to the early seventh, and there are books in Greek, Coptic and Latin. Twenty-four of the volumes include biblical texts, of which 12 are in Greek. There is a notable group of classical texts, especially Homer but including Menander, Thucydides and Cicero. These seem so unexpected in a Christian devotional library that it has been wondered if these might be parts of two hoards, added together to make the total more saleable. It is simplest, however, to accept that they do indeed belong together, and that early Christians in Upper Egypt were intimate with the Greek and Roman classics. That too gives a valuable context for the studying the early circulation of the Bible. There are a couple of apocryphal texts, including the book of James, a detailed account of the birth and childhood of Jesus, and the unique Greek text of a third letter to the Corinthians. Saint Paul himself alludes to another Epistle to the Corinthians, not now known (I Corinthians 5:9), but probably the Bodmer manuscript, which dates from the third century, represents a text invented to fill a known gap rather than an authentic lost book of the Bible. It was preserved independently, in translation, in the biblical canon of the Armenian Church.

The papyri of regular Bible texts among the Bodmer Papyri include some of the most textually important ever found. One is a Gospel of Saint John dating from approximately 200 AD (now P. Bodmer II, Pl. 233). It is the earliest intact manuscript of any part of the New Testament so far discovered, only about 75 years later than the reputed date of the little Rylands fragment. The Bodmer Saint John is in codex form, very fragile but with part of its original stitching intact. Another volume comprises the Gospels of Luke and John together, written in a tall narrow format (P. Bodmer XIV–XV). It dates from the third century.

Its text is extremely pure. Even in its smallest variants it corresponds so closely to the Gospel text of the *Codex Vaticanus* that it has even been suggested that it might have been the actual exemplar for the scribe of *Vaticanus* a century later.

Let us now take stock, at least of the New Testament. Exactly a hundred years had passed between the publication of Darwin's *Origin of Species* and the acquisition of the final papyrus by Dr Bodmer. The quantity of available material for understanding the origins and evolution of the Bible was totally transformed during that century. It is reasonable to look for some conclusions on three essential questions. They are the accuracy of the Bible as it has been preserved; the context in which the early Bible was disseminated; and the date and authorship of the texts themselves.

Firstly, all evidence confirms that the text of the Christian Bible as we have it today has been maintained and transmitted with extraordinary accuracy since the late second or early third century AD. Anxious believers can be enormously reassured by the almost exact similarity between even the earliest of the biblical papyri from Egypt and the text as it has survived during its descent through countless scriptoria and printing shops of Europe. Here and there the odd word or phrasing may exist in variant forms. Occasionally a few extra words have crept into the text or a slightly different emphasis has emerged from a translation. Modern textual emendation can usually put these right. No significant variations or deliberate falsifications have ever been found to shake public confidence in the Bible as a whole. No other text of comparable antiquity has come down to us with so few uncertainties about its transmission. As a generalization, words are more likely to have been added to a text than lost from it. There is an old maxim of textual criticism, '*lectio brevior lectio potior*', a shorter reading is a more likely reading. This applies to the Bible as to any other text. There are a few passages where the received text has almost certainly been expanded slightly since the earliest manuscripts. One of the oldest textual controversies concerns the authenticity of the story of the woman taken in adultery (John 8:3-11). These nine verses represent one of the few extended doubtful passages in the New Testament. As we encountered in Chapter 2 above (p. 61), this passage was always regarded as being of uncertain authenticity in medieval Greek Bibles. It has some early champions, such as the fifth-century *Codex Bezae* and early Latin translations of the Bible, but the incident does not occur in *Sinaiticus*, *Alexandrinus* or *Vaticanus*, and it finds no support in the fifth-century Freer Gospel Book discovered in 1906 or in the Sahidic or Old Syriac translations or in the Greek text of P. Bodmer II, the oldest papyrus codex of all, copied *c.*200 AD. On those grounds, then, it should probably be deleted from the Gospel. Another clause which varies in early manuscripts of the Gospels is Luke 11:4. This is the final petition of the Lord's Prayer in Saint Luke's account, 'But deliver us from evil'. The sentence occurs in *Alexandrinus* and the Freer Gospels but it is not found in *Sinaiticus*, *Vaticanus* or the Sahidic papyri or in P. Bodmer XIV. There is an explanation. The Lord's Prayer also occurs in Matthew 6:9-13, authentically ending there 'But deliver us from evil'. When the author of Luke did not include it (as he probably originally did not), some early reader helpfully inserted the clause by analogy with the earlier citation in Matthew. It can only have been interpolated at a period of history when the two Gospels were available simultaneously. Modern scholarship would remove it. A final example is from the famous hymn of the angels in sky above the shepherds in the field outside Bethlehem (Luke 2:14). Did they sing 'Glory to God in the highest and on earth peace [and] good will to men'? or was it '… and on earth peace to men of good will'? The difference is in only a single letter of the Greek, *eudokia* ('good will') or *eudokias* in the genitive ('of good will'). The former is the reading of very many Greek manuscripts, the Syriac, the Boharic, and the *Diatessaron* of Tatian in the second century. The latter is the word used by the Sahidic papyri and by *Sinaiticus, Vaticanus, Alexandrinus*, the Old Latin and the Vulgate text of Saint Jerome. Possibly the genitive is slightly more logical but both variants make grammatical sense.

The second question raised by the biblical discoveries of the twentieth century is that of the context in which the books of the Bible circulated in the early Church. There is no surviving evidence of the books of the Bible ever being written out together in a double compendium of the Old and New Testaments earlier than the three great codices of the fourth century. Before that, biblical books were made instead in short units of one or two texts, quite often mingling books of the Old and New Testaments without evident distinction. They were uninhibitedly translated into Syriac, Boharic, Sahidic, Latin, Ethiopian and other languages, without undue self-consciousness or fear of heresy, and single deposits of manuscripts often included biblical texts in more than one language. Minor variants within the manuscript traditions suggest that there was no single authoritative text which scribes felt obliged to follow. More importantly, the books of the Bible were not alone. This is the most unexpected revelation about the discoveries from the Egyptian desert. All early archaeological finds of biblical texts and many early oriental translations present the familiar books of the Bible in the company of a considerable mass of similar texts which we would now dismiss as merely apocryphal. The canonical texts were read with books such as those of Enoch and James, the Gospels of Peter and Thomas, the Acts of Peter, III Corinthians, and the Apocalypse of Peter. Some of these are very like parts of the Bible used now. Early manuscripts do not seem to distinguish the relative authenticity of genuine and spurious books of the Bible. These are books in free circulation before the promulgation of an official canon of the New Testament in the late fourth century and the suppression of rival texts. The *Diatessaron* of Tatian shows that four principal Gospels already existed by about 170 AD. Chester Beatty II reveals that most, at least, of the Epistles of Saint Paul were being copied as a unit by about 200 AD (the manuscript lacks its end and we cannot know if it included II Thessalonians or Philemon, for example). The Gospels and apocryphal Gospels circulated singly for much longer. The process of weighing up the many other Christian texts was still continuing after the Roman Empire became Christian, and some early translations, such as the *Peshitta*, had already been made before the scriptures were pared down and bolstered up into their present definitive form. This probably happened about 300 AD.

What, if anything, does this tell us about the authorship of the New Testament? No autograph manuscripts are ever likely to be discovered, or to be recognized if they are found. There will probably never be agreement as to whether Matthew, Mark, Luke and John were actual historical figures who knew Jesus at first hand, or whether these are merely invented names attached to collections of stories which were finally committed to writing only when the last living witnesses had died. The generally accepted hypothesis is that the principal letters of Saint

Paul are the earliest New Testament books, mostly composed about 50-60 AD. Nowhere in the works of Saint Paul are there references to any written Gospels. The latest texts of the New Testament, such as I–II Timothy, Titus and II Peter, are assumed to be second-century. Saint John's Gospel must have existed by about 125 AD, if the early dating of the Rylands fragment is right. This brings the origin of the Gospels far earlier than some nineteenth-century critics believed. The three 'Synoptic' Gospels – Matthew, Mark and Luke – are textually dependent on each other. It is usually assumed that the Gospel of Mark was written first, perhaps about 65–70 AD, and that this Gospel was then used by the authors of Matthew and Luke. Extremely close parallels between the narratives make this both probable and logical. It was first suggested in the very late nineteenth century that these two Gospel writers also drew upon a lost written source, commonly designated as 'Q'. This hypothetical text would have to have comprised an anthology of sayings and parables of Jesus, with other stories such as that of the Temptation of Christ (Matthew 4:2–11, Luke 4:2–13). The discovery of the Gospel of Thomas at Nag Hammadi raised initial hopes that this might be a version of 'Q' itself. It is not, but it does at least confirm that a written reservoir of sayings of Jesus is a plausible reality. Beyond 'Q', the authors of Matthew and Luke must have had other sources of information. Luke 1:1 says that 'many' had undertaken to write about Jesus, which suggests an awareness of a variety of sources. Probably the author used other collections, oral or written, such as an anthology of traditions about the birth and childhood of Christ which furnished material for his opening chapters. The apocryphal book of James among the Bodmer Papyri is an example of such a collection. All this brings us nearer to the moment when the Gospels were first written down. We are not yet back into the first century or to the country where the Bible was written, but we are close. Archaeological discoveries of papyri do not contradict the theory that the Gospels were initially created by evolution and selection.

With the Dead Sea Scrolls we return to ancient Palestine and, in all probability, to the lifetime of Jesus. In 70 AD, Jerusalem was destroyed by the Romans and the Jews were dispersed. This catastrophic event may have affected the necessity to record the Gospels but, more certainly, it led to the adoption of a definitive Hebrew Bible for what the Christians call the Old Testament. We saw in Chapter 2 how a fixed text of the Hebrew Bible was promulgated for Jewish use during the council of Jamnia, around 100 AD (above, p. 42). Until 1947, it was acknowledged that it would never be possible to confront any substantial versions of the Hebrew Bible earlier than the 'Masoretic' text which descended from those enigmatic meetings at Jamnia.

The accounts of the discovery of the Dead Sea Scrolls are among the most famous archaeological tales ever told. Like all oral traditions, the stories vary in their details. Jewish and Jordanian versions assign the credit for discovery slightly differently but all agree on the immense value of the find. Briefly, the first Scrolls

234
The first of the Dead Sea Scrolls were found by Bedouin shepherds in caves near Qumran to the north-west of the Dead Sea in 1947. These are the caves above Qumran

brought to light were found some time in 1947 by a group of Bedouin shepherds of the Ta'amireh tribe, one of whom was lobbing stones through an aperture in the cave-filled hills north-west of the Dead Sea (Pl. 234). Instead of the sound of the stone hitting sand far below, he heard the crack of pottery. Eventually the scrolls which the Bedouins removed from the cave were brought to a local merchant in Bethlehem. There is something rather satisfying about this modern parallel with the Gospel story (Luke 2:15), when the shepherds went to Bethlehem to verify their good news. From Bethlehem, the Scrolls were mostly consigned to the Syrian convent of St Mark in Jerusalem for possible sale. Three were bought rapidly by Professor Eleazor L. Sukenik for the Hebrew University in Jerusalem. Negotiations took place during the very days that the state of Israel was being created at the end of November 1947. The three scrolls were a part of the book of Isaiah (Pl. 235) and two unique texts, a prophecy now called the *War Scroll*, or the *War of the Sons of Light against the Sons of Darkness*, and a collection of verses rather like the biblical psalms, published as the *Thanksgiving Scroll*. The convent, alerted by the ease of this sale, consulted the American School of Oriental Research in Jerusalem, and began to suspect that the finds might be extremely valuable indeed. The four remaining scrolls from the cave were sent to America.

מהרה בוא וצל מרוה את ירושלם מנוה ... ואורישו ולוא עם אותוא ולבי לוא מענות
דבק חק לספור לוא מעמד

ויבוא אליקים בן חלקיה על הבית ושובנא המופר ויואח בן אמף המוזיר אל
חזקיהו קרועי בגדים ויגידו לוא את דברי רב שקה ויאמר שמוע חזקיהו ויקרע
ויקרע את בגדיו ויתכסם בשק יבוא בית יהוה וישלח את אליקים אשר על הבית
ואת שובנא המופר ואת זקני הכוהנים מתכסים בשקים אל ישעיהו בן אמוץ הנביא
ויאמרו אליו כוה אמר חזקיהו יום צרה ותוכחה ונאצה היום כי באו בנים
עד משבר וכוח אין ללדה אולי ישמע יהוה אלוהיך את דברי רב שקה אשר שלחו
מלך אשור אדוניו לחרף אלוהים חי והוכיח בדברים אשר שמע יהוה אלוהיך ונשאת
תפלה בעד השארית הנמצאה ויבואו עבדי המלך חזקיהו אל ישעיהו
ויאמר אליהם ישעיהו כוה תאמרון אל אדוניכם כוה אמר יהוה אל תירא מפני הדברים
אשר שמעתה אשר גדפו נערי מלך אשור אותי הנני נותן בוא רוח ושמע שמועה ושב לארצו
והפלתיו בחרב בארצו וישב רב שקה וימצא את מלך אשור נלחם על לבנה כי שמע כי נסע מלכיש וישמע

אל תרהרסאר מלך כוש לאמור יצא ללחום אתך וישמע וישלח מלאכים אל
חזקיהו לאמור כוה תאמרון אל חזקיהו מלך יהודה לאמור אל ישיאך אלוהיך אשר
אתה בוטח בוא לאמור לוא תנתן ירושלם ביד מלך אשור הנה אתה שמעתה את אשר
עשו מלכי אשור לכל הארצות להחרימם ואתה תנצל הצילו אותם אלוהי הגואים
את גוזן ואת חרן ורצף ובני עדן אשר בתלאסר איה מלך חמת ומלך ארפד ומלך לעיר ספרוים הנע ועוה

ויקח חזקיהו את הספרים מיד המלאכים ויקראם ויעל בית יהוה ויפרשהו חזקיהו
לפני יהוה ויתפלל חזקיהו אל יהוה לאמור יהוה צבאות אלוהי ישראל יושב
הכרובים אתה הוא האלוהים לבדך לכל ממלכות הארץ אתה עשיתה את השמים
ואת הארץ הטה יהוה אזנך ושמע פקח יהוה עיניך וראה ושמע את כל דברי
סנחריב אשר שלח לחרף אלוהים חי אמנם יהוה החריבו מלכי אשור את הגואים
ואת ארצם ונתן את אלוהיהם באש כי לוא אלוהים המה כיא אם מעשה ידי
אדם עץ ואבן ויאבדום ועתה יהוה אלוהינו הושיענו מידו וידעו כול
ממלכות הארץ כיא אתה יהוה לבדך ...

וישלח ישעיהו בן אמוץ אל חזקיהו לאמור כוה אמר יהוה אלוהי ישראל אשר
התפללתה אלי אל סנחריב מלך אשור זה הדבר אשר דבר יהוה עליו בזה לך

A few pieces fell off. When no buyer was found, the scrolls were advertised in the *Wall Street Journal* for 1 June 1954, under the heading 'Miscellaneous for sale', between offers of stoves in Kalamazoo and welding equipment in Murphysboro, Illinois, as 'Biblical Manuscripts dating back to at least 200 BC', with a box number. They were bought immediately by the government of Israel for $250,000. The Prime Minister telegraphed 'Mazal-tov', the Jewish cry of congratulation. The four scrolls were a second manuscript of Isaiah, this one complete, a commentary on the prophet Habakkuk, a sectarian rule known as the *Manual of Discipline* (or *Rule of the Community*), and an Aramaic retelling of the opening of the Bible, now called the *Genesis Apocryphon*.

In the meantime, attention had shifted back to the site itself by the Dead Sea, then still part of Jordan. A series of searches and excavations promoted by the Jordanian Department of Antiquities between 1949 and 1956 revealed a total of eleven different caves which contained scrolls or fragments of scrolls. Some were in clay jars, and others were filtered out of the sand on the floor of the caves. Further pieces were recovered from the original cave. For convenience, the caves with manuscript deposits were numbered as they were found, I–XI. One of the most extensive deposits was in the so-called Cave IV, found in 1952, with more than 15,000 fragments of manuscripts, including parts of 127 biblical scrolls. Other sites along the western shores of the Dead Sea, including Masada, delivered further fragments in the early 1960s. The term 'Dead Sea Scrolls' does not simply refer to a single hoard but to a whole series of similar discoveries made over a wide area. Following the Six-Day War of 1967, many of the finds were taken into the custody of Israel. They are mostly now housed in a very striking modern building, the Shrine of the Book, adjacent to the Israel Museum in the suburbs of Jerusalem.

The Dead Sea Scrolls have so far furnished parts of 175 biblical manuscripts, including fragments of every Old Testament book except Esther. Nine of the

235 opposite

By far the best preserved of the biblical texts from the Dead Sea Scrolls is the manuscript of Isaiah, dating from c.100 BC. It is one of the manuscripts from the initial Dead Sea hoard found in 1947 (JERUSALEM, ISRAEL MUSEUM)

236 below

Many of the Dead Sea Scrolls are small fragments and pieces of manuscripts. This portion comprises the text of Judges 4:5–6 in Hebrew (OSLO AND LONDON, THE SCHØYEN COLLECTION, MS. 2861)

eleven caves contained at least some biblical texts. About 70 scrolls are from parts of the Pentateuch, especially Deuteronomy. Among the prophets, Isaiah is exceptionally well represented. Most are written on leather, usually in various forms of Hebrew or Aramaic. Some are on parchment or papyrus. A few are in Greek, including, for example, 93 tiny pieces of papyrus with fragments of the Septuagint translation of Leviticus found in Cave IV. Another site at Nahal Hever furnished a text of the Minor Prophets in Greek. The earliest Dead Sea Scrolls may well date from as early as the second century BC; many are datable to about the first third of the first century AD, more or less the lifetime of Jesus, which co-incidence has provoked many speculative fantasies. It should be emphasized that most of the Dead Sea Scrolls are extremely fragmentary. Out of about 800 scrolls with about 600 different texts, only about 15 to 20 are reasonably intact. The remarkable condition of the Isaiah scroll from Cave I should not lead us to expect that all others are beautiful soft scrolls ready to be unrolled and published. Many of the Dead Sea finds comprise little more than crumbs of dark brown leather confetti, each with a few letters or even less in the Hebrew alphabet.

It is assumed that the original concealment of the scrolls had something to do with safekeeping of texts during or after the Roman conquest of Judea, between the destruction of Jerusalem in 70 AD and the final overthrow of Masada beside the Dead Sea in 73 AD. By the chance that one of the first scrolls found was the so-called *Manual of Discipline*, with rules for the initiation of members into an ascetic Jewish sect, it was quickly suggested as early as 1948 that the Dead Sea Scrolls had probably belonged to a community of Essenes. This was a pious sect living in deliberate poverty in the Judean wilderness in expectation of the imminent end of the world and the coming of the Messiah. There is some case that Saint John the Baptist might have been an Essene. Several contemporary writers, including Pliny, describe the Essenes as inhabiting the desert near the Dead Sea. The excavation of a group of ancient buildings at Khirbet Qumran, near the foot of the hillside by Cave I, led rapidly to the common assumption that Qumran was the home of the Essene community and that its members had owned and buried the Dead Sea Scrolls.

The attribution of the Dead Sea Scrolls to an origin at Qumran is similar to the supposition that the Nag Hammadi and Bodmer Papyri had been owned and hidden by the monks of the neighbouring Pachomian monastery near where the papyri were found. Both are convenient and plausible explanations which do not entirely fit the complexity of the manuscripts found nearby. In the 1960s, when the Nag Hammadi and Dead Sea finds were first being published, the idea of New Age communities was fashionable and credible. Both the Dead Sea Essenes and the Egyptian Gnostics evidently withdrew from a materialistic world which seemed at that time to be on the brink of disaster. In the public imagination of the second half of the twentieth century, the Essenes were understandable. However, the passing of time has not strengthened the association between the Dead Sea

Scrolls and a community at Qumran, not least because some of the caves with
scrolls are situated far from the Qumran site. There is a case, probably too tempting to be realistic, that the Dead Sea Scrolls might be salvage brought from the
treasury of the Temple in Jerusalem, hidden for safekeeping by Jews escaping the
Roman siege. Other theories, less plausible, are that the ascetic sect of the *Manual
of Discipline* was actually a very early community of Christians. Pieces of another
scroll commonly called the Damascus Document are invoked in support of
such interpretations, for they describe a struggle between a certain 'teacher of
righteousness' and his ideological opponents. The teacher has been variously
explained as alluding cryptically to John the Baptist, Jesus himself, or his brother
James. No such interpretations are accepted by serious scholarship, but they tell
us a great deal about the Bible in our own time and the fundamental desire to
rearrange it into a world justified by tangible archaeological evidence.

It is possible that the extant Dead Sea Scrolls were not the only such manuscripts originally hidden in the wilderness of Judea in the first century AD. There
are several historical references to finds of ancient Hebrew manuscripts which,
with hindsight, sound extraordinarily like similar deposits. In Chapter 2 above,
we looked at the *Hexapla* text of Origen (d. *c.*250). Eusebius reports that Origen
made use of a Greek translation which, he said, had been found with other Hebrew
and Greek books in a jar near Jericho in the reign of Caracella (211–17). Origen
was in Palestine in 216. These could have been Dead Sea Scrolls. Another reference dates a find to about 790. A letter from the Nestorian patriarch in the late
eighth century refers to a recent discovery of many manuscripts in Hebrew script
hidden in a cave near Jericho. The books were said to have been not only biblical
works of high textual value but also uncanonical texts such as a collection of more
than 200 psalms, fifty more than in the Bible. This combination of authoritative
and apocryphal texts sounds remarkably similar to the finds we now call Dead
Sea Scrolls. A final puzzling event occurred as late as 1883. In that year a Jewish
dealer, Moses Shapira, offered to sell to the British Museum for a million pounds
a group of leather manuscript fragments of the Hebrew Bible, purportedly
several thousand years old, which had been found in caves near the Dead Sea.
The outrageousness of Shapira's claim attracted great interest. Even Gladstone,
who had attended Smith's lecture on cuneiform tablets in 1872, now came to
inspect these Hebrew curiosities. However, 1883 was just too early for manuscripts of such reputed antiquity to be accepted as credible, and neither public
nor scholarly opinion could be persuaded of their possible authenticity. The
manuscripts were universally denounced as fakes; Shapira shot himself. The
pieces were sold instead for £25, apparently to a collector in Sydney, Australia,
where they are said to have destroyed by fire in 1899.

Whether or not the Dead Sea Scrolls found in 1947–56 are unique among
Hebrew manuscripts originally concealed, it seems increasingly likely that they
are not necessarily the freakish books of an eccentric sect but may be more widely

representative of the written culture and religion of first-century Palestine. Like the Nag Hammadi papyri, moreover, they encompass texts seemingly beyond the edges of the orthodox. This is where they are so endlessly fascinating and disconcerting. Besides parts of several copies of the apocalyptic *War Scroll* from Caves I and IV, there are apocryphal psalms, for example, like the unique *Apostrophe to Zion* found in Cave XI; hymns, like the *Words of the Luminaries* from Cave IV (this is an original title – *Dibre hamme'orot* – written in Hebrew on the back of the scroll); and ancient fictional texts, such as the *Testaments of Levi and Naphtali*, also from Cave IV, in which the sons of Jacob bequeath advice to their descendants on virtuous conduct. There are many biblical commentaries, like that on Habakkuk from Cave I, applying the words of the biblical prophet to the imminent last days of the first century BC and the expectation of a Messiah. There are many books of the Bible, as mentioned. Some correspond to the Hebrew Bible as it has survived into modern times; others are texts now downgraded to the Apocrypha, like the original Hebrew text of the book of Enoch. Others are close paraphrases of biblical books, or are from different traditions, like the Samaritan Pentateuch, or present the psalms (for example) in a different order, or are anthologies of quotations from the prophets, or translations, like the Aramaic version of the book of Job, found in Cave XI. Others are no closer to the Bible than alternative renditions of biblical narratives, like the *Genesis Apocryphon* in Aramaic from Cave I, or eight little scraps in Hebrew from Cave IV with what appears to be a new account again of Noah and the Flood. All these suggest the availability of a body of Jewish biblical and semi-biblical material much more extensive than was ever imagined, all mixing freely with regular books of the Old Testament.

When the news of the discovery of the Dead Sea Scrolls was first announced in 1948, it was expected or dreaded by many that the received text of the Hebrew

237

This is a substantial fragment of Acts in the Sahidic dialect of Coptic, excavated in Egypt. It is approximately fifth-century (NEW YORK, PIERPONT MORGAN LIBRARY, M. 910)

Bible was about to be overturned. It was anticipated that the sacred texts might well prove to have been altered or corrupted by the rabbinical reforms at Jamnia around 100 AD and then by 800 years of subsequent transmission between that time and the survival of the earliest substantial Hebrew manuscripts from the late ninth century. Nothing could be further from reality. The discovery of the Dead Sea Scrolls was extremely reassuring. The Isaiah scroll from Cave I, for example, is by far the most complete of the scrolls and was one of the first to be published. Word by word, verse by verse, it corresponds exactly to the text as we have it now. Very occasionally, the odd word is added or subtracted, usually negligible explanatory phrases, characteristic of even the most careful scribes at all periods. What is quite apparent from the Dead Sea Scrolls is that the edition which emanated from Jamnia did not alter the text: it simply selected good texts, promoted them to the canon of the Hebrew scriptures, and dismissed all others as apocryphal. What it chose, it launched on a safe journey of two thousand years. What it rejected, it eliminated utterly.

Both the Dead Sea Scrolls and the early Christian papyri from Egyptian desert tell almost the same story. Both the Old and the New Testaments initially circulated in a variety of versions and in the company of many texts which might, in different circumstances, have become parts of the Bible. The books which we now regard as authentically biblical were sifted after the fall of Jerusalem in 70 AD and after the conversion of the Roman Empire to Christianity. It became necessary to endorse them as canonical. They have been preserved and disseminated ever since, more or less exactly, more widely than any other texts ever written. They have become the Bible. They are now a single book. Many fundamental questions about the actual origins of the text are still matters of faith, or limitless scholarly conjecture. Archaeology since Darwin, however, has taught us a great deal about the evolution of the Bible. It has given us real manuscripts. It has filled out the libraries of early Christianity, and has given us a prehistory. The beginnings of the Bible are set in an increasingly secure context. Its first centuries can now be documented. In the end, then, in the late fourth century, Saint Jerome translated the books of the Bible from Hebrew and Greek into Latin. This is exactly where we began.

Bibliography

INTRODUCTION

There is no single source for the breadth of the subject covered by this book. There is a survey of the literature of the medieval period in A. Vernet, *La Bible au Moyen Âge, Bibliographie*, Paris, 1989. Throughout the whole book I have often used the composite volumes of *The Cambridge History of the Bible*, 3 volumes, Cambridge, 1963–70. Volume II was edited by G.W.H. Lampe, *The West from the Fathers to the Reformation*, Cambridge, 1969, and volume III by S.L. Greenslade, *The West from the Reformation to the Present Day*, Cambridge, 1963. I bought volume II on publication in 1969, for I wanted to know about medieval Bibles. I was disappointed to find it was full of complicated discussions of text and it encompassed a range of biblical problems so diverse that it was hard to disentangle any sequential narrative. The more manuscript Bibles I saw over the years, the more I came to appreciate the skill in gathering such encyclopaedic material into one volume. No other book has managed it. Many years later I acquired a second-hand copy of volume III in New York, and these well-thumbed books, bound in blue and red respectively, have now been beside me ever since. A wonderfully old-fashioned book, in print for more than 60 years (a tribute to its appeal) is F. Kenyon, *Our Bible and the Ancient Manuscripts, being a History of the Text and its Transmission*, London, 1895, with many subsequent editions, especially the fourth, fully updated, 1939, and the fifth, revised by A. W. Adams, 1958. The author was Director of the British Museum; the book is written almost entirely from an English (and Christian) standpoint. I am almost ashamed by how often I have come back to it, however, to share Kenyon's evident delight in manuscripts and the fascination of what they can reveal. For the standardization of names and the relentless checking of dates, I have resorted to the magisterial *Oxford Dictionary of the Christian Church*, second edition, edited by F. L. Cross and E. A. Livingstone, London, 1974, and, where that has failed me, the *Encyclopaedia Judaica*, 17 volumes, Jerusalem, 1971–82. A book with a tantalizing title was published while the present work was in proof, *The Oxford Illustrated History of the Bible*, edited by J. Rogerson, Oxford, 2001, with essays by 18 authors. It proves not to be a history of Bibles as artefacts but an account of biblical theology and of the ever-changing application of the Bible text in different situations, contrasting the ancient world with our own times. The whole of the Middle Ages and Renaissance are reduced into 12 pages, about a third of which are plates. I feared it would overlap with the present book; it complements it splendidly.

I was exposed to many Bibles during the 25 years I spent at Sotheby's, and some of the most important biblical manuscripts in Britain have now passed into my care at Corpus Christi College in Cambridge, including the Bury Bible, which is appropriately Plate 1. I am grateful to both institutions for the opportunities afforded by easy access to manuscripts and good reference collections. Seven chapters of this book were written during two enjoyable terms as a Visiting Fellow of All Souls College in Oxford. One was written on holiday near Skagen in Denmark. The others were constructed during spare moments in a busy life, to the inconvenience of my good-natured wife and my work colleagues, especially Camilla Previté, to all of whom I am enormously grateful.

CHAPTER 1

I have used *The Cambridge History of the Bible*, II, especially chapter 4, E. F. Sutcliffe, 'Jerome', pp.80–101, and chapter 5, R. Loewe, 'The Medieval History of the Latin Vulgate', pp.102–54. There is a densely packed and engaging essay and collection of plates with commentaries by M. T. Gibson, *The Bible in the Latin West*, Notre Dame (Indiana), 1993. Anything by Margaret Gibson is worth reading, and if she had not died young in 1994 she could and probably should have written my book. There is a succinct narrative summary of the evolution and circulation of the Latin Vulgate in W. Cahn, *Romanesque Bible Illumination*, Ithaca (New York), 1982, especially chapters 1–2, pp.11–60. The old heavy-going classics are still S. Berger, *Histoire de la Vulgate pendant les premiers siècles du moyen âge*, Nancy, 1893 (reprinted, Hildesheim, 1976), and H. Quentin, *Mémoire sur l'établissement du texte de la Vulgate*, I, Rome and Paris, 1922. They can be supplemented by P. McGurk, *Latin Gospel Books from AD 400 to AD 800*, Paris and Brussels, 1961, B. Fischer, *Lateinische Bibelhandschriften im frühen Mittelalter*, Freiburg, 1985, and the valuable article by P.-M. Bogaert, 'La Bible latine des origines au moyen âge, Aperçu historique, état des questions', *Revue théologique de Louvain*, XIX, 1988, pp.137–59. A remarkably readable and exhilarating study of the early period is H. Y. Gamble, *Books and Readers in the Early Church, A History of Early Christian Texts*, New Haven, 1995. Nicholas Poole-Wilson drew my attention to it. I have also quarried the essays in *The Early Medieval Bible, Its Production, Decoration and Use*, ed. R. Gameson, Cambridge, 1994; for the beginning of this chapter, I have used especially chapter 1, P. McGurk, 'The Oldest Manuscripts of the Latin Bible', pp.1–23, and for the end, chapters 3–4, D. Ganz, 'Mass Production of Early Medieval Manuscripts: the Carolingian Bibles from Tours', pp.53–62, and R. McKitterick, 'Carolingian Bible Production: the Tours Anomaly', pp.61–77. For individual manuscripts, I have relied heavily on the great illustrated volumes edited by E. A. Lowe, *Codices Latini Antiquiores, A Palaeographical Guide to Latin Manuscripts Prior to the Ninth Century*, 11 volumes, Oxford, 1934–66, with *Supplement*, 1971, and addenda by B. Bischoff and V. Brown in *Mediaeval Studies*, XLVII, 1985, pp.317–38. As it happens, the Turin and Verona manuscripts compared on p.16 here occur together on the same page of

C.L.A. (as Lowe's work is commonly abbreviated) with almost adjacent numbers, vol. IV, 1947, p.18, nos.465 and 467. My example of Matthew 10:21 was made by comparing the detail from the *Vercelli Codex* in F. Ehrle and P. Liebart, *Specimina Codicum Latinorum Vaticanorum*, Bonn, 1912, Pl.5c, with the facsimile of fol. 74v of the Turin manuscript in C. Cipolla, *Il Codice Evangelico 'k' della Biblioteca Universitaria Nazionale di Torino*, Turin, 1913. Pl.5 on p.17 here is *C.L.A.* no.162; Pl.8 on p.25 is *C.L.A.* no.984 (it is also discussed in C.H. Turner, *The Oldest Manuscript of the Vulgate Gospels*, Oxford, 1931); Pl.9 on p.26 is *C.L.A.* no. 197; the beautiful *Codex Brixianus*, Pl.10 on p.27, is *C.L.A.* no.281; the fifth-century fragments which are Pl.11 on p.28 are part of *C.L.A.* no.1174, listed when they were still at Donaueschingen (I described them for Sotheby's, 21 June 1982, lot 1); Pl.13 on p.30 is *C.L.A.* no.313; pls.14–15 on p.31 are *C.L.A.* nos.126 and 1423; the *Codex Amiatinus*, pls.16–17 (pp.33 and 34) is *C.L.A.* no.299; the Echternach Gospels (Pl.18, p.35) is *C.L.A.* no. 578; and the volume of the Maudramnus Bible here, Pl.19 on p.36, is part of *C.L.A.* no.707. The Bible of Borso d'Este illustrated in Pl.6, p.18, is now in facsimile with a commentary by F. Toniolo, *La Bibbia di Borso d'Este*, Modena, 1997. Pl.7 on p.19 is from a Bible once at Pipewell Abbey, lot 12 in the Chester Beatty sale at Sotheby's, 3 December 1968, and afterwards S. Fogg, catalogue 16 (1995), no.39; it is now privately owned in Japan. The Vulgate on the Internet, cited on p.21, can be found at *http://bible.gospelcom.net/cgi-bin/bible?language=latin.* It is extremely useful in that it allows a word search. The tables on pp.22–4 owe much to F. Stegmüller, *Repertorium Biblicum Medii Aevi*, I, *Initia Biblica, Apocrypha, Prologi*, Madrid, 1950 (misprinted '1940', reprinted 1981).

CHAPTER *2*

Some of the general texts used for chapter 1 were used here too. Chapters 1 and 2 of *The Cambridge History of the Bible*, II, were useful, B. J. Roberts, 'The Old Testament: Manuscripts, Texts and Versions', pp.1–26, and C. S. C. Williams, 'The History of the Text and Canon of the New Testament to Jerome', pp.27–53. I read H.H. Rowley, *The Growth of the Old Testament*, London, 1950, 3rd edn., 1967. For manuscripts in Hebrew, I consulted in addition B. Narkiss, *Hebrew Illuminated Manuscripts*, Jerusalem, 1969, R. Posner and I. Ta-Shema, eds., *The Hebrew Book, An Historical Survey*, Jerusalem, 1975, and two exhibition catalogues, *A Visual Testimony: Judaica from the Vatican Library*, ed. P. Hart, Miami and New York, 1987, and the short but helpful publication of the Jewish National and University Library, *The Bible in Manuscripts and Printed Books*, ed. R. Weiser, Jerusalem, 1994. David Breuer-Weil genially answered unexpected questions about the Bible in modern Jewish culture. John Lowden kindly talked me through the literature on the early Bible in Greek. His own publications include J. Lowden, *Illuminated Prophet Books, A Study in Byzantine Manuscripts of the Major and Minor Prophets*, and *The Octateuchs, A Study in Byzantine Manuscript Illustration*, University Park (Pennsylvania), 1988 and 1992 respectively, and his excellent entry on Greek manuscript illumination in the Macmillan *Dictionary of Art*, IX, 1996, pp.604–19. For the text of the Greek Bible, I looked at J. K. Elliott, *A Bibliography of Greek New Testament Manuscripts*, Cambridge, 1989, and used especially B. M. Metzger, *The Text of the New Testament, Its Transmission, Corruption, and Restoration*, 2nd edn., Oxford, 1968, the same author's *Manuscripts of the*

Greek Bible, An Introduction to Greek Palaeography, New York and Oxford, 1981, and J. Finegan, *Encountering New Testament Manuscripts, A Working Introduction to Textual Criticism*, Grand Rapids (Michigan), 1974. There are fine illustrations with commentaries in W. H. P. Hatch, *The Principal Uncial Manuscripts of the New Testament*, Chicago, 1939, and in the same author's *Facsimiles and Descriptions of Minuscule Manuscripts of the New Testament*, Cambridge (Mass.), 1951. I made considerable use of the lists of manuscripts in K. Aland and B. Aland, *Der Text des Neuen Testament*, Stuttgart, 1981, translated by E. F. Rhodes as *The Text of the New Testament, An Introduction to the Critical Editions and to the Theory and Practice of Modern Textual Criticism*, Grand Rapids (Michigan) and Leiden, 1987; every known Greek biblical manuscript has an 'Aland' number. Pl.20 on p.41 was chosen after consulting O. Mazal, *Kommentar zur Wiener Genesis, Faksimile-Ausgabe des Codex theol. Gr. 31 der Österreichischen Nationalbibliothek in Wien*, Frankfurt-am-Main, 1980. Pl.25 on p.43 is from a manuscript in the Sassoon sale at Sotheby's, 21 June 1994, lot 27. The discussion of the origins of the codex on pp.48–9 here owes much to H. Y. Gamble's book, *Books and Readers in the Early Church*, cited above. Pl.30 on p.49 is part of a magnificent and little-known manuscript of the *Liber Insularum Archipelagi* of Cristoforo Buondelmonti in the private collection of Mr Kenneth Nebenzahl, to whom I am very grateful for permission to see and reproduce the book. The three great early Greek codices discussed on pp.50-2 are widely published. In addition to works cited already, I have used especially H.J. M. Milne and T. C. Skeat, *Scribes and Correctors of the Codex Sinaiticus*, London, 1938, and T. S. Pattie, 'The Creation of the Great Codices', *The Bible as Book, The Manuscript Tradition*, ed. J. L. Sharpe and K. Van Kampen, London and New Castle (Delaware), 1998, pp.61–72. Scott McKendrick is working on the origins of the *Codex Alexandrinus* and I owe to him the suggestion that it may have been made in Ephesus. The two early illustrated manuscripts described on p.53 can be consulted in K. Weitzmann and H. L. Kessler, *The Cotton Genesis, British Library Codex Cotton Otho D.VI*, Princeton, 1986, and in the facsimile of the Vienna Genesis, edited by Mazal, Frankfurt-am-Main, 1980, cited above. For later Byzantine biblical illumination, see K. Weitzmann, *Late Antique and Early Christian Book Illustration*, New York, 1977; R.G. Calkins, *Illuminated Books of the Middle Ages*, New York and London, 1983, especially the Introduction, 'From the Earliest Bibles to Byzantine Manuscripts', pp.15–29; A. Cutler, *The Aristocratic Psalters in Byzantium* (Bibliothèque des Cahiers Archéologiques, XIII), Paris, 1984 (this is simply a list, with good plates, for the promised accompanying text volume has never appeared); the exhibition catalogue for the Metropolitan Museum of Art, *The Glory of Byzantium, Art and Culture of the Middle Byzantine Era, A.D. 843-1261*, ed. H. C. Evans and W. D. Wixom, New York, 1997; and recently *Imaging the Early Medieval Bible*, ed. J. Williams, University Park (Pennsylvania), 1999, which includes essays by J. Lowden, 'The Beginnings of Biblical Illustration', pp.9–59, and K. Kogman-Appel, 'Bible Illustration and the Jewish Tradition', pp.61-96. The Rossano Gospels, cited here on p.54, illustrated as Pl.35 on p.55, has been published in a facsimile with commentary by G. Cavallo, J. Gribomont and W. C. Loerke, *Codex Purpureus Rossanensis*, Rome and Graz, 1985-7. The suggestion on pp.54–5 that the word 'uncials' is a mis-reading of 'initials' is described by F. Kenyon, *Handbook to the Textual Criticism of the New Testament*, London, 1926, p.49, n.1. On Lectionaries specifically, I have looked at E. C. Colwell and D. W. Riddle, eds., *Prolegomena to the Study of the Lectionary Text of the Gospels* (Studies in the

Lectionary Text of the Greek Gospels, I), Chicago, 1933, and J. C. Anderson, *The New York Cruciform Lectionary*, University Park (Pennsylvania), 1992. The details of scribes and dated manuscripts on pp.60-1 almost all derive from I. Spatharakis, *Corpus of Dated Greek Illuminated Manuscripts to the Year 1453* (Byzantina Neerlandica, VIII, I), Leiden, 1981. I owe to its plates my knowledge of the images reproduced here as pls.36-7 (pp.56–7). Pl.39 (p.60) derives from the excellent little book, T. S. Pattie, *Manuscripts of the Bible, Greek Bibles in the British Library*, London, 1979, new edn., 1995. The bequest of books in 1059, cited on p.63 here, is published by S. Vryonis, 'The Will of a Provincial Magnate, Eustathius Boilas (1059)', *Dumbarton Oaks Papers*, XI, 1957, pp.263–77. Finally, I must recount that I lent an early draft of this chapter to Miss Ruth Barbour, who kindly read and annotated it with the meticulous care of a retired civil servant and returned it while I was abroad and (here is the terrible part) I never acknowledged it; I do so now, bewailing, like a medieval Greek scribe, my unworthiness and inability to profit properly from all I have learned.

CHAPTER *3*

Without doubt, the book I have consulted most often is W. Cahn, *Romanesque Bible Illumination*, 1982, already mentioned above. It is a stout square-shaped book, and it is not immediately obvious if it was intended as a picture book for the general reader, an illustrated census of eleventh- and twelfth-century Bibles, or an academic study. It is said that Professor Cahn wrote a much longer and more profound work (and there is no one better qualified to do so) and that his publishers barbarously reduced it to its present truncated state, like the torso of a once-great Romanesque ivory Crucifix. What remains is still unsurpassed. The early part of the chapter owes much also to L. M. Ayres, 'The Italian Giant Bibles: Aspects of their Turonian Ancestry and Early History', chapter 6 in the volume already cited, *The Early Medieval Bible*, ed. Gameson, 1994, pp.125–54. The opening quotation ascribed to Bernard of Chartres derives from a first-hand reminiscence by John of Salisbury in his *Metalogicon*, III:4. The St-Maximin Bible cited on p.71 was sold at Sotheby's, 6 December 1983, lot 46. The reference from the Schaffhausen catalogue is from G. Becker, *Catalogi Bibliothecarum Antiqui*, Bonn, 1885 (reprinted, Hildesheim and New York, 1973), p.154. The name of the Carilef Bible, Pl. 49 on p. 72, needs explaining. The donor had been a member of the monastery of St-Carilef, near Le Mans, in Maine. That name is now spelled St-Calais, and the bishop is usually called William of St-Calais. His Bible, however, commonly retains the archaic spelling of the 'Carilef' Bible. The identification of its scribe, pp.71–2 here, was made by M. Gullick, 'The Scribe of the Carilef Bible: A New Look at some Late-Eleventh-Century Durham Cathedral Manuscripts', *Medieval Book Production, Assessing the Evidence, Proceedings of the Second Conference of The Seminar in the History of the Book to 1500, Oxford, July 1988*, ed. L. Brownrigg, Los Altos Hills (California), 1990, pp.61–83. Throughout the writing of this book, Michael Gullick has frequently sent me telegraphic notes on biblical oddities he has encountered. The chronicler's account of Abbot Olbert of Gembloux, p.72 here, is printed in A. Derolez and B. Victor, eds., *Corpus Catalogorum Belgii, The Medieval Booklists of the Southern Low Countries*, II, *Provinces of Liège, Luxembourg and Namur*, Brussels, 1994, p.191. The identification of Bishop Robert, donor to Reading Abbey, p.72, is

made by R. Sharpe, J. Carley, R. Thomson and A. Watson, *English Benedictine Libraries, The Shorter Catalogues* (Corpus of British Medieval Library Catalogues, IV), London, 1996, p.421; these compulsive catalogues have provided further small references for this and the following two chapters, including the notes on Alexander, preceptor of Rochester (p.76 here, from *English Benedictine Libraries*, p.527), and on books at Burton-on-Trent (p.98 here, from p.35) and Glastonbury (p.119 here, from p.169), and so on. The abbey chronicle of St-Pierre-le-Vif, quoted here on pp.73 and 75, is taken from Becker, *Catalogi Bibliothecarum Antiqui*, as above, pp.194–5. The Bible of Stephen Harding, pp.76–7, is discussed in Y. Zaluska, *Manuscrits enluminés de Dijon*, Paris, 1991, pp.49–56, nos.22–3; and W. Cahn, *Romanesque Manuscripts, The Twelfth Century* (*A Survey of Manuscripts Illuminated in France*, ed. F. Avril and J. Alexander, III), London, 1996, pp.70-2, no.58. For Christian interest in Hebrew in twelfth-century France, see B. Smalley, *The Study of the Bible in the Middle Ages*, 1952, reprint, Notre Dame (Indiana), 1970, pp.149–56. Many of the great Romanesque Bibles listed telegraphically on pp.78–9 have been the subject of specialized studies, including, for example, in order of citation here, R.M. Thomson, *The Bury Bible*, Woodbridge (Suffolk), 2001; R. Dodwell, *The Great Lambeth Bible*, London, 1959; A. Cohen-Mushlin, *Making of a Manuscript, The Worms Bible of 1148 (British Library, Harley 2803–2804)* (Wolfenbütteler Forschungen, XXV), Wiesbaden, 1983; W. Oakeshott, *The Two Winchester Bibles*, Oxford, 1981, and C. Donovan, *The Winchester Bible*, London and Winchester, 1993; F. Garnier, *Le Langage de l'image au moyen âge*, II, Paris, 1989 (on the Souvigny Bible); together with the entries in the two books by Walter Cahn. The inscription from the Bonne-Espérance Bible, summarized on p.82, is printed in F. Masai and W. Wittek, ed., *Manuscrits datés conservés en Belgique*, I, *819–1400*, Brussels and Ghent, 1968, pp.18–19. On travelling artists in the twelfth century, see (for example) W. Oakeshott, *Sigena: Romanesque Paintings in Spain and the Artists of the Winchester Bible*, London, 1972, and W. Cahn, 'St. Albans and the Channel Style in England', *The Year 1200, A Symposium*, New York, 1975, pp.187–230. The family of Manerius, mentioned on p.86, is identified on the advice of William Urry in C. R. Dodwell, *The Canterbury School of Illumination, 1066–1200*, Cambridge, 1954, p.110. The account of the requisition of a Bible by Leopold of Austria, p.87 here, is from T. Gottlieb, *Mittelalterliche Bibliothekskataloge Österreichs*, I, *Niederösterreich*, Vienna, 1915, p.83. The story of Henry II and Witham is in W. Oakeshott, *The Artists of the Winchester Bible*, London, 1945, p.2, with a summary in the same author's *Two Winchester Bibles*, p.33. My account of the Calci Bible on pp.88–91 is derived from the transcription in K. Berg, *Studies in Tuscan Twelfth-Century Illumination*, Oslo, 1968, pp.226–7.

CHAPTER *4*

A chapter-by-chapter bibliography, like a medieval Bible commentary, is based on cumulating sources. Many of the principal books listed above were used here too. From *The Cambridge History of the Bible*, II, I added now the two parts of chapter 6, 'The Exposition and Exegesis of Scripture', the first part by G. Lampe, 'To Gregory the Great', pp.155–83, and the second by J. Leclercq, 'From Gregory the Great to St Bernard', pp.183–97. There are excellent summaries of the contributions of patristic writers in L. Light, *The Bible in the Twelfth Century, An Exhibition of Manuscripts at the Houghton Library*, Cambridge (Mass.), 1988, and in G. Bray, *Biblical Interpretation, Past and Present*, Downers Grove (Illinois) and Leicester, 1996, esp. pp.79–164 on the Middle Ages. Primary sources are easy to use in comparing biblical commentaries in Latin before about 1200 from the famously unreliable but very accessible series of 222 big volumes of small print edited by J.-P. Migne, *Patrologia Latina* (*Patrologiae Cursus Completus*), Paris, 1844–55. Bible commentaries, at least as they emerged in the twelfth-century Gloss, were the subject of my doctoral thesis, published as *Glossed Books of the Bible and the Origins of the Paris Booktrade*, Woodbridge (Suffolk), 1984, and I have raided old notes. The first plate here, Pl.63 on p.93, was originally reproduced there. The thesis was examined at the time by Beryl Smalley. I have now frequently referred back to her own elegant and ground-breaking works, including *The Study of the Bible in the Middle Ages*, mentioned above, *The Gospels in the Schools, c.1100–c.1280*, London and Ronceverte (W. Virginia), 1985, and a collection of her essays, *Studies in Medieval Thought and Learning from Abelard to Wyclif*, London, 1981. Pl.64 shows Hereford, the most perfect medieval library in England, before its move to an even more noble building in May 1996; my computations of the ratio of biblical commentaries there were made from R. A. B. Mynors and R. M. Thomson, *Catalogue of the Manuscripts of Hereford Cathedral Library*, Cambridge, 1993. The library lists on p.99 are from Becker, *Catalogi Bibliothecarum Antiqui*, pp.3, 24, 54–5, 143, 154 and 207 respectively. The example of Gregory's *Moralia* on pp.102–3 was taken from the introduction and text in G. Gillet, ed., *Grégoire le Grand, Morales sur Job, Livres I–II* (Sources Chrétiennes, 32bis), Paris, 1989. An important but complicated discussion of how the differences between monastic and secular methods of reading texts are reflected in the format and organization of the books is M. B. Parkes, 'The Influence of the Concepts of *Ordinatio* and *Compilatio* on the Development of the Book', *Medieval Learning and Literature, Essays presented to Richard William Hunt*, ed. J. J. G. Alexander and M. T. Gibson, Oxford, 1976, pp.115–41. The uses of coloured inks and other methods of citation (pp.103–6) were built from the volumes of Lowe, *Codices Latini Antiquiores*, and from E. A. Lowe, 'More Facts about our Oldest Latin Manuscripts', in Lowe, *Palaeographical Papers, 1907–1965*, ed. L. Bieler, I, Oxford, 1972, pp.251–74, esp. p.273; P. McGurk, 'Citation Marks in Early Latin Manuscripts', *Scriptorium*, XV, 1961, pp.3–13; and from references in M. B. Parkes, *Pause and Effect, An Introduction to the History of Punctuation in the West*, Aldershot, 1992. Pl.71 on p.104 is from a manuscript of Peter Lombard in the Abbey sale at Sotheby's, 19 June 1989, lot 3010. The account of the Gloss derives from my own book, already cited, supplemented now by the introduction by M. T. Gibson and K. Froehlich to *Biblia Latina cum Glossa Ordinaria, Anastatical Reproduction of the First Printed Edition*, Turnhout, 1992, and from M. T. Gibson, 'The Place of the *Glossa Ordinaria* in Medieval Exegesis', *Ad Litteram, Authoritative Texts and their Medieval Readers*, ed. M. D. Jordan and K. Emery, Notre Dame (Indiana) and London, 1992, pp.5–27. The teaching methods of Hugh of St-Victor, p.111, are evoked in I. Illich, *In the Vineyard of the Text, A Commentary to Hugh's Didascalicon*, Chicago and London, 1993. For Peter Comestor, pp.111–12 here, see J. H. Morey, 'Peter Comestor, Biblical Paraphrase, and the Medieval Popular Bible', *Speculum*, LXVIII, 1993, pp.6–35. For Peter Riga, see the partial edition, P. E. Beichner, ed., *Aurora Petri Rigae Biblia Versificata, A Verse Commentary on the Bible*, Notre Dame (Indiana), 1965. The *Interpretation of Hebrew Names*, pp.112–13 here, is described in A. d'Esneval, 'Le perfectionnement d'un

instrument de travail au début du XIIIe siècle: les trois glossaires bibliques d'Étienne Langton', *Culture et travail intellectuel dans l'occident médiéval*, ed. G. Hasenohr and J. Longère, Paris, 1981, pp.163–75. The final quotation on p.113 is from L. Delisle, *Le Cabinet des manuscrits de la Bibliothèque Nationale*, III, 1881, p.3.

CHAPTER 5

First of all, note the number of illustrations in this chapter taken from thirteenth-century Bibles in private hands. Such manuscripts were made in such enormous numbers and were launched into commerce so professionally that they are still available 750 years later. Pl.81 on p.116 was Sotheby's, 18 June 1991, lot 76; pls.84 and 87 on pp.121 and 125 are from a Bible formerly in the Harry Walton collection, Virginia; Pl.88 is from lot 10 in the Ritman sale, Sotheby's, 19 June 2001; Pl.90 on pp.126–7 was Sotheby's, 20 June 1989, lot 36; Pl.91 on p.128 was lot 8 in the Ritman sale again (a convenient last-minute source for pictures), 19 June 2001; Pl.92 on p.131 is a detail from Sotheby's, 19 June 1990, lot 17; Pl.93 on p.132 was Sotheby's, 21 June 1988, lot 50; and Pl.96 on p.137 was lot 13 in the Beck sale, Sotheby's, 16 June 1997. There is no standard history of the thirteenth-century Bible and there should be. Some of the best work on the subject is by Laura Light, including three major articles: L. Light, 'Versions et révisions du texte biblique', *Le Moyen Age et la Bible*, ed. P. Riché and G. Lobrichon, Paris, 1984, pp.55-93; L. Light, 'The New Thirteenth-Century Bible and the Challenge of Heresy', *Viator*, XVIII, 1987, pp.275–88; and L. Light, 'French Bibles, c.1200-30: a New Look at the Origins of the Paris Bible', *The Early Medieval Bible*, ed. Gameson, 1994, cited above, pp.155-76. I have used all three extensively. There is still useful material in H. Glunz, *History of the Vulgate in England from Alcuin to Roger Bacon*, Cambridge, 1933. I have taken some details from the slightly disappointing unpublished B. Litt. thesis by J. Case Schnurman, 'Studies in the Medieval Book Trade from the late Twelfth to the Middle of the Fourteenth Century with Special Reference to the Copying of Bibles', Oxford, 1960. For the whole context of making thirteenth-century Bibles, we are now graced by the long-awaited two-volumed R. H. Rouse and M. A. Rouse, *Illiterati et Uxorati, Manuscripts and their Makers, Commercial Book Producers in Medieval Paris, 1200–1500*, Turnhout, 2000. I am grateful to the Rouses for more than 25 years of discussions about biblical manuscripts in Paris. Some observations on thirteenth-century Bibles are in my own book, *A History of Illuminated Manuscripts*, 2nd edn., London, 1994, pp.118–23. The reference to Newenham Abbey on pp.118–19 is from D. Bell, *The Libraries of the Cistercians, Gilbertines and Premonstratensians* (Corpus of British Medieval Library Catalogues, III), London, 1992, p.84. For Cardinal Guala Bicchieri on p.119, now see Rouse and Rouse, pp.29–30. The standard account of the Dominican *Correctiones Bibliae* is still H. Denifle, 'Die Handschriften der Bibel-Correctorien des 13. Jahrhunderts', *Archiv für Literatur- und Kirchen-Geschichte des Mittelalters*, IV, 1888, pp.263-311 and 471-601. The texts are Stegmüller, *Repertorium Biblicum*, I, 1950, p.310, nos.854-6, and II, 1950, p.402, no.2817 (as by the Franciscan, Guilelmus Brito). Eton College MS. 25 (pp.122-3 here) is described in N. R. Ker, *Medieval Manuscripts in British Libraries*, II, 1977, p.652. For the adoption of chapter numbers (pp.124-5), I have used Smalley, *The Study of the Bible in the Middle Ages*, 1970 edn., pp.223–4, and A. d'Esneval, 'La Division de la Vulgate latine en chapitres dans l'édition Parisienne du XIIIe siècle', *Revue des sciences philosoph-iques et théologiques*, LXII, 1978, pp.559–68. On the introduction of running-titles and other devices for readers, see R. H. Rouse, 'L'Évolution des attitudes envers l'autorité écrite: le developpement des instruments de travail au XIIIe siècle', *Culture et travail intellectuel*, ed. Hasenohr and Longère, as above, 1981, pp.115–44, and R. H. Rouse and M. A. Rouse, '*Statim invenire*: Schools, Preachers, and New Attitudes to the Page', *Renaissance and Renewal in the Twelfth Century*, ed. R. Benson and G. Constable, Cambridge (Mass.), 1982, esp. pp.221–4. The pioneering if provisional classification of early illuminators' workshops is R. Branner, *Manuscript Painting in Paris during the Reign of Saint Louis*, Berkeley and Los Angeles, 1977. The first 'workshop' mentioned on p.130 here is that named by Branner as the Almagest Shop, pp.201–2 in his book, and the second is what he calls the Alexander shop, his pp.202–3. For the friars and Paris, I have drawn on H. Rashdall, *The Universities of Europe in the Middle Ages*, ed. F. M. Powicke and A. B. Emden, I, Oxford, 1936. On the portability of friars' books, see D. d'Avray, *The Preaching of the Friars, Sermons Diffused from Paris before 1300*, Oxford, 1985, esp. p.57. The private library in Liège in 1269, mentioned on p.132, is recorded in the will of Henry of Tongeren, canon of the collegiate church of St John in Liège; see Derolez and Victor, *Corpus Catalogorum Belgii*, II, 1994, p.71. The friars' systems of concordance, described here on p.133, are explained in R. H. and M. A. Rouse, *Preachers, Florilegia and Sermons: Studies on the Manipulus florum of Thomas of Ireland*, Toronto, 1979, pp.9–13. Other revolving bookmarks, like that illustrated in Pl.94 on p.134, are listed by Mynors and Thomson, *Manuscripts of Hereford Cathedral Library*, 1993, p.107. The Franciscan constitutions of 1338, cited on p.135, are from K. W. Humfreys, *The Book Provisions of the Medieval Friars, 1215–1400*, Amsterdam, 1964, pp.58–9. The examples from Majorca are from an island remarkably well documented; the contract of 1242 is in J. N. Hillgarth, *Readers and Books in Majorca, 1229–1550*, Paris, 1991, p.342. The classic account of copying books from *peciae* is J. Destrez, *La Pecia dans les manuscrits universitaires du XIIIe et XIVe siècles*, Paris, 1935; see also the papers in L. J. Bataillon, B. G. Guyot and R. H. Rouse, eds., *La Production du livre universiaire au moyen-âge, Exemplar et Pecia (Actes du symposium tenu au Collegio San Bonaventura de Grottaferrata en mai 1983)*, Paris, 1988, especially R. H. Rouse and M. A. Rouse, 'The Book Trade at the University of Paris, ca.1250–ca.1350', pp.41–114, and L. J. Bataillon, 'Les Textes théologiques et philosophiques diffusés à Paris par *exemplar* et *pecia*', pp.155–63. The Rouses' article says that *pecia* copies of the Bible are 'virtually unknown' (p.62) and the three copies in Paris supposedly produced by the method are cited in Bataillon's article, p.161, n.13. For thirteenth-century Bibles from Bologna, see the PhD. thesis of M. B. Norris, 'Early Gothic Illuminated Bibles at Bologna, the *prima maniera* phase, 1250–1275', University of California at Santa Barbara, 1993 (reduced scale photocopy, Ann Arbor, 1994), and examples in F. Avril and M.-T. Gousset, *Manuscrits enluminés d'origine italienne*, II, *XIIIe siècle*, Paris, 1984, nos.97 (pp.81–2), 98 (pp.82–3), 103 (pp.85–7), 118bis (pp.94–6), 124 (pp.101–4), etc., and in G. C. Mariani and P. F. Vettore, *Calligrafia di Dio, La Miniatura Celebra la Parola*, Modena, 1999, esp. pp.134–63, nos. 21–32. The quotation from Roger Bacon on p.138 is discussed and indeed quoted in the title of Rouse and Rouse, *Manuscripts and their Makers*, 2000, pp.32–3. The observations on the medieval library of the Sorbonne, p.138 here, are from Delisle, *Cabinet des manuscrits*, III, 1881, pp.9–11. The concluding examples of thirteenth-

century Bibles in use in late medieval England are mostly from Ker, *Medieval Manuscripts in British Libraries*, I, 1969, p.95, and II, 1977, pp.215–16 and 775, and IV, 1992, p.701.

CHAPTER **6**

The Bible has probably provided more subject-matter for artistic endeavour than any other written source. All books on medieval art and Western manuscript illumination include examples of pictures with biblical themes. In touching only briefly on the illustration of Psalters and Books of Hours and in ignoring paintings and sculpture, for example, I am aware of neglecting some of the most important biblical art of the Middle Ages. We are looking simply at books, and especially books where the sequence of illustrations follows and interprets that of narratives in the Bible. This bibliography must similarly be very selective. What follows is by no means all I have seen or everything that would be of interest for further reading. There are overviews by F. Wormald, 'Bible Illustration in Medieval Manuscripts', *The Cambridge History of the Bible*, II, chapter 8, pp.309–37, and by O. Pächt, *Buchmalerei des Mittelalters, Eine Einführung*, Munich, 1984, translated by K. Davenport as *Book Illumination in the Middle Ages, An Introduction*, London and Oxford, 1986, esp. chapter 3, 'Bible Illustration', pp.129–53. The Holkham Bible Picture Book, quoted on p.142, was published in a black-and-white facsimile of the same name edited by W. O. Hassall, London, 1954. For Psalters, I used the magnificent catalogues of V. Leroquais, *Les Psautiers, manuscrits latines des bibliothèques publiques de France*, Mâcon, 1940–1. The quotation from Pseudo-Alcuin on p.143 is from F. Wormald, 'Continental Influence on English Medieval Illumination', reprinted in the author's *Collected Writings*, II, *Continental Art of the Later Middle Ages*, ed. J. J. G. Alexander, T. J. Brown and J. Gibbs, London, 1988, p.14. The Psalter cycle of which Morgan M. 724 is a part (Pl.101 on p.145 here) is discussed by T. A. Heslop and G. Henderson in *The Eadwine Psalter, Text, Image, and Monastic Culture in Twelfth-Century Canterbury*, ed. M. Gibson, T. A. Heslop and R. W. Pfaff, London and University Park (Pennsylvania), 1992, pp.25–42. For the Ingeborg Psalter, see F. Deuchler, *Der Ingeborgpsalter*, Berlin, 1967, and F. Avril, 'L'Atelier du psautier d'Ingeburge: problèmes de localisation et de datation', *Art, objets d'art, collections: Hommage à Hubert Landais*, Paris, 1987, pp.16–21. For the Psalter of Blanche of Castile, see still H. Martin, *Psautier de Saint Louis et de Blanche de Castile (Les joyeaux de l'Arsenal)*, Paris, 1909. The great royal Psalters of this period are discussed in P. Stirnemann, 'Quelques bibliothèques princières et la production hors scriptorium au XIIe siècle', *Bulletin archéologique du comité des travaux historiques et scientifiques*, n.s., XX–XXI, 1984–5, pp.7–38. A new and engrossing book on the *Bible Moralisée* is J. Lowden, *The Making of the Bibles Moralisées*, I, *The Manuscripts*, II, *The Book of Ruth*, University Park (Pennsylvania), 2000. Until that publication, the best sources were commentaries to facsimiles: by R. Haussherr, *Bible Moralisée, Faksimile-Ausgabe im Originalformat des Codex Vindobonensis 2254 der Österreichischen Nationalbibliothek*, Graz, 1973; G. B. Guest, *Bible Moralisée, Codex Vindobonensis 2254, Vienna, Österreichische Nationalbibliothek*, London, 1995; and H.-W. Stork, *Die Bibel Ludwigs des Helgen, Vollständige Faksimile-Ausgabe im Original-format von MS. M.240 der Pierpont Morgan Library, New York, Kommentar*, Graz, 1995. Because there are two facsimiles of ÖNB. cod. 2254, the Nationalbibliothek are reluctant to rephotograph the original manuscript; the transparency they supplied for Pl.105 on p.149 was evidently taken from the reproduction. The most easily available text on the Shah Abbas Bible (pp.150–2) is an old one: S. C. Cockerell, *Old Testament Miniatures, A Medieval Picture Book with 283 Paintings from the Creation to the Story of David*, London, 1969 (a reissue, with a preface by J. Plummer, of the earlier Roxburghe Club edition of 1927). There is also a full facsimile with commentary by D. Weiss and W. Voelkle, *Die Kreuzritterbibel, Die Bilderbibel Ludwigs des Heiligen*, Luzern, 1998. I owe the tale of William of Rubruck to J. J. G. Alexander, *Medieval Illuminators and their Methods of Work*, New Haven and London, 1992, p.54. The text is edited and translated into French by C. and R. Kappler, *Guillaume de Rubrouck, Voyage dans l'empire Mongol (1253–1255)*, Paris, 1985. My account of the Eton Roundels on pp.153-4 is derived almost entirely from A. Henry, *The Eton Roundels, Eton College, MS.177 ('Figurae bibliorum'), A Colour Facsimile with Transcription, Translation and Commentary*, Aldershot and Brookfield (Vermont), 1990. Thirteenth-century Apocalypses (pp.154–7) have been much discussed in print. References include L. Delisle and P. Meyer, *L'Apocalypse en français au XIIIe siècle* (Société des anciens textes français, 44), Paris, 1909; M. R. James, *The Apocalypse in Art*, The Schweich Lectures, London, 1931; B. McGinn, *Visions of the End, Apocalyptic Traditions in the Middle Ages*, New York, 1979; P De Winter, 'Visions of the Apocalypse in Medieval France and England', *Bulletin of the Cleveland Museum of Art*, LXX, 1983, pp.396–417; S. Lewis, *Reading Images, Narrative Discourse and Reception in the Thirteenth-Century Illuminated Apocalypse*, Cambridge, 1995. There are also a number of full or partial facsimiles, including P. H. Brieger, *The Trinity College Apocalypse*, London, 1967; F. Deuchler, J. M. Hoffeld and H. Nickel, *The Cloisters Apocalypse, Commentaries on an Early Fourteenth-Century Manuscript*, New York, 1971; *Apokalypse: MS Douce 180 der Bodleian Library, Oxford*, Graz, 1982; and N. Morgan, *The Lambeth Apocalypse, Manuscript 209 in Lambeth Palace Library*, London, 1990. On the Peterborough Psalter, p.158 here, see L. F. Sandler, *The Peterborough Psalter in Brussels and other Fenland Manuscripts*, London, 1974. Texts on the *Biblia Pauperum* (pp.158–61) include H. Cornell, *Biblia Pauperum*, Stockholm, 1925; G. Schmidt, *Die Armenbibeln des XIV. Jahrhunderts*, Graz and Cologne, 1959; G. Schmidt, introduction to F. Unterkircher, ed., *Die Wiener Biblia Pauperum, Codex Vindobonensis 1198*, Graz, Vienna and Cologne, 1962; R. L. P. Milburn, 'The People's Bible: Artists and Commentators', *The Cambridge History of the Bible*, II, chapter 7, pp.280–308; and A. Henry, *Biblia Pauperum, A Facsimile and Edition*, Aldershot, 1987. There are good parallel observations in M. Caviness, 'Biblical Stories in Windows: Were they Bibles for the Poor?', *The Bible in the Middle Ages: Its Influence on Literature and Art* (Medieval and Renaissance Texts and Studies, 89), ed. B. S. Levy, Binghamton (New York), 1992, pp.103–47. On the relationship of Books of Hours to Bibles, cited on pp.161–2, I might just mention my own article, 'Books of Hours: Imaging the Word', *The Bible as Book, The Manuscript Tradition*, ed. Sharpe and Van Kampen, 1998, pp.137–43. Publications on the *Speculum Humanae Salvationis*, pp.163–4, include M. R. James and B. Berenson, *Speculum Humanae Salvationis, being a Reproduction of an Italian Manuscript of the Fourteenth Century*, Oxford, 1926; A. Wilson, *A Medieval Mirror: Speculum Humanae Salvationis, 1324–1500*, Berkeley, 1984; and B. Cardon, *Manuscripts of the Speculum Humanae Salvationis in the Southern Netherlands (c.1410–c.1470): A Contribution to the Study of the 15th Century Book Illumination and of the Function and Meaning of Historical*

Symbolism (Corpus of Illuminated Manuscripts, 9, Low Countries), Louvain, 1996. For blockbooks, pp.164–5, see G. Bing, 'The Apocalypse Block-Books and their Manuscript Models', *Journal of the Warburg and Courtauld Institutes*, V, 1942, pp.143-58; S. Mertens and C. Schneider, eds., *Blockbücher des Mittelalters: Bilderfolgen als Lektüre, Gutenberg-Museum, Mainz, 22. Juni 1991 bis 1. September 1991*, Mainz, 1991; and N. F. Palmer, 'Biblical Blockbooks', *The Bible as Book, The First Printed Editions*, ed. P. Saenger and K. Van Kampen, London, New Castle (Delaware) and Grand Haven (Michigan), 1999, pp.23–30. The leaf of a blockbook Apocalypse, illustrated as Pl.115 on p.165, was sold at Christie's, 24 November 1993, lot 57.

CHAPTER 7

The great edition of the Wycliffite Bible with a long introduction is that of J. Forshall and F. Madden, *The Holy Bible, Containing the Old and New Testaments, with the Apocryphal Books, in the Earliest English Versions made from the Vulgate by John Wycliffe and his Followers*, Oxford, 1850. Despite the comments of S. L. Fristedt, *The Wycliffe Bible, Part 1, The Principal Problems Connected with Forshall and Madden's Edition* (Stockholm Studies in English, IV), Stockholm, 1953, the large old Victorian volumes are still the essential reference books for the history of the Wycliffite Bible. I have especially used Forshall and Madden's detailed catalogue of the 170 manuscripts of the text which were then known, pp.xxxix-lxiv. This list was updated by C. Lindberg, 'The Manuscripts and Versions of the Wycliffite Bible: A Preliminary Survey', *Studia Neophilologica*, XLII, 1970, pp.333–47, and there are still corrections and additions to be made. I have also used M. Deansley, *The Lollard Bible and other Medieval Biblical Versions*, Cambridge, 1920; M. Deansley, *The Significance of the Lollard Bible*, London, 1951; H. Hargreaves, 'The Vernacular Scriptures', iv, 'The Wycliffite Versions', part of chapter 9 in *The Cambridge History of the Bible*, II, pp.387–415; and M. Aston, *Lollards and Reformers*, London, 1984. In recent decades, Anne Hudson has emerged as the apostolic authority on Wycliffe and his teaching in her own university of Oxford. Among her many publications are a collection of essays, A. Hudson, *Lollards and their Books*, London and Ronceverte (W. Virginia), 1985; A. Hudson, 'Wyclif and the English Language', *Wyclif and his Times*, ed. A. Kenny, Oxford, 1986, pp.85–103; A. Hudson, *The Premature Reformation: Wycliffite Texts and Lollard History*, Oxford, 1988; A. Hudson, 'Lollard Book Production', *Book Production and Publishing in Britain, 1375–1475*, ed. J. Griffiths and D. Pearsall, Cambridge, 1989, pp.125–42; and A. Hudson, *Selections from English Wycliffite Writings*, Toronto, 1997, reprinted, Cambridge,1998, esp. 'The Lollards and the Bible', pp.162–77. I am grateful for many agreeable conversations with Dr Hudson. She is far too courteous to deny my radical suggestion that MS. Bodley 959 was copied in Italy (pp.171–2 here) but I think it is fair to record that she has done no more than listen kindly, without either agreeing or disagreeing. On that manuscript, see the series of fascicles edited by C. Lindberg, *MS Bodley 959: Genesis–Baruch 3.20 in the Earlier Version of the Wycliffe Bible* (Stockholm Studies in English, VI, VIII, X, XIII and XX), Stockholm, 1959–69. On the royal copies of the Wycliffite Bible, pp.173–4 here, see A. I. Doyle, 'English Books in and out of Court from Edward III to Henry VII', *English Court Culture in the Later Middle Ages*, ed. V.

J.Scattergood and J.W.Sherborne, London, 1983, pp.163–81, esp. pp.168–9. N.R.Ker identified Eborall and Ive (p.178 here) in *Medieval Manuscripts in British Libraries*, III, Oxford, 1983, p.404, n.1. The manuscript in Pl.127 on p.181 was sold at Sotheby's, 22 June 1993, lot 83. I owe the explanation of its alphabetical symbols to P. Saenger, 'The Impact of the Early Printed Page', *The Bible as Book, The First Printed Editions*, ed. Saenger and Van Kampen, 1999, pp.31–51, esp. pp.37–8. On the absence of pictures in Wycliffite Bibles, pp.182–3 here, see K. Scott, *Later Gothic Manuscripts, 1390–1490* (*A Survey of Manuscripts Illuminated in the British Isles*, VI), I, p.45. I thought I had first discovered the pictures pasted into BL. Arundel MS.104 (Pl.129 on p.183) but while this book was in proof Stella Panayotova kindly sent me an offprint of her article, 'Cuttings from an Unknown Copy of the *Magna Glossatura* in a Wycliffite Bible (British Library, Arundel MS. 104)', *The British Library Journal*, XXV, 1999, pp.85–100. The Wycliffite New Testament which is Pl.132 on p.186 is in a private collection in California. On its last leaf is an ownership inscription of a Thomas Downe, apparently of *c*.1500, *Iste liber constat Thome Downe de haloghton*. This associates the manuscript tantalizingly with accusations laid against Richard Hunne, a free-thinking merchant tailor of London, who was murdered in December 1514 in his cell in the Lollards Tower, beside St Paul's Cathedral, and was then posthumously tried for heresy. Among the charges against Hunne were that he had smuggled into his cell a Wycliffite Bible which 'was one Thomas Downe's' (cf. W. R. Cooper, 'Richard Hunne', *Reformation*, I, 1996, pp.221–51, esp. p.229). I owe this reference, and permission to reproduce the book, to the generosity of its owner. The quotation from Thomas More on p.187 is taken from T. M. Lawler, G. Marc'hadour and R.C. Marius, *The Complete Works of St Thomas More*, VI, i, New Haven and London, 1981, p.317. Richard III's reputed ownership of New York Public Library MS.67 (pp.188–9) is accepted by A. F. Sutton and L. Visser-Fuchs, *Richard III's Books, Ideals and Reality in the Life and Library of a Medieval Prince*, Stroud (Gloucestershire), 1997, no.III, pp.281–2. The manuscript which is Pl.134 on p.189 is described in A. H. Reed, *A XV Century MS of the Wyclif-Purvey Gospels: An Introduction to the Dunedin Public Library's Copy*, Dunedin, 1956.

CHAPTER **8**

There are only about four or five unambiguous contemporary references to Johann Gutenberg as a historical figure. Nonetheless, there are many ingenious accounts which attempt to construct a life and a personality for the inventor of printing. About 50 copies of the original Gutenberg Bible still survive (a large number) but these are so famously valuable that access to the originals is not always easy. I am quite proud to have glimpsed about half the extant copies and to have handled about 10 per cent of them. Most accounts of the origins of printing in Mainz have no choice but to take the same information and repeat or re-interpret it in different ways. There is a recent bibliography in E. König, *Gutenberg-Bible, Handbuch zur B42, Zur Situation der Gutenberg-Forschung, Ein Supplement*, Münster, 1995. The most up-to-date census of copies of the Gutenberg Bible is I. Hubay, 'Die bekannten Exemplare der zweiundvierzigzeiligen Bibel und ihre Besitzer', *Johannes Gutenbergs zweiundvierzigzeiligen Bibel, Faksimile-Ausgabe, Kommentarband*, ed. W. Schmidt and F. Schmidt-Künsemüller, Munich, 1979,

pp.127–55, to which can now be added several changes of ownership (such as the Doheny copy moving from California to Keio University, Tokyo) and the discovery an incomplete first volume of an unrecorded Gutenberg Bible in the church of Rendsburg in Schleswig, Germany. Popular but sound accounts in English which I have used include D. McMurtrie, *The Gutenberg Documents*, New York, 1941; C. F. Bühler, *The Fifteenth-Century Book, The Scribes, The Printers, The Decorators*, Philadelphia, 1960; J. Ing, *Johann Gutenberg and his Bible, A Historical Study*, New York, 1988; A. Kapr, *Johannes Gutenberg, Persönlichkeit und Leistung*, Munich, 1988, translated by D. Martin as *Johann Gutenberg, The Man and his Invention*, Aldershot, 1996; and M. Davies, *The Gutenberg Bible*, London, 1996. By far the most innovative work on the Gutenberg Bible in recent years has been by Paul Needham who has gone back to examine and compare the original copies with remarkable results. For a quietly-spoken man of gentle manners, he is not afraid of provocative originality. I am grateful for more than a decade's friendship with Dr Needham and many exhilarating conversations on Gutenberg. He gave me copies of the following articles, all of which I have used extensively: P Needham, 'The Compositor's Hand in the Gutenberg Bible: A Review of the Todd Thesis', *The Papers of the Bibliographical Society of America*, LXXVII, 1983, pp.341–71; P. Needham, 'The Paper Supply of the Gutenberg Bible', *ibid.*, LXXIX, 1985, pp.303–374; P. Needham, 'Division of Copy in the Gutenberg Bible: Three Glosses on the Ink Evidence', *ibid.*, LXXIX, 1985, pp.411–26; P. Needham, 'The Text of the Gutenberg Bible', *Trasmissione dei testi a stampa nel periodo moderno*, II, *Il seminario internazionale Roma-Viterbo 27–29 giugno 1985*, ed. G. Crapulli, Rome, 1987, pp.43–84; and P. Needham, 'The Changing Shape of the Vulgate Bible in Fifteenth-Century Printing Shops', *The Bible as Book, The First Printed Editions*, ed. Saenger and Van Kampen, 1999, pp.53–70. I owe most of my account of the Aachen pilgrimages, pp.193–4 here, to B. Spencer, *Pilgrim Souvenirs and Secular Badges* (Museum of London, Medieval Finds from Excavations in London, 7), 1998, esp. pp.13–24. On the manuscript Bibles of the fifteenth century, cited here on pp.195–6, see (for example) S. Schutzner, *Medieval and Renaissance Manuscript Books in the Library of Congress*, I, *Bibles, Liturgy, Books of Hours*, Washington, 1989, pp.41-7; W. G. Bayerer, *Handschriftenkataloge des Universitätsbibliothek Giessen*, 4, i, Wiesbaden, 1980, pp.34–4; Masai and Wittek, eds., *Manuscrits datés conservés en Belgique*, III, *1441–1460*, 1978, p.79, no.354; H. L. M. Defoer, A. S. Korteweg and W.-C. M.Wüstefeld, *The Golden Age of Dutch Manuscript Illumination*, Stuttgart, 1989, pp.245–7; and J. P. Gumbert, *Die Utrechter Kartäuser und Ihre Bücher in Frühen Fünfzehnten Jahrhundert*, Leiden, 1974, pp. 134–6 and 342. On the printing associated with news of the fall of Constantinople, see also M. B. Stillwell, *The Beginning of the World of Books, 1450 to 1470*, New York, 1972, nos.5, 8–11 and 14–15; E. Simon, *The Türkenkalendar (1454), attributed to Gutenberg, and the Strassburg Lunation Texts*, Cambridge (Mass.), 1988. The letter of Enea Silvio de' Piccolomini, described here on pp.198–9, was recognized only as recently as 1982, although it had been in print since about 1480; cf. E. Meuthen, 'Ein neues frühes Quellenzeugnis (zu Oktober 1454?) für den ältesten Bibeldruck', *Gutenberg-Jahrbuch*, 1982, pp.108–18; and M. Davies, 'Juan de Carvajal and Early Printing: The 42-line Bible and the Sweynheym and Pannartz Aquinas', *The Library*, 6th series, XVIII, 1996, esp. pp.193–201. The analysis of Gutenberg's ink, mentioned on p.201, is summarized by R. N. Schwab, T. A. Cahill, R. A. Eldred, B. H. Kusko and D. L.Wick, 'New Evidence on the Printing of the Gutenberg Bible: The Inks in the Doheny Copy', *The Papers of the Bibliographical Society of America*, LXXIX, 1985, pp.375–410. The question of how Gutenberg cast his type, outlined on pp.204–5 here, represents some of newest and most original work of Paul Needham using computerized enhancement devised by Blaise Agüera y Arcas; their preliminary findings were announced in *The New York Times*, 27 January 2001, pp.B9 and B11, and in *The Times* in London on 7 March 2001. The parchment leaf of a Gutenberg Bible, illustrated as Pl.147 on p.206, was first recorded in a sale at Venator, Cologne, 22 June 1977, lot 42. On p.207 I give the weight of Gutenberg Bibles: I owe these figures to Stephen Massey who persuaded the Pierpont Morgan Library to weigh their copies for me in December 1999. On the decoration of Gutenberg Bibles after they were printed, pp.211–12, the important study is E. König, 'Die Illuminierung der Gutenbergbibel', *Johannes Gutenbergs zweiundvierzigzeiligen Bibel, Kommentarband*, as above, 1979, pp.71–125; I am grateful to Professor König for sending me a copy to which he has added notes and further localization of illuminators' workshops. I have also benefited from his observations in E. König, 'The Influence of the Invention of Printing on the Development of German Illumination', *Manuscripts in the Fifty Years after the Invention of Printing, Some Papers read at a Colloquium at the Warburg Institute on 12–13 March 1982*, ed. J. B. Trapp, London, 1983, pp.85–94, and E. König, *The 1462 Fust and Schoeffer Bible, An Essay, Introduction by Christopher de Hamel*, Akron (Ohio) and Evanston (Illinois), 1993, esp. pp.7–10. For the survival of the first press, see H. Lehmann-Haupt, *Peter Schoeffer of Gernsheim and Mainz, with a List of his Surviving Books and Broadsides*, Rochester (New York), 1950. The discovery that the Cambridge University Library copy of the Gutenberg Bible was used as printer's copy (p.215) was characteristically made by Dr Needham (P. Needham, 'A Gutenberg Bible used as Printer's Copy by Heinrich Eggestein in Strassburg, ca.1469', *Transactions of the Cambridge Bibliographical Society*, IX, 1986, pp.36–75).

CHAPTER 9

I began serious reading for this chapter during a winter break in the Austrian Alps, which seemed to give an appropriately Central European perspective. I started with volume III of *The Cambridge History of the Bible*, 1963, especially chapter 1, R. H. Bainton, 'The Bible and the Reformation', pp.1–37; chapter 2, B. Hall, 'Biblical Scholarship: Editions and Commentaries', pp.38–93; and chapter 3, H. Volz, 'Continental Versions to c.1600', i, 'German', pp.94–109. Exhibition catalogues have been helpful to me in sketching out a mental picture of Reformation Bibles, especially two substantial American catalogues, D. S. Berkovitz, *In Remembrance of Creation, Evolution of Art and Scholarship in the Medieval and Renaissance Bible*, Waltham (Mass.), 1968; and J. Pelikan, *The Reformation of the Bible*, and V. R. Hotchkiss and D. Price, *The Bible of the Reformation, Catalog of the Exhibition*, New Haven, London and Dallas, 1996. For a general introductory survey, it would be hard to improve on chapter 4, 'The Bible', pp.90–111 in A. G. Thomas, *Great Books and Book Collectors*, London, 1975. A further volume in *The Bible as Book* series, often cited above, was published too late for consultation here but is probably too important to ignore. It is O. O'Sullivan and E. N. Herron, eds., *The Bible as Book, The Reformation*, London, New Castle (Delaware) and Grand Haven

(Michigan), 2000, and includes D. Daniell, 'William Tyndale, the English Bible, and English Language', pp.39–50; G. Latré, 'The 1535 Coverdale Bible and its Antwerp Origins', pp.89–102, and W. S. Campbell, 'Martin Luther and Paul's Epistle to the Romans', pp.103–14. For Lorenzo Valla, introduced on pp.218–19, I consulted A. Perosa's edition of the *Collatio Novi Testamenti*, Florence, 1970. I am an admirer of A. K. Offenberg, *Hebrew Incunabula in Public Collections, A First International Census*, Nieuwkoop, 1990, and I drew too from A. K. Offenberg, 'Hebrew Printing of the Bible in the XVth Century', *The Bible as Book, The First Printed Editions*, ed. Saenger and Van Kampen, 1999, pp.71–7. My accounts of the Complutensian Polyglot and of the Greek text of Erasmus owe much to J. H. Bentley, *Humanists and Holy Writ, New Testament Scholarship in the Renaissance*, Princeton, 1983. The accepted assumption that Erasmus had begun working on the New Testament by 1505 is ingeniously refuted by A. J. Brown, 'The Date of Erasmus' Latin Translation of the New Testament', *Transactions of the Cambridge Bibliographical Society*, VIII, 1984, pp.351–80. Martin Dorp's letter to Erasmus urging caution, p.225 here, is no.304 in F. M. Nichols, *The Epistles of Erasmus*, II, London, 1904, pp.168–70; the letter of Erasmus to Budé, pp.226–6 here, is no.409, p.282 in the same edition. For German Bibles and their woodcuts of the fifteenth century, I have made use of W. Eichenberger and H. Wendland, *Deutsche Bibeln vor Luther, Die Buchkunst der achtzehn deutschen Bibeln zwischen 1466 und 1522*, Hamburg, 1977. For Luther, in addition to texts already cited, I consulted H. Bornkamm, *Martin Luther in der Mitte seines Lebens*, Göttingen, 1979, translated by E. T. Buchanan as *Luther in Mid-Career, 1521–1530*, London, 1983; H. Bluhm, 'Luther's German Bible', *Seven-Headed Luther, Essays in Commemoration of a Quincentenary, 1483–1983*, ed. P. N. Brooks, Oxford, 1983, pp.178–94; and M. Brecht, *Martin Luther, Ordnung und Abgrenzung der Reformation, 1521–1532*, Stuttgart, c.1986, translated by J. L. Schaaf as *Martin Luther, Shaping and Defining the Reformation, 1521–1532*, Minneapolis, 1990. I visited the Wartburg with Graham Wells. In plotting the editions of Luther's Bible, I have used H. Reinitzer, *Biblia deutsch, Luthers Bibelübersetzung und ihre Tradition*, Wolfenbüttel, 1983, and the invaluable T. H. Darlow and H. F. Moule, *Historical Catalogue of the Printed Editions of Holy Scriptures in the Library of the British and Foreign Bible Society*, II, *Polyglots and Languages other than English*, London, 1911, in which editions of Luther's translations appear as nos.4188–4489, pp.486–550. On the profligacy of publications by Luther, pp.236-7 here, see J. Benzing, *Lutherbibliographie, Verzeichnis der Gedruckten Schriften Martin Luthers bis zu dessen Tod*, ed. H. Claus, Baden-Baden, 1966. Pl.237 on p.237 shows my wife, Mette, who is Danish, with the folio Danish Bible we bought once in Hay-on-Wye. Since then, Peter Raes has kept me constantly informed of his ongoing discoveries about Danish editions of the Bible and sent me his handsome book, P. E. Raes, *På sporet af Gamle Bibler, En nordisk antologi, De tre danske foliobibler fra 1550, 1588–89 og 1632–33, og De tre islandske Hólar bibler fra 1584, 1644 og 1728*, Copenhagen, 1995. For other translations following Luther, I have especially used the Darlow and Moule catalogues and further sections of chapter 2 of *The Cambridge History of the Bible*, III, K. Foster on Italian versions, pp.110–13, R. A. Sayce on French versions, pp.113–22, E. M. Wilson on Spanish versions, pp.125–9, and chapter 4, S. L. Greenslade, 'English Versions of the Bible, 1525-1611', pp.141-74. There is a great deal of old-fashioned and patriotic literature about the translations of the Bible in the English Reformation, including A. W. Pollard, *Records of the English Bible, The Documents relating to the Trans-*

lation and Publication of the Bible in English, 1525-1611, Oxford, 1911, which is still useful. For Tyndale himself we now have D. Daniell, *William Tyndale: A Biography*, New Haven and London, 1994; the same author is working on a full-length history of the Bible in English, for publication by Yale University Press. I owe to Richard Linenthal the news of the discovery of the 1526 Tyndale in Stuttgart in November 1996; it has now been published by E. Zwink, 'Confusion about Tyndale: The Stuttgart Copy of the 1526 New Testament in English', *Reformation*, III, 1998, pp.28–47.

CHAPTER **10**

The skeleton of this chapter is the revision and expansion by A. S. Herbert of T. H. Darlow and H. F. Moule, *Historical Catalogue of Printed Editions of the English Bible, 1525–1961*, London and New York, 1968. It gives detailed bibliographical entries but is supplemented by historical notes on the publishing history of Bibles. One can spend happy hours with Darlow and Moule. It is the sort of book from which one longs to read out interesting and unexpected facts to one's friends. For the earlier period, I have used G. Henderson, 'Bible Illustration in the Age of Laud', *Transactions of the Cambridge Bibliographical Society*, VIII, 1981–4, pp.173–216 (reprinted in the author's *Studies in English Bible Illustration*, I, London, 1985, pp.254–85); G. E. Bentley, Jr., 'Images of the Word: Separately Published English Bible Illustrations, 1539–1830', *Studies in Bibliography*, XLVII, 1994, pp.103–28; and the engagingly recondite exhibition catalogue for the Museum of the History of Science, Oxford, *The Garden, the Ark, the Tower, the Temple: Biblical Metaphors of Knowledge in Early Modern Europe*, ed. J. Bennett and S. Mandelbrote, Oxford, 1998. Mr Scott Mandelbrote gave me a number of very helpful references when I first entered these difficult waters, including copies of his two articles, S. Mandelbrote, 'John Baskett, the Dublin Booksellers, and the Printing of the Bible, 1710–1724', *The Book Trade and its Customers, 1450–1900*, ed. A. Hunt, G. Mandelbrote and A. Shell, Winchester, 1997, pp.115–31; and S. Mandelbrote, 'The Bible and National Identity in the British Isles, c.1650–c.1750', *Protestantism and National Identity*, ed. A. Claydon and I. McBride, Cambridge, 1998, pp.157–81. On the trade in Bibles in the seventeenth century, see D. McKitterick, 'Customer, Reader and Bookbinder: Buying a Bible in 1630', *The Book Collector*, XL, 1991, pp.382–406. For Ogilby's Bible, pp.251–2 here, see *The Garden, the Ark*, etc., no.1, pp.16–20, and M. Schuchard, *A Descriptive Bibliography of the Works of John Ogilby and William Morgan*, Berne and Frankfurt, 1975. For the Macklin Bible and much else, pp.255–7, I have used T.S.R. Boase, 'Macklin and Bower', *Journal of the Warburg and Courtauld Institutes*, XXVI, 1963, pp.148–77. The three copies of the expanded Macklin Bible listed on p.257 are described in Sotheby's, Chancery Lane, 8 February 1973, lot 1 (a reference I owe to Paul Quarrie); D.R. Farmer, *The Holy Bible at the University of Texas*, Austin, 1967, no.47, pp.34–6; and A. Sparke, *The Bowyer Bible, A Monograph*, Bolton (Lancashire), 1920, from which Pl.187 is reproduced. Mr Julian Edison gave me advice on miniature or 'thumb' Bibles, with a list of references back to W. M. Stone, *Snuffbox full of Bibles*, Newark, 1926. I have especially used S. Roscoe, 'Early English, Scottish and Irish Thumb Bibles', *The Book Collector*, XXII, 1973, pp.187–207; R. E. Adomeit, *Three Centuries of Thumb Bibles, A Checklist*, London and New York, 1980; and interesting references from R. B. Bottigheimer, *The Bible for Children, from the Age of*

Gutenberg to the Present, New Haven and London, 1996. For American Bibles, from p.259, see M. T. Hills, *The English Bible in America: A Bibliography of all the Editions of the Bible and the New Testament Published in America, 1777 to 1957*, New York, 1962. An excellently researched account is P. C. Gutjahr, *An American Bible, A History of the Good Book in the United States, 1777–1880*, Stanford (California), 1999, with a magnificent bibliography. D. Morgan, *Protestants and Pictures: Religion, Visual Culture, and the Age of American Mass Production*, New York and Oxford, 1999, is less readable but pp.61–6 furnished information on *Harper's Illuminated and New Pictorial Bible*. The Bibles illustrated with early photographs, described on pp.263–4, are recorded in H. Gernsheim, *Incunabula of British Photographic Literature, A Bibliography of British Photographic Literature, 1839–75, and British Books Illustrated with Original Photographs*, London and Berkeley, 1984, nos. 88, 130 and 180–1. The little Bible illustrated as Pl.195 on p.268 was bought with his pocket money in 1902 by my grandfather, who gave it to me in 1963.

CHAPTER **11**

I have already acknowledged the detailed lists of Bibles made by Darlow and Moule, *Historical Catalogue of the Printed Editions of Holy Scriptures in the Library of the British and Foreign Bible Society*, 1911. The second part of the catalogue, on Bibles in languages other than English, is so extensive that it fills three volumes. Almost every page of this chapter owes something to those books. The Society has now shortened its name to the Bible Society and its splendid library is still flourishing, now on deposit at Cambridge University Library. The Society has published specialized bibliographies, G. D. Dance, *Oceanic Scriptures, A Revision of the Oceanic Sections of the Darlow and Moule Historical Catalogue of Printed Bibles, with Additions to 1962*, London, 1963; G. E. Coldham, *A Bibliography of Scriptures in African Languages*, London, 1966; H. W. Spillet, *A Catalogue of Scriptures in the Languages of China and the Republic of China*, London, 1975; and G. E. Coldham, ed., *Historical Catalogue of Printed Christian Scriptures in the Languages of the Indian Sub-Continent, A Revision to 1976*, London, 1976. I am especially grateful to the Fondation Martin Bodmer, Cologny, Geneva, for allowing me to examine large numbers of printings of the Bible in exotic languages, and to the librarians of the Bible Society for the use of many Bibles for illustrations here. I used, though perhaps not greatly, E. Fenn, 'The Bible and the Missionary', chapter 11 in *The Cambridge History of Bibles*, III, pp.383–407. Names and dates have been checked and standardized against the huge *Biographical Dictionary of Christian Missions*, ed. G. H. Anderson, Grand Rapids (Michigan) and Cambridge, 1998. Some of the activities described there are so recent that it is difficult to judge yet whether or not the work of European missionaries will have benefited the world in the long term, but, looking through almost a thousand pages of quite extraordinary lives in the *Biographical Dictionary*, it is impossible to doubt the phenomenon which drives many people, against all rational odds, to disseminate Christianity and its Bible. For the Eliot Indian Bible, pp.270–7 here, my principal sources have been the documents printed in G. P. Winship, *The Cambridge Press, 1638–1692, A Re-examination of the Evidence Concerning the Bay Psalm Book and the Eliot Indian Bible as well as other Contemporary Books and People*, Philadelphia, 1945, esp. chapter 10, pp.208–44. I used the census of copies in J. C. Prilling, *Bibliographic Notes on*

Eliot's Indian Bible and on his other Translations and Works in the Indian Language of Massachusetts, Washington, 1890; there seems to be no more recent version. The volume of the Indian Bible illustrated as Pl.199 on p.275 was in the Doheny sale at Christie's, New York, 21 February 1989, lot 1705; it is currently on deposit at the Houghton Library, Harvard University. The copy with annotations in the Indian language, mentioned on p.276, was sold at Sotheby's, New York, 7 November 1994, lot 40. For Boyle, p.277, see R. E. W. Maddison, *Robert Boyle and the Irish Bible*, Manchester, 1958; and M. Hunter, ed., *Robert Boyle, by Himself and his Friends*, London, 1994. On the early activities of the Society for Promoting Christian Knowledge, pp.278–80, I used W. K. Lowther Clarke, *A History of the S.P.C.K.*, London, 1959, supplemented by S. Neill, *A History of Christian Missions* (Pelican History of the Church, VI), 2nd edn., Harmondsworth, 1986, and (as throughout this chapter) the faithful volumes of Darlow and Moule. The Bible societies described on pp.281–2 are commemorated in R. Lovett, *The History of the London Missionary Society, 1795-1895*, London, 1899; J. M. Rice, *A History of The British and Foreign Bible Society, 1905–1954*, London, 1965; G. G. Findlay and W. W. Holdsworth, *The History of the Wesleyan Methodist Missionary Society*, London, 1921–4; F. Tschudi, 'La Société biblique de Bâle au XIXᵉ siècle: Les lignes de force de son action missionnaire', *La bible en Suisse, Origines et histoire*, ed. U. Joerg and D. M. Hoffman, Basel, 1997, pp.257–66; H. O. Dwight, *Centennial History of the American Bible Society*, New York, 1916; and A. J. Brown, *The Word of God among All Nations: A Brief History of the Trinitarian Bible Society, 1831-1981*, London, 1981. I used T. Thomas, 'Foreign Missions in Victorian Britain', *Religion in Victorian Britain*, ed. J. Wolff, V, Manchester, 1997, pp.101–34. On the Bible Society in the 1820s and 1830s and the part of George Borrow, pp.287–91, I drew much of my account from A. M. Ridler, *George Borrow as a Linguist: Images and Contexts* (Ph.D. thesis for the Council for National Academic Awards), privately printed, Wallingford, 1996, esp. pp.352–69. There is apparently an account of his St Petersburg experiences by Borrow himself, which I have not seen, in *The Bible Society Reporter*, 1899, pp.230–4. On the Binghams, pp.291–292, see C. Miller, *Fathers and Sons: The Bingham Family and the American Missions*, Philadelphia, 1982. For the missions to the South Pacific, see N. Gunson, *Messengers of Grace: Evangelical Missionaries in the South Seas, 1797–1860*, Melbourne and Oxford, 1978. There is a vast amount of material on Livingstone and the evangelism of Africa, from all perspectives. Perhaps the best accounts are C. Northcott, *David Livingstone, His Triumph, Decline and Fall*, Guildford, 1973; and T. Holmes, *Journey to Livingstone: Exploration of an Imperial Myth*, Edinburgh, 1993.

CHAPTER 12

This chapter is dedicated to Martin Schøyen. His fascination for the Bible and the history of writing has led him to form what is almost certainly the most comprehensive and wide-ranging private collection of early biblical manuscripts ever assembled. Mr Schøyen is well known as a generous lender to exhibitions and as a sponsor of the most recent publications of the Dead Sea Scrolls. I have known him since 1986; he has watched the preparation of this book since its inception and I owe much to his patient advice. Before beginning this last chapter, I invited myself to Oslo and settled with my notebooks in his superb reference library. I am grateful to him and Bodil for hospitality unlike that offered by any other library in the world. Martin Schøyen would suddenly appear upstairs where I was sitting and would produce, like a conjurer, an original artefact or manuscript for whatever I was reading about, an unknown cuneiform tablet on the Flood, a fourth-century codex of Matthew in an unrecorded Coptic recension (p.215 and Pl.230), the lid of the actual jar in which the Nag Hammadi hoard was found (p.316), a Dead Sea Scroll (Pl.236). It was a dazzling and unforgettable performance. The background reading for this chapter included Kenyon, *Our Bible and the Ancient Manuscripts*, various editions, and Gamble, *Books and Readers in the Early Church*, 1995, both already cited, and the wise and captivating book by E. G. Turner, *Greek Papyri, An Introduction*, Oxford, 1968, paperback ed., 1980, given to me by John Collins. A sense of excitement for archaeology and deduction is evoked by J. Romer, *Testament, The Bible and History*, London, 1988, reprinted 1996. I devoured the book but found some its statements difficult to verify independently. For the cuneiform accounts of the Creation and Noah's Flood, I began with R. W. Rogers, *Cuneiform Parallels to the Old Testament*, 2nd edn., New York, 1926; W. G. Lambert and A. R. Millard, *Atra-Ḥasīs, The Babylonian Story of the Flood*, Winona Lake (Indiana), 1969, reprinted 1999; R. S. Hess, 'One Hundred Fifty Years of Comparative Studies on Genesis 1–11: An Overview', *'I Studied Inscriptions from before the Flood', Ancient Near Eastern, Literary, and Linguistic Approaches to Genesis 1–11*, ed. R. S. Hess and D. T. Tsumura, Winona Lake (Indiana), 1994, pp.3–26; and A. George, *The Epic of Gilgamesh, The Babylonian Epic Poem and other Texts in Akkadian and Sumerian*, London, 1999. All these and others I found on Martin Schøyen's shelves. For the recovery of texts such as the *Diatessaron* of Tatian, pp.305–7 here, I used B. M. Metzger, *The Early Versions of the New Testament, Their Origins, Transmission and Limitations*, Oxford, 1977, and the two other books by Professor Metzger cited earlier, *The Text of the New Testament*, 1968, and *Manuscripts of the Greek Bible*, 1981, and Aland and Aland, *The Text of the New Testament*, 1987, as above too. I owe the localization of Pl.224 on p.308 to Sam Fogg. On the forays for manuscripts in the abandoned and neglected sites of Egypt, pp.308-10, I drew information from S. Emmel, 'The Coptic Manuscript Collection of Alexander Lindsay, 25th Earl of Crawford', *Coptology: Past, Present and Future, Studies in Honour of Rodolphe Kasser* (Orientalia Lovaniensia Analecta, LXI), ed. S. Giversen, M. Krause and P. Nagel, Louvain, 1994, pp.317–25; S. Emmel, 'Reconstructing a Dismembered Coptic Library', *Gnosticism and the Early Christian World, in Honor of James M. Robinson* (Forum Fascicles, II), ed. J. E. Goehring *et al.*, Sonoma (California), 1990, pp.145–61; and S. Emmel, 'Robert Curzon's Acquisition of White Monastery Manuscripts', *Actes du IVᵉ congrès copte, Louvain-la-Neuve, 5-10 septembre 1988* (Publications de l'Institut orientaliste de Louvain, XLI), ed. M. Rassart-Debergh and J. Ries, Louvain-la-Neuve, 1992, pp.224–31. The Genesis fragment in the Morgan Library, cited on p.312, is described in B. P. Grenfell and A. S. Hunt, *The Amherst Papyri, being an Account of the Greek Papyri in the Collection of the Right Hon. Lord Amherst of Hackney, F.S.A., at Didlington Hall, Norfolk*, I, London, 1900, pp.30–1; I owe my knowledge of it to the kindness of William Voelkle. The quotations on p.313 about uncertain provenances are from W. H. Worrell, ed., *The Coptic Manuscripts in the Freer Collection*, New York, 1923, p.x, and A. S. Hunt, *Catalogue of the Greek Papyri in the John Rylands Library, Manchester*, I, *Literary Texts (Nos. 1–61)*, Manchester and London, 1911, p.vii. For the Hamuli finds

(Pl.227, p.313) I used P. Needham, *Twelve Centuries of Book-bindings, 400–1600*, New York and London, 1979, pp.5–21, nos.2–4. There is an ideal introduction to the three great hoards of Chester Beatty, Nag Hammadi and Bodmer, pp.314–19, in N. Van Elderen, 'Early Christian Libraries', *The Bible as Book, The Manuscript Tradition*, ed. Sharpe and Van Kampen, 1998, pp.45–59. The quotation on p.314 is from F. G. Kenyon, *The Chester Beatty Biblical Papyri, Descriptions and Texts of Twelve Manuscripts on Papyrus of the Greek Bible*, I, *General Introduction*, London, 1933, p.5. Schøyen MS.2650 (p.315 and Pl.230 on p.316) is hitherto unpublished. It is potentially of extraordinary importance. It comprises the Gospel of Matthew but in a version apparently not otherwise known. There are a number of unverifiable early Christian allusions to an original text of Saint Matthew's Gospel in Aramaic, first used by Jewish Christians (as cited, for example, in Eusebius, *Historia Ecclesiastica*, III.16) and Mr Schøyen tells me that Professor Hans-Martin Schenke has suggested that this might be a Coptic translation from a Greek version of that lost proto-text of Matthew. On the discovery of the Nag Hammadi codices, p.316 here, I used J. M. Robinson, ed., *The Facsimile Edition of the Nag Hammadi Codices, Published under the Auspices of the Department of Antiquities of the Arab Republic of Egypt in Conjunction with the United Nations Educational, Scientific and Cultural Organization, Codex I*, Leiden, 1977, and J. M. Robinson, ed., *The Nag Hammadi Library in English, Translated and Introduced by Members of the Coptic Gnostic Library Project of the Institute for Antiquity and Christianity*, Claremont, California, 3rd edn., San Francisco, 1988, esp. pp.1–10. On the finding of the Dishnā (or Bodmer) papyri and their subsequent adventures, see J. M. Robinson, 'The Manuscript's History and Codicology', *The Crosby-Schøyen Codex MS.193 in the Schøyen Collection* (Corpus Scriptorum Christianorum Orientalium, 521, Subsidia 85), ed. J. E. Goehring, Louvain, 1990, pp.xix–xlii; R. Kasser, 'La Collection de papyrus de Martin Bodmer, à l'occasion du centième anniversaire du collectionneur', *Librarium, Revue de la Société Suisse des Bibliophiles*, III, 1999, pp.157–73; and M. Bircher, 'Avant-Propos', and R. Kasser, 'Introduction', *Bibliotheca Bodmeriana, la collection des Papyrus Bodmer, Manuscrits de texts grecs classiques, grecs et coptes bibliques et de littérature chrétienne, du 2ᵉ au 9ᵉ siècle*, Munich, 2000. I am grateful to Dr Bircher for copies of these two most recent articles. The quotations from the *Sayings of Jesus* on p.318 are from the translations by T. O. Lambdin in Robinson, ed., *The Nag Hammadi Library*, 1988, as above, pp.126–38. On the enigmatic text 'Q' (p.322), see B. H. Streeter, *Oxford Studies in the Synoptic Problem*, Oxford, 1911. The literature on the Dead Sea Scrolls, pp.322–9, is enormous. Among other texts, I have consulted J. Allegro, *The Dead Sea Scrolls, A Reappraisal*, 2nd edn., Harmondsworth, 1964, reprinted 1990; F. M. Cross, ed., *Scrolls from the Wilderness of the Dead Sea, A Guide to the Exhibition The Dead Sea Scrolls of Jordan*, London, 1965; J. C. Trever, *The Dead Sea Scrolls, A Personal Account*, 2nd edn. (the first was published as *The Untold Story of Qumran*), Grand Rapids (Michigan), 1977, reprinted 1988; G. Vermes, *The Dead Sea Scrolls, Qumran in Perspective*, London, 1977; M. Pearlman, *The Dead Sea Scrolls in the Shrine of the Book*, Jerusalem, 1988; H. Scanlin, *The Dead Sea Scrolls and Modern Translations of the Old Testament*, Wheaton (Illinois), 1993; and E. Tov, 'Scribal Practices and Physical Aspects of the Dead Sea Scrolls', *The Bible as Book, The Manuscript Tradition*, ed. Sharpe and Van Kampen, 1998, pp.9–33. I have used the many-volumed editions of the Scrolls published as *Discoveries in the Judaean Desert*, with plates and descriptions arranged according to the caves where the pieces were found, from volume I (Cave 1), Oxford, 1955, to XXXIV (Cave 4, part ii), Oxford, 1999, and still continuing. The argument that the Scrolls are salvage from the Temple of Jerusalem is presented eloquently in N. Golb, *Who Wrote the Dead Sea Scrolls? The Search for the Secret of Qumran*, London, 1995. On attempts to associate the Dead Sea Scrolls with Christianity and events and people known from the Gospels (p.327 here), see G. Vermes, *Jesus and the World of Judaism*, London, 1983, and C. P. Thiede, *The Dead Sea Scrolls and the Jewish Origins of Christianity*, Oxford, 2000. Such implausible theories were first argued by J. L. Teicher in a series of articles in the *Journal of Jewish Studies*, II–IV, 1950–4. Among the more extreme publications are M. Baigent and R. Leigh (authors of *The Holy Blood and the Holy Grail*, which fact should be enough to discredit anything which follows), *The Dead Sea Scrolls Deception*, London, 1991, described on the cover as 'The sensational story behind the religious scandal of the century'; L. Star, *The Dead Sea Scrolls, The Riddle Debated*, Sydney, 1991; B. Thiering, *Jesus and the Riddle of the Dead Sea Scrolls, Unlocking the Secrets of his Life Story*, San Francisco, 1992 (based on the false claim that scraps from Cave 7 include part of the New Testament); E. M. Cook, *Solving the Mysteries of the Dead Sea Scrolls*, Grand Rapids (Michigan), 1994; N. A. Silberman, *The Hidden Scrolls, Christianity, Judaism and the War for the Dead Sea Scrolls*, London, 1995; and R. Price, *Secrets of the Dead Sea Scrolls*, Eugene (Oregon), 1996. The titles of such books alone may place the Scrolls in the Loch Ness Monster class of journalism but they reveal a great deal about the Bible in late twentieth-century popular culture. On the unexplained scrolls which were offered for sale in 1883 (p.327), see J. M. Allegro, *The Shapira Affair*, London, 1965, and B. S. Hill, 'Ephraim Deinard on the Shapira Affair', *The Book Collector, Special Number for the 150th Anniversary of Bernard Quaritch*, 1997, pp.167–79.

Index of Manuscripts

Specifically identified copies of printed books are included in this index. Plate references are in **bold**

Plate references are in **bold**

Photographic acknowledgements

Phaidon would like to thank all those private owners, museums and galleries and institutions credited in each caption who have kindly provided material for publication. Additional credits and providers of images are as follows:

AKG London 167, 168, 193; AKG London/Hilbich 164; The Ancient Art & Architecture Collection 64, 234; The Art Archive 3, 113, 161; The Pierpont Morgan Library/Art Resource, NY 38, 98, 101, 103, 141, 144, 227, 237; Bayerische Staatsbibliothek, Munich 41, 111; Benediktinerkloster Engelberg, Stiftsbibliothek 50; Bibliothéque de Troyes (photo: P. Jacquinot) 75; Bibliothèque du Séminaire de Tournai (photo: Olivier Desart/CRAL) 45; Bibliothèque Interuniversitaire de Montpellier, Section Médecine 99; Bibliothèque municipale de Dijon, France (photo: F. Perrodin) 52, 68; Collection de la Bibliothèque municipale de Rouen (photo: Didier Tragin/Catherine Lancien) 47; Bibliothèque municipale de Tours 70; Bibliothèque nationale de France 18, 19, 21, 26, 34, 37, 59, 76, 80, 83, 102, 143; Bibliothèque publique et universitaire de Genève (photo: Jean Marc Meylan) 43; Bibliothèque Sainte-Geneviève, Paris (photo: Studio Dupif) 60; Bildarchiv Preussischer Kulturbesitz 118, 137, 201; Bodleian Library, University of Oxford 56, 65, 119, 120, 125, 126, 128, 131, 181, 184, 185, 198, 200, 130; Courtesy Bolton Libraries 187; Maidstone Museum & Art Gallery, Kent/Bridgeman Art Library, London 214; Stapleton Collection/Bridgeman Art Library, London 220; The British Library, London 5, 9, 20, 24, 27, 31, 33, 39, 40, 46, 58, 69, 73, 85, 114, 116, 129, 136, 151, 174, 175, 177, 178, 182, 186, 189, 221, 223; © The British Museum, London 219; By permission of the Syndics of Cambridge University Library 121, 155, 225; By permission of the Syndics of Cambridge University Library and of the British and Foreign Bible Society 156, 160, 162, 163, 165, 166, 169, 173, 179, 180, 183, 188, 190, 192, 194, 203, 204, 207, 208, 209, 210, 211, 212, 213, 215, 216, 218; Reproduced by kind permission of the Trustees of the Chester Beatty Library Dublin 229; © Christies Images Ltd. 2001 114, 115, 199; © Richard T. Nowitz/Corbis 28; © The Master and Fellows of Corpus Christi College, Cambridge 1, 14, 51, 53, 54, 72, 77, 78, 82, 94, 106, 109, 112, 123, 172; Diözesan- und Dombibliothek Cologne (Fotostudio Hilch, Cologne) 66; Alfred and Isabel Reed Collections, Dunedin Public Libraries (Bill Nichol Photography, Dunedin) 134; Durham Cathedral 49; Courtesy of the Egypt Exploration Society 226; Reproduced by permission of the Provost and Fellows of Eton College 108, 149; Mary Evans Picture Library 159, 197, 202, 205, 206, 217; © Fitzwilliam Museum, University of Cambridge 12; Sam Fogg, London 7; Reproduced by kind permission of the Fondation Martin Bodmer, Cologny-Geneva 233; © 2001 Michael Freeman 2; Germanisches Nationalmuseum, Nürnberg 138; The J. Paul Getty Museum, Los Angeles 29; Giraudon 100; Gutenberg Museum, Mainz 145; © Sonia Halliday and Laura Lushington 42, 107; Sonia Halliday Photographs (photo by F.H.C. Birch) 74; Herzog August Bibliothek Wolfenbüttel 122; The Huntington Library, San Marino 48, 135; INDEX, Florence 4, 10, 13, 16, 17, 32, 36, 62, 153, 222; Institute for Antiquity and Christianity, Claremont, California 232; The Israel Museum, Jerusalem 235; Lambeth Palace Library 97, 152; Library of Congress, Washington, D.C. 139; Kenneth Nebenzahl Collection 30; Arents Collectios, The New York Public Library, Astor, Lenox and Tilden Foundations 191; Manuscripts and Archives Division, The New York Public Library, Astor, Lenox and Tilden Foundations 133; Copyright © 2000/01 Niedersächsische Staats- und Universitätsbibliothek, Göttingen (SUB)154; Österreichische Nationalbibliothek, Wien (photo: Bildarchiv, ÖNB Wien) 22, 146, 105; Oxford University Press 196; Pepys Library, Magdalene College, Cambridge 124; By kind permission of the Provost and the Fellows of The Queen's College Oxford 117; Copyright Brussels, Royal Library of Belgium 95; The Royal Library, National Library of Sweden, Stockholm 57; Reproduced by courtesy of the Director and Librarian, the John Rylands University Library of Manchester 104, 148, 150, 228; Scala 6, 23, 35, 142, 157; Scala/Art Resource, NY 170; The Schøyen Collection, Oslo and London 231, 236, 230, 224; Sotheby's 25, 96, 11, 71, 81, 86, 88, 89, 90, 91, 92, 93, 127; Berlin, Staatsbibliothek zu Berlin - Preussischer Kulturbesitz, Handschriftenabteilung 158; Stadtarchiv Trier (photo: Anja Rünkel) 67; Stiftsbibliothek St. Florian (photo: Diözesanbildstelle, Linz) 44; Stiftsbibliothek St. Gallen (photo: Carsten Seltrecht) 8; Reproduced by permission of the Master and Fellows of Trinity College, Cambridge 63, 110; Universitäts-Bibliothek, Erlangen 61; Universitätsbibliothek Würzburg 15; Universiteitsbibliotheek Utrecht 140; The Dean and Chapter of Winchester 55; © Württembergische Landesbibliothek, Stuttgart (photo: Joachim Siener) 176.